RESHAPING TORONTO'S WATERFRONT

Edited by Gene Desfor and Jennefer Laidley

Toronto's waterfront is at a critical juncture. The area is undergoing a much-anticipated revitalization in the form of major public and private development. Yet in the shadow of this latest wave of change, and a rich, complex, and important history, Toronto's waterfront has a long legacy of unfulfilled plans, conflicting interests, and missed opportunities. Social and economic developments have gone awry, biophysical environments have been damaged, and ecological relationships have been upset.

In cities around the world, policymakers, planners, and developers have looked to waterfronts as spaces of promise and prime locations for large-scale development within global urban hierarchies. This collection of essays looks at these processes of development and brings together different disciplinary perspectives around the theme of nature–society relations. The volume features analyses of Toronto's waterfront past and present, and draws on insights from urban and environmental history, urban planning, political ecology, human geography, sustainability and environmental studies, governance and politics, resource management, and population biology. Contributors from this wide range of disciplines study and interpret the ways environmental, economic, and political processes mutually transform one another on the city's waterfront. The authors examine waterfront struggles over the past one hundred and fifty years, while also attending to the underlying biophysical conditions that have shaped and constrained possibilities. Together the essays address the interdependence of social and natural processes in myriad ways, exploring the potential and limitations of human intervention within these dynamic spaces.

GENE DESFOR is a professor emeritus and senior scholar in the Faculty of Environmental Studies at York University.

JENNEFER LAIDLEY holds a master of environmental studies degree in urban planning from the Faculty of Environmental Studies at York University.

Reshaping Toronto's Waterfront

Edited by Gene Desfor and Jennefer Laidley

UNIVERSITY OF TORONTO PRESS
Toronto Buffalo London

ISBN 978-1-4426-4027-6 (cloth)
ISBN 978-1-4426-1001-9 (paper)

∞

Printed on acid-free, 100% post-consumer recycled paper with vegetable-based inks.

Library and Archives Canada Cataloguing in Publication

Reshaping Toronto's waterfront / edited by Gene Desfor and Jennefer Laidley.

Includes bibliographical references and index.
ISBN 978-1-4426-4027-6 (bound). – ISBN 978-1-4426-1001-9 (pbk.)

1. Waterfronts – Ontario – Toronto – History.   2. City planning –
Ontario – Toronto – History.   3. Toronto (Ont.) – History.   I. Desfor,
Gene   II. Laidley, Jennefer, 1969–

FC3097.4.R47 2011   971.3'541   C2011-900582-4

University of Toronto Press acknowledges the financial assistance to its
publishing program of the Canada Council for the Arts and the Ontario
Arts Council.

 Canada Council   Conseil des Arts   ONTARIO ARTS COUNCIL
for the Arts   du Canada   CONSEIL DES ARTS DE L'ONTARIO

University of Toronto Press acknowledges the financial support of the
Government of Canada through the Canada Book Fund for its publishing
activities.

Contents

Figures

Tables

Acknowledgments

The editors would like to acknowledge the support of the Social Science and Humanities Research Council of Canada, Standard Grant #410-2005-2071.

Jennifer Bonnell wishes to acknowledge the helpful comments received at the Canadian Historical Annual Meeting in Vancouver, BC, in June 2008, and the insightful critical commentary provided by members of her dissertation committee: Dr Ruth Sandwell, Dr Cecilia Morgan, and Dr William J. Turkel. The research and writing of this chapter were conducted with generous support from the Social Sciences and Humanities Research Council's Canada Graduate Scholarship. Image purchases were made possible with support from the Changing Urban Waterfronts project, directed by Dr Gene Desfor with support from the Social Sciences and Humanities Research Council. Bonnell also wishes to acknowledge the Toronto and Region Conservation Authority, the City of Toronto Archives, the Todmorden Mills Museum, and Jordan Hale for providing the images used in chapter 5.

Susannah Bunce would like to thank the editors of this volume and the support of Social Science and Humanities Research Council, Standard Research Grant #410-2005-2071, in the production of doctoral dissertation research from 2005–7. She also wishes to acknowledge the permission granted by Waterfront Toronto to reproduce the image in chapter 12.

Tenley Conway would like to acknowledge insights provided by Stefan Cermak, and technical-data gathering and map-classification work completed by Mike Lackner and Namrata Shrestha. She would also like to thank Gene Desfor and Jennefer Laidley for sharing their knowledge of the Toronto waterfront and providing insightful comments on earlier versions of this chapter. This work was supported by Social Sciences and Humanities Research Council of Canada Grant #510382.

Gene Desfor would like to thank the Toronto Port Authority for permission to reproduce the images in chapter 2, the Toronto Port Lands Company (formerly the Toronto Economic Development Corporation) for permission to reproduce the image in chapter 10, and Waterfront Toronto for permission to reproduce the image in chapter 13.

Gene Desfor and Lucian Vesalon gratefully acknowledge permission from Blackwell Publishing Ltd. to use parts of the article 'Urban Expansion and Industrial Nature: A Political Ecology of Toronto's Port and Industrial District' in chapter 2. The original article was published in *International Journal of Urban and Regional Research* 32(3): 586–603.

Paul S.B. Jackson thanks W. Scott Prudham, Gene Desfor, and the entire Changing Urban Waterfronts Project for supporting this research, both financially and intellectually. Jackson also acknowledges the Toronto Public Library for its provision of the images used in his chapter.

Jennefer Laidley acknowledges an earlier version of chapter 8 published in the journal *Cities* (24:4 [2007], 259–72), entitled 'The Ecosystem Approach and the Global Imperative on Toronto's Central Waterfront.' Permission for reprinting in this edited collection has been granted by Elsevier, licence 2104310014436. Both were based on the author's Masters of Environmental Studies major paper, entitled 'Constructing a Foundation for Change: The Ecosystem Approach and the Global Imperative on Toronto's Central Waterfront,' available at www.yorku.ca/fes/research/students/outstanding/index.htm.

Michael Moir wishes to thank Jeff Hubbell, records manager and archivist for the Toronto Port Authority, for his assistance and support while accessing the records of the Toronto Harbour Commission, and Carolyn King, cartographer with York University's Department of Geography, for her work on the maps in figures 1.4 and 1.5. Moir also wishes to acknowledge the generous support of York University Libraries through a Library Research Grant and research time to prepare his chapters, and the contribution of Mark Gulla, who, as research assistant for this project, located many of the newspaper clippings cited as references. He also acknowledges the permission granted by the City of Toronto Archives for the use of the image in chapter 1.

Chris Sanderson and Pierre Filion wish to acknowledge SSHRC Major Collaborative Research Initiative funding for the project 'Public Policy in Municipalities,' through which the research on which their chapter is based was conducted.

RESHAPING TORONTO'S WATERFRONT

Introduction

GENE DESFOR AND JENNEFER LAIDLEY

In the summer of 2008, we loaded two dozen graduate students into a rented yellow school bus to tour Toronto's waterfront. The students had come on a field trip from Germany to learn about urban development processes in North America and arrived in Toronto after a visit to Boston. As we bumped along the streets lining the edge of Lake Ontario, we pointed out the highlights of Toronto's ever-changing waterfront – high-rise office and residential towers, expanding public cultural facilities, repurposed industrial buildings, underutilized marine terminals, a downtown airport, elaborate sports complexes, and landscaped recreational areas. We directed the bus to the West Don Lands, a downtown area just minutes south-east of the central business district that is being prepared for large-scale redevelopment. These preparations include construction of the West Don Lands berm, a raised landform intended to provide flood protection from the Don River. Before passing through a gate in the hoardings that surround the area, an official with the Ontario Realty Corporation, the provincial agency charged with constructing the berm, boarded our bus to explain the processes involved in this complex socio-ecological project. We wanted the students to witness the intricate relationships that are involved in the production of a major urban development project, and to understand how its completion will provide the foundation for a new phase in Toronto's waterfront development.

The berm is just one small part of a thirty-year, multi-billion-dollar socio-ecological waterfront development project that seeks to reconnect the city with the lake, opening up the West Don Lands and other waterfront lands to a variety of new uses. This four metre tall, 190,000 cubic metre mound of clay and soil signals the impending transformation of

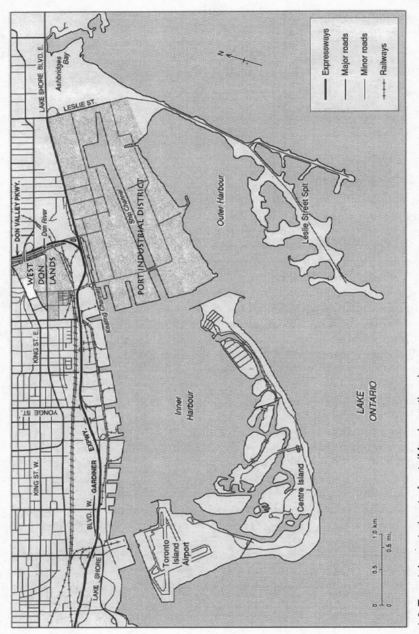

1.0 Toronto's central waterfront. (Map by authors)

this formerly industrial waterfront area just minutes from the central business district, as well as the deep interconnectedness between urban life and ecological processes. Officially called a 'flood protection landform' (Urban Design Associates 2005: 28), its scale and height is specifically engineered to provide protection from a 'once-in-a-century' storm (see www.hurricanehazel.ca), highlighting the irony of re-employing a technological solution to resolve the impacts of a nineteenth-century techno-engineering project – the straightening and channelizing of the Don River more than a century earlier.

Completion of the berm will allow a thirty-six hectare area immediately west of the southern reaches of the Don River to be brought out of a development limbo imposed in 1997 (City of Toronto 1997a). Planners and politicians hope to attract developers to the area to invest in the construction of 'a new mixed-use precinct with an emphasis on urban living,' a downtown live-work community of more than 5800 new residential units and 93,000 square metres of new employment space (Urban Design Associates 2005: 6). The centrepiece of the West Don Lands will be the seven hectare Don River Park, for which the flood control berm assumes centre stage. The flattened top surface of the berm will become both active and contemplative recreation areas and its sloping sides will be traversed by a network of trails and natural habitats (Waterfront Toronto n.d.a). The berm/park will become the 'principal organizing element' for the area (Urban Design Associates 2005: 47), intended to transform a contaminated and underutilized industrial site into dynamic new urban neighbourhoods aspiring to serve Toronto's competitive ambitions in the global hierarchy of cities.

But the berm is just one of the latest examples of the socio-ecological change that has characterized Toronto's waterfront since the early days of colonial settlement. Despite a lingering popular sentiment that a knot of outdated politics has tied up change on the city's twenty-five kilometre stretch of Lake Ontario, Toronto's waterfront has been anything but static. Particularly over the past hundred years, 'things' have been constantly changing: new landforms have been produced; a river has been straightened; shipping and shipbuilding facilities expanded and contracted; manufacturing plants established and demolished; water mains and sewers laid; grain silos built and razed; housing torn down and condominiums constructed; streets built and rebuilt; commercial and office buildings have sprouted; city beaches appear and disappear; parks and gardens come and go; cultural and entertainment venues are fabricated; an airport built; and more. Just as noteworthy as the physical transformations are the major and frequently contentious struggles for change in the processes and institutions that defined and produced them – changes in government structures, public participation in decision making, jurisdictional authorities, planning processes, and regulatory mechanisms. For those of us who insist on doing research on Toronto's waterfront, 'things' are constantly changing. For sure, the waterfront is never dull.

This volume's explorations of socio-ecological change on Toronto's waterfront are particularly timely for a number of reasons. First, the waterfront is at a critical juncture. The city has a long legacy of unfulfilled plans and cantankerous relationships among a multitude of government agencies and development organizations. Social and economic developments have gone awry, biophysical environments have been damaged, and ecological relationships upset. But large-scale investments in development projects – like the ones we showed to our visiting students – are once again making Toronto's waterfront a leading edge in changing the city. Over the last few decades, policymakers, planners, and developers in North America, Europe, and Asia have, despite fierce competition from suburban areas, looked to waterfronts as locations for massive investments that contribute to elevating particular metropolitan regions within globalized urban hierarchies. Supporters of this most recent wave of development have envisioned waterfront projects as spaces of promise and marketed them as crucial territorial wedges for competitive-city growth strategies for the twenty-first century. Waterfront developers in Toronto, as elsewhere, are pledging to convert problem spaces into opportunity spaces. As this newest transformation continues, we argue, it is crucial to reflect on the history of the waterfront to see how and why it has been transformed and to understand better the critical role of nature–society relationships in these processes of change.

Second, although a large amount of scholarly and popular work has focused on Toronto's port and waterfront in the last two or three decades, this is the first book to bring together multidisciplinary scholarship on the socio-ecological aspects of the city's current and past waterfront development. This fresh body of scholarly work expands traditional disciplinary boundaries and makes available new timely insights into the ways natural and social processes are intertwined in the development of Toronto's waterfront.

Third, conventional wisdom has it that Toronto's waterfront has been ensnared in its past – snarled by outdated politics – and has not embraced a fundamental need for change. This volume demolishes conventional wisdom about Toronto's unvarying and immovable waterfront, and analyses change as a dynamic and interactive process during which the social and the natural have been constantly remaking one another. Understanding the rich history of reconfiguring Toronto's waterfront will allow us to be better equipped to ask intelligent questions about proposals for future change.

And finally, and most important from our perspective, this volume appears at time when a major re-examination of society's relationships with nature is under way. A near-unanimous consensus exists about the reality of climate change, although none exists on how to avoid the ecological, social, and economic ruin that is likely to follow. Scientists, politicians, journalists, and non-professionals continue to debate the correct response to the impact of human activity on natural processes. A new discussion has emerged about whether human activity at the global scale has so affected the planet that a new geological epoch, much like the well-known Cambrian, Jurassic, and Pleistocene periods, has begun. Paul Crutzen, the 1995 Nobel laureate in chemistry, has coined the term 'Anthropocene' to describe this epoch, in which rising CO_2 levels, increasing urbanization, global temperature increases, changes in sedimentation materials and levels, and oceanic changes due to acidification and rising temperatures and sea levels have all been triggered or exacerbated by human activity, leaving behind a layer of material that future geologists will be able to identify as distinctly our own. The Anthropocene, as described by Crutzen and a group of leading scientists, is 'a new phase in the history of both humankind and of the Earth, when natural forces and human forces became intertwined, so that the fate of one determines the fate of the other' (Zalasiewicz et al. 2010: 2231). While debate continues on when the Anthropocene may have begun – at the start of the Industrial Revolution or with the start of the 'Great Acceleration' of the post-war years – we agree that natural and societal forces have become so deeply intertwined during the contemporary period that it is currently impossible to distinguish one from the other. It is this intertwining of the natural and the social that the students witnessed in the construction of the berm and that is fundamental to our approach to studying change on Toronto's waterfront.

Waterfront Scholarship and Socio-Ecological Perspectives

Port cities and their waterfronts have long been the subjects of substantial academic exploration. Urban ports and their administrations have been studied for their maritime, development, transportation, and naval importance (e.g., Brown 2009; Harms 2008; Meyer 1999; Konvitz 1978; Bird 1963), their associations with commerce and industry (e.g., Wang 2007; Oliver and Slack 2006; Hoyle and Pinder 1981), and the changing technologies that led to growth, decline, and shifting port-city geographies around the world (e.g., Hoyle 1990; Hoyle et al. 1988, Tweedale 1988; Hayuth 1982; Norcliffe 1981; Slack 1980; National Research Council 1980; Moss 1976). Hoyle's (1988) framework of successive stages of waterfront development (primitive cityport, expanding cityport, industrial cityport, retreat, and redevelopment) has been used by many scholars to describe spatial and functional relations that have arisen from changing economic activities and technological developments. Although Hoyle's framework provides a useful periodization of waterfront changes, it tells us little about the dynamic relationships among the human and non-human actors who produce these waves of development. We need to investigate further the large-scale social, biophysical, political, cultural, economic, and technological changes that have done much to redirect the flows of goods, wealth accumulation, and shipping activity in ways that have fundamentally altered relationships between ports and their cities.

Over the past fifty years in particular, urban waterfronts have experienced tremendous transformations in shape, form, and function – such that cities have witnessed the emergence of what is being called a 'post-industrial waterfront' (Norcliffe et al. 1996). Indeed, the same kinds of transformations that we have recently seen on Toronto's waterfront are also occurring on urban waterfronts throughout the world – from London to New York, from Boston to Shanghai, and from Hamburg to Melbourne. Further, a new academic literature has emerged as these changing waterfronts have received a resurgence of scholarly interest (Desfor et al. 2011; Lehrer and Laidley 2008; Bunce and Desfor 2007; Dovey 2005; Swyngedouw 2004; Bassett et al. 2002; Gordon 1997a; Fainstein 1994; Brownill 1993)

Toronto's waterfront has been the focus of its fair share of scholarly research. This body of work has focused to a large extent on analyses of the urban planning and development regimes under which waterfront change has taken place (Bunce 2009; Laidley 2007; Kipfer and Keil 2002, 2000; Hartmann 1999; Goldrick and Merrens 1996, 1990; Greenberg 1996; Reeves 1992; Lemon 1990; Desfor 1988; Desfor et al. 1989, 1988; Merrens 1988; Moir 1989; Norcliffe 1981; Schaeffer 1981; Gemmil 1978), and of the institutional structures which facilitated these changes (Todd 1996; Desfor 1993; O'Mara 1984, 1976), but has also examined the more normative aspects of urban waterfront development and planning (Gordon 1997a). We also note that during its just over three-year existence, the Royal Commission on the Future of the Toronto Waterfront produced an extensive array of important reports and studies in support of its inquiries (see, for example, Royal Commission on the Future of the Toronto Waterfront 1992, 1990, 1989b; Stinson and Moir 1991; Greenberg and Secheri 1990; Merrens 1989; Munson 1990). And Toronto's waterfront has most recently been the subject of several studies concerned with nature–society relationships (Keil and Whitehead forthcoming; Bonnell 2010; Desfor and Vesalon 2008; Bunce 2007; Desfor et al. 2006; Desfor and Keil 2004; Keil and Desfor 2003; Keil and Graham 1998).

The work in this volume builds on this recent scholarly foundation, but originates with the 'Changing Urban Waterfronts' research project. This multidisciplinary project, which was housed at York University and funded by the Canada Social Sciences and Humanities Research Council from 2005–10, focused on developing an understanding of how Toronto's waterfront has changed over the last 150 years. Seven main researchers from four different universities with very different disciplinary backgrounds came together in this project. And while some of the contributions in this volume did not arise directly out of the project, virtually all the authors have been connected with it in some way.

The theme of this volume – socio-ecological change on Toronto's waterfront – draws on a body of literature that characterizes urban change as arising from networks of socio-ecological processes involving biophysical forces – including hydrological, biological, and geological – as well as social, economic, political, and cultural ones. In other words, processes of change intertwine social actors and institutions as they combine with ecological dynamics. And the complex and co-evolving relationships between these human and non-human forces produce urban spaces. At the same time, these processes focus attention on the ways actors, institutions, and ecological dynamics are immersed in broader imperatives, not least of which is the global political economy and its attendant environmental implications.

Our theme is informed by this conceptualization, with which all the authors in this volume engage, although they approach the topic of socio-ecological change from a diverse range of perspectives. They are concerned with debates about the history of institutional arrangements for governance over and uses of space, the changing role of biophysical nature in support of various kinds of capital accumulation, and broad currents of political thought concerned with the production and reproduction of particular environments (e.g., urban neighbourhoods, energy landscapes, urban rivers, green spaces, and port lands). Chapter authors are both academics and practitioners, with disciplinary backgrounds in urban and environmental history, physical and social geography, political science, urban planning, and urban political ecology. The different approaches, diverse perspectives, and varying sets of methodological tools that they bring to our study of Toronto's waterfront complement each other and give this volume its distinct understanding of the processes by which socio-ecological change has been occurring on Toronto's waterfront for more than a hundred years.

Conceiving of urban change as a distinctly socio-ecological process presents a major challenge, from an analytical standpoint, in that it subverts a deep divide between the natural and social sciences (Wallerstein 2000). Only in recent years has this divide been questioned, by debates and developments within a wide range of literatures, including cultural ecology and ecological anthropology (Descola and Pálsson 1996); environmental sociology (Goldman 2001, 1998; Redclift and Benton 1994); human ecology (Steiner and Nauser 1993); environmental history (Cronon 1996, 1990; R. Nash 1982; White 1995; Worster 1993, 1990); political ecology (Peet and Watts 1996; Escobar 1995; Peluso 1992; Blaikie and Brookfield 1987; M. Watts 1983); and environmental cultural and literary studies (Herzogenrath 2001; Kollin 2001). This broad literature has shaken the epistemic and political division between the biophysical and the socio-cultural by subverting the obviousness or naturalism of nature and exposing the ideological, political, and cultural influences on the ways nature is understood and represented. At the same time, biophysical processes have been afforded a new role in social, cultural, and political economic analyses (see Davis 2001) that emphasize nature as an important source of constraint and contingency (Prudham 2003; Boyd et al. 2001; Demeritt 2001; Bridge 2000). This leads us in the direction of a distinctly urban form of political ecology, emphasizing the ways in which the city and nature are inextricably interwoven through processes of mutual transformation (Desfor and Keil 2004; Gandy 2005, 2004, 2002; Keil 2003; Swyngedouw 2004, 1999; Davis 1998; N. Smith 1996). The variety of disciplinary approaches in this volume is a critical strength in helping to untangle and understand this complexity.

Our socio-ecological approach to studying urban change must be distinguished from the well-known Chicago School of Urban Ecology, for whom the city was understood as an ecological unit composed of adjacent niches occupied by human groups in a series of concentric rings around the central core (Park et al. 1925). Urban ecology conceived of society as a collection of spatially separated and territorially distributed individuals capable of independent locomotion, and of spatial relationships as the products of competition and selection, continuously in process of change to facilitate mobility. Although the approach made important conceptual and methodological advances in urban studies, we agree with Gottdiener's (1988) several critiques: that urban ecology possesses a biologically framed reductionist view of human relations that ignores the influences of class, status, and political power; that it was technologically deterministic in its reliance on innovations in transport and communication as the explanation for urban growth and change; and that it inadequately treated the importance of the state's interventions in the economy. Although more recent advances in urban ecology have expanded and enlarged its interests and understandings, the approach still does not adequately integrate society's relationships with nature and the rise of knowledge-based technologies in urban development processes.

Instead, we take four key ideas from the broad intellectual movement described above: (1) nature is inescapably political and politicized; (2) biophysical nature is an important and active participant in shaping and constraining social geographies and histories; (3) places are continually being transformed by social processes, not least by their articulation with a broad, and increasingly globalized, political economy; and (4) transforming and representing nature is constitutive of society, social justice, and power relations, so that making and remaking nature is inextricably linked to social reproduction.

Historical Context for Waterfront Development

Toronto, the capital of the province of Ontario, is the largest city in Canada, and its urban region is home to 5.5 million people. For many years, Toronto has played the leading role in integrating the region and the nation into the global economy (Friedmann 1995; Friedmann and Wolff 1982). Even in its earliest years, the city and its waterfront connected the local area to broader regional and international networks (Careless 1984; Lemon 1985). The city began as a military outpost, its location chosen in the mid-eighteenth century largely for its harbour, protected by a sandy spit and buttressed by rivers on two sides. From its military origins, the Town of York, as Toronto was formerly known, grew quickly into a bustling port city. The early decades of the nine-teenth century saw its population increase exponentially as the city spread north, west, and east from the water's edge; from 456 inhabit-ants in 1803, the area's population swelled to 9254 in 1834, the year York formally became the City of Toronto (Toronto Harbour Commis-sioners 1985). While Toronto's harbour could initially handle only shal-low-draft vessels, extensive and repeated dredging beginning in 1833 enabled larger and larger ships to access city docks (Wickson 2002). As ships became larger and economic endeavours more complex, activ-ity around the docks changed over the years, from the early retailers, wholesalers, brokers, and import and export dealers to the industrial and manufacturing firms and bulk storage yards that came later. Toron-to was a vital part of trade on the Great Lakes and St Lawrence River, with shipbuilding yards servicing both trade and military needs (see Moir, chapter 4, this volume). In the 1850s, a railway corridor was built directly across the lakefront, giving the increasingly powerful railways access to the movement of both goods and people in and out of Toron-to's city core (Mellen 1974). But water remained a vital transportation and trade route; in 1889 more than 1.25 million passengers and 600,000 tonnes of marine cargo travelled through the port (Wickson 2002).

By 1901, the city's population had grown to 208,040 (City of Toronto Archives n.d.) and between 1891 and 1911 Toronto's manufacturing output increased by 243 per cent (Careless 1984). Growing industriali-zation gave rise not only to accelerating commodity production, con-solidation and concentration in manufacturing, and an increasingly powerful banking and finance sector in Toronto (Careless 1984: 154), but also to engineered sea walls along the waterfront, replacing the harbour's extensive marshes with the hard edges required for indus-trial and maritime activity. Across the entire span of the city's central waterfront, huge tracts of land produced by a widespread practice of lakefilling over many decades extended the city southward from the railway tracks. On the western waterfront, parks and recreational facili-ties, including an amusement park and bathing pavilion, were erected. To the east, a first-rate art-deco water treatment facility, a major sewage processing plant, and a network of energy infrastructure was built (see Prudham et al., this volume) was built.

A suburban boom was beginning to increase population outside the city, and by 1951 Toronto's population swelled to nearly 700,000 within a region of 1.1 million (City of Toronto Archives n.d.). Starting in the late 1950s and 1960s, elaborate city planning processes began to identify new and 'best' uses for waterfront lands as the relevance of industrial and port activity began to wane (Desfor, Goldrick, and Merrens 1989). But even as the public sector planned for change, industrial firms moved out or closed down on the waterfront and the private sector proceeded with its own initiatives for development. For example, the *Toronto Star*, one of Canada's largest circulation newspapers, purchased a prime waterfront site in 1962 on which it built a new head-office tower in 1971. At about the same time, Canada Steamship Lines announced it was closing down its central waterfront location, and a developer purchased the site for commercial and residential uses. And the Gooderham and Worts distillery, which in the late nineteenth century was the largest producer of grain spirits in the Commonwealth, stopped production in 1990, leaving its architecturally significant buildings vacant for nearly twenty years until being adapted for artists' studios, art galleries, new media production facilities, lofts, entertainment complexes, and high-end restaurants.

While activity at the Port of Toronto peaked in 1969 (Ramlalsingh 1975), efforts to create new plans for increasingly underused waterfront lands met with opposition and roadblocks. As industrial activity was attracted to suburban sites, a 'territory of availability' was being created on the waterfront (Greenberg 1996). Though the transition to a post-industrial waterfront had begun in the 1950s, the dominance of port- and industrial-oriented activity would not come to an end until the late 1990s (see Laidley, this volume).

At the beginning of the twenty-first century, Toronto's waterfront has taken a decisive step towards a new wave of development. In 2001, the city's population reached 2.5 million (Statistics Canada 2007) and the Port of Toronto's cargo handling declined to 1.8 million tonnes, far behind Vancouver, Montreal, and Hamilton, its neighbour to the west (Statistics Canada 2003). In that same year, an enormous, multi-year waterfront 'revitalization' scheme began taking shape, spurred initially by Toronto's ambitions to host the Olympic Games (see Laidley; Eidelman, this volume). 'Mixed-use development' and 'sustainability' (see Bunce, this volume) are the mantra of this thirty-year, multi-billion-dollar project (City of Toronto 1999a: 2), which promises to soften the waterfront's hard edges by 're-naturalizing' nature. Waterfront Toronto, currently the lead waterfront development corporation with support and funding from three levels of government, has taken major strides towards changing the waterfront.

The waterfront transformations recounted above have taken place in the context and under the direction and influence of a changing array of institutions, regimes of governance, and economic imperatives. The British North America Act of 1867, under which the Dominion of Canada was first established, gave the federal government exclusive jurisdiction over navigation and shipping. And public harbours, also under federal jurisdiction, have been managed through a number of different organizational systems throughout Canada's history (Manning et al. 1968: 6). As described by Moir (this volume) the Harbour Trust, established in 1850, led port and harbour management in Toronto for more than half a century. But by the early twentieth century it was clear the Trust was incapable of ushering in an impending industrial wave of development. The formation of the Toronto Harbour Commission in 1911 marked a new era in Toronto's waterfront development (see Moir; Desfor et al., this volume). While the commission's jurisdictional hold over the waterfront continued for nearly eighty years, inter-jurisdictional strife with provincial and municipal agencies characterized much of its existence, which came to an end in 1999 with the creation of the Toronto Port Authority (see Sanderson and Filion, this volume). With the emergence of a post-industrial-oriented economy in the late twentieth and early twenty-first centuries, a new action model of planning and development has become prevalent that features public-private partnerships and publicly financed urban development corporations (see Bunce; Eidelman; Laidley, this volume).

Toronto's waves of waterfront development have had an enormous impact on the landscape at the water's edge (see Conway, this volume), while providing both support for and constraint on urban growth. For example, the Don River, with its headwaters some fifty kilometres north of the city and running just east of the downtown, has been a space that has been regarded with a great deal of ambiguity as both an asset to the city and a barrier to the city's expansion. Since European settlement, the Don has featured prominently in the city's waterfront development – celebrated both for its beauty and habitat for flora and fauna, but also used for waste disposal. The river valley became a rather complex liminal space: not only a marginal and undesirable place, but also offering refuge, limited subsistence, and relative freedom from authorities (see Bonnell, this volume). Straightening and encapsulating of the river during the mid- and late-nineteenth century was done, at the insistence of a major railway company, to provide a more efficient landscape for transportation facilities and the location for industry. These 'improvements' to the Don resulted in a significant decline in biological connectivity across the land-water interface (see Conway, this volume), and are now seen as impediments to mixed residential, commercial, and entertainment development projects designed to propel the area forward in an era of competitive and creative city-formation. Currently, major efforts are under way to remove those earlier 'improvements' and to unleash the 'natural' potential of the lower Don valley for twenty-first-century 'sustainable' development (see Bunce; Desfor and Bonnell, this volume).

The vast southern expansion of the city into Lake Ontario at the beginning of the twentieth century propelled the city's industrialization ambitions, but constrained later developments. A new hybrid landscape, the Port Industrial District, was constructed as a site for industrial, warehousing, port, commercial, and, to a lesser extent, recreational activity, with the intention to resolve a complex combination of economic, political, environmental, and public health concerns (see Moir; Desfor et al.; and Jackson, this volume). New shipping and industrial facilities both required and profited from a landform that was solid and stable and adjacent to deep water (see Desfor et al., this volume). But waterfront sites constructed for this early-twentieth-century district now bear the scars of industrialism, a period when ecological relationships were often ignored by or subordinated to production practices and urbanization strategies aimed at maximizing profit. Many of these sites are currently the object of the most recent wave of development (see Laidley; Bunce, this volume), which has long been delayed by struggles to overcome the health risks and financial liabilities arising from industrial contamination, and are now central to efforts to revitalize urban spaces and modernize ecology. Political, economic, and regulatory processes and institutions have been reconfigured (see Eidelman; Sanderson and Filion, this volume) in an attempt to provide 'win-win' solutions for converting and reshaping devalued landscapes into newer forms that can again serve as productive urban sites (see Bunce; Lu and Desfor, this volume).

One of these 'win-win' approaches to development is captured in the term 'sustainability,' an often loosely defined notion that has been used to mean the coupling of economic growth with the maintenance of ecological viability in order to maintain future productive capacity (see Bunce, this volume). Sustainability differs from 'improvement,' a concept frequently used in the late nineteenth and early twentieth centuries to refer to making 'nature' more efficient and productive, but without a concern for long-term productivity or ecological viability. Another contemporary 'win-win' approach is embodied in the vast amount of effort that has gone into both biophysical procedures and social processes for the remediation of contaminated sites (see Lu and Desfor, this volume). Scientific-oriented (or, perhaps more precisely, liability-oriented) practices have focused on identifying dangerous levels of contaminants and procedures for cleaning up soil and groundwater. Equally important are economic and political processes for putting in place regulations to guide the determination of how clean is clean, liability issues, jurisdictional authority, who pays for a clean-up, and attempts to ensure that contamination is not repeated. Another current 'win-win' socio-ecological development strategy, 're-naturalization,' involves intimately interlacing nature and society by returning a site to earlier conditions that were understood to be more 'natural' and thus presumably ecologically healthy (see Desfor and Bonnell, this volume).

But the success of all these strategies has been constrained, in large part due to the 'nature' of nature, in its relations with urbanization. As Raymond Williams contends (see Harvey 1996a), the production of space and the production of nature cannot be independently analysed; nature and society, particularly in an urban setting, are locked in a dialectic relationship that facilitates dynamic processes of capitalist accumulation and influences the social relations by which 'things' are produced. At the water's edge, we see many such 'things' that are the products of a historical interweaving of nature and society: landforms, wharves, piers, electricity generating stations, parks, cormorants and their breeding areas, water filtration plants, coal storage areas, 'native' and 'non-native' flora and fauna, waste disposal sites, and much more. Drawing from the insights of the growing literature in urban political ecology concerned with the social 'production of nature' (see, for example, Swyngedouw 2007, 2004; Kaika 2005; Braun 2005; Gandy 2002; Castree 1995; N. Smith 1984; and Harvey 1982), we agree that these hybrid 'things' have embedded within them the biophysical forces, political and economic ideologies, and social and institutional relations by which they were produced. But the underlying dialectic relation between nature and society may limit the production of 'things' and, at times, even threaten the social relations that have been the basis for economic growth (J. O'Connor 1988). Toronto's changing waterfront attests to underlying and often out-of-sight social and biophysical specificities that have shaped, reshaped, and constrained the possible, and have often bedevilled attempts to control it. Whether it was an elite group of Torontonians' ambitions for industrialization that inspired the filling of a deltaic marsh, the annual flooding of the Don River, silt and urban run-off that accumulated in the harbour and gave rise to obstacles for shipping, contaminated soil and groundwater jeopardizing human and environmental health, the construction of hard-edged surfaces intended to eliminate socially problematic but highly biologically productive riparian areas, or plans to construct sustainable mixed-use neighbourhoods, waterfront change, as many authors in this volume discuss, has been centrally influenced by relationships between nature and society.

Structure of the Book

The volume has been divided into two parts, which roughly correspond with the periods of time on which the chapters focus. It is these two periods – the decades spanning the end of the nineteenth and the beginning of the twentieth centuries, and those marking the transition from the twentieth to the twenty-first – during which major socio-eco-logical changes to the waterfront were being contemplated, struggled over, planned for, and undertaken. With this division, we do not intend to indicate an abrupt or clear delineation between the industrial and the post-industrial waterfront. The transition from the former to the latter has been a decades-long and very contentious process that in many instances continues today. Nonetheless, and while some chapters span the time frames of the two parts (see Conway; Prudham et al., this volume), we believe it is instructive to situate our explorations within the context of these two periods, in no small part because dominant societal relationships with nature in these two periods tend to be distinguished one from the other as 'industrial' and 'post-industrial.'

The chapters in the first part, 'Forging the Industrial Waterfront,' explore changes to the waterfront during the late nineteenth and early twentieth centuries that were concerned with producing an industrial-oriented space. These include changes to the waterfront's physical shape, its vegetation, and its social history, as well as the institutions formed to oversee the socio-ecological relationships by which new port and waterfront lands were produced, public health issues managed, land uses determined, and major infrastructure projects built. In chapter 1, Moir investigates the challenges presented by the interactions between urban growth and ecological flows in the Toronto Harbour from the late eighteenth century through to the early twentieth, where commissions of varying structure and influence have been at work. The establishment of the Toronto Harbour Commission in 1911 and its 1912 Waterfront Development Plan is explored by Desfor, Vesalon, and Laidley in chapter 2. The chapter unravels the issues associated with the social production of solid land by lakefilling, the primary mechanism for urban territorial expansion in the 1912 Plan.

Chapter 3 investigates interactions between public health concerns and the reshaping of Toronto's waterfront. Jackson demonstrates that an inadequate and often internally contradictory science of disease contributed to a fear of a filthy city. Thus, Jackson adds not only a public health dimension but also a rhetorical foundation for the destruction of the marshes of Ashbridge's Bay. And as Moir presents in his history of shipbuilding in chapter 4, the socio-ecology of the waterfront was highly influenced by the growth and decline of this industry and its connection to extra-local political and economic events. In chapter 5, Bonnell presents a social history of a changing environment, demonstrating that the connections between the Don River and two transient groups, Roma immigrants and a population of unemployed single men, are bound up in a broader project of liberal enculturation. And in chapter 6, Conway investigates the Lower Don River and Ashbridge's Bay from a physical geography perspective. She explores the dynamism of the changes in ecological connectivity between land and water that have accompanied the transitions from a pre-industrial economy, through industrialization, and into the post-industrial period. Chapter 7 surveys the geography of networked energy systems in Toronto and, as Prudham, Gad, and Anderson argue, the role of the nineteenth- and early-twentieth-century waterfront as an 'energy hub' rather than a space of manufacturing.

In the second part of the book, 'Shaping the Post-Industrial Waterfront,' we focus on more recent changes to the Toronto waterfront – those beginning with the 1960s and continuing into the twenty-first century. This part is concerned with the many aspects of the waterfront's transformation from an urban space largely devoted to industrial-oriented activities and governance arrangements to those associated with a globally oriented and knowledge-based economy. In chapter 8, Laidley asserts that an 'ecosystem approach' to waterfront development in the period of transition from an industrial to a post-industrial waterfront was not only a novel ecological planning paradigm, but also the foundation for the pursuit of a 'world-class' waterfront for the twenty-first century. Chapter 9, by Sanderson and Filion, investigates the role of the federal government in waterfront planning and development in Toronto, contending that selective federal intervention on the waterfront is a central factor in ongoing conflict between various governance bodies. The authors demonstrate that waterfront policy at the federal level contains major socio-ecological considerations, most apparently in the form of institutional arrangements, for waterfront development. In chapter 10, on cleaning up contaminated waterfront sites, Lu and Desfor document how new collaborative arrangements between public- and private-sector actors have been able to redefine the regulatory processes by which an environmental clean-up has been undertaken, literally preparing the waterfront's ground for the new uses critical to a post-industrial economy. The issue of 'jurisdictional gridlock' is examined in detail in chapter 11, in which Eidelman maps the conflicts that precipitated the creation of a quasi-public development corporation and continue to influence waterfront planning and policy processes, and what this means for notions of democratic responsiveness, public accountability, and political legitimacy. He notes that jurisdictional issues reflect competing visions of society's relationships with nature that have both driven and thwarted processes of waterfront change. In chapter 12, Bunce argues that sustainable development, one of the most prevalent and influential strategies in use in contemporary waterfront planning policy and practice, is a key site of intersection between public-sector policy goals and private-sector, property-led revitalization processes. And, finally, in chapter 13, Desfor and Bonnell return to the Don River to explore the ways that socio-ecological dynamics support urban growth, comparing the nineteenth-century period, during which nature was 'tamed' in support of industrialization, with the twenty-first century period, in which nature is being reconverted to a wilfully engineered state of 'wildness' to sustain a post-industrial economy.

PART ONE

Forging the Industrial Waterfront

1 Planning for Change: Harbour Commissions, Civil Engineers, and Large-scale Manipulation of Nature

MICHAEL MOIR

European settlement in North America began at the water's edge, where sheltered harbours offered protection for water-borne vessels essential for the basic needs of colonial expansion: defence and the movement of people, information, and commodities between empires and their outposts. Settlement was drawn to locations surrounded by rich agricultural land that could support a growing population and generate surplus produce for trade. Access to a regional network of waterways promoted the exchange of staples and manufactured goods, and as commerce increased, so did the size of vessels. These boats and ships required an infrastructure of wharves, quays, cranes, and yards that became a port, an area where ships could be loaded or unloaded, tendered, repaired, and berthed when not in service. Over time, ports took on a look of permanence. As Gordon Jackson remarked in his history of British ports, 'Few things in the world of modern redundant industry are quite so vast, solid and impressive as docks and their related works. They look, for the most part, as if they have always been there and always will be' (1983: 10). Such appearances are deceiving. Ports are developed within the context of an environment that changes through the interaction of land, wind, and waves. Because of the constancy of these forces, harbours will never be the same tomorrow as they are today. Erosion and alluvial deposits relentlessly reshape coastlines and harbour beds, confounding those who require a stable platform to operate and sustain the port's infrastructure. Regulatory and development bodies, be they private corporations or public agencies, have been established to manage this interaction between nature and socio-economic expectations of permanence.

The historical study in this chapter examines such relationships between nature and society within the context of Toronto's waterfront, where commissions of varying structure and influence have been at work since 1833. The Toronto Harbour Commission is the best known of these organizations because of its longevity and the dramatic changes it effected to the waterfront's configuration and land use as the result of its Waterfront Plan of 1912. Accounts of its creation by the federal government in 1911 have largely attributed the Commission's considerable development powers to the ineffectiveness of its predecessor, the Harbour Trust, and in particular to the failure of the Trust to stop Toronto's port from deteriorating into a series of ramshackle wharves that discouraged shipping (Careless 1984; O'Mara 1976; Mellen 1974). The port, however, was not the focus of the Trust nor of the previous committee of commissioners. These nineteenth-century bodies were occupied with the harbour and, in particular, its preservation as a safe and navigable body of water. Merchants, manufacturers, and civil engineers struggled to react to natural changes and human abuses of the harbour, until rapid industrialization and the increasing involvement of municipal and federal governments led to a transition in governance from harbour commission to port authority, and the almost complete reconfiguration of Toronto's waterfront.

Military Arsenal to Commercial Port, 1793–1850

Even before he set eyes on the place, John Graves Simcoe, the lieutenant governor of Upper Canada, selected Toronto as a location for permanent settlement. After examining maps of the colony and speaking with those acquainted with its geography, Simcoe described Toronto as 'the natural arsenal of Lake Ontario,' offering a much more defensible place than either Kingston or Niagara (Firth 1962: xxxiii–xxxiv). While he intended to focus his attention on the development of London as the site of Upper Canada's capital, Great Britain's home secretary, Henry Dundas, made it clear that the settlement of York (as Simcoe had named Toronto) was the priority, since Simcoe's primary objective was the maritime defence of the colony. When Simcoe finally visited Toronto in May 1793, he found a place very much to his liking. A narrow spit guarded the harbour's western entrance, and it could be fortified by a few heavy canons to control the movement of vessels. The harbour offered 'a Situation admirably adapted for a Naval Arsenal and Dock Yard,' and, mentioned in passing almost as an afterthought, 'a place for a Town on the main Shore' (ibid.: 4). The scene was later described by

Joseph Bouchette, who surveyed the harbour in November 1792 on the orders of Simcoe (see figure 1.1):

> The harbour of York is nearly circular, and formed by a very narrow peninsula stretching from the western extremity of the township of Scarborough in an oblique direction, for about six miles, and terminating in a curved point nearly opposite the garrison; thus enclosing a beautiful basin about a mile and a half in diameter, capable of containing a great number of vessels, and at the entrance of which ships may lie with safety during the winter. The formation of the peninsula itself is extraordinary, being a narrow slip of land, in several places not more than sixty yards in breadth, but widening towards its extremity to nearly a mile; it is principally a bank of sand with a very little grass upon it; the widest part is very curiously intersected by many large ponds, that are the continual resort of great quantities of wild fowl; a few trees scattered upon it greatly increase the singularity of its appearance; it lies so low that the wide expanse of Lake Ontario is seen over it: the termination of the peninsula is called Gibraltar Point, where a blockhouse has been erected. (Bouchette 1815: 606–7)

Sixteen years later, Bouchette wrote of 'the untamed aspect which the country exhibited when I first entered the beautiful basin ... Dense and trackless forests lined the margin of the lake,' sheltering two families of the resident Mississauga people (Bouchette 1831: 89). To the east, the Don River meandered into marsh of almost 525 hectares, entering the bay through a cut in the sandbar running from the north shore to the oblique peninsula that separated the bay and wetlands from Lake Ontario. Simcoe, his family, colonial officials, and the Queen's Rangers established a community under canvas on the north shore near the Don River in July 1793, marking the beginning of a permanent, continuous settlement.

Serving as the centre of government and military command and connected to the interior by Yonge Street, Toronto's merchant community prospered in the service of colonial officials and outlying settlements. Growth accelerated after the War of 1812 and the Napoleonic Wars, when immigration from Great Britain and Ireland significantly increased. By the early nineteenth century, Toronto was a gathering place for shipmasters, shipwrights, and mariners, whose schooners took wheat, flour, potash, lumber, and farm produce to ports that included Kingston, Cobourg, Rochester, and Oswego. They returned with manufactured goods for distribution through the hinterland (Careless 1984).

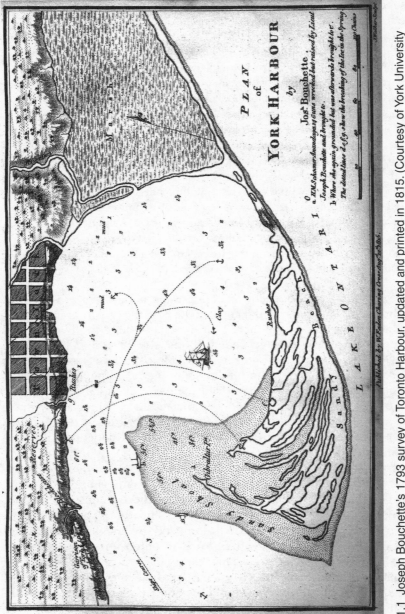

1.1 Joseph Bouchette's 1793 survey of Toronto Harbour, updated and printed in 1815. (Courtesy of York University Libraries)

Construction of three wooden wharves began along the harbour's north shore in 1816, which later appeared on Lieutenant George Philpott's 'Plan of York' of 1818 (Hayes 2008). The wharves with their storehouses, ship carpentries, and yards gave the waterfront a commercial appearance, despite the close proximity of residential buildings, gardens, and a shoreline that was still a sandy beach (Careless 1984).

The growing town's livelihood was directly influenced by the cycles of economic decline and prosperity that began in Britain and the United States. The early 1820s were very lean times and, after a brief recovery between 1822 and 1825, the town was hit by another commercial slump. When James Grant Chewett prepared his 'Plan of the Town of York' in 1827, no new wharves had been added to the piers at Peter, Church, and Frederick streets, but the projection of water lots south from the shore between Jarvis and Sherbourne streets and into the bay suggests that schemes for development were under consideration (Hayes 2008). As the city's population increased nearly fourfold between 1825 and 1833, the boom years returned, until the depression of 1837 (Careless 1984).

Nature, however, threatened to throttle maritime trade, which was so essential for commercial growth, by closing the entrance to the harbour. Those who studied the harbour's contours, such as surveyors and shipmasters, noticed with alarm the changing dimensions of the peninsula, and the encroachment of a shoal upon the western channel. This concern led the colonial government to appoint a committee of three commissioners, the first of several bodies charged with Toronto harbour's maintenance and improvement.

The commissioners were Chewett, a surveyor who remained closely involved with harbour affairs until his death in 1862; William Chisholm, a lumber merchant, owner of a fleet of schooners, and shipbuilder responsible for laying out nearby Oakville and developing its harbour; and Captain Hugh Richardson, an owner and operator of steamships who paid to light and buoy Toronto harbour at his own expense. Granted £2000 by the Legislative Assembly of Upper Canada, the commissioners started work on a new pier, the Queen's Wharf, on the east side of Garrison Creek. By the time the commissioners reported to the legislature in January 1834, another £500 were required to raise the pier 1.8 metres above the water line (which was always a moving target because lake levels fluctuated over a range of 1.6 metres; Worts 1878), fill the cribbing with stone, erect a pier light, and maintain the wharf until a fund could be established for this purpose.

The commissioners' report made recommendations on three other issues. The first was to redirect the Don River into the marsh. The original mouth of the Don had been joined by another channel to the north that was likely created as a defensive measure during the American invasion of 1813; surveys suggested that by 1834 the two openings were of almost equal size (Speight and Van Nostrand 1930). The commissioners saw the river as nothing more than 'a vehicle for the transport of alluvium into the bed of the harbour,' a problem that could be solved by a dam that would 'arrest the very progress of ruin to the port' (in Langevin 1881: 2–3). The second recommendation was to construct a breakwater from the tip of the peninsula west across the top of the shoal to prevent silt from reaching the harbour's entrance. Third, the commissioners called for the legislature to appoint 'a permanent and scientific commission' which would be given responsibility 'to prosecute works in their opinion so urgently called for to secure to the country the best yet most perishable harbour on Lake Ontario' (ibid.: 3).

Before it could respond to these recommendations, the Legislative Assembly had other positions to consider. Hugh Richardson wrote an open and polemic letter to the residents of York concerning the Don. It eschewed the moderate language of the harbour commissioners to attack the river as 'a monster of ingratitude,' 'the destroying cancer of the port' whose 'destructive mouths' threatened to turn 'this beautiful sheet of water into another marshy delta' (ibid.: 3–10). Captain (later Sir) Richard Bonnycastle of the 1st Royal Engineers used more temperate words in his report to the legislature of 14 January 1834, arguing that the Don had little effect on the condition of the harbour; but he too advocated redirecting the river so its silt would fill up the marsh, 'such a fertile source of unhealthiness to this city' (ibid.: 10–17). Like Richardson, Bonnycastle noted the relationship between farming and deforestation along the Don valley and the increase in the amount of sediment brought south by the river. His report also addressed plans to create a permanent eastern entrance to the harbour at the narrows of the peninsula, where storms had left a temporary breach in 1830. While Bonnycastle felt strongly that an unfinished gap would result in the harbour's ruination by opening the basin to yet more sand, a small canal with flood gates and piers could prove useful for trade (ibid.: 12–13).

After weighing these opinions, William B. Jarvis, the legislative representative of the Town of York, reported to the legislature on 13 February 1834 that while the government had granted funds to finish the Queen's Wharf, no additional monies would be granted pending incorporation of York as a municipality the following month. It would be left 'to the local authorities under the municipal government to make such improvements towards effecting the desired object as to them may appear necessary' (ibid.: 1), likely Toronto's first but certainly not its last experience with higher levels of government downloading responsibilities without the funding required to carry them out. Before Confederation, municipal incorporation was frequently used to create a political infrastructure that could raise taxes and support major public works (D. Baldwin 1988). But the animosity between Reformers and Tories on Toronto's newly elected city council precluded action on such pressing issues as contaminated water and sewerage, let alone harbour improvements. Nothing was done in response to the harbour commissioners' recommendations in 1834, and while Chewett and Chisholm were reappointed to their posts to expand the Queen's Wharf in 1837 with a grant of £2500, the onset of another depression precluded action on the Don, western shoal, or eastern entrance.

Despite its constricted entrance, the harbour accommodated increased activity during the 1840s. The economy improved in 1841, leading to a rise in exports and imports as harbour dues rose almost 25 per cent between 1843 and 1844 (W.H. Smith 1846). Increased traffic led to growth in the port's fleet. Donald Bethune, who owned eight steamships, operated the largest number of such vessels in Canada West[1] out of Toronto harbour (Careless 1984). Private-sector confidence in the viability of the harbour was also evident in its changing contours as traced by surveyors in 1842 and 1850. Seven private wharves, clustered primarily between Peter and Jarvis streets, were mapped by James Cane in 1842. Within the next eight years, several new piers were built at the east end of the north shore (including at the Gooderham and Worts distillery), as were retaining walls that replaced the shore of low bluff and beach with timber cribbing (Hayes 2008). This uncoordinated expansion of the port was driven by private commercial interests that began the city's push south into the bay in the search for additional space close to established businesses.

Preservation by Trust, 1850–1880

The discovery of gold in California and the industrialization of western Europe and the eastern United States brought a close to the economic depression of the late 1840s and a encouraged strong demand for staples. Toronto flourished as the trade centre for a region extending from Peel County in the west to Durham County in the east, and north to Barrie. The Reciprocity Treaty of 1854 opened American markets to wheat and lumber shipped through Toronto, and trans-lake trade led to an increase in imports from $1.2 million in 1849 to $6.6 million in 1856 (Careless 1984). The arrival of railways in Toronto during the 1850s had a negative effect on the port later in the nineteenth century, but as early as 1845 it was recognized that Toronto's harbour, along with its wealth and relatively large population, made the city the logical terminus for railways in Canada West (*Globe* 1845). Recent completion of the St Lawrence, Erie, and new Welland canals meant that bulk freight such as wheat, flour, and lumber travelled more cheaply by major lakes and rivers to reach markets in Canada East, the Maritimes, and the United States, and water-borne transportation retained a competitive edge over rail throughout the decade (Passfield 1988).

Public investment in harbour improvements in Toronto, as in other trans-shipment nodes on the Great Lakes, was essential to maintain the link between ship and shore in a region where water-borne transportation played a vital role in the export of staples and the import of finished items from distant manufacturers. The grants to construct and expand the Queen's Wharf had actually been loans to be paid off by harbour dues, a toll on cargo. The debt lingered into the 1840s, yet dues collected by provincial officials were used neither to discharge this burden nor to fund necessary improvements (*Globe* 1847b). Working through the Toronto Board of Trade in 1844, the city's merchants launched a campaign to transfer responsibility for management of the harbour to a trust (Stanford 1974). Their persistence was rewarded in 1850, when the provincial legislature created the Commissioners of the Harbour of Toronto, more commonly known as the Harbour Trust. Five commissioners (two nominated by city council, two by the Toronto Board of Trade, and one by the provincial government) were given responsibility for preparing plans and estimates for the improvement of the harbour, managing these works, and regulating vessels in the harbour. Revenues to pay for harbour improvements and the small staff of a harbour master, deputy harbour master (later two), and consulting engineer would come from harbour dues and the power to issue debentures. J.G. Chewett, one of the three original harbour commissioners of 1833, was appointed to the Harbour Trust by the provincial government, and was elected its first chairman. Hugh Richardson, another of the original commissioners, was made harbour master.

The Trust had much to consider. The Canadian Institute was established in Toronto in June 1849 by Frederick Cumberland, Kivas Tully, Sandford Fleming, and others as a scientific society dominated by engineers, architects, and surveyors. Fleming, a Scottish surveyor who emigrated to Upper Canada in 1845, was particularly adept at using the organization to advance his professional interests, which, between 1850 and 1855, were focused on Toronto harbour (Creet 2000). Addressing members of the Institute on 1 June 1850, Fleming attributed Toronto's rapid rise in commerce to 'the unequalled excellence of this harbour ... To maintain this harbour in its original state, or if practicable, to improve thereon so as to ensure a continuance of prosperity, becomes, therefore, of the utmost importance' (Fleming 1853–4: 105). An examination of old charts, however, revealed an old problem: natural forces were quickly closing the harbour's western entrance. Challenging Sir Richard Bonnycastle's 1835 assertion that its distinctive peninsula was one of several ridges left behind by the retreat of Lake Iroquois thousands of years earlier, Fleming undertook a detailed analysis of coastal hydrology, concluding that the harbour originated as a delta of the Don River. Since Bouchette's 1792 survey, Fleming noted, more than twelve hectares had been added to the peninsula by the wind and waves that eroded the Scarborough Bluffs and brought sediment westwards. 'It seems ... that the same natural agents which have raised up a breakwater, and formed one of the most capacious harbours on the Lake, are as actively engaged in its destruction, by fencing in, as it were, the whole smooth water basin they have made' (ibid.: 226–7). About 8410 cubic metres of sand were added to the peninsula each year, reducing the width of the navigable three-metre-deep channel by three-quarters, from 439 metres in 1796 to 110 metres in 1850. The channel was notoriously difficult to enter for sailing vessels when the wind came from the southwest, making this growing constriction a significant concern.

Dredging was effective as a temporary solution, but it involved 'unceasing attention and endless outlay; it should be accordingly dreaded as a permanent restorative' (ibid.: 228). Unlike with tidal ports, lake currents did not provide sufficient force to scour the encroaching shoal. Groynes and a breakwater could be effective, and Fleming called for their construction in three places, including the south side of the channel. He was also concerned about the silt from the Don – which, as a result of spring freshets, broke through the marsh and into the harbour – as well as the city's drains and sewers that emptied into harbour, 'making [Toronto bay], in truth, the grand cess-pool for a population of probably 30,000 inhabitants, with their horses and cattle' (ibid.). He called for an interceptor sewer to carry the effluence east to the marsh, where new British technology would strip away the noxious qualities and convert it to 'a marketable commodity of the highest value to the farmer' (ibid.). Fleming also recommended that the Don's entrance to the harbour be blocked, and that the proposition put forward in 1835 to construct an eastern entrance to the harbour be revived. He dismissed Bonnycastle's fears that such a canal would bring ruination of the harbour, and instead argued that the new entrance would purify its waters and slow the growth of the western shoal by using the canal's piers to intercept passing silt. Fleming's remarks were the first thorough and analytical study of the forces shaping Toronto harbour, specifically the interaction of waves, wind, and land features that resulted in constant change to the physical environment – change that threatened to rob Toronto's commercial sector of the 'natural' asset that had given its merchants and shipowners a competitive advantage.

Fleming's paper launched more than three decades of engineering reports that provided a foundation for public works that began in the 1880s. In January 1852, harbour master Hugh Richardson asked Walter Shanly, another member of the Canadian Institute and a civil engineer, to furnish proposals for the westerly extension of the Queen's Wharf and improvements to the harbour's entrance. Shanly had only a brief acquaintance with the harbour, but he reiterated many of Fleming's recommendations. The western shoal would eventually close the entrance unless a pier was constructed from the peninsula to stem the deposit of silt. The Don was 'a less potent, but insidious and impatient enemy' that could be beaten by channelling its mouth through the marsh to reclaim the wetlands for buildings and other purposes; remnants of the river's flow would be flushed into Lake Ontario. Repeated breaches in the peninsula pointed the way to an eastern entrance that would be a great advantage to shipping (in Langevin 1881: 19–21). Kivas Tully, the superintendent engineer for the Esplanade, joined the debate a year later in a letter to the *Patriot* and a subsequent petition to the mayor, arguing that an eastern entrance could be opened with considerable commercial advantage, and that the city's sewers should be connected to a proposed channel under the Esplanade that would lead to the Don River and eventually the marsh (Tully 1853a, 1853b).

Hugh Richardson reported to the Harbour Trust in January 1854 on steps necessary to preserve the harbour, particularly in terms of the need to maintain a navigable western channel and a breach in the peninsula. The need for more information led the Trust to offer awards of £100, £75, and £50, co-funded by city council, for the best reports on the 'means to be adopted for the improvement and preservation of Toronto Harbour,' paying particular attention to the breach in the peninsula, and the advisability of connecting the harbour with Ashbridge's Bay or Ashbridge's Bay with the lake (*Globe* 1854). The award-winning essays by Henry Youle Hind (professor of chemistry at the University of Trinity College), Sandford Fleming, Kivas Tully, and Hugh Richardson clearly illustrated that there was no agreement among the experts regarding the formation of the harbour, or what to do with it. Hind, who won first prize, provided a thorough geological analysis of the Scarborough Bluffs and the peninsula, challenged Fleming's earlier conclusions, and recommended the diversion of sewage to the Don and then into the marsh, where it would become inoffensive (Hind 1854). Fleming stood behind his previous work, and challenged the assumptions by Hugh Richardson that construction and expansion of the Queen's Wharf would accelerate currents and scour the channel (Fleming 1854). Tully reiterated his case for directing sewage to the Don, diverting the river into Ashbridge's Bay, extending the Queen's Wharf, and creating an eastern entrance flanked by lengthy piers to keep silt out of the bay (Tully 1854). Richardson, who would have been given second prize were it not for his position of harbour master with the Trust, strongly opposed a second entrance as an unjustifiable expense and pointed out that shutting out the Don was no longer an option because it would affect private interests. He appealed to the inhabitants of Toronto to 'appreciate the great value of their Harbour *as it is*' and to oppose 'delusive and costly projects of innovation which oppose the *operations of nature*' (Richardson 1854: 38).

Perhaps the most striking aspect of this literature on Toronto harbour is not its lack of consensus, but its lack of influence. Henry F. Perley, chief engineer for the federal Department of Public Works, observed in a confidential memorandum, prepared on 11 April 1881, that

> for nearly half a century it has been the desire of those interested in the welfare of the harbour that steps should be taken to ensure its preservation for the future: that, though many reports have been made and suggestions and estimates of cost submitted, none have been adopted nor acted upon, even in part; and the same forces of Nature which have acted through past years are still acting unchecked to the detriment and possible destruction of the finest harbour on Lake Ontario. (in Langevin 1881: xiii)

Part of the problem likely lay in public indifference. As Letty Anderson observed in her study of urban water supply in Canada, 'attention seems to be drawn only by crisis' in many areas of public works, and once a solution has been found, the problem ceases to be an issue (1988: 217). This attitude may explain why Toronto voters twice voted down expenditures on improved sewage facilities during the 1880s, despite a history of deaths from cholera and typhoid linked to drinking water fouled by sewage in the harbour, a problem that lingered for another twenty years (D. Baldwin 1988; Sing et al. 1912). Apathy was clearly evident when Mayor Adam Wilson called a public meeting on 29 April 1859 to urge the government to adopt immediate measures for the preservation of the harbour in view of a permanent breach that had turned the peninsula into an island. Wilson and Alexander Manning expressed surprise at the poor attendance, particularly among the commercial classes (*Globe* 1859). A large part of the responsibility for inaction, however, lay with the Trust itself. James Gooderham Worts, a harbour commissioner since 1856 and chairman of the Trust from 1865 to 1882, informed Toronto's mayor and council in 1878:

> I consider reports on the Harbour to be of very little value. No person, be he ever so learned, can foresee with any certainty the effects the different currents and winds will have, but one thing we do know, that if the Harbour is kept out of debt and the tolls at the lowest possible rates, we may expect a fair share of business to remain, but should the opposite course be adopted, the expenditure of large amounts of money and increase of the tolls to pay interest, will have the effect of causing our trade to fall more and more to the railways. (1878: 3)

Worts saw little point in works to protect an island that he conceded would eventually succumb to the lake, since timber cribbing required an immense outlay and costly regular repairs. He also opposed spending any of the Trust's revenue to protect the East Gap, and instead proposed a toll on all craft that passed through it for the Gap's maintenance as a navigable waterway. As for the western entrance, Worts supported the government's efforts to maintain a dredged channel equal in depth to 'all the water that the Welland Canal will afford' (ibid.).

Worts's fiscally conservative approach to managing the harbour was reflected in the narrow focus of the Trust's activities during his tenure. As Sandford Fleming had predicted, dredging had been an unceasing obligation since the early 1850s, and the demands for dredging significantly increased during the late 1860s. By 1876 dredging had put the Trust in debt by close to $10,000, and it took several years to eradicate this liability. This was by no means unusual, since shipping berths were notoriously difficult to maintain, deposits of silt in ports lacking a tidal scour could be measured in centimetres per month, and the deliberations of other harbour commissioners were preoccupied by dredging during the late nineteenth century as ships became larger (G. Jackson 1983; Trump 1974). The problem was exacerbated in Toronto by sewers that drained garbage, household and animal waste, and other filth directly into the harbour. During the year 1869, about 3100 cubic metres of silt and sewage were dredged from the Yonge Street slip. Twenty-two years later, approximately 18,700 cubic metres of sewage were discharged each day into Toronto bay and vicinity by a population of 181,000, and Kivas Tully estimated that almost 19,000 cubic metres of material were dredged from the harbour during 1891 (Harbour Trust 1892). The city's faith in the natural powers of large bodies of water to diffuse and purify such wastes, although quite conventional for a Victorian urban centre that made sanitation a higher priority than concern for the natural environment (Winter 1999), created significant problems in terms of port operations and quality of life.

In the case of A. & S. Nairn, importers and shippers of coal, its letter-head in 1879 advertised a depth of twelve feet (or 3.7 metres) at its Church Street wharf (see figure 1.2), conveying the notion that schooners carrying this bulk cargo could berth at its dock without having to find deeper water elsewhere, thereby avoiding lightering charges. A year later, however, new letterhead no longer boasted of this capacity, and Nairn informed the harbour master that the Church Street slip offered between only 1.2 and 2.6 metres of water. Nairn urged that the Trust finish its dredging of the slip in view of the significant amount of harbour dues and municipal taxes paid by the company (Nairn 1880). While there is merit in maritime historian Adrian Jarvis's observation that 'for shipowners the water was always deeper on the other side of the dock' (1994: 125) – Nairn complained a year earlier when the Trust dredged the slip of his neighbour, the Sylvester Brothers – the number of complaints submitted by businesses located between the Yonge and Sherbourne Street slips indicate that sewage deposits were a serious problem, particularly when the time and expense of lightering could drive importers into the hands of the railways. And, at a time when people believed that disease spread through the miasma of polluted waters, the Yonge Street slip was particularly offensive; wharfingers

1.2 Letterhead of A. & S. Nairn, importers and shippers of coal, 1879; the advertised depth at its Church Street wharf was 3.7 metres (12 feet). (Courtesy of Toronto Port Authority Archives, RG/14, box 1, folder 9)

complained of the deposit's 'foul and putrid nature, generating large quantities of offensive and poisonous gases' that endangered the lives of those who did business on the wharf (Milloy et al. 1882: [1]). This problem would not be remedied until the completion of two interceptor sewers to carry waste to a treatment facility near the east end of Ashbridge's Bay in 1913. Until then, the Trust was often ordered by provincial health officials to dredge sewage from the slips and transport it on scows for dumping several miles into Lake Ontario (a strong candidate for one of the nineteenth century's foulest jobs; see figure 1.3), and its officials spent considerable energy pursuing financial relief from the City for costs associated with dredging slips affected by municipal sewer drains.

The expense of dredging drove the Trust to pursue its only major infrastructure project of the 1870s: the Don Breakwater. A deep-water

PRINCESS ST DOCK Nov 16 1912 R&B 50

1.3 Toronto Harbour Commission dredging sewage from the Princess Street dock in 1912. (Photograph courtesy of City of Toronto Archives, series 372, subseries 84, item 50)

channel privately dredged between 1854 and 1858 connected the harbour with the Rolling Mills wharf via the Don's much-enlarged northern channel (Speight and Van Nostrand 1930). Ships were often prevented from entering the northern channel by silt that entered the harbour through the East Gap and by the Don when in flood, but an attempt by the Trust to remove the sand was abandoned in 1866 because of how quickly the alluvium was replenished. By 1868 the Rolling Mills factory had been unable to use its dock for three years, and while the high cost of dredging was offset by high amounts of harbour dues paid by Gooderham and Worts, a gasification company, and other businesses in this area of the harbour, the Trust did not wish to make this activity a regular expenditure. In 1869, Kivas Tully began advocating for a breakwater to protect the southern side of the Rolling Mills channel, extending westwards from the remnants of the sandbar that separated the harbour from Ashbridge's Bay. The breakwater was completed in 1871 at a cost of $24,804, with the expectation that it would accommodate a spur of the Toronto & Nipissing Railway. Dredging to widen the channel was completed the next year, and in 1873 the harbour master reported that tolls collected on goods moving through the channel rose by $1895 to $3365, an amount that represented more than 25 per cent of that year's harbour dues (Harbour Trust 1873).

Despite the prospect of a reasonable return on this investment, the Don Breakwater became a focal point for criticism. The *Globe* hinted at a 'particular benefit to certain private parties' – presumably James Gooderham Worts who, in addition to being chairman of the Trust, was also a prominent east-end distiller and major shareholder in the Toronto & Nipissing (*Globe* 1870). Another daily newspaper, the *Express*, was much more virulent in its attacks on the Trust and its chairman. Opening salvos came in June 1871, when it criticized the Trust for allowing the East Gap to expand uncontrollably without constructing piers to reduce the impact of easterly waves, despite more than $10,000 sitting idle in its bank account and in building society stocks. By October, the *Express* focused on the Trust's allocation of a disproportionate share of funds to a project that benefited Worts and the Toronto & Nipissing Railway while leaving the deteriorating breach in the sandbar to its own devices. A letter from 'An East End Man' published the next day assailed the structure of the Trust, accusing the municipal appointments of taking no interest, letting harbour business fall into the hands of Worts, and allowing public funds to be spent for the benefit of private interests instead of the protection of the harbour. Much to the paper's disgust, the

Board of Trade reappointed Worts to the Trust in January 1872. Under pressure from the railways to improve the navigability of wharves, the City's Committee of Wharves and Harbours sent a strongly worded message to Toronto's three members of Parliament in 1874 that eventually resulted in an appropriation of $20,000 for dredging – on the condition that the work not be delegated to the Trust (Mellen 1974).

Gooderham and Worts directly benefited from the Don Breakwater and access to a protected deep-water channel, which suggests that enlightened self-interest played a key role in the involvement of business interests on public bodies (a theme that also dominated the negotiations between city council and the railways for construction of the Esplanade; Mellen 1974). Moreover, the anonymous east-end resident raised an important point regarding the Trust's commissioners: they were short-term appointments who were seldom on the Trust long enough to have meaningful input in decision making, since issues often took several years to unfold (Toronto Harbour Commissioners 1934). Only six men served ten years or more, with Worts serving twenty-seven years and Arthur B. Lee, a hardware merchant and proprietor of the St Lawrence Foundry, serving twenty-three. The two men were chairmen of the Trust from 1865 to 1902, providing constancy in representing Toronto's mercantile community, for whom a safe and navigable waterway was paramount. So long as wharves remained accessible and harbour tolls were low, shipping remained competitive with railway transport, leading few to question the work of a harbour authority that was basically reactive to hydrological forces while leaving port development to uncoordinated private interests.

From Harbour Trust to Harbour Commission, 1881–1914

The 1880s were the years that many of the decades-old schemes for large-scale reconfiguration of the waterfront began to take form, bringing together the Harbour Trust with the municipal and federal governments in a chain of events that would forever change waterfront governance in Toronto. The north shore of the harbour continued to evolve in the piecemeal, ad hoc manner that started in the 1840s, and accelerated in the 1850s with the arrival of the railways to compete with wharfingers, lumber and coal yards, shipbuilders, ferry operators, recreational boaters, and each other for the creation and use of new waterfront property. Its hard edge was moved south by more than three hundred metres by 1900, consuming 180 hectares of the bay

(O'Mara 1976). The other three quadrants of the harbour still bore features shaped by wind and waves similar to those recorded in George Philpott's 1818 survey (see 1818 contour in figure 1.4). The peninsula had become an island, and by 1882 the site of Privat's Hotel, which lay to the west of the original 1858 breach, was a considerable distance off shore. The western shoal hugged Gibraltar and Hanlan's points much more closely than forty years earlier, but was steadily closing the Queen's Wharf's channel. The northerly channel of the Don River, dug out in 1813 but closed again by 1818, was much more prominent by 1882, and the sandbar to the south much less stable as currents moving through the East Gap disrupted the marsh (see figure 1.5). Civil engineers in this Victorian age had spent the previous thirty years exploring and attempting to understand the natural waterfront; their successors would spend the next thirty years attempting to subdue it and render it productive (Ball 1988).

The Trust's principal contribution to this process was the Commissioners' Cut, otherwise known as the Don Diversion (see the upper-right corner of the 1911 map in figure 1.5). In an attempt to reduce expenditures by eliminating the need for dredging the silt and refuse delivered into the harbour by the Don after heavy storms, the Trust obtained permission from the City to excavate a channel south from the Grand Trunk Railway bridge into the river's northerly channel, so that it would flow directly into Ashbridge's Bay and eventually into Lake Ontario. This project was also seen as an opportunity to realize the recommendations of Fleming, Shanly, and Tully to channel the city's sewage into the Don, have it be filtered by reeds in the marsh, and then diffused by the lake. The channel was cut from the river to the marsh in 1883, but the Grand Trunk refused to allow stop logs to be placed along the west bank of the Don where it flowed into the northern channel. The Trust decided not to proceed further the following year. Attempts were occasionally made by City officials in the 1890s to revive plans to bring the Don's mouth south to the lake, with no success. Tully's work on this project did not achieve his original design, but he did establish the river's course between the railway bridge and the Keating Channel that would be its permanent path by 1914.

The Don Diversion project did not reduce the demand for dredging in the north-east section of the harbour, but assistance was forthcoming from the federal government to deal with challenges elsewhere. Dredging the Queen's Wharf channel was always problematic; when the firm of Hamilton & Pearce worked this location in the summer of 1875, they encountered so much rock that a large portion of the dredge had to be replaced and its crane end strengthened in dry dock in St Catharines (Hamilton & Pearce 1875). The situation was studied in April 1876 by William Kingsford, a civil engineer, to give advice on the most effective ways of spending the federal government's allocation of $17,700 for harbour works. Kingsford pointed out that the western entrance was too shallow and too difficult for ships to enter with ease, particularly during bad weather. While he recommended bringing contracts for dredging the channel under the purview of the federal Department of Public Works, he thoughtfully suggested nitroglycerine as an effective tool for dealing with the rock bottom of the channel (*Globe* 1876).

The federal government's continuing interest in Toronto harbour led to a visit by Hector Langevin, minister of public works, in July 1880. Discussions with Worts made it clear that while Langevin's department would remove obstructing boulders from the Western Channel, they could do nothing to deepen the harbour below bedrock (*Globe* 1880b). Langevin was also adamant that federal funds would not be forthcoming until Toronto stopped draining its sewage into its harbour – a pledge repeated by his successor, Joseph Israel Tarte (*Globe* 1901). Langevin had announced in May 1880 that a thorough survey of the harbour was needed to determine why the harbour filled up with silt as fast as the federal government was removing it (*Globe* 1880a). His department recruited James Buchanan Eads, an American civil engineer renowned for his design of a jetty system to control silting along the Mississippi River. Eads's report called for major public works along the natural edges of the harbour: closure of the East Gap with a dyke of sheet piling; breakwaters to protect the island from erosion; a new Western Channel cut through the shoal south of the existing channel, which would be filled; and a dyke of light sheet piling or earth to close communication between Ashbridge's Bay and the harbour to stop floating vegetative matter from moving west and disrupting navigation (Eads 1882).

His recommendations received a positive reception, with the exception of closing the East Gap. The harbour's increased current improved its water quality and, since the sewers still drained into its water, the Gap's benefits outweighed its shortcomings. The Department of Public Works initiated two contracts that got under way in February 1883. The first created a substantial double wall of sheet piling 2000 metres along the island's south shore, giving protection to the badly worn coast. The second involved constructing a dyke, later known as the Government Breakwater, that ran from the northerly channel of the Don to the south edge of the marsh and then west to the East Gap. Unfortunately, as

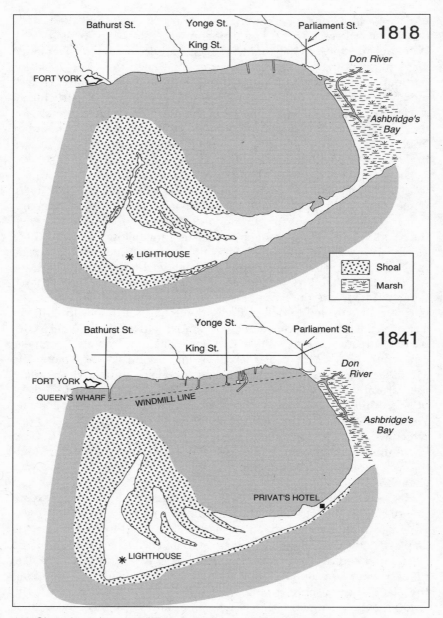

1.4 Changing contours of Toronto Harbour, 1818 and 1841.
(Map by C. King, Cartographic Lab, Department of Geography, York University)

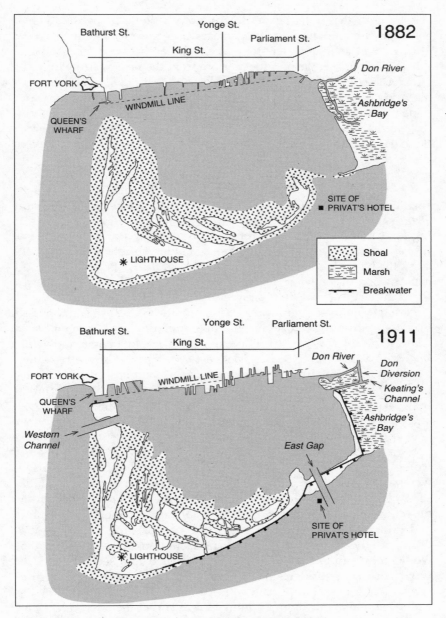

1.5 Changing contours of Toronto Harbour, 1882 and 1911.
(Map by C. King, Cartographic Lab, Department of Geography, York University)

Adrian Jarvis has noted, government intervention was 'bound to have some effect, but not necessarily any that was foreseen or intended' (2007: 181). While the breakwater stopped circulation between the two bays, it also trapped sewage and the manure from the nearby cattle byres of Gooderham and Worts. Typhoid broke out in the 1890s, leading to an alarming rise in the city's death rate. In response to 'the unsanitary and dangerous condition of Ashbridge's Bay' (see Jackson, this volume), the Provincial Board of Health ordered that a channel be dredged from the harbour into Ashbridge's Bay, and then into Lake Ontario. Sewers discharging into Ashbridge's Bay were to be extended into deep water, and Gooderham and Worts was instructed to find another destination for its manure (*Globe* 1892a). City engineer Edward Keating created such a channel through sheet piling and dredging between 1893 and 1895 as part of his plan for the reclamation of Ashbridge's Bay, providing some but not much relief from this unintended conflict between nature and society. The next decade brought federal public works that still mark the harbour's entrances: piers to protect the East Gap in 1901 and construction of a new and deeper Western Channel some 305 metres south of the Queen's Wharf between 1908 and 1911 (see figure 1.5).

Perhaps the most significant change in Toronto during this period was its rapid industrialization. As the population rose from 96,196 in 1881 to 376,538 in 1911, the number of people employed in manufacturing rose from 13,245 to 65,274 (Mellen 1974). The waterfront remained a strategic location due to its proximity to fuel supplies, customs, warehousing, and connections between water and land-based transportation networks, but competition with the railways had resulted in wharves and retaining walls in exceedingly poor repair. Space for new industry was also in short supply, as the railways had tied up most available property and urban growth had already brought the city up against well-established outlying communities. The unproductive, expansive wetlands of Ashbridge's Bay, so long considered a major source of disease, became the focus of many schemes to reclaim its marshes for industry and a modern deep-water port, starting with the plan by Beavis and Browne in 1889 (Desfor 1988; Mellen 1974). Progress in negotiations with the railways to raise its waterfront tracks onto a viaduct that would return to grade at Parliament Street led to a second round of proposals for Ashbridge's Bay in 1907 and 1908. These ambitious designs shared several important concepts, including a channel allowing water to circulate through an industrial area that included docks and parkland, but the plan by the Board of Trade set the tone for the ensuing

debate by proposing public ownership of the waterfront and that properties be leased and not sold. The passage of City by-laws for a trunk
sewer and water treatment facility in June 1908 cleared the way for
federal involvement in these harbour works. Residents expressed their
support for this new approach to waterfront development through a
referendum in January 1911 that effectively placed the reclamation of
Ashbridge's Bay in the hands of a harbour commission. In view of this
consensus, the Toronto Harbour Commission was created by an act of
Parliament on 19 May 1911.

The choice of this governance structure is surprising given that strong
dissatisfaction with the Trust had been expressed since the 1860s. The
Board of Trade championed a commission because it offered more stability than a council-run authority, an arrangement that promoted long-
range planning instead of the previous disjointed, piecemeal approach
to managing the waterfront. The situation was also aided by the appointment of two municipal politicians, Francis Spence and Thomas Church,
to the Trust for several years. Spence had chaired the Trust since 1904 as
well as council's Special Committee on Water Front Improvements that
proposed most of the terms that made up the 1911 legislation. There was
considerable debate at council over the powers that should be given to
the new commission, particularly as this governance model put a costly program of public works into the hands of appointees who were at
arm's length from government and not directly accountable to elected
representatives. The special committee stood firm, conceding only that
the commission's surplus revenues would go to the City, and that the
commission would be audited on an annual basis. The Harbour Trust's
principal shortcoming (besides its reticence to expend funds on dredging and other works) had been its lack of powers (Mellen 1974). Spence
and his supporters addressed this shortcoming by giving the commission the right to hold land in trust for the City, to build and operate
docks and railways, to expropriate and develop property, and to issue
debentures worth up to $30 million secured by its property holdings.
The commission's role as a land development agency would be its most
enduring and significant legacy (Merrens 1988).

Work on this role began with the Waterfront Plan of 1912 (Toronto
Harbour Commissioners 1913b). It was sweeping in its breadth and
scope, calling for reclamation across the waterfront between Toronto's
boundaries to create land for industrial, commercial, and recreational
uses. Modern dock facilities in the central and eastern sections could
accommodate vessels with a draught of up to eleven metres in anticipa-

tion of further work on the St Lawrence canals and the arrival of larger ocean-going freighters. Few sections of shoreline would be spared the engineer's attention. Portland cement, invented in England in 1824 but not in widespread use in Canada until after 1900, gave permanence and quality to massive dock walls that could never be achieved by the timber sheet piling of the nineteenth century (Ball 1988). Hydraulic steam dredges built at the Polson Iron Works in Toronto reclaimed not only the Port Industrial District from Ashbridge's Bay, but also the western beaches at Sunnyside and 263 hectares of parkland added to Toronto Island. The work was led by Edward L. Cousins, who had been the City's assistant engineer in charge of railways, bridges, and docks. Hired by the Toronto Harbour Commission in May 1911, he represented a new generation of Canadian-born and -trained civil engineers who combined an education in the pure and applied sciences with practical experience in the field. Equipped with a plan to raise $25 million through debenture offerings (Cousins 1921) and a small army of engineers, surveyors, machinists, and labourers unavailable to his predecessors, Cousins set about eradicating the remaining vestiges of the harbour, as Sandford Fleming, Kivas Tully, and their contemporaries knew it, in the pursuit of a modern port and industrial district.

Conclusion

As noted by J.R. Millard, 'Engineers viewed Canada as a vast engineering frontier,' replete with unbridled forces and stores of natural assets waiting to be turned into wealth through progress (1988: 13). This chapter captures a sense of Toronto harbour during the nineteenth century, when Simcoe's arsenal played a crucial role in the emergence of the city as a regional centre for trade and commerce. Engineers such as Sandford Fleming saw the harbour as being in 'a constant state of development' (ibid.), one that required scientific study to understand the hydrological forces at work in order to intercede by redirecting nature through groynes and breakwaters to preserve the source of Toronto's prosperity. In the language of mid-nineteenth-century engineers and harbour officials, nature was personified as a wilful creature that, having given Toronto an asset so perfect as its harbour, threatened to destroy it through erosion and alluvial deposits as 'a monster of ingratitude.'

Such language failed to stir the hearts of businessmen such as J.G. Worts, particularly when there was considerable dissent among the interpretations and recommendations of engineers at a time when the

reputation of the profession was far from established. Worts's long tenure as chairman of the Harbour Trust inspired a fiscal conservatism that
limited harbour works to dredging and projects such as the Don Breakwater that provided benefits to those who had a direct interest in the
port, such as distillers, shipowners, and railway investors. This was not
an unusual arrangement. By 1913, harbour trusts handled 40 per cent of
trade in the United Kingdom and had become a standard governance
structure with international success (Jarvis 1996). Trusts prospered elsewhere because they represented the interests of the port's stakeholders,
but in the case of Toronto, the sensibilities of east-end manufacturers
placed a higher priority on maintaining low harbour tolls and high financial assets than on improving the harbour through initiatives that
addressed problems of sewage and public welfare. When pressed by
the City's board of health in 1886 to remove filth from slips along the
central waterfront, the Trust replied that it was not its responsibility to
ensure the purity of the harbour, only its depth (Mellen 1974).

As control of the Trust changed hands in 1904, so did its priorities.
The City and the federal government became much more involved in
harbour works than they had been in the 1880s, and the Trust became
engaged with these initiatives as City appointees, particularly Francis
Spence and Thomas Church, became more actively involved in its deliberations. This dialogue eased the transition from harbour commission to
port authority, from an agency that procrastinated in reacting to the impending closure of the Western Channel and East Gap to a highly structured organization with objectives directly linked to the City's need to
turn 'wasted' wetlands into profitable industrial sites. When compared
against several decades devoted to gathering engineering reports that
led to few permanent harbour works, it is remarkable that only two
years passed between E.L. Cousins's appointment as chief engineer for
the Toronto Harbour Commission and the first sale of debentures of a
planned $25 million based on the Waterfront Plan of 1912.

There are several reasons for this accomplishment. The spate of ambitious water and sewage works that occurred in North America during
the 1890s and early twentieth century created a level of comfort among
the public that would have made the commission's plan seem quite
reasonable. Cleveland had spent almost $14 million on its waterworks
by 1905, and Buffalo had expended more than $11 million on a similar
project, with another $4 million worth of works under way. Toronto's
water system cost around $10 million by the end of 1910, more than
half of the preliminary cost for the 1912 Plan (Sing et al. 1912). Projects

on this scale required a centralized, permanent bureaucracy that could support long-range, comprehensive planning, leading to the emergence of the engineer as a neutral expert and the public's implicit acceptance of this advice in the context of urban planning (Schultz and McShane 1978). In addition, engineers drew inspiration from working within a commission form of government, where conflict with politicians, the 'popularly elected amateurs,' was reduced and the organization was allowed to run on business principles featuring clear lines of authority, long-term planning, continuity in management, and decisions based on expert advice (Millard 1988). In the case of Toronto, this approach to governance facilitated the transition from reactive attempts to preserve the harbour from the forces of nature to a wholesale reconfiguration of nature to initiate industrial and commercial growth.

NOTE

1 The Constitutional Act passed by the British parliament in 1791 created the province of Upper Canada (largely the area now known as southern Ontario), its Legislative Assembly, and the office of lieutenant governor, with a similar arrangement for Lower Canada (Québec). Following the Rebellion of 1837 and Lord Durham's report recommending responsible government for the colonies in 1838, the British parliament passed the Act of Union in 1840, creating the United Province of Canada and renaming Upper Canada as Canada West.

2 Establishing the Toronto Harbour Commission and Its 1912 Waterfront Development Plan

GENE DESFOR, LUCIAN VESALON, AND
JENNEFER LAIDLEY

Michael Redhill's recent novel *Consolation* tells the story of a late-twentieth-century university historian who was convinced that a diary he found in the rare book library of the University of Toronto suggested where the earliest photos of Toronto might be found. The photos, the historian believed, had been stored in the strongbox of a ship, which was wrecked by a storm just off Toronto's shore and then buried by lakefilling as the waterfront crept southward. About 150 years after the storm, the story goes, remnants of the wrecked ship were unearthed while digging out the foundations for a new hockey palace. Commenting on the extent of land created along Toronto's central waterfront, Redhill's narrator says, 'The docks are two hundred and forty feet out from the lake's original shoreline. Landfill pushed everything forward. Buildings erupted out of it like weeds. The city, walking on water' (2006: 2).

Landfill, in this novel, is not only a literal but also a symbolic process to hide, preserve, and then reveal relationships between the past and the present. This chapter is also concerned with unearthing hidden aspects of city building processes, but our main exploration takes a different tack on the production of the very solid land that enabled the city to 'walk on water.'

We are concerned with critically analysing the establishment of the Toronto Harbour Commissioners, a nationally legislated body, as an important local state institution that obtained a mandate to formulate policy for the dual yet highly interrelated concerns of land development, including the production of new waterfront land, and port and harbour management. In May 1911, the Dominion Government of Canada adopted legislation establishing the Toronto Harbour Commissioners (Canada 1911).[1] The new commission represented a major change in governing arrangements for the port and waterfront, and during its eighty-eight years in existence it was the lead organization in changing the shape of Toronto's waterfront.[2] The commission's development policy, enshrined in its *Toronto Waterfront Development, 1912–1920* plan, reshaped Toronto's waterfront and guided processes that resulted in the city 'walking on water' (see figure 2.1).

At the outset, we note that the commission's plans relied on some very tricky business – what we call a 'walking on water' strategy. This development strategy involved the production of approximately five hundred hectares of solid land and deep water, primarily by filling in Ashbridge's Bay and the central harbour area. To be successful, the plan required an understanding of both biophysical and social processes and the highly interrelated socio-ecological dynamics embedded in city building generally, and particularly in land constructed by lakefilling. The Harbour Commission's development strategy, we argue, is tricky because the financial arrangements were unusual, the socio-ecological processes by which the land was to be built were, at best, incompletely understood, and the interrelationships among those processes not adequately acknowledged.

In this chapter, the Harbour Commission's ambitious 1912 planned waterfront development (see figure 2.2), intended to catapult the city into becoming a leading industrial centre, is represented as an example of what Swyngedouw has called 'socio-nature' (1996: 68). Lakefilling weaves together a hybrid landscape through chemical, littoral, biological, cultural, economic, political, and spatial processes. Such a landscape is neither entirely socially constructed nor within the control of society. Despite attempts to make it manageable by and subordinated to social processes, it escapes full social, political, and economic control. It is tricky, and its trickiness will be made evident through this chapter's analysis of the commission's establishment and focus on the production by lakefilling of solid land and deep water (Toronto Harbour Commissioners 1913b: n.p.).[3]

We begin this chapter with a discussion of Canada's emerging industrial economy at the beginning of the twentieth century and its influence on urban government, and particularly the ways by which the political economy of this period influenced Toronto's new form of port and harbour administration. An examination of the influences of municipal politics on the formation of the Harbour Commission follows. This discussion focuses on two particular aspects of political practices

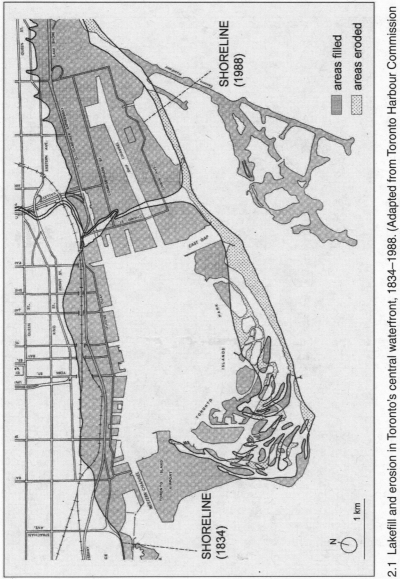

2.1 Lakefill and erosion in Toronto's central waterfront, 1834–1988. (Adapted from Toronto Harbour Commission drawing 15879 by C. Blundell, Department of Geography, University of Toronto)

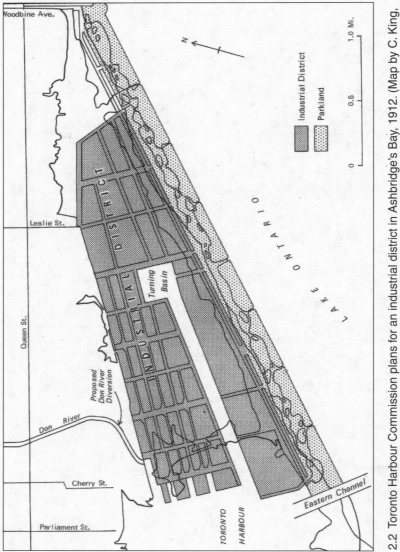

2.2 Toronto Harbour Commission plans for an industrial district in Ashbridge's Bay, 1912. (Map by C. King, Cartographic Lab, Department of Geography, York University)

at the municipal level: first, the discursive construction of a strategy for waterfront development; and, second, the referendum that sought to determine the extent to which Torontonians supported development of their waterfront. The production of waterfront land, the subject of the following section, analyses some fundamental aspects in the lakefilling process in the Port Industrial District. Finally, we end the chapter with a discussion of the 1911 Harbour Commissioners Act, its ambiguities, and some of the controversies and continuing problems that it generated.

Modernizing Toronto's Waterfront at the Beginning of the Twentieth Century

The emergence of Canada's industrial era, in the decades spanning the end of the nineteenth and beginning of the twentieth centuries, marks a turning point in the history of the country's urban settlements. As was the case in many colonial countries, industrialization in Canada was built on a thriving agricultural sector and expanding resource extraction, and was propelled by new technologies such as steam-powered machinery in manufacturing. As Innis documented, Canada's staples trade was a key supplier of empires, first through its colonial ties to Britain and, increasingly, to the emerging economic giant to the south (see Drache 1995). The growth of major Canadian urban settlements fed on an extensive network of staples trading and improved transportation linkages.

In the province of Ontario, servicing the expanding mineral, forestry, and agricultural sectors of the province's northern hinterland was important in fuelling urbanization in the south. Toronto, in particular, achieved phenomenal growth in both population and industrial activity during this time. The city's population tripled between 1871 and 1901 from 86,000 to more than 234,000 people, fuelled by increasing industrial employment, an influx of immigrants, and the annexation of suburban neighbourhoods. Over the same period, industrial output rose from over $13 million to over $58 million (Goheen 1979). Industrial growth was particularly rapid between 1880 and 1890. A growing financial sector serviced not only resource extraction in remote areas but also industrial production in the city. Prominent among the emerging firms were the Massey Manufacturing Company, which moved to Toronto in 1879 to make agricultural implements (Careless 1984), and the Gooderham and Worts distillery, located at the mouth of the Don River and, by the late nineteenth century, producing more proof spirits than

54 Gene Desfor, Lucian Vesalon, and Jennefer Laidley

any other company in Canada. As J.M.S. Careless, a prominent Toronto historian, put it, 'Manufacturing advances in the now thickly settled southern Ontario region partly centred in Toronto because of its large amounts of capital and labour, its well-developed entrepôt structure and radiating transport network' (1984: 105). A central hub of this radiating transport network was Toronto's port and waterfront area around the mouth of the Don.

By the turn of the twentieth century, visions for an extensive industrial expansion of Toronto began to take hold. Ambitious plans led to a search for new sites on which to locate manufacturing plants, expand transportation routes, store coal and other energy supplies, and build commercial facilities. In the pursuit of these expansion plans, the development of Toronto's waterfront figured prominently.

The growth of industrial-based urbanization in Canada set in motion not only a search for new sites, but also the need for new forms of governance to regulate and support this mode of production with its particular spatial ordering of the city. One such institution, which governed over the largest single reshaping and restructuring of Toronto's waterfront in the city's history, was the Toronto Harbour Commission. The commission represented a major reformation of the previous harbour minding authority, the Commissioners of the Harbour of Toronto (known as the Harbour Trust; see Moir, chapter 1, this volume).

The commission's development policy was published in its 1912 waterfront plan, less than a year after the organization was established (Toronto Harbour Commissioners 1913b). The logic of development was based on a speculative strategy: a major industrial district for manufacturing and warehousing firms would be constructed; firms located on this land would generate a need for more shipping and an expanded harbour; and increased shipping tolls and land rents would repay the expense of constructing the industrial land. The newly created land was intended to be a hive of industrial activity linked to modern rail, road, and water transportation facilities, and, as was noted some decades earlier, was expected to 'well repay the projectors' for their $25 million investment (Bonnycastle in Langevin 1881) (see figure 2.3).

The idea of filling in the marsh was not new; as early as 1853, Kivas Tully, a prominent engineer and member of city council, had recommended reclaiming the marsh for industrial land, as did virtually every plan submitted since his time (Desfor 1988). While an industrial district had long been envisioned for the area, realizing the massive development scheme for filling in Ashbridge's Bay – and, most important,

2.3 A concrete cap is being constructed for the dock wall as part of the production of the Port Industrial District. (Courtesy of Toronto Port Authority,
number PC/4/359)

creating the new institution that would be mandated to carry it out
– ultimately required a major campaign on the part of its proponents.

That campaign derived much of its power from Toronto's boosterish
political and economic elite, who were anxious to propel the city forward, particularly in relation to Montreal, and who saw the waterfront
as strategic in this effort. They argued that bringing in and transporting
out goods in the service of the city and industry required major improvements to transportation facilities. Earlier lakefilling had created
solid land on the waterfront that served as a foundation on which to
lay railway tracks, thereby giving the railways a significant locational
advantage. Businesses complained bitterly about the high transport
rates stemming from the railroads' monopoly on transport facilities,
and many central areas of the waterfront saw major battles among
residents, shipping interests, and the railroad companies for valuable

locations and strategic sites (see Mellen's 1974 analysis of the first rail-way penetration in the mid-1880s). The scale of the new opportunities for capital circulation provided by such grand infrastructure projects was evident in massive railway development across Ontario; by 1911 the railways employed 36,700 people and were largely determining the growth of several towns and the development of numerous industries (Drummond 1987). Manufacturers, however, and particularly the own-ers of heavy industry, considered improving or expanding waterway transportation equally important. Well-known examples of such water-related projects are the various stages for deepening the Welland and St Lawrence canals, and the modernization of several ports, such as St John's in Newfoundland.

Industrialists and commercial interests took note of the opportunities these investments in transportation infrastructure projects presented for Toronto. If significant new port facilities, built on solid land and giving access to deep water, were constructed, then Toronto's position in Great Lakes shipping would be enhanced. To achieve this goal, in-dustrial interests and city boosters rallied around the filling in of Ash-bridge's Bay and marsh. Supporters of waterfront development began to combine and redefine a number of issues into a single public-agenda item – a 'waterfront problem' that encompassed an array of interrelated issues of differing magnitudes, including a need for expanded port fa-cilities, a desire for industrial growth, a need for a more powerful port and harbour governing body, a concern for public health, high trans-port rates stemming from a veritable railway monopoly, and a need for more public parks.

Constructing the 'Waterfront Problem'

During a period of a decade or so at the beginning of the twentieth cen-tury, groups of politicians, businessmen, property owners, newspaper owners and reporters, public health officials, and other prominent in-dividuals contributed to the discursive construction of a development agenda that had at its core the 'waterfront problem.' Issues incorporat-ed within this one problem were to some extent spatially and function-ally related, but were institutionally disconnected and not necessarily of equal importance from the public's perspective. Supporters of the development agenda most loudly proclaimed the city's need for 'deep water and good land' (Gourlay 1914a: 2) to fuel its industrial ambitions, but other issues were also included in the problem. One of the immediate consequences of constructing a development agenda based on the 'waterfront problem' was to justify establishing an institution invested with the extensive powers purportedly needed to address such a wide array of issues.

We concur with those who suggest that having the authority to define a problem, or determining the process by which it is defined, reflects important power relations in society (Laclau and Mouffe 1985; Lukes 1974). According to this understanding, power relations are manifested not only through the formalized interactions between state institutions and individuals, but also through the discursive mechanisms involved in controlling the agenda and the language of public debates. Although less obviously apparent, this form of power represents a fundamental dimension of social control and a key element in mobilizing public support for specific collective projects. Decoding the contribution of political power in defining public agenda items, therefore, allows for a better understanding of how complex social relations influence policy formation processes.

Discussion of the major dimensions of Toronto's waterfront problem began with the inadequacy of the extant port regulatory authority and difficulties with shipping in the harbour (see Moir, chapter 1, this volume). The Harbour Trust was responsible for keeping the harbour free from obstructions and for dredging slips, but as early as the 1870s complaints were commonly heard about obstructions that made the harbour unsafe for shipping (Middleton 1923: 446). Ship captains and owners reported serious and enduring problems with both floating logs and shallow water – conditions that were so dreadful that they avoided using the harbour. The commercial viability of the port was being jeopardized, they claimed, and the competitive position of shipping was losing out to the railway companies. The Trust was denounced both for its inability to ensure a safe shipping harbour and for its limited authority to raise funds needed to alleviate this problem. Moreover, charges of corruption were levelled against the Trust (Middleton 1923), bringing the agency into further disrepute. These and other problems made it clear that, by the turn of the twentieth century, the Trust 'had ceased making any positive contributions to the improvement of the harbour' (O'Mara 1976: 15). If a 'modern' port and harbour were to be created, a new regulatory body would have to be established.

As important as the lack of an adequate governing body was for a turn towards a new institutional arrangement for waterfront development, this was only one of the representations of the waterfront problem. Another was the general distrust of local government's ability to handle the complexities of a large and rapidly growing industrial, financial, and commercial city. A number of prominent citizens and groups suggested that neither the Trust nor the City of Toronto was adequate for the task at hand, and that therefore a new body outside municipal government had to be established. One of these prominent groups was the Toronto Board of Trade. As the most effective organization promoting the interests of merchants in the city, the board of trade was interested in creating an organization that could promote waterborne shipping, thereby strengthening a transportation system that could compete with the then extremely powerful railway companies. Management of the large capital investments required for construction of an expanded port and harbour, the board argued, would have to be independent of the vicissitudes of political life, function in a businesslike way, and have adequate jurisdictional authority to deal with a broad range of problems. These qualities, which reflect the then prevalent ideas of the urban reform movement, helped to shape public debate (see both Rutherford and Weaver in Stelter and Artibise 1979 for a discussion of this movement). This particular institutional structure was, however, not agreed upon by all concerned and was the subject of considerable and sometimes heated deliberations (Desfor 1988; O'Mara 1976). Indeed, some members of the City government and the public vociferously objected to giving over port management and city-owned waterfront lands to an independent special-purpose body.

The waterfront problem was also constructed to include a perceived need to deal with a serious public-health issue. The Ashbridge's Bay marsh, which for years had been referred to as a cesspool (Tully 1853a), had become seriously polluted, for three related reasons: in the 1880s a breakwall had been constructed that reduced the flow of water through the bay; the city emptied its sewers directly into these congested waters; and industries disposed of their waste into the marshlands – in particular, the refuse from a large number of nearby cattle byres and dairy and beef-fattening yards. Fear of cholera epidemics was prevalent, and the provincial health officer and property owners threatened to take the City to court for allowing such conditions to exist (see Jackson, this volume, for a discussion of cholera and its influences on the filling in of Ashbridge's Bay).

The emergence of the Harbour Commission as the dominant actor for regulating, managing, and transforming the waterfront should be understood precisely as a response to various representations of the multi-issued waterfront problem. The commission that was legislated into existence in 1911 was given an unprecedented degree of institutional authority, combining powers usually provided by a state agency with those of a private corporate body. Like a corporation, it had the authority to own, lease, and sell land and to raise required financial resources. But it was also able to enjoin actions typical of the state, such as exercising the power of eminent domain (Canada 1911). And its Waterfront Development Plan (Toronto Harbour Commissioners 1913b) codified a massive transformation of the waterfront, with the Port Industrial District as its centrepiece.

While much of the boosterism and political manoeuvring among various interests involved in the establishment of the commission has been documented elsewhere (Goldrick and Merrens 1990; Desfor 1988), we focus in the next section on a previously unexamined part of the campaign – the municipal referendum that paved the way for the commission's creation.

The Referendum

On 2 January 1911, Toronto's duly registered electorate went to the polls to elect a new city government. At the same time, a referendum asked voters to express their preferences on a series of development issues. Among the referendum questions on that election day, two addressed the 'waterfront problem.' One was concerned with funding particular infrastructure improvements, while the other focused on the creation of a new waterfront development institution, asking voters: 'Are you in favor of the control and development of Ashbridge's Bay and the waterfront in the city's interest by a commission having a majority of its members appointed by the city?' (City of Toronto 1911: 129).

As framed by this question, control over and the accountability of such a commission were vaguely, ambiguously, and, in some respects, misleadingly presented. The reference to the 'city's interest' says nothing about the particular mechanisms that would be used to define the public interest in the context of Toronto's waterfront development. Similarly, the organization of a new commission and its place within local-state structures were not explicitly mentioned in the referendum question. It is likely that the public had little access to relevant information for determining the extent to which 'a commission having a majority of its members appointed by the city' would mean that the commission would be controlled by city council and thus accountable to Torontonians. And, as discussed in the final section of this chapter, the ambiguity of the referendum question was not satisfactorily resolved in the enabling legislation, giving rise to considerable tensions and controversy, particularly towards the end of the twentieth century.

Nonetheless, the referendum question on the ballot that day sounded too good to oppose. This was acknowledged fifteen years later in the report of a royal commission to examine Toronto's waterfront development,[4] which noted that the form of the question seemed to be favourable to those who wished the improvements to be made. The report stated plainly: 'There are some ratepayers, however, who would like to know by whom and by what methods public opinion was created in favour of this large undertaking' (Canada 1927: 8). Three important institutions in Toronto – the board of trade, local newspapers, and Toronto City Council – all engaged in fervent discussions about the waterfront problem and the merits of a new waterfront development authority leading up to the referendum vote. An examination of their discussions, which undoubtedly had some influence on public opinion, begins to respond to the question in the royal commission's report.

The Toronto Board of Trade, representing the interests of the business community, brought together a group of influential businessmen and labour leaders, including the Canadian Manufacturers' Association, the Retail Merchants' Association, and the District Labour Council, to run a well-financed and organized political campaign. As part of this campaign, the board published and widely circulated a leaflet proclaiming in bold points that voting 'Yes' to the referendum would benefit Torontonians in five primary ways: Toronto's 'greatest asset' would be developed; Ashbridge's Bay would become worth many millions of dollars; the harbour would be made into 'the finest harbour on the Great Lakes'; Toronto would become one of the greatest industrial centres on the continent; and the harbour would be managed like a business (Wickson 2002: 38). All of this could be achieved, the leaflet claimed, by creating a new commission that would be run on a business-like basis. Such an organization would avoid the ineptitude and corruption that reformers associated with local government, but would seemingly keep the benefits of development in public hands.

The board of trade and its allies supported the formation of a 'national' harbour commission – that is, a commission established under national legislation with the majority of its board members being appointed by the national government. Two issues were fundamental to this position: first, they thought that a 'national' commission was a necessary precondition for the Dominion government to contribute financially to the development scheme; and, second, they wanted to ensure that profits from land development would be reinvested specifically in port and harbour development – rather than other city projects (*Toronto Daily Star* 1910a).

This latter point is central to the board of trade's view that the city's economic growth depended upon efficient and competitively priced transportation facilities, and that a new urban development corporation could manage this venture so as to ensure continuing productive capacity at the waterfront. The board had long-standing positions supporting both the establishment of commissions outside city government and the systematic development of the waterfront for industrial and commercial purposes. Its rhetoric prominently described the way that Toronto could build the finest port and harbour on the Great Lakes and become a major urban region. In their view, a waterfront industrial district full of water-related manufacturing activities and warehousing firms was not only integral to an expanded port, but also provided the basis for general urban expansion. But critics of the board of trade's approach were not convinced that its position would be of benefit to the general public. They argued (see O'Mara 1976) that the board's position was intended to privilege the business community's position in policy formation and to direct development projects for the benefit of its members.

The second institution contributing to public debates with articles and editorials about Toronto's 'waterfront problem' was the media – Toronto's three daily newspapers. In their articles and editorials, the *Toronto Daily Star*, the *Globe*, and the *Evening Telegram* helped to consolidate a negative public perception of the marsh and supported proposals to transform Ashbridge's Bay into an industrial district. However, each newspaper took a different position with respect to whether the new waterfront commission should be part of the 'local' or the 'national' government.

The *Toronto Daily Star* favoured a local commission. In a prominent editorial, the *Star* argued: 'There seems to be no reason why the elected representatives of the people should not remain in direct control of the waterfront. To elect men to control the city's fund, and then to hand over the spending power to other sets of men, seems somewhat of an anomaly' (*Toronto Daily Star* 1910a: 6). The *Star* would not support the establishment of a non-elected commission, fearing that board members would fall prey to the influence of businessmen and thus that corruption similar to that associated with the earlier Harbour Trust would result (*Toronto Daily Star* 1910b: 1). The *Star* did recognize the importance of ensuring Dominion government funding for waterfront development, but suggested that the City should proceed with its own plans even if federal funds were not forthcoming.

The *Globe* was the most enthusiastic supporter of a 'national' harbour commission that was based mainly on its belief that the city needed rapid industrial expansion to become a dominant economic centre of the region. This position linked the creation of an industrial district at Ashbridge's Bay with the city's industrial ambitions. As a *Globe* editorial urged, voters should 'answer the Commission question with a "Yes" and vote for the harbour improvement money by-law' (*Globe* 1910d: 4). In terms of the commission's structure, the *Globe* favoured a board of directors composed of three City representatives and two representatives of the Dominion government, stating that such a structure would make the 'Toronto harbour the finest on the Great Lakes, and make the city one of the great industrial centers of the continent. An improved harbor means more work, more wages, cheaper freight, while a commission would secure a wise, businesslike and continuous management' (*Globe* 1910c: 8). In a 1906 article, the *Globe* extolled the 'national importance' of an initiative by the industrialists Messers Mackenzie and Mann to invest in a manufacturing establishment at Ashbridge's Bay, and supported the idea of providing 'suitable lands' in the area by filling Ashbridge's Bay (*Globe* 1906b: 12).

The *Telegram*, with its outspoken populist publisher John Ross Robertson, gave more attention to Toronto's waterfront development than the other newspapers. The *Telegram* commented on various methods by which board members could be appointed, issues of financial accountability, and the powers of the future commission. It recommended voting against the referendum question and, while remaining supportive of filling in Ashbridge's Bay, the *Telegram* advocated 'a Dominion Government commission working to secure navigable water for deep vessels in the port of Toronto and a civic commission working to plan docks and otherwise develop the city's property' (*Telegram* 1910a: 14). This two-commission solution, it argued, would encourage Dominion government participation in the project, and allow the City to control its waterfront lands in its interest.

In sum, Toronto's three daily papers all supported the radical transformation of the waterfront through socio-ecological processes, particularly the filling in of Ashbridge's Bay and marsh to create an industrial district, but each held a somewhat different position about the structure of the institution that should govern the district's construction and operations. They supported the idea that major changes in the management of the waterfront were urgently needed, that private developers should not be in charge, that the financial worth of Ashbridge's Bay as a marsh was negligible, and that filling it in was the only possibility for 'making the marsh of any real value for the city' (*Globe* 1907a: 1).

The third institution to influence public opinion was Toronto City Council. During the period leading up to the referendum, council focused its attention more on the structure and control of a possible harbour commission than on detailed plans for filling in the marsh. Council generally agreed that management of waterfront development should be given over to a commission outside city government – indeed, an interesting position for a city council to hold, but it continued to debate, even in the final weeks leading to the referendum, whether the commission should be 'local' ('civic') or 'national.' About a month before the referendum, Toronto's Mayor Geary expressed opposition to the establishment of a 'national' harbour commission. He wanted a civic commission in which all board members would be appointed by city council (*Globe* 1910b: 1, 4). He took the position that taxpayers' property should only be administered by a civic commission with exclusive representation from the City, and that the City's land should be developed in the City's interests. If the City-owned Ashbridge's Bay were to become an industrial district, the mayor argued, then the profits from development should be controlled by a civic commission for the benefit of the city. And he countered the argument that national representation was necessary for funding by suggesting that the Dominion government was not 'so small as to refuse assistance if we have a civic commission' (ibid.: 4). Only weeks before the referendum, however, Mayor Geary succumbed to pressure from industrial and economic influences, reversed his position, and supported the board of trade, saying, 'These are public-spirited gentlemen, and we feel it is due to them to let their plan go before the ratepayers unmarred by any scars of contest. Therefore we will not oppose the by-law' (*Telegram* 1910b: 1).

When voters went to the polls that 2 January, there could have been little doubt about the outcome of the referendum question. While a small amount of opposition to the referendum came primarily from landowners who stood to lose their direct access to the lake from filling in the marsh, the prevailing tide ran decidedly the other way. With the Toronto Board of Trade leading a well-run campaign for the 'yes' side, the failure of resistance in city council, only a single newspaper voicing opposition to the referendum, and very favourable wording of the referendum question, a resounding 76 per cent of voters (City of Toronto 1911: 133) indicated they did indeed wish both to have Ashbridge's Bay developed and to have control of this development put into the hands of a commission that would be outside the usual structures of city government.

Land Production in Toronto

Following its establishment, the Harbour Commission quickly turned its attention to formulating plans to meet its dual mandate of, on the one hand, waterfront land development and, on the other, port and harbour minding. Central to these plans was the construction of the Port Industrial District, a massive undertaking based primarily on lakefilling.

At the outset of the chapter, we noted that in our analysis we represent lakefilling as a network of interwoven natural and social processes that are neither distinctly 'natural' nor 'social'; rather, they are simultaneously both 'natural' and 'social' (Swyngedouw 1996). And we suggested that lakefilling is a particularly good example for unravelling the ways that 'natural' and 'social' processes are interwoven in urban development.

In our analysis of lakefilling as a socio-natural project, we pay special attention to the political, economic, and social dimensions of its production. As revealed in the growing urban political economy literature, the production of socio-natures serves economic and political interests, reflects the ideological preferences of dominant groups in society, and acts as a condition of possibility for societal change (see Heynen et al. 2006; Keil 2005, 2003; Swyngedouw 2004; Heynen and Swyngedouw 2003; Castree and Braun 2001; Harvey 1996a; Castree 1995). Speaking about the transformation of Spain's hydraulic system under the authoritarian regime of Franco, for example, Swyngedouw observed that 'every political project is also an environmental project' (2007: 24) – and we add that every environmental project is also political. This is especially true for situations where the environmental project is expected to produce an economically productive asset and a means of supporting the emergence of a new mode of development – as in the Toronto case, the production of land to propel the city's industrialization ambitions.

One of the important lessons from political ecology dialectics is that attempts to dominate and control socio-nature can never be complete

(Harvey 1996a; N. Smith 1984). Such attempts are always vulnerable to ideological contestation, political opposition, social transformation, economic change, and, of course, unknown or unpredictable ecological relationships. Although socio-natural projects are produced in specific historical contexts, their forms and manifestations are not inert material objects which can be arbitrarily manipulated. Rather, socio-natures provide material conditions for new social relations and impose limits on the economic factors underpinning these relations. In capitalist societies, these limits can subvert the logic of capitalist accumulation and even pose a 'threat to the social relations that have underpinned growth' (Boyle 2002: 173). In other words, socio-natures function both to facilitate the establishment of capitalist relations and to impose limits on the circulation of capital. In our case, examining the production of lakefilling is instructive for better understanding the circulation of capital in urban development processes.

Torontonians' support for a development strategy based on industrialization and filling in Ashbridge's Bay had been building for years both before and after the turn of the twentieth century. An article in one of Toronto's dailies, the *Globe*, provides a fine example of the language used to represent the 'despised' Ashbridge's Bay marsh and the wonders of 'great iron and steel plants' that would lead Toronto's industrialization ambitions:

> Toronto is to become the Pittsburgh of Canada. That heretofore despised region known as 'The Marsh' is to be the site of one of the great iron and steel plants in America, the headquarters of the manufacturing industries that will supply the cars and the equipment for the Canadian Northern [Railway], and the pig iron for the foundries and factories of the city. Toronto has been a city of light manufacturing up till the present time. It will soon be the biggest producer in Ontario of the basic material of twentieth century prosperity – iron and steel. (*Globe* 1907a: 1)

The Toronto Harbour Commission, the lead organization in making this vision real, undertook and managed an impressive socio-ecological production system that began in 1913 and lasted for the better part of two decades (Canada 1927). It was guided by its chief engineer, E.L. Cousins, in planning, organizing, and implementing a highly capital-intensive and mechanized process intended to closely control production and dominate 'nature.'[5] The processes and labour relations that constructed the land, as well as the form and function of the landform

itself, reflected industrial capitalism. Dock walls outlined linear boundaries creating regular geometric shapes consistent with the proposed
grid pattern of streets behind which solid land was to be created to
facilitate manufacturing, warehousing, and commercial sites, all supported by piped infrastructure, accessible to electricity, and connected
to railroad sidings. The dock walls were constructed using fir trees
that had been harvested in British Columbia, transported more than
3000 kilometres, machined into 'tongue and grooved close sheet piling' (Cousins 1948: n.p.), and reinforced with concrete. The commission
also committed capital-intensive equipment to hydraulically dredge
the lake bottom, both to raise much-needed material for filling in the
lake and to create a navigable depth of nine metres in the harbour. The
largest dredge on the Great Lakes at the time churned its huge blades
to stir up the lake bottom, and powerful pumps moved this dredgeate
through an extensive system of pipes to its desired location. In addition
to the approximately 27 million cubic yards of dredged material, earth
was hauled from outside the city and dumped behind the dock walls.

Funding such a massive project required a particularly stable institutional environment and points to an important relationship between
the state and private financing in opening up new opportunities for the
circulation of capital (Harvey 1982). To finance construction of the plan,
the commission issued approximately $25 million in debentures that
were secured by property and developments that had not yet been created – primarily the solid land in its Port Industrial District. Arrangements for raising these funds were set forth in a trust deed involving
the Harbour Commission, the City, and two Toronto banks. The City
signed onto the deed as a guarantor, ensuring that it would pay off
the debentures if the commission failed to meet its obligations (Toronto
Port Authority Archives n.d.; O'Mara 1984)

The commission mediated the flow of international funds for the
construction of the new territory. The arrangements for issuing the $25
million of debentures – the 2009 equivalent of almost one half billion
Canadian dollars – benefited considerably from the work of R. Home
Smith, a member of the first board of the Harbour Commission and
one of the people centrally responsible for the 1912 plan. He was the
general manager of the National Trust bank and sat on the board of the
Toronto General Trusts Company (O'Mara 1976).[6] Smith's close connections with the banking sector were key to the commission's operations
within an international economic and financial system. It is not surprising that the commission arranged to have its debentures sold through

the National Trust Company, and the Toronto General Trusts Company, as well as the Dominion Securities Corporation (Toronto Port Authority Archives n.d.; O'Mara 1976). With both the authority and the connections to attract funds domestically and from Canada's dominant colonial centres, the United Kingdom and the United States, the commission sold its debentures in London, New York, and Toronto (Toronto Port Authority Archives n.d.).

As with other colonial situations, investment opportunities in the periphery (e.g., Toronto) provided private capital in colonial centres with productive outlets. In the first decade of the twentieth century, European economies grew significantly and the major European banks were particularly active in funding large industrial projects and infrastructure development internationally (Crouzet 2001: 130). European exports of capital were particularly high during this period, with the United Kingdom's investments abroad being the highest and reaching, in some periods, more than half of its financial surplus (ibid.: 156–9). Toronto's strong banking sector, coupled with rising productivity, made it possible for both the United Kingdom and the United States to strengthen their roles and positions in the Canadian economy. In relative terms, foreign investments in 1911 made by UK companies in Canada made up approximately 77 per cent of total foreign investments, while US companies' investments reached 20 per cent (in Norrie and Owram 1996: 321–2).

Although the commission was quite successful in producing industrial land, its track record in attracting firms to locate in the Port Industrial District was less impressive. A systematic analysis of the commission's record in leasing or selling its newly created waterfront lands is not available, but partial analyses have been compiled. For example, by 1929, the commission had created about 182 hectares of land on which oil-tank storage companies, grain elevators, ship builders, coal processors and storage companies, ice companies, metal fabricators, a sewage treatment plant, fishing companies, construction companies, and gas companies had located. These companies had leased or purchased about fifty-three hectares of the total land available, only 29 per cent of the land that had been produced (Desfor et al. 1988). Manufacturing firms clearly did not locate on the waterfront to the extent expected by the Harbour Commission (see discussion in Prudham et al.; Moir, chapter 1, this volume). With the exception of two major sales of land for industry in 1949, the industrial wave of waterfront land development that had begun with the 1912 plan was largely spent by the end of the 1940s (see Laidley, this volume, for a discussion of the politics of the transition away from industrial land uses on the waterfront).

Ambiguities of a Local-State Organization

As noted earlier, the wording of the 2 January 1911 referendum was vague and ambiguous, particularly regarding how the City's interests would be represented and what the new commission's position would be within government structures. The Toronto Harbour Commission Act did not resolve some of the ambiguities found in the referendum, particularly in terms of accountability.

Briefly, the act established the Toronto Harbour Commission with unprecedented real-estate development powers, giving it a status unique in Canada's port administration system. It stipulated that the commission had authority to 'hold, take, develop and administer on behalf of the City of Toronto' the lands and property under its jurisdiction (Canada 1911: sect. 15-1). While the commission was not entirely outside, or independent of, local and national government structures, neither was it within the standard government framework with a procedure for unambiguous institutional accountability (Olson 1988). The commission's unprecedented powers to raise capital, expropriate land, and operate largely independently of city, provincial, or national governments were accompanied by its ownership of virtually all waterfront lands, acquired through purchases, expropriation, or exchange (Canada 1927).

The development powers of the new commission were clear. But, accountability of the Toronto Harbour Commission to Torontonians, the City, and the national government, we argue, is a complicated matter for at least two main reasons. The first is that, in some important ways, commissions are not intended to be accountable: they are outside the usual structure of government, intended to operate in a business-like fashion and hence be disciplined primarily by market forces, and frequently composed of unelected officials.

The notion of conducting public business through commissions outside of government was influenced both by a public administration ideology 'built on the concept of blue ribbon panels' (O'Mara 1976: 7) and by related concepts in the urban reform movement. The blue-ribbon ideology advocated establishing semi-independent agencies composed of the city's 'best and brightest' citizens, who would direct municipal government. This ideology was applied to harbour commissions and, in a 1922 analysis of the Montreal harbour commission, Robert M. Dawson, a leading twentieth-century scholar of public administration and government in Canada, advocated that the Montreal 'Harbour Commission should be absolutely free from interference by government ... I would like to see it composed of men who would act for themselves without the government being held responsible for their actions' (in O'Mara 1976: 9). Dawson's recommendations are important for Toronto because its enabling legislation was modelled on Montreal's. Even though so-called blue-ribbon panels are still appointed by current governments, more recent public administration scholars point out that this approach to public administration is seriously lacking in democratic processes. These analysts have argued that semi-independent agencies remove control of policy formation processes from the electorate, encourage irresponsibility, and, importantly for our argument, do not permit the public to hold these agencies accountable (see Silcox 1973).

The early-twentieth-century urban reform movement in Canada was based on a perceived need for a systematic transformation of unhealthy conditions in newly industrializing cities. It sought to save city dwellers from the negative results of rapid expansion and unregulated housing and manufacturing. Urban reform was based on a utopian vision that included programs to improve public health, child welfare, and public transportation, and provide good public administration (Rutherford 1979). Public administration, they emphasized, should be undertaken by commissions in which unelected administrators would be free from the encumbrances of politics to act in the public interest. Public policy would become essentially a technical management matter. Accountability, therefore, would not be an issue as long as a governing body was composed of 'right-thinking,' disinterested individuals whose decisions were independent from political processes. Critiques of this movement (see Weaver 1979) have observed that, although some of its programs were successful, a full assessment of the urban reform approach must go beyond analysing its rhetoric. Weaver notes, for example, that newly structured urban governments 'were designed to afford business interests a greater opportunity to mould city development' (393) rather than defending the public interest. He also notes that the movement tended to 'perpetuate a stratified society based upon traditional patterns of deference and morality, patterns which clashed with the ways of newcomers who resided in urban slums' (394).

The second reason that the accountability of the Harbour Commission is problematic is associated with the commission's ownership of virtually the entire waterfront and a mandate to develop all these lands. In fulfilling its dual mandate it had to deal with a complex array of interrelated and multi-scaled urban issues including the planning and development of land reclamation, railways, roads, water transportation facilities, parks and recreation, provision of facilities for energy generation and storage, manufacturing plants and warehouses, and of course shipping. A single authority dealing with all these aspects of development could provide integrated and efficient administration. However, maintaining accountability for such a vast array of interrelated developments could be cumbersome and time-consuming and give rise to inordinate delays and intractable jurisdictional problems. Moreover, the board and its staff would have to scrupulously identify and adhere to a distinction between the public interest and its own institutional or private-members' interests.

A third reason that the accountability of the commission became problematic should also be mentioned. This reason, however, relates less to the commission's enabling legislation and more to its historical particularities. In 1922, after allegations of faulty construction and corrupt business practices were made, a royal commission was established to inquire into the operations of the Harbour Commission. The so-called Denton inquiry lasted about two years and identified incidences of political favouritism, construction incompetence, and some significant business irregularities (Canada 1927). Although no criminal charges were laid, the Harbour Commission became defensive, secretive, and 'retreated into their board rooms' with little concern for providing public accountability (O'Mara 1976: 45).

In the late 1980s, as questionable land sales made headlines, the Harbour Commission's accountability was again brought into question, becoming a concern of a second royal commission, established in 1988. The Royal Commission on the Future of the Toronto Waterfront analysed the Harbour Commission Act, and found that three types of accountability were at play: political, financial, and functional (Royal Commission on the Future of the Toronto Waterfront 1989d). According to the royal commission, the act established political accountability by having the City and federal governments appoint the members of the board of the Harbour Commission. The act gave the City power to appoint the majority of the five-member board – the only such case in Canada – but was silent on whether elected politicians could become commissioners. To complicate the accountability issue, the act required that, upon assuming office, board members would take an oath of impartiality in executing their duties, creating confusion about how members could or should represent the interests of their appointing bodies.

In the act, financial accountability was provocatively ambiguous. It did give the City power to annually examine the board's books; however, it also provided for considerable financial independence. It stipulated that the Harbour Commission was not subject to the federal Financial Administration Act, a cornerstone of the legal framework for general financial management that 'sets out a series of fundamental principles on the manner in which government spending may be approved, expenditures can be made, revenues obtained, and funds borrowed' (Treasury Board of Canada 2010).

The royal commission reported that in the act, functional accountability, that is, the obligation to have harbour-minding operations and development policies reviewed, was diffuse. The disposition of land did receive attention: the board was required to obtain the consent of the federal Governor-in-Council to sell or dispose of any land it had acquired. It also required the Governor-in-Council to confirm the transfer of previously owned city property. It recognized that the Harbour Commission's land development activities would involve railway rights-of-way, and thus made its operations subject to the terms of the Railways Act, intended to ensure safe railway operations. The commission was also required to satisfy the Customs Act, regulating the movement of goods and services across international borders. It seems, however, that the commission act did not provide for functional accountability in other systematic ways.

Although the royal commission did identify these types of accountability in the act, it pointedly reported that the actual accountability of the board of the Harbour Commission was 'entirely another' matter (Royal Commission on the Future of the Toronto Waterfront 1989d: 73). The royal commission noted that in its early years the board accounted to the public for its actions primarily through the newspapers and its own communications. For example, the board's early development policy was extensively covered in Toronto newspapers with the publication of the 1912 plan. And, the royal commission reported, 'the 1912 plan can be seen as the THC's method for establishing a frame of reference within which it could be held accountable' (73). But some land sales in the 1980s, questionable development projects, and the falling off of shipping traffic left municipal, provincial, and even some federal officials wondering how the commission could be made accountable for its actions. Indeed, the establishment of the Royal Commission of

the Future of the Waterfront arose, in part, from controversies in which
the Harbour Commission was embroiled.

In sum, the new commission's enabling legislation provided broad
powers not only to mind the port and harbour, but also to develop waterfront lands – a process requiring its participation in multi-party and
multi-scalar networks of groups and individuals with waterfront interests. The commission's ambiguous accountability has been highly
problematic for decades.

Conclusions

With a development mandate secured from Toronto's electorate in January 1911 and enabling legislation passed in May, the Harbour Commission set about preparing its Waterfront Development Plan. The
commission's establishment marked the beginning of a period during
which it was the lead organization for managing a many-faceted 'waterfront problem.' With its then unconventional institutional structure,
the commission was responsible for shepherding in massive industrial,
transportation, and park infrastructure projects to support increased industrial development in a rapidly changing city at the beginning of the
twentieth century.

There is no doubt that the establishment of the Toronto Harbour
Commission was a defining moment in the history of Toronto's waterfront. From its establishment in 1911 to its dissolution and restructuring
in 1999 (see Sanderson and Filion, this volume), the commission created
more than eight hundred hectares of new land spanning nearly twenty
kilometres of shoreline (Pankratz, in Wickson 2002: 9) and, in the process, fundamentally reshaped both the terrestrial and jurisdictional terrain of Toronto's waterfront. Indeed, the commission's influence over
its newly created lands continued until its dissolution, contributing
to some of the most hotly contested episodes on the waterfront in the
twentieth century (see Laidley; Sanderson and Filion, this volume).

The socio-ecological processes examined in this chapter lead us to
make five conclusions. First, we challenge the merit of the speculative
'walking on water' strategy. We agree with E.L. Cousins, the Harbour
Commission's chief engineer and a prime mover of the 1912 plan, who,
in a 1931 interview, questioned the strategy he himself had promoted.
Although the commission was earning significant revenues through
the lease of its industrial lands, he said, the harbour tolls, shipping fees,
and land rents which the commission earned did not meet its financial
obligations to its creditors. It was being forced to sell the very land that

it had gone into debt to create. The strategy of constructing solid land as a location for industrial firms that would, in turn, create a demand for extensive shipping facilities was not yielding an adequate return on investments. As Cousins sadly and ironically observed, 'no sane man' would spend as much as the commission did on Toronto's ambition to be a lake port (*Toronto Star Weekly* 1931: n.p.). The 'walking on water' strategy revealed, we believe, the tensions and complexities inherent in dynamic networks of socio-ecological development projects and the fundamental contribution of political power to urban expansion.

Second, in analysing the discursive strategy that constructed the 'waterfront problem' at the end of the nineteenth century, and the public discussions that framed the debate over how this problem should be resolved, this chapter reinforces the notion that the way a problem is resolved often has much to do with the way it is defined. The discursive construction of a complex waterfront problem was pivotal in the establishment of a multi-scaled institution with a multi-scaled mandate, ambiguous accountability, and powers the likes of which had never before been seen on Toronto's waterfront.

Third, the establishment of the Toronto Harbour Commission institutionalized a new set of social relations supporting industrialization in the city. The process by which the commission was established brought together a variety of different players, with as disparate interests as the manufacturers, merchants, and labour leaders who contributed to the Toronto Board of Trade's successful campaign in favour of the January 1911 referendum.

A fourth conclusion relates to the matter of 'jurisdictional gridlock' – an issue that gained prominence in debates over the waterfront in the late twentieth century (see Eidelman, this volume). While jurisdictional gridlock has been blamed for myriad problems on the waterfront, the conflict that lies at the heart of this gridlock – that is, determining who gets to decide on the waterfront's shape and future – was, as demonstrated in this chapter, inherent in the very mandate and structure of the Toronto Harbour Commission. The lack of a clear definition, in both the referendum question that authorized the commission and the legislation that created it, of 'the city's interest' and, perhaps more importantly, of which body or agencies were empowered to determine it, laid the foundation for nearly a century of antagonism, most particularly between the City of Toronto and the commission, but also among other organizations with competing waterfront mandates. In essence, the underlying issue revolved around the question of who determines the City's interests – a question of power and authority. That is, the commission was mandated to act on behalf of the City to develop its waterfront lands, but the City and the commission frequently had very different ideas about what the City's interests were.

And fifth, for much of its existence the Harbour Commission defined waterfront development policy, initially articulated in its 1912 waterfront plan. Although the plan was constructed at the local level, its formation was influenced by political, economic, and ecological processes at municipal, regional, national, and even international scales. We believe that the commission should thus be considered part of the 'local state,' despite its establishment by national legislation. This conclusion may go some way to explaining the near-continuous enmity that existed between the City of Toronto and the Harbour Commission, in that the primarily municipal interests of City government may necessarily have been at odds with the multi-scalar concerns of a local state body.

NOTES

1 The formal name is the Toronto Harbour Commissioners, but throughout the chapter we refer to it as the Toronto Harbour Commission, its more commonly used name.

2 While we distinguish local state organizations from municipal government, we also recognize that such organizations are not branches of the national state with specific functions or delegated responsibilities having their origin with the national scale of governing (Desfor and Keil 2004). Rather, we understand a local state body as a government organization whose policies, planning, and practices are focused on activities at the local level, but its policy and operations are established by organizations originating at local, regional, and the national scales (see Kipfer and Keil 2002; Magnusson 1996; Jessop 1990; Duncan and Goodwin 1985).

3 Though Redhill refers to the filling in of the lake as landfilling, we prefer the more technically correct term, lakefilling, which we use throughout the chapter.

4 See below for additional discussion of this inquiry.

5 We put nature in quote marks to distinguish it from socio-nature.

6 R. Home Smith was a man with many talents, one of which was being a land developer. His position with the Harbour Commission provided him with information about future directions of waterfront developments and he used this information to enrich himself through speculative land purchases (O'Mara 1976).

3 From Liability to Profitability: How Disease, Fear, and Medical Science Cleaned Up the Marshes of Ashbridge's Bay

PAUL S.B. JACKSON

George Henry, in his 1831 book *The Emigrant's Guide, or Canada as it is*, introduced Europeans to the town of York, favourably describing its local attractions. Yet Henry warned:

> There is a great drawback on the score of its unhealthiness of situation on the eastern side of the town, which, it is much to be feared, is irremovable. At the head of the bay, which comes to the east side of York, are some very extensive stagnant marshes; they extend for six or seven miles; and are considered to be the principal agents in germinating the local diseases felt more or less in and about the town. (in Firth 1966: 332)

However, Henry was mistaken about the irremmovability of the stagnant marshes; in less than one hundred years this 'unhealthy' marsh called Ashbridge's Bay had been completely removed. By 1930, Toronto's promotional material triumphantly declared that the 'Ashbridge's Bay and Marsh have entirely disappeared and in their place the Toronto Harbour Commissioners have created a modern industrial area, known as the Eastern Harbour Terminals'; a new waterfront had been 'created out of lands which were covered by water and non-revenue producing' (Toronto Harbour Commissioners 1930: 5). In one hundred years Ashbridge's Bay had been transformed, from liability to profitability.

Yet Toronto's marshy liability was actively produced through intertwining the fear of disease, medical science, and dreams of a sanitary city. During the nineteenth century, five international cholera pandemics affected North America, frequently infecting Toronto. These foreign diseases seemed to spring out of the urbanized and polluted local waterfront ecology. But the doctors and scientists of the time were bewildered by the persistent myths surrounding the origins of disease and by the new developments in bacteriological science. At the same time, doctors, engineers, and moral reformers became integrally involved in the planning and sanitation of cities. And as the discipline of public health became institutionalized in city governments, the fear of a cholera crisis in 1892 helped consolidate the power of the medical official in Toronto, particularly in the push for the industrial development of Toronto's waterfront. All of these trajectories converged to destroy Ashbridge's Bay.

This chapter asserts that in the summer of 1832, when cholera arrived in Toronto, the relationship that had already been drawn between marsh and disease became a key rationale for how the city should be improved. While the presumption that Ashbridge's Bay was the cause of disease was based on conjecture, the arrival of cholera in the city appeared to confirm these fear-ridden connections. But why cholera? Why and how did cholera help set in motion the industrial redevelopment of Toronto's waterfront? This chapter will show how the recurring cholera epidemics ruptured the politics and culture of nineteenth-century Toronto, which in turn enabled investment in urbanization to become a viable option to cure urban disease. While other diseases had infected many people in Toronto, the institutional response to cholera set a new standard for urban health governance. Cholera transmission by water contributed to Toronto's fears of marshy shorelines and untameable rivers and, while no direct causal link can be established between cholera and the development of what we now call the Port Industrial District, I contend that cholera, as the pre-eminent disease of the nineteenth century, set the stage for how reformers could deal with such unwanted places and environments. Cholera's many accumulated negative associations made the destruction of the marsh a presupposed and assumed collective benefit. Yet these associations were built on confusion and fear. Cholera was scary; an infected person could die in a day, sometimes hours. Cholera was messy; it produces copious watery diarrhea and vomiting while the body cramps painfully, and the rapid loss of bodily fluids leads to dehydration, shock, and finally death. Cholera was emblematic of all urban evils; as O'Connor summarizes: 'Over the course of the [nineteenth] century, Asiatic cholera became the master trope for urban existence' (2000: 26; see also Gilbert 2008). While grandiose, this claim is not completely unfounded. The obsessive desire among urban reformers and medical experts to determine what, where, or who caused cholera, and the public-health cures that would arise from these determinations, would enable a massive urban transformation. Cholera inspired excessive fear that overwhelmed Toronto's health reformers, so that by the end of the nineteenth century the reclamation of Ashbridge's Bay was assumed to be a positive benefit. Cholera accumulated such a mass of cultural associations that they must be parsed out before illustrating how the 1892 outbreak influenced Toronto's waterfront transformation.

Cholera: Myths, Theories, and Sites of Infection

Asiatic cholera is a bacteria spread by infected human faeces in drinking water; a human host is necessary to carry the disease over long distances. Between 1832 and 1871, cholera broke out in various Canadian cities and towns, having arrived in migrant shipping vessels often called coffin ships, with an estimated death toll of 17,000 to 20,000. During this time, Canadian newspapers regularly reported on the disease's movements from the Middle East to Russia to Germany to Britain (see Atkinson 2002; Bilson 1980). Cholera first crossed the Atlantic on a ship that set sail in April 1832 from Dublin with 167 emigrants aboard. By the time the ship arrived in Canada on 3 June, forty-five people had died. Five more passengers died on Grosse Île, the makeshift quarantine island near Quebec City. The ship continued to Montreal and the disease moved further inland, with fatalities in Cornwall, Prescott, and Kingston. Mr Filgiano, a merchant tailor, fled Montreal to escape the disease, but on 21 June he was the first case of cholera to arrive in Toronto (Fenwick and Campbell 1866). The diary entry of James Lessile on 29 June 1832 described the fearful situation in Toronto:

> 9 new Cases of Cholera & 6 deaths since yesterday! – the alarm excited by it very great so that but few persons are found coming in from the Country but many leaving & going to a distance – the most active measures adopted by the Magistracy to prevent its spreading – *all drunkards* found on the Streets taken up & put either in Jail or in the Stocks – Houses occupied by poor persons cleaned & washed in Lime ... The burning of Tar, Pitch – Sulphur &c recommended & adopted by many & ... anti-Contagion Hand Bills circulated to persuade people not to use Brandy – opium &c as *preventatives* ... (in Firth 1966: 241–2; emphasis in original)

This report speaks volumes: the flight to the countryside; the moral overtones of blaming 'drunkards'; and useless attempts at cleansing the air of impurities by burning tar. Yet the 1832 epidemic in Toronto was not as dire as the situation in other parts of Canada. In Quebec City and Montreal, panic was more widespread, and had even more dire impacts (Bilson 1980). But the next epidemic hit Toronto harder. In 1834, cholera seemed more virulent and caused even more panic throughout Canada, perhaps because more cities and towns were affected. The outbreaks that occurred in Canada between 1849 and 1871 inflamed both panic and calls for reform. Once cholera had arrived, Toronto could no longer be seen as a small, isolated outpost of the British Empire. The city had become enmeshed in the central debates of myth, medicine, and morality that surrounded the cholera mystique.

But cholera was only one of many diseases that affected North American cities in the mid-to-late 1800s. In contrast to endemic diseases like ague and fever (malaria and tuberculosis; see Bonnell, this volume, for a discussion of the role of malaria in Toronto's waterfront), cholera was an epidemic crisis that came upon (*epi*) the people (*demos*) of Toronto and inspired political manoeuvres to reclaim the marshes. Many 'filth diseases' were a part of daily life and became associated with cholera, such as diphtheria, diarrhea, dysentery, typhoid, croup, bronchitis, and pneumonia (Rosenberg 1987; Bilson 1980; Godfrey 1968). For scientists, doctors, and urban reformers, the sheer variety of diseases affecting urban populations fostered debate about diagnosis and treatment. We now know the epidemiological vectors responsible for these diseases; however, at the time science and medicine were in disarray because of the fear, conjecture, and confusion resulting from uncertainty. Medical and science journals reflected these fears. As this chapter will argue, rather than being a hindrance, the confusion over and lack of scientific consensus about the cause of cholera enabled significant political and public health reforms. This confusion, which existed throughout the majority of the nineteenth century, did not create a deadlock in the medical community. Instead, cholera's origins were highly debated. These debates hinged on whether cholera was imported from abroad or arose from local environmental conditions. Contagion theory assumed that cholera was spread through immigrants who brought the disease into new cities. Miasma theory, by contrast, stated that there were elements inherent to local ecological conditions that allowed the disease to burst forth. The assumed cause for the cholera outbreak, be the source immigrant, marsh, or pollution, was abstracted and rationalized, then written into theory itself. And the ambiguity between cholera as a local problem and cholera as an imported problem allowed for disease theories to be used for political ends.

Cholera's Myths and Foreignness

A historical account of recurring cholera outbreaks cannot demonstrate the social impact these events had on cities. To place these events in context, one has to delve into the realms of science, morality, literature, and politics – only when read together does the fear-laden alignment of city, marsh, and disease cohere. In an article entitled *How shall we treat cholera?* Dr Johnson, professor of medicine at King's College, stated that 'the cholera poison, whatever may be its nature and source, whether it be "ponderable" or not, is a reality, and no figment of the imagination' (1866: 561). In contrast, the historian Delaporte has suggested that, in Paris, 'people ... spoke of cholera as of a creature of the imagination. Fear led irresistibly to fantasy and, at times, to remarkable bluster and bravado' (1986: 47). In the historical documents, there is a consistent tension between the tendency to fearfully mythologize cholera and a scientific focus on the disease's biology and transmission. Cultural and scientific imaginations ran wild, for no other reason than that cholera was new and unknown, and hence feared. The scientific facts of the period were intertwined and mutually reinforced the already prevalent and fear-mongering myths.

Cholera was constructed as foreign, carried in its very name – *Asiatic* cholera – and things foreign were feared. John A. Benson, a professor of physiology in Chicago, epitomizes the uninhibited imagination surrounding cholera's origins. His 1893 account of the cholera creation myth begins:

> Up from the depths of hell, in the early part of this century, arose the Goddess of Filth, and she wandered around over the face of the globe, seeking a home to her liking. And coming to the delta of the Ganges, in this low, insalubrious and festering locality, where so many noxious and noisome diseases are generated, and where so many epidemics have arisen and so often swept over the earth with most fatal and desolating effects, – here she met, one dark and stifling night, with gaunt Despair. And surrounding her with his bony arms, Despair threw her on the foul, dark and slimy ground, and had his will of her. And when the day of her reckoning was reached, here in the neighborhood of Jessore – a town in the center of the delta – in agony and in shame and in desolation, Filth gave birth to the monstrosity yclept, – Asiatic cholera. (in E. O'Connor 2000: 21)

The quote evokes many of cholera's oft-repeated associations: India and Orientalism; myths and fears; ecology and environment. Importantly, the story ends with a scientific definition. While Jessore, a city in Bangladesh, was considered the endemic origin of cholera, Benson's mystifying portrayal obscured the existing science of the time. This fiction was written in 1893, after the end of the major cholera outbreaks in Europe and North America. By that time the cholera bacterium had been discovered and cholera's transmission through water had been proved. Benson's imaginative 'origin' was based on fear and, as such, served to further entrench cholera's deadly foreign mystique. Throughout the 1800s, therefore, the medical journals' writings consistently blamed the cholera epidemics on the people of India, their poor sanitation, and their practice of burning and disposing of dead bodies in the Ganges. Cholera, no matter where epidemics broke out, was reconnected to India.

Yet cholera travelled. Immigrants, be they Irish, Russian, Jewish, or Asian, were blamed for carrying diseases into other nations and cities. The contagion theory of disease transmission provided the rationale necessary to keep these and other stigmatized populations separate from their host communities (see Fong 2003; Markel and Stern 2002; Craddock 2000; Kraut 1994). Cholera, in particular, invoked an 'Oriental raider, a barbaric force whose progress westward exposed the weak spots of an expanding industrial culture' (E. O'Connor 2000: 22). In Europe, migration was restricted and monitored as a protection against the 'diseased' Middle East (see Ogawa 2000; P. Baldwin 1999). In Canada, after the 1832 cholera epidemic, the Montreal *Gazette* declared, 'When I see my country in mourning and my native land nothing but a vast cemetery, I ask what has been the cause of all these disasters? … The voice of thousands of my fellow citizens responds from their tombs. It is emigration' (Bilson 1980: 50; see figure 3.1). Diseases were transported by the steamships and railroads that connected global empires, but the scapegoats of the outbreaks were those peoples exposed to the consequences of expanding capital and colonialism.

Cholera's Local Filthiness: Miasma and Bacteriology

Miasma was the opposing theory of disease transmission. This theory was dominant long before the 1800s and, while largely debunked by the 1880s, it held significant sway throughout much of the nineteenth century. As British epidemiologist and founder of medical statistics William Farr stated in his 1868 report on the origin of cholera:

3.1 'An undesirable emigrant.' (From *Evening News*, 31 August 1892, 1; courtesy of Toronto Public Library)

Like species of the animal kingdom plagues lie hidden in the strata of past history; they live, they flourish, they perish like organic forms, because they are in their essence successive generations of organic forms at enmity with the corpuscles of which the human race consists. If the algid cholera can be spontaneously generated in Asia, why ... not ... in Africa, in Europe, in America? We know the summer cholera is generated in London ... Why resort to the theory of importation? (in Gilbert 2004: 149)

The nebulous hypothesis of miasma theory was that diseases arose spontaneously with the right local ecological conditions. Medical scientists who believed in miasma claimed that disease itself existed as a fog, stain, or vapour, and that these vapours were unleashed from local environments. Miasma scientists gathered evidence to show that cholera had a predilection to certain landscapes: damp low-lying areas; neighbourhoods located near water; and along rivers, streams, or canals. As such, the swamps of India were not the origin of cholera; rather, any local marsh could be its birthplace. The growing fears of cyclical outbreaks and the affinity among disease, water, and marshy soils led the miasma theory camp to declare that instituting a healthy city would require the elimination of all ecologies that fostered disease. As paved areas, which also happened to be in the wealthier neighbourhoods (Delaporte 1986: 87–9), appeared to be bypassed by the epidemics, the cure for the high mortality rate became clear: filling in and paving the city.

Yet Delaporte suggested that the theory of disease origin shifted from natural environments to a single cause, a single local 'agent' that could be isolated and then eradicated. Disease was no longer just a mysterious fog, but instead came to be seen as an element or particle that became integrated into marshes, houses, bodies, together forming a 'morbid environment' (1986: 85–6). The disease particles that inhabited specific places were the cause of morbidity, rather than weather, soil, or any natural process. The famous scientists Koch and Pasteur's discoveries in the 1880s debunked the environmental theories and ushered in the era of bacteriology. Yet this transition was neither smooth nor complete. The discovery of bacteria did not automatically eliminate existing ideas or theories from the entire medical discipline or its many supporting professions. The mobilization of new scientific facts and theories into existing institutions takes political work (Worboys 2000; Hamlin 1990; Latour 1988). In turn, debunked theories eliminate existing circles of expertise. But this is an incomplete process and, as we will see below in Toronto's case, contradictory understandings of disease can be held at the same time. Moreover, these contradictory theories can support each other, allowing diverse objects and people to be linked in support of urban reform.

Yet scientific theories, at their core, contain an analysis of cause and effect. In the case of theories of disease origin, this cause and effect was a narrative that described how diverse places, objects, and peoples produced sickness, through their connection with an identifiable microscopic organism. The scientific imagination then visualized these interconnected relations of disease. In 1854, one of the fathers of epidemiology, Dr John Snow, created maps that made cholera's infection vector in London's water supply perceptible (see Koch 2004; McLeod 2000). Making the enemy visible in this way (see Latour 1988: 33; Foucault 1994) allowed Koch and Pasteur's bacteriology to triumph over the other theories of disease origin.

While visualizing disease in this way was vital to validate their theories, the scientists of the late nineteenth century cannot take all the credit for the microscopic imagination. Almost two hundred years before bacteriology, the Dutch naturalist van Leeuwenhoek, after inventing the microscope, observed small living 'animalcules' in water (Wainwright 2001). Cambridge professor Charles Kingsley stated in his treatise *The Water Supply of London* that when one drinks water, 'you are literally filled with the fruit of your own devices, with rats and mice and such small deer, paramecia, and entomostraceae, and kicking things with horrid names, which you see in microscopes at the Polytechnic' (in E. O'Connor 2000: 41). Yet these were allegorical illustrations of disease, imagined as insectile, monstrous, ghostly, or alien (see figure 3.2). Science sought to understand the relations of cause and effect and then eradicate those agents that caused sickness, be they immigrants, swamps, human contact, or dirty pipes. Scientific knowledge therefore made visible the heretofore invisible elements of illness – how disease lived and moved in cities, what conditions fostered the existence of bacteria, and the best way to eradicate what could not be seen.

When the microscopic elements of disease became visible, in either allegorical or scientific descriptions, the stigma of disease could be liberally applied. Stigmatized ecologies, places, and bodies could then be slotted into a world described by Derrida as a 'well-computed binarism,' one that was 'rigorously divided into remedies and poisons, seeds of life and seeds of death, good and bad traces' (in Clark 2002: 108). As cholera became increasingly understood to be a microscopic

3.2 'No alien need apply.' (From *Evening News*, 5 September 1892, 1; courtesy of the Toronto Public Library)

bacteria that travelled in the urban sewer infrastructure, water, so vital to life, now potentially contained the seeds of death. Water, sewers, swamps, and rivers became animated with the cholera poison. To garner influence over municipal water policies, scientists and sanitarians used speculation and conjecture regarding the consequences of filth.

Filth, disease, and speculations on their relationship filled books and journals. Indeed, the notion of filth allowed multiple disease theories to be held at the same time, accompanied often by moral disgust. And filth as a cultural construct could be applied to anything. Filth became an intermediary between invisible diseases and very observable landscapes such as a polluted swamp. Cholera eroded the borders between filth and the body, as seen in the diarrhea that inevitably accompanied the disease. Indeed, cholera illustrated a 'logic of material disintegration,' forcing the body to break down, stop working, and eliminate vital fluids (E. O'Connor 2000: 49; see also Hamlin 1985). In the words of Victorian social reformer George Godwin, in framing disease

> there are certain diseases, of which it is hardly a metaphor to say, that they consist in the extension of a putrefactive process from matters outside the body to matters inside the body – diseases of which the very essence of filth, – diseases which have no local habitation except where putrefiable air or putrefiable water furnishes means for their rise or propagation, – diseases against which there may be found a complete security in the cultivation of public and private cleanliness. (Godwin 1972: 69)

Filth was not merely passive, rejected waste; instead, it was 'animated and hostile' (Gilbert 2004: xii). Cholera was thought to be enabled by filth, to inhabit piles of waste, dirty water, smelly sewers, and especially polluted marshes.

Swamp Fixation

The swamp or marsh fixation that overtook public health authorities in the nineteenth century epitomized Victorian culture's civilizing mission. The reformer George Godwin exemplified this in his conflation of urban redevelopment and social transformation. He begins his 1859 book *Town Swamps and Social Bridges* with the claim that 'there are dark and dangerous places – swamps and pitfalls – in the social world which need bridging over, to afford a way out to the miserable dwellers amidst degradation and filth' (1972: 1). For Godwin, urban swamps not only represented the breakdown of social organization, they also fostered further degeneration. Swamps were equated with crime, poverty, bad drainage, noxious industries, sickness, unemployment, economic distress, and disease. Equally, swamps could represent ignorance, superstition, overcrowding, pollution, the lack of recreation and education, and especially alcohol – swamp in a cup (Godwin 1972: 15; see Gilbert 2008, 2004; Choi 2001).

The urban swamp became a highly visible symbol of urban filth. Constructed as foreign, filthy, and cholera-friendly, the swamp was a local piece of the Ganges. Gilbert explains that 'low-lying, damp areas in England were seen as unhealthy' through connections to 'India, and the people and behaviors that were mapped onto the land were considered by many to constitute an ecological entity productive of evil' (2004: 145). These conclusions did not depend on specific scientific testing or research, but rather on superficial observations that conflated these marshy 'evils.' The British social reformer Henry Mayhew could call Jacob's Island in the East End, the 'very capital of cholera, the Jessore of London' because this island was his 'image of an English India, or an Indian England, an environment whose filth causes an exotic change in the inhabitants complexions' (E. O'Connor 2000: 47). This foreignness became localized and naturalized into the very landscape of a swamp.

In newspaper articles and government reports of the time, a rhetorical race to the bottom took place as each city claimed to be the filthiest, the most stagnant, the most in need of transformation. In 1832, the Montreal board of health stated: 'Perhaps there are few other cities more exposed to the operation of all the causes which create or aggravate such disease. Low and marshy grounds, stagnant waters filled with all the elements of miasma (pestilential effluvia), in circumstances most favourable to their malignant influences meet us in every part of this city' (in Bilson 1980: 33). In Toronto, the swamp of Ashbridge's Bay was a local pool of stagnant, damp, filth where excrement and industrial waste were dumped. Public health officials and urban reformers positioned Toronto's marshy waterfront as a stand-in for East London, where the Don River became akin to the Thames, which was similar to the Ganges. All became comparable and all needed redevelopment.

These swamps exemplified 'a boundary experience with its spatiality rooted in anxieties of displacement and disorientation,' a zone 'between the rational and irrational, nature and culture, male and female, the visible and invisible' (Gandy 1999: 34; see also Sibley 1995; Stallybrass and White 1986). As Gandy has suggested, 'the "cesspool" city of the nineteenth century was a place where metaphors of disease and moral degeneration mingled with the threat of women and the labouring classes to middle-class society' (1999: 36). A cesspool swamp was ambiguous, and disoriented social reformers' notions of a modern city. Gandy calls this the urban uncanny, 'a spatial[ly] defined sense of dread' which hinges on an object of fear's visibility or lack thereof. Filth and sewage were visible in the water, yet cholera was invisible. The swamp was a potential site of sickness; disease could originate there and then travel through sewers and water systems. Sewers, urban rivers, and pumps, just as water itself, became feared. Diseased places became sites where the bacteriological city (Gandy 2004) could be eradicated. The pollution of urban waterways activated municipal reformers and social movements to push for sanitary change.

Every river, water well, lake, and water cart became suspect and a site to reform. Since immigrants travelled along rivers, disease outbreaks followed water-based transportation systems (Bilson 1980: 46). Canadian Dr Robert Godfrey in his 1866 speech 'Cholera: A Few Practical Remarks on Its Prevention,' stated: 'Every casual observer must have noticed that cholera travels inland, along the different navigable rivers and canals; for in its several visits to this continent it has always followed this course … This choleraic poison, when thrown into water, increases its contagious power so rapidly as to effect a river for miles down' (Godfrey 1866: 344). Healthy drinking water was possible if municipalities had the political will and financing to build appropriate urban water systems; even so, the persistent fear of water-borne disease led to other, speculation-fuelled responses. Proximity to water spatialized fear and illness, so in Toronto the huts and shanties of the waterfront were targeted for demolition owing to their poor state of upkeep and the 'low moral fortitude' of their inhabitants (in Bilson 1980: 77). As the then mayor of Toronto described these shanties, 'I never saw anything in Europe to exceed the loathsome sights met with in Toronto' (ibid). Nonetheless, cities did begin to promote the construction of a public water supply. Toronto even held a planning and design competition to improve its water quality (131–2). However, the city government also turned its attention to Ashbridge's Bay, using science to determine the foulness or healthiness of the swamp's ecology. But science could not treat or eradicate the cultural and political myths that had accumulated on the waterfront.

Public Health: Dreaming Concrete Dreams

Throughout the nineteenth century, the inhabitants of Toronto were fixated on the problem of Ashbridge's Bay's marsh ecology. The Port of York's first medical officer arrived in May of 1832 because, as the *Canadian Freeman* reported, much 'sickness prevails at present, and the approach of warm weather is likely to increase the evil. – Therefore, the cleanliness of the town, or rather its filthiness, ought to engage the first attention of this officer ... The state of the bay, from which a large portion of the inhabitants are supplied with water, is horrible' (in Firth 1966: 238–9). A constant debate existed within government circles and in public forums over how to solve the problem of the swamp. What was the best method to clean the water? Where should Toronto dump its sewage? Was it possible to engineer the filling in of Toronto's marshlands? Various measures to solve the problem were proposed, but the underlying question of whether the marsh should remain was never discussed.

In 1835, the worlds of public health and urban development came together in proposals to resolve the problem. Captain Bonnycastle, a strong advocate of shipping improvements in the harbour, suggested that, since the Don River was dumping silt into Lake Ontario, the city must reclaim 'the great marsh' – but he underscored his proposal by reminding Torontonians that Ashbridge's Bay was 'a fertile source of unhealthiness to the city' (in Desfor 1988: 79). Twenty years later, engineer and city council member Kivas Tully wrote about the worsening condition of the harbour (*Patriot* 1853). The sewers of Toronto and the wastes of the Gooderham and Worts distillery and cattle byres now emptied into the marsh, and the place had become a cesspool. In addition, the bay waters were filling with silt and shipping was becoming nearly impossible. Tully proposed to resolve these problems by completely reshaping the ecology of the marsh, deepening the bay waters and dredging the bay floor. The shallower areas could then be reclaimed for industrial development. To push his plan, Tully emphasized that the 'source of these endemic diseases (e.g., cholera) which afflict the citizens would be thus destroyed and what is now a *positive evil* would be converted into a benefit – and a profit to the city' (in Desfor 1988: 80; my emphasis). Tully was just one in a long line of engineers, politicians, health officers, and citizens who dreamed of transforming the waterfront. This persistent dream was that the evil, disease infested swamp could be converted into beneficial, healthy, and profitable land.

If Toronto could do this, the entire city would be renewed and a brighter future would be assured.

By the end of the 1800s, fear of disease arising from Ashbridge's Bay had become obsessive. The City was criticized for its constant foot dragging. When change did take place on the waterfront it was piecemeal rather than comprehensive, such as construction of the government breakwater and shipyards, and granting land and water lots. Different levels of government reviewed these changes, made up new plans, and entered into public discussion about future directions. But the partial reshaping of the shoreline actually made water quality worse by containing the silt and waste, rather than releasing the sewage into Lake Ontario. Nuisance complaints from citizens mounted. Ashbridge's Bay's reputation as an extensive health menace only increased (see Desfor 1988; Brace 1995, 1993). The city commissioner, the Board of Works and Markets, and the Health Committee had to deal with growing complaints of inefficiency and demands for a healthy Toronto from a wide variety of sectors (H.A. MacDougall 1982: 7).

During this time, both the agents and discourses of public health administration began to have effects on Toronto's waterfront. The public health sector had grown substantially and loudly demanded reform. Public health in Canada was moving away from a triage model, dealing solely with emergencies and epidemics, towards the creation of a permanent institution, fully embedded in the workings of municipal and provincial governments (see Valverde 1991; Roland 1984; for North America see Platt 2005; Melosi 2000). With the establishment of the Provincial Board of Health in 1882, the province became a vital player shaping the health governance of cities, and in 1883 a permanent medical health officer was instituted in Toronto.

By the 1870s, public-health professional associations were formed for Ontario, Canada, and North America. Toronto doctors were members of all three organizations and attended conferences in the United States, Europe, and throughout the world. In turn, doctors in Canada relied on British and European medical science expertise. British-trained sanitarians, such as Drs Canniff, Covernton, and Bryce, made up the elite of the medical profession in Toronto (H.A. MacDougall 1982: 166). These sanitarians obsessed over filth diseases, particularly cholera. Indeed, the story of combating cholera paralleled the institutionalization of medical science in government (Hardy 1993; Pelling 1978) and its application to the colonies (see M. Watts 2006 ['Empire']; Ogawa 2000; Paneth et al. 1998).

Throughout the 1880s health reformers attacked Toronto's government for permitting such unsanitary conditions. Open conflict over the condition of the city's sewers took place between Toronto's health department and the city engineer's office. In 1886, Dr Canniff was so disgusted with City Hall that he declared that Toronto had the worst sanitation in the civilized world, citing as an example the pollution of Ashbridge's Bay (Bator 1979). Toronto's Municipal Health Board added to the condemnation, calling the waterfront an open sewer. In 1888, the medical health officer wrote to Mayor Edward Clarke, saying, 'Year after year, I have pointed out the unsanitary state of Ashbridge's Bay and the necessity of abating the evil. Beyond this I have not authority to proceed without instruction' (H.A. MacDougall 1982: 385; for more background on Toronto's sanitary conditions see Allen 1892). While public health had become integrated within city government, it took the power of the 1892 cholera epidemic to solidify the authority of these institutions and professions.

The Power of a Cholera Outbreak

In the summer of 1892, a massive cholera epidemic infected European cities, most notably Hamburg. In North America, cholera landed only in Hamburg's largest trading partner, New York City. Yet when the ship that carried infected Russian Jews docked in that city, fear gripped the entire continent. Cholera had returned (see Markel 1997; Evans 1987). In Toronto, the years of debate crystallized into an immediate call to fill in Ashbridge's Bay. Toronto's officials predicted that cholera would infect the city within the next year; improvements to Ashbridge's Bay therefore had to begin during the 1892 season (Desfor 1988: 83). No one in Toronto was infected – or has been infected since – and even before 1892 the cholera epidemics were under control in Europe and North America (Bilson 1980). Yet the assumption at the time was that the crisis would continue for years. Cholera was inevitable, it was thought, and therefore Toronto must take steps to prepare. The call to prepare gave an urgency and validity to the reconstruction and sanitation of Toronto's waterfront. Plans were approved. Inspections were made. More sewage systems and filtration plants were demanded (Brace 1995; Desfor 1988). But there were delays, budgetary constraints, and drawn-out planning procedures. Most of the redevelopments were completed twenty years after the cholera outbreak, stalled in part owing to an ongoing economic depression. Even so, by 1911, while the threat of cholera had long since passed, fears of a health emergency arising from the bay remained an implicit rationale supporting the development of the Port Industrial District.

During the 1892 international cholera crisis, the secretary of the Provincial Board of Health, Dr Peter Bryce, jumped at the opportunity to enact reforms. In an interview with the *Toronto Evening News* on 2 September, Bryce prescribed improvements to the city's sanitary conditions. In particular, he declared that Ashbridge's Bay must be put in the 'best possible condition before 1893 when it is feared cholera may reach Canada' (*Evening News* 1892c: 1). He called for the purification of the bay: removal of the causes of pollution, such as the cattle byres; sanitizing of the lake's shores; and destruction of the swamp. Bryce declared that sewage should not be allowed to go into the city's water supply untreated, and all health officials agreed. Bryce's frustration with the city's government was palpable.

Dr Bryce epitomized the public health officials' perspective on the 1892 cholera epidemic. Trained as a doctor, he pursued a career in government and became the official spokesperson of the Provincial Board of Health. His 1891 report to the board, *A Hundred Years of Sanitation in Ontario*, focused exclusively on cholera, illustrating how concerned medical professionals were about the disease. But Bryce's expert recommendations seem to have been based on his health agenda in a time of potential crisis, mixing and invoking a variety of disease theories to validate his reforms. In the Toronto newspapers, Bryce claimed cholera could live in a trunk for weeks and be destroyed by sunshine and running water (*Evening News* 1892a: 1). Yet he also seems to have believed in contagion theories, calling for the surveillance of all immigrants. Simultaneously he called for the purification of the swamp, perpetuating the notion that local environments caused disease. During the 1892 cholera outbreak Bryce convened the International Conference of State Boards of Health in Toronto. The group, which included representatives from the United States and Mexico, surveyed the eastern seaboard, examining maritime quarantine stations and repeatedly calling for sanitary reforms. Bryce used the cholera crisis, along with his political and professional connections, to institute change locally, nationally, and internationally.

Yet no consensus existed on the diagnosis of Toronto's sanitary conditions. On 15 September 1892, during the outbreak, the *Evening News* ran a story called 'Toronto is Ready.' Dr Allen, the medical health officer of Toronto, declared that a cholera epidemic occurring in Toronto in 1892 was impossible. He went on to say:

> And it [the city] is prepared ... There are no fever spots in this city and no especially dirty slums. Since the first of the month we have had 20 extra inspectors hard at work ... They have disinfected the premises themselves in many cases and have distributed over a ton of disinfectant in two weeks. I venture to say that there are few cities in America so well prepared to resist cholera as Toronto is. Cleanliness and proper disinfection are the greatest enemies of cholera.

Mayor Fleming backed Dr Allen's position. Toronto bacteriologist Professor Thomas Hayes took water samples at the intake of the pumping house and in his laboratory on King Street and, through 'exhaustive analysis,' showed that the water was 'first-class and almost entirely free of impurities. So there is one cause of fear removed' (*Evening News* 1892e: 1). Oddly, this contradicted Allen's sanitary assessment of the marsh the year before, when he urged that an extensive clean-up be 'commenced at once, as any delay may give rise to a serious epidemic' (Allen 1892: 13–14). Local doctors and scientists working for the City of Toronto had a very different view than provincial health authorities about the city's susceptibility to cholera. But Dr Allen's dissent was short lived. At the beginning of 1893 he came under attack over the mismanagement of finances by the new Local Board of Health, while simultaneously the Provincial Board of Health laid charges against him over the dereliction of duties. Dr Allen was dismissed by February of 1893 and the call for sanitary reform was consolidated (City of Toronto 1893).

During 1893, cholera broke out in smaller cities in eastern Europe. Toronto's media reported these events, along with the unsatisfactory and unsanitary nature of federal quarantine procedures. Chairman Cassidy's 1893 annual address to the members of Provincial Board of Health declared:

> To-day the most striking fact in the sanitary world is the deep-seated and universal dread of cholera both in Europe and North America ... Recognizing as we do the imminent danger that is present in the use of sewage polluted water and all the readiness with which it becomes charged with the comma bacilli [cholera] ... we cannot but look with positive dread at the condition of Toronto's city water supply.

For him the municipal authorities were 'trifling with the grave danger at their gates' by not taking well-known, efficient precautions (*Evening News* 1893a: 1). Accordingly, the Provincial Board of Health requested new extensive powers from the provincial government to force the dredging of Ashbridge's Bay, under a clause in the Ontario government's recently passed order-in-council regarding contagious disease. Provincial heavyweights Cassidy and Bryce were appointed to a committee to carry out these health regulations. Passed on 11 April 1893, this regulation gave the Provincial Board of Health immense power to dictate to cities a particular medical regime. Provincial health officials, without the consent of any local authority, could enter a municipality and close up wells, order privy pit removal, remove slaughterhouses, and procure sanitary technologies, and the cost for such changes would have to be borne by the local municipality (*Evening News* 1893b, 1893c). Yet the provincial health officers never used these extensive new powers to change Toronto's waterfront, as unsanitary as they claimed it to be.

The reason these new provincial powers were not used against the City of Toronto is unclear. One possibility was that the city's water was indeed healthy, at least according to Toronto's newspapers. The *Evening News* stated that 'the Quality of the Water is at Present the Best Toronto Ever Had' and 'the city's health, so far as contagious disease are concerned, continues to be first-class' (1893d: 1). The incidence of typhoid fever, diphtheria, and scarlet fever had all been reduced. Another reason could be that the reshaping of Ashbridge's Bay was now moving forward under its own momentum, albeit strongly propelled by the cholera crisis. Importantly, the financing of the marsh reclamation had been secured. Even though putting the costs onto the city's debt load was rejected in a city-wide general vote, provincial and Toronto reformers used their legislative powers to make sure the city engineer's plans would be paid for (City of Toronto 1893). A jetty and other public works were constructed, and new land was produced. Newspaper editors hoped that 'if this land is dealt with in an intelligent way it will be the source of considerable revenue for the city' (*Evening News* 1893e: 1). Provincial health reformers did not have to enforce their extensive new health powers – the fear of cholera and the constructed liability of the swamp had already provided enough leverage. The outbreak did demonstrate, however, that a crisis could be used by health professionals to consolidate their political and institutional powers, and once legislated, these powers could be used at any future time.

The question then arises as to which health expertise was to be believed: was Toronto ripe for an outbreak or not? No answer is helpful for understanding historical shifts on the waterfront, as epidemiological facts may matter less than the conditions propelling waterfront transformation. Was Toronto's water free of disease? No, Toronto's water supply did carry diseases such as diphtheria, although such chronic water-borne diseases were finally eliminated by the construction of Toronto's filtration plant and the institutionalization of chlorine. Then was it the case that Toronto's sanitary condition and Ashbridge's Bay could indeed foster cholera? My contention is that scientific 'facts' may be less important to understanding waterfront change than cultural fears. At the turn of the twentieth century Toronto was dealing with a range of social uncertainties: a confusing and distrusted new science of bacteriology; threats that were visible and yet invisible; various social 'ills' that preoccupied moral reformers; and increasing urbanization and pollution. Bacteria counts could not compete with the interdisciplinary and totalizing rhetoric of reformers like Bryce, who could condemn with science while fostering fears with myth. Urban reformers could use any medical theory to make a case for urban transformation. Crusading against cholera and for the filling in of Ashbridge's Bay was less about the spread of disease and more about fulfilling the dream of Toronto becoming a clean and modern city.

Godwin, the crusader against swamps, ended his book with a triumphant call to 'Drain the Swamps and increase the Bridges,' but he also quoted the poet Longfellow as having called for 'God's blessing on the architects who build' (1972: 1). Bridges were the 'cure' to swamps, but also represented everything that was essential for a modern urban society. The bridge as an urban ideal invoked the reform movement, productive industry, commerce, and public infrastructure. The promise of industry was integral to transform Toronto's waterfront. This push to build was not isolated to Toronto, but instead 'reflected the needs of an urban mercantile class who faced the consequences of modernity, not by an escape into romantic anti-urbanism, but through a celebration of the possibilities for the technological mastery of urban space and the search for progressively greater degrees of social and spatial order' (Gandy 1999: 29; see also Otter 2004). Bridges were not only order, but also the ensemble of acts of construction that would heal the city.

Godwin also reminds the Victorian reader that change is not immediate: 'Improvement is not so easily obtained when the evil is of monster size: it takes a long time to make the public appreciate the necessity of it, and they must be told a thing many times before they will even hear, still oftener before they move' (Godwin 1972: 1). Similarly, the constantly repeated insistence that cholera was sure to come again is where the political power of crisis resided. The litany of 'The swamp is unhealthy, the city is filthy' intersected with 'Cholera is coming' and, joined together, created a chorus of urban transformation that was loud and inescapable. The urban reformers insisted that waterfront development was necessary since cholera was always just over the horizon; if every corner of the city was not cleaned, then the evil monster of disease could spring forth. Repetition, confusion, and fear led to transformative action.

Conclusion

Kivas Tully called cholera a 'positive evil.' Even as an oxymoron, the meaning of this statement is clear: the battle against the 'evils' of disease enabled the development of 'positive' – that is, profitable – enterprises. Evils, such as a filthy, diseased urban swamp, were socially constructed and in need of public health management. And doctors and scientists created methods to manage and patrol the microscopic worlds within the city's waters and the citizens' bodies. Instituting urban cleanliness also required a political call for investment in infrastructure such as sewers, filtration plants, and water testing, as demanded by authorities informed by scientifically based studies. Yet the manipulation of urban space, seen through the creation of a concrete industrial waterfront, was one particular response to the human vulnerability that cholera invoked in Toronto. The reshaping of Toronto's waterfront was one aspect of implementing the sanitary city. And the paving and transforming of the physical environment was justified as enriching both the health and finances of Toronto. Ashbridge's Bay's concrete future was constructed as an integral piece in solving the problems of nineteenth-century Toronto.

One consistent feature of a disease crisis is that, after the trauma, the memory of the event fades. After the first cholera outbreak in Toronto, local citizen James Lessile nicely summarized matters: 'The period of this terrible visitation is perhaps now terminated. Confidence is now restored ... and all moves on as if it had not been' (in Firth 1966: 245). Similarly, in the early twentieth century, the fear of cholera waned, yet the consequences of the cholera epidemics remained socially imprinted in the city for years. Indeed, in European and North American cities, the fear of immigrant neighbourhoods as constituting a primary source of disease continues. The association among disease, fear, and unseemly urban spaces persists, just as did Toronto's obsession with public health reform.

The confidence expressed in Lessile's statement was strengthened through investment and reform. Toronto built a water filtration plant. Vaccination became institutionalized. Toronto's health, during the 1910–29 reign of Dr Charles Hastings as medical officer of health, was internationally toasted, and the city became a model of public health administration. Yet the airborne 1918 Spanish Flu caught everyone off guard, setting a new standard for crisis preparation. Developments in public health had parallels on the waterfront. Confidence in the new modern waterfront was assumed once the new Port Industrial District was built. Through urban development on Toronto's shore, profit and progress were trumpeted and a bright industrious future was thought to be ensured. But these hopes and dreams eroded with time.

Toronto's waterfront of today still retains the tension between dreams of investment and threats from the unknown. Toronto's port lands have lost their confident lustre. A polluted wasteland on the city's shoreline is lamented again, albeit under different conditions. Hopes are now attached to tourism, condos, and ecological wetland restoration. Yet rehabilitated wetlands are niches for mosquitoes and bird nesting, disease vectors for avian influenza and West Nile virus. The diseased city was thought to be a problem of the past. Yet 'the outbreak' has returned in North American cities, with recent examples such as SARS and the H_1N_1 swine flu. As public health crises become reincorporated into visions for Toronto's urban future, a dominance of science in the discussion is a cause for concern. As history has shown, science and health are constantly in flux and revised, dominated by cultural biases and political agendas. Once 'expertise' is humbled, decisions about the future of the city become primarily political, like all changes on the waterfront.

4 From Feast to Famine: Shipbuilding and the 1912 Waterfront Development Plan

MICHAEL MOIR

Long before road, rail, and air seemingly shortened the distance between communities, humanity depended on water to connect regions and continents. Settlement usually proceeded inwards from the shorelines of rivers, lakes, and oceans, starting from natural features that provided sheltered anchorage for vessels. This was the case in Canada where, as Garth Wilson noted in his history of Canadian shipbuilding, 'Transportation by water was the most efficient (and for almost two hundred years the fastest) means of moving people and goods. Thus, the construction and repair of water craft soon became a functional imperative for the new colonists' (Wilson 1994: 1). This activity matured over time, producing increasingly larger and more complex wooden ocean-going ships to carry bulk cargoes during its 'golden age' in the mid-nineteenth century. The production of these ships was indicative of the close relationship between socio-economic development and nature, particularly in terms of the availability of timber, fertile land to produce surplus grain and other produce for trade, and access to water where vessels could be launched and sent on their way to international ports of call. The emergence of new technologies, iron and steel as building materials, and scientific ship design shifted the advantage to Britain, and traditional centres of shipbuilding in Canada, such as Quebec and St John, waned by the end of the nineteenth century.

The settlement of the Canadian west, railway expansion, increased exports, and the growth of manufacturing instead shifted the locus of economic development inland to the Great Lakes and St Lawrence River, providing the conditions needed for the industrialization of Canadian shipbuilding and the production of large steel vessels during the opening decade of the twentieth century. The First World War was a powerful catalyst in this process, as submarine warfare instigated a rapid expansion in the country's shipbuilding capacity (Wilson 1994).

Shipbuilding has been identified as 'a neglected topic in Canadian maritime history' (ibid.: vi, 2), and Garth Wilson's work broke new ground by examining its relationship to the history of science. This study explores another aspect of this activity that has received little attention: the relationship between shipbuilding and urban planning. Wilson noted how large towns and cities in central Canada had the labour, markets, and capital required to alter the nature of shipbuilding, but in the case of Toronto – Canada's second largest manufacturing centre at the start of the twentieth century – shipbuilding was invoked by politicians, pundits, and port authorities as an instrument of change in waterfront development. The need for shipyards was often cited in calls to turn the 526-hectare marsh of Ashbridge's Bay into a new socio-ecological landscape – a productive industrial property. And these calls culminated in the Toronto Harbour Commission's Waterfront Plan that was submitted to city council in November 1912 (see Desfor, Vesalon, and Laidley, this volume, for a discussion of the politics surrounding the establishment of the Toronto Harbour Commission). The plan featured large-scale reclamation for commercial, industrial, and recreational uses, an ambitious program of public works that was expected to pay for itself through cargo dues and, in particular, property rentals. The commission fell well short of the mark in its attempts to establish revenue-producing industries on reclaimed properties, a situation attributed to a strategy that was 'too expansive and too unfocussed' (Lemon 1990: 1). Although shipbuilding and ship repair have been discounted as activities of no importance in the development of the port of Toronto (Norcliffe 1981: 239), this industry was placed in the vanguard of the commission's promotion and implementation of the plan. An examination of shipbuilding in Toronto during the nineteenth and early twentieth centuries offers a clearer understanding of its role in urban planning, and the impact of national and international developments on the viability of plans for Toronto's waterfront.

Attempts at Shipbuilding before 1890

Reflecting the origins of the settlement, shipbuilding in Toronto began in defence of a military garrison. The armed yacht *Toronto* was launched in 1799 near the King's Mill on the Humber River, where carpenters had access to a ready supply of sawn timber. Construction of more substantial vessels, however, required deeper water. After a heated dispute regarding the appropriate location for shipbuilding – Lieutenant Colonel Ralph Bruyères of the Royal Engineers favoured Kingston because Toronto Harbour was too shallow and 'totally incompetent for the purpose,' while others considered Kingston to be indefensible due to its proximity to the United States – the keel of the thirty-gun frigate *Sir Isaac Brock* was laid in the spring of 1813 just west of Bay Street on a site now occupied by Union Station (Firth 1962: 288–9). The quarrel foreshadowed troubled times ahead; in April, the *Brock* was torched at the hands of the British before it could be seized by the invading Americans. George Williams mapped the burnt frigate in his sketch of Toronto in November 1813, and also noted the 'Merchants Shipyard' east of the principal settlement and north of the mouth of the Don River (Firth 1962: plate before lxxxi; see figure 4.1). Both landmarks disappeared by the time of George Philpott's survey of the harbour in 1818, but commercial shipbuilding reappeared on the waterfront as the military rationale for the town gave way to prosperity based on maritime trade.

A list of approximately two hundred vessels under Canadian ownership plying the Great Lakes was published by the *Daily Globe* on 4 August 1856, and included fourteen schooners and brigantines built in Toronto between 1832 and 1855. Despite contemporaneous complaints about Toronto's meagre efforts at shipbuilding due to a lack of oak, and especially its merchants' lack of industry compared with their counterparts in Niagara (*Globe* 1855), this number is comparable to the output of yards in Kingston and Montreal and is surpassed only by Oakville and St Catharines. The launch of the square-rigged *City of Toronto* from the Hayes Brothers' Front Street yard on 3 April 1855 was the local industry's high point in the construction of wooden hulls until the next century (see figure 4.1). The ship was designed for the timber trade between Quebec City and Liverpool, and was the city's first vessel built for ocean navigation. It was also the last significant vessel to be built in Toronto for several decades, reflecting the city's growing reliance upon the railways for economic development.

The changing contours of Toronto harbour provided a new incentive for shipbuilding. Settlement of the Don valley led to deforestation, erosion, and the southerly conveyance of significant amounts of silt whenever storms increased the river's flow. These deposits threatened to turn the harbour into an alluvial plain, preventing ships from reaching wharves along the eastern waterfront. The problem was aggravated

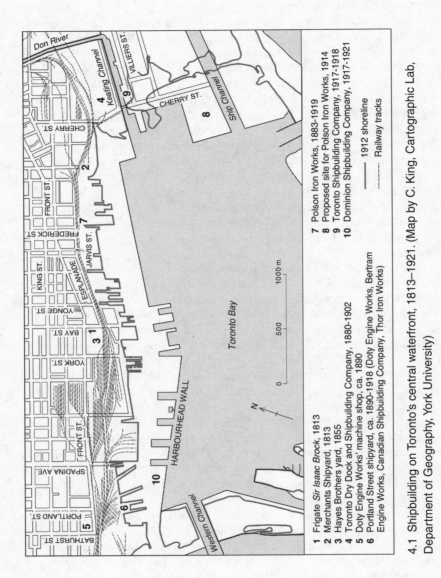

1 Frigate *Sir Isaac Brock*, 1813
2 Merchants Shipyard, 1813
3 Hayes Brothers yard, 1855
4 Toronto Dry Dock and Shipbuilding Company, 1880-1902
5 Doty Engine Works' machine shop, ca. 1890
6 Portland Street shipyard, ca. 1890-1918 (Doty Engine Works, Bertram
   Engine Works, Canadian Shipbuilding Company, Thor Iron Works)
7 Polson Iron Works, 1883-1919
8 Proposed site for Polson Iron Works, 1914
9 Toronto Shipbuilding Company, 1917-1918
10 Dominion Shipbuilding Company, 1917-1921

———— 1912 shoreline
———— Railway tracks

4.1 Shipbuilding on Toronto's central waterfront, 1813–1921. (Map by C. King, Cartographic Lab,
Department of Geography, York University)

by an opening in the narrows of the peninsula along the south edge of the harbour (now known as the Toronto Islands) that was made permanent by a violent storm in 1858. The Harbour Trust (the port authority created in 1850; see Moir, chapter 1, this volume) dealt with this problem through works that included a breakwater built south of the Don's northerly channel. Sheet piling and cribbing for the Don Breakwater were completed in 1871, giving rise to speculation about the potential to turn the neighbouring barren and unproductive marshes of Ashbridge's Bay into a site for industry. Kivas Tully, engineer for the Harbour Trust, raised this possibility with his board in 1872:

> When the advantages of the improvement of the Eastern end of the Harbor become known, there can be no doubt that the facilities offered on the completion of the permanent channel, will lead to the construction of ship yards, and buildings for manufacturing purposes, on the vacant land in the possession of the City, south of the River Don, as the demands for such improvements increase. (Tully 1872: 56)

The constant need for dredging Toronto harbour provided support for Tully's optimistic prediction the following summer. The 'first launch of any kind which has taken place in this city in a great number of years' (*Daily Leader* 1873: 3) was that of the steam dredge *Nipissing*, constructed on the Don Breakwater by Hamilton & Pearce. Unlike previous vessels intended to carry goods and people, the *Nipissing* was built to sustain trade by maintaining the harbour as a safe and navigable waterway.

Further demand arose five years later, when William Donaldson and Alexander Coghill (a ship's carpenter trained in yards on the Clyde River and a contractor for dredging and dock construction, respectively) petitioned the City for a grant of slightly more than two hectares at the mouth of the Don River, exempt from taxes for ten years and with a loan of $5000, to build and repair ships (Donaldson and Coghill 1877). Negotiations dragged on until 1880, when city council approved a twenty-one-year lease with the Toronto Dry Dock and Shipbuilding Company for 2.8 hectares of marsh facing onto the harbour and the Don estuary at a rate of eight dollars per year. Coghill had less than three years to construct a dry dock 'with all necessary approaches, connections and appertenances [*sic*]' to cost no less than $10,000. The arrangement drew praise in the *Globe* newspaper, which observed: 'For many years it has been a source of just complaint among vessel-owners calling at this port that, though compelled to come here for cargoes, they could not get repairs done here to their ships' (*Globe* 1880c: 6). Vessels were forced to sail on to Port Dalhousie, Ogdensburg, or some other American port for repairs. 'The importance of the scheme to Toronto can hardly be over-estimated,' added the *Globe*. Not only did the arrangement offer the opportunity to redirect money spent on ship repairs elsewhere into the pockets of Toronto's citizens, augmented by a shipyard that would keep workers busy when the dry dock was not in use, but 'a portion of the marsh, which has so long been an object of discussion, will be reclaimed, and made valuable. This, it is to be hoped, will be the precursor of a large number of industries to be established upon this spot' (ibid.).

But Coghill and his partners struggled to live up to these ambitious expectations. They failed to construct the dry dock, and the property reverted to the City. Toronto's growth in population and industry, however, along with municipal efforts to improve the lower Don River by straightening its course and diverting its outfall into Ashbridge's Bay, made the venture more attractive. The company was revived in 1888 by D.S. Keith, A.R. Boswell, and Thomas Davies, who raised money based on the increased value of the property and, by 1890, had built and were operating a dry dock (*Globe* 1888a and 1888b). Success, however, was short lived. The City's property commissioner observed in 1901 that the dry dock 'was a failure from the beginning, and was very little used' (Coatsworth 1901: n.p.). Its decrepit ruins lay at the foot of Cherry Street as the City negotiated a surrender of the lease in 1902 to permit filling of the Don's northerly channel into the harbour.

The brief and unhappy history of this company demonstrates the high degree of risk associated with investment in shipbuilding. It also suggests several tenets that influenced waterfront planning during the second half of the nineteenth century: shipbuilding and ship repair were intrinsic to a competitive and viable port; these activities would play a major role in schemes to turn harbour and marsh into productive industrial land; property created for industrial purposes would be leased so that it remained in public control; and tenants would be attracted by public works that created borrowing power for investors using leasehold property in newly developed industrial districts as collateral. It was also clear that shipbuilding was being pushed to the outlying areas of the port. When William E. Redway, a naval architect, submitted a proposal to the City's property committee to build a dry dock on the central waterfront in 1894, he was directed by its chairman to consider the east of the harbour. Property near John Street, taken up with passenger terminals and freight sheds that required access to the city's growing commercial district, was too valuable. The City would, however, lease land to the east 'on very liberal terms' (*Globe* 1894a: 2). Gone were the days when the shipwrights building the *Sir Isaac Brock* and the *City of Toronto* could command centre stage on Toronto's waterfront.

Beginnings of Steel Shipbuilding in Toronto

Shipbuilders developed a firm foothold at the harbour's western end without the need of municipal encouragement and assistance. William Armstrong, the skilled artist who recorded much of the city's waterfront development during the nineteenth century, painted a scene showing wooden hulls under construction at the foot of Bathurst Street in 1865 (Campbell 1971). John Doty moved his machine shop from Oakville to the Yonge Street wharf in 1875, but by 1885 he had relocated to the corner of Front and Bathurst streets, where he specialized in building marine boilers, upright engines, and machinery for yachts and other vessels. By 1890, the company expanded to the north and east and took over the Northern Railway's wharf south of Portland Street to build ships (see figure 4.1). Doty's company produced passenger vessels such as the *Garden City* to run between Toronto and St Catharines, which fit well with his other business as a ferry operator on Toronto harbour.

The Doty Engine Works was purchased in September 1892 by hardware merchants John and George Bertram, two of Doty's major creditors. On 1 November 1893 the new owners announced the appointment of Arendt Angstrom, a naval architect from Sweden and formerly chief engineer of the Cleveland Ship Building Company, as manager of the Bertram Engine Works Company. Diversity was important to keep a workforce of skilled and general labour occupied throughout the year – by 1894, the company was giving 'special attention' to the manufacture of mining machinery (*Globe* 1894a and 1894c) – but the Bertram Engine Works was best known for the palatial passenger steamers designed by Angstrom for inland navigation companies. It also had success with prefabricated hulls, such as the steamer *Keenora* (built in the Toronto yard, disassembled, shipped in pieces by rail to northern Ontario, and re-erected for launch at Rat Portage in 1897) and the sternwheeler *Moyie* (operated by the Canadian Pacific Railway after its assembly at Nelson, British Columbia). Despite strikes over wages and a major fire in 1898, the company prospered. It had built more than twenty-five passenger ships, tow barges, and grain carriers by 1899, when it reorganized its capital to accommodate new contracts that required expansion as the workforce doubled to five hundred workers between 1895 and 1900 (*Globe* 1899b, 1899c, and 1900). The company remained active in all branches of its operations – shipbuilding, boilers, and stationary and marine engines – after the passing of George Bertram in 1900, but John's death in November 1904 left the company in a vulnerable position.

Sustained domestic demand for new vessels in the early 1900s attracted the attention of venture capitalists. Frederic Nicholls, head of Canadian General Electric and an investor in several power and railway companies, joined with William Mackenzie (a driving force behind the transcontinental Canadian Northern Railway), Wilmot Deloui Matthews (a shrewd financier known for sound investments), and others to form the Canadian Shipbuilding Company with capital of $1 million and 'powers to construct and navigate vessels, do a general forwarding and wrecking business, and acquire the rights of other companies' (*Globe* 1902: 8). The investors lured Angstrom from the Bertram Engine Works in February 1903, and by March 1905 the company had secured a contract from the Niagara Navigation Company to build a steamship for the Toronto-to-Lewiston route at its new Bridgeburg yard on the Niagara River. Angstrom returned to Toronto just months later when the company purchased the Bertram Engine Works to build canal-size freighters and excursion steamers. The yard thrived under his guidance. After the launch of passenger vessel *Cayuga* on 3 March 1906, Nicholls remarked that he never had any reason to regret his connection with this enterprise (*Globe* 1906a). Within a year, however, a deepening recession, strikes by machinists and plumbers, and tightening money markets convinced the company to turn down offers of new contracts. Declaring 'this was the worst possible time for workers to select to advance claims for wages,' Nicholls suggested that 'even if the demand does not slacken a healthful contraction should prove beneficial' (*Globe* 1907b: 12). The yard closed after completion of the railway car ferry *Ontario No. 1*, and its plant was sold in August 1908 to pay for a dry dock in Bridgeburg.

A more enduring venture was located near the foot of Sherbourne Street on the harbour's east flank. William Polson and his son, Franklin Bates Polson, started the Polson Iron Works in Toronto in 1883 to manufacture marine engines and boilers. They expanded their operation in 1888 by establishing a shipyard in Owen Sound, a facility best known for the launch in May 1889 of the passenger steamer *Manitoba* for service on the Canadian Pacific Railway's Port Arthur Line. The vessel was reputed to be the largest ship in fresh water, and the first steel steamship built in Canada (Adam 1891; Wilson 1994). The company was taken over by Franklin Polson and John Bellamy Miller (a lumber merchant from Parry Sound) in 1893, who sold the yard in Owen Sound the following year to focus on its Toronto operations. By 1907, when Miller took over as president of the firm following the death of Polson, the Frederick Street yard employed five hundred people who turned out a wide variety of vessels: launches, dredges, car ferries, a prefabricated steamboat hull bound for the Klondike, side-wheel passenger ferries such as the *Trillium*, lighters for the Hudson's Bay Company, light ships for use in the Gulf of St Lawrence and Bay of Fundy, and the armed fisheries-protection cruiser *Vigilant*, the country's first home-built, steam-powered warship slated for service on the Great Lakes. The demand for new vessels led to the reclamation of a water lot south of the yard in 1903, and starting in 1906 the company pressed municipal officials to expand east of Sherbourne Street (Polson Iron Works 1910). Constrained by legislative limits on development of the north shoreline, the Polson Iron Works applied to the City for a lease of twenty hectares of undeveloped marsh in the harbour's east end (*Globe* 1909; *Toronto Daily Star* 1909) – the same area that had previously caught the attention of Tully, Coghill, and Redway.

The Polson Iron Works appeared poised to capture an even larger share of the market, yet its financial position was precarious. The company was financed by a bond issue of $500,000 circulating in the United Kingdom, which represented a significant liability. Competition within the shipbuilding industry had also taken its toll in recent years, and the constant undercutting of tenders led to prices that Miller could not accept. He became increasingly reticent to discuss his firm's financial affairs (Bradstreet 1914). Miller was not alone in this predicament. The federal Department of Marine and Fisheries could name only seven Canadian shipbuilding companies when pressed for advice (Johnston 1911). The Polson Iron Works was the lone survivor in Toronto, and contemporaneous literature by the shipbuilding industry revealed that the challenges faced by Miller's firm were shared by yards across the country (Wilson 1994; *Shipbuilding in Canada* 1913; McDougall 1907). Chafing at federal support given to railways by way of grants, guarantees of credit, and tariffs to promote east–west trade and subsidiary industries such as rolling mills and locomotive works, shipbuilders complained that there was virtually no protection for their yards. Short navigation seasons and improvements in hull design allowed owners to drive vessels harder, resulting in repairs that were more extensive. Ships were not insured for time lost, so repairs also had to be expedited to satisfy the requirements of operators.

Shipyards needed good dry docks, boiler shops, foundries, cranes and associated plant, a supply of steel worth between $50,000 and $100,000 close at hand, and workforces of between three hundred and one thousand highly specialized workers to attract the repair business that could sustain them between contracts for new vessels. Shipbuilding was highly vulnerable to competition from protected yards in the United States, as well as from firms in the United Kingdom that paid their trades close to 70 per cent less than their Canadian equivalents. Just as Toronto yards sent hulls in sections to the west coast for assembly, competitors in the United Kingdom could use the same technique to bring large vessels through the St Lawrence canals. The future was not bright for shipbuilders as proposals for tariffs, bounties, subsidies, and a merchant marine were disregarded by federal officials with very different priorities.

Impact of the Waterfront Plan of 1912

Toronto was facing similar prospects for its port. Decades of domination by the railway companies had cut the waterfront off from the central business district through a wide band of tracks that stretched across the city parallel to the shore (see figure 4.1). Pedestrians were frequently killed as they walked to the passenger terminals at the Yonge Street Wharf, and the movement of goods was interrupted by rolling stock parked across roads leading north from the docks. As level crossings choked the commercial vitality out of wharf operations, docks fell into disrepair. Even if vessels were inclined to call at ramshackle wharves, it was frequently difficult to make their way through the sediment brought down by the Don River. In 1898, it was impossible to move vessels in or out of Polson's slip due to the silt (Caswell 1898). Dredging became a political football between the City and the Harbour Trust as each group fought to preserve limited financial resources. Further east, the marsh of Ashbridge's Bay presented serious health concerns after decades of abuse (see Jackson, this volume), and it was generally agreed that the area should be reclaimed for industrial purposes (Desfor 1988). As with most of the issues facing the waterfront, the lack of a strong, central agency to coordinate redevelopment left it unclear who would carry out this ambitious task.

Into this vacuum stepped the Toronto Board of Trade, buoyed by its recent success in convincing the Board of Railway Commissioners to order railway companies to construct a viaduct that would eliminate the waterfront's level crossings. The board launched a similar campaign to reorganize the Harbour Trust into a powerful agency with the mandate and powers to deal with the problems facing the city's waterfront (see Desfor, Vesalon, and Laidley, this volume). After winning the support of the municipal and federal governments, the board's objectives were achieved when the Toronto Harbour Commission was established through an act of Parliament on 19 May 1911 (Schaeffer 1981; O'Mara 1976; Mellen 1974). In addition to the usual responsibilities given to any port authority that had to maintain the navigability of a harbour, the commission was also given extraordinary powers in the area of land development – a role that would dominate its work for decades to come (Merrens 1988). Urban planning and development was the commission's primary focus for the next eighteen months as it prepared a comprehensive program that would reshape the waterfront.

The Harbour Commission's recommendations were assembled in the Toronto Waterfront Plan of 1912, which was presented to city council in November and soon released to the public (City of Toronto 1913; Toronto Harbour Commissioners 1913b). The port was slated for three types of land use: commercial and dock development in the central waterfront and along new retaining walls constructed in Ashbridge's Bay; parks, bathing beaches, and other recreational activities in each section of the waterfront; and industrial development concentrated in a nearly nine-hectare site at the foot of Bathurst Street and in an industrial district reclaimed from Ashbridge's Bay.

The creation of new land for industrial purposes was the primary objective of the plan, addressing an acute shortage of space for a rapidly expanding manufacturing sector where the number of employees expanded from 26,242 in 1891 to 65,274 in 1911 and an estimated 78,581 in 1914 (Toronto Harbour Commissioners 1915a: 27). As Robert Gourlay, a manufacturer appointed to the commission's board, pointed out to the Empire Club in January 1913, it was 'almost impossible at any price to get a factory site at the heart of the city' (Gourlay 1913: n.p.). Constrained by geography, established neighbouring communities that limited outward expansion, and the growing preference for single-storey plants that required a much larger footprint than existing three- to four-storey factories, there was only one place left to develop: Ashbridge's Bay (Beeby 1984). The commission pointed out in an advertisement to

Canadian manufacturers in June 1915 that 341 factories had been built in Toronto over the previous four years to bring the city up to 1445 industries, and that the new industrial district in Ashbridge's Bay offered room for a thousand more (Toronto Harbour Commissioners 1915b).

The 1912 plan was an ambitious undertaking originally estimated to cost $19 million, which was increased to $25 million when the initial bond issue was sold the following year. The debentures were unusual in that they were based on serviced property not yet created; as James O'Mara so neatly put it, 'The security for the debentures, in effect, was the 1912 Plan, its projected developments, and the assumed ability of the Board to carry the Plan to a successful conclusion. The reality in 1913 was that the Commissioners, in effect, had mortgaged waterlots and swamp land' (1984: 5; see also Desfor, Vesalon, and Laidley, this volume). The commission's presentation to council in November 1912, however, assured the City that 'a careful estimate of business possibilities of the plan warrant the assurance that the ultimate annual revenue … will be such as to meet the interest and sinking fund charges on the money borrowed, and to leave a handsome surplus to be handed over to the city to aid in the reduction of the tax rate' (*Toronto Daily Star* 1912: 6–7). Mayor George Geary expressed concern about handing over millions of dollars to a board not absolutely under the control of the City (*Globe* 1910a), but the *Toronto World* newspaper hailed 'an entirely new spirit in civic affairs … In the harbor scheme there is the first real dawn of a new day in Toronto, and the enterprise and business-like methods which distinguish its management are distinctly of the new school' (1913: 8).

The plan was not specific about the types of industry to be developed on land made from harbour and marsh, but comments by Robert Gourlay provide some clues as to where shipbuilding fit within the commission's intentions. Speaking before the National Conference on City Planning held in Toronto in 1914, he remarked that provision would be made for 'the construction and repair of all classes of water-borne craft; industries of this nature able to manufacture the smallest pleasure craft or the largest inland freight or passenger steamer should be indigenous to the development of a water-front property' (Gourlay 1914b: 21). Although he did not indicate precisely where such industry would be located, the diversion of the Don River through a concrete channel then under construction (the Keating Channel) offered an ideal opportunity to provide frontage along the south dock wall for the city's boat builders (ibid.: 19, 26). Toronto was not alone in making shipbuilding a priority in port development; a month after the Waterfront Plan was unveiled, the Montreal Harbour Commission announced arrangements with the great English firm Vickers Limited to establish a modern shipyard on a twelve-hectare site to be reclaimed from its waterfront in response to the Naval Service Act of 1910 (Wilson 1994; *Globe* 1912).

The 1912 plan was most vague when dealing with the central waterfront due to ongoing negotiations with the railways over the viaduct, but by April 1912 the proposals were causing concern at the Polson Iron Works. The limit of expansion from the harbour's north shore would have to be shifted south to place the central waterfront under public ownership, and to accommodate the arrival of deep-draught vessels without having to blast bedrock. This scheme had serious implications for the Polson site, threatening to strand its yard behind a plain of lake-fill. J.B. Miller's plans for a concrete pier, a swinging dock-side derrick, and steel floating dry dock would entail considerable expense, a waste of scarce capital if the site was landlocked (Miller 1912). The company would have to vacate its yard, and negotiations began for its resettlement in the industrial district being reclaimed from Ashbridge's Bay. A tentative deal was presented to the commissioners in July 1914. An eleven-hectare site north of the Ship Channel would be leased to the company for forty-two years at a competitive rental, with the commission and the federal government assisting the shipbuilder by picking up the $400,000 tab for construction of new dock walls (see figure 4.1). Satisfied that this arrangement would ensure the survival of an important waterfront industry, the commissioners endorsed the proposal (Cousins 1914; Toronto Harbour Commissioners 1914). Within weeks, however, the situation was significantly altered by the start of the First World War. The commission met in early August, and decided that in view of the ample funds at hand through its recent bond issue, all works should proceed without interruption. The Polson Iron Works was not so fortunate. The war made it extremely difficult to arrange financing, and it was agreed to put off matters until the situation in Europe was clearer or until the railways expropriated the Frederick Street property for the new viaduct (Lewis 1914).

Shipbuilding and the First World War

The war temporarily stalled efforts to solidify the position of shipbuilding in Toronto, but it soon became a major catalyst for change in the nature of the industry and the landscape of the waterfront. The Brit-

ish minister of munitions established the Imperial Munitions Board
to oversee the procurement of military equipment and supplies on 29
November 1915, and Canada became a major supplier of munitions
throughout the war. The Polson Iron Works secured a contract for manufacturing shells that helped it struggle through these difficult times,
and several buildings were given over to the production of shrapnel.
The firm was less successful in obtaining similar work from the French
government, probably as a result of the Imperial Munitions Board's persistent efforts to centralize war-related purchasing in Canada through
its staff (Amos 1916).

Any disappointment at such developments was soon offset by work
of a more suitable nature. Merchant shipbuilding in Britain had ground
to a halt in late 1914 when yards were commandeered to construct naval vessels. The anticipated battles at sea never materialized and Britain
became desperate for merchant vessels as a result of the heavy toll exacted by German submarines, which sunk 3,149 ships with a capacity
of nine million gross tons between 1914 and 1918 (Wilson 1994). Yards
were returned to the construction of freighters by December 1915, but
Britain lacked the labour and the materials needed to maintain its navy
while restoring the merchant marine (J.R. Smith 1919). Submarines
emerged as the chief menace to the war effort, and the Imperial Munitions Board raised the possibility of placing contracts with the shipbuilding yards in Canada.

It turned out to be a lengthy and difficult campaign. The Admiralty
repeatedly rebuffed requests by Canada's prime minister, Sir Robert
Borden, to have warships built in Canadian yards well into 1915, and
there was growing annoyance within Canada at the British practice of
giving orders for shells and ships to the United States while looking
to Canada for significant financial support and armed forces (Hadley
and Sarty 1991). Lord Brand, the Imperial Munitions Board's representative in London, continually stressed with his superior, Winston
Churchill, and other British officials the importance of placing orders
for munitions in Canada (Flavelle 1917; Brand 1916). After the United
States entered the war in April 1917 and took possession of most of the
vessels commissioned by the Imperial Munitions Board, the Ministry of
Shipping requested the Imperial Munitions Board to turn to the one remaining source for ships by implementing a shipbuilding program limited to the capacity of existing Canadian yards (Wilson 1994; Heal 1992;
Carnegie 1925). Steel freighters were the first priority, and contracts for
six vessels were awarded to the Polson Iron Works. In response to the

need for patrolled shipping lanes that offered a modicum of protection from German submarines, the firm was also involved in negotiations with Canada's minister of naval service and Vickers of Montreal for the production of armed steam trawlers. The project went ahead with the support of the Admiralty, and Polson received contracts for six steel 'battle class' trawlers to serve with the Royal Canadian Navy (Hadley and Sarty 1991).

With work in hand, the company could pursue its new site with vigour. In a pointed letter to Robert Gourlay, the harbour commissioner who had spoken so supportively about the place of shipbuilding in the development of Toronto's waterfront, J.B. Miller took the commission to task in January 1917:

> Both the Canadian and British Government want us to build vessels and do work of different descriptions, and if we were now in use of our new property, there would have been an amount running into the millions spent here on this work. As it is, we will have to be satisfied with a fraction of the work we might otherwise have taken. This not only means a serious loss to ourselves, but also a loss to the city and the country. (Miller 1917: n.p.)

The war had tightened European money markets, putting the company in a position where it was unable to pursue expansion. The government contracts for merchant and naval vessels eliminated this financial roadblock, but Polson ran into another obstacle. The discovery of over 305 metres of faulty dock-wall substructure prevented occupation of the new site until its replacement in 1918. Faced with this delay and the need to start work on orders that would increase Polson's workforce by some 400 per cent to 1700 employees within the year, Miller ordered the expansion of the Frederick Street plant that he knew would eventually be left high and dry.

While it was unable to expedite development of Polson's new site, the Toronto Harbour Commission's support for the city's shipbuilding industry was otherwise demonstrated during the next two years. In July 1917 city council requested the commission to pursue the development of a shipyard to take advantage of a spate of contracts from the Imperial Munitions Board. While its chairman, Sir Joseph Flavelle, declined the commission's invitation to build a national shipyard in Toronto comparable to British Forgings (the board's electrical steel mill that had been completed on lands reclaimed from Ashbridge's Bay), private concerns had more success pursuing the board's business. John Russell, a contractor for Toronto's harbour improvements, purchased the shipyard at the foot of Portland Street in September 1915 as the base for his new company, the Thor Iron Works. In addition to winning contracts to construct two steam trawlers for the Royal Navy, Thor built two freighters for Norwegian interests. But while Polson's site at the east end of the harbour would remain undisturbed for many years, the Toronto Harbour Commission was constructing the harbourhead wall east from the Western Channel just as Thor's orders were due for delivery. A temporary channel was made to launch these ships, but the yard would soon be landlocked.

John Russell expanded his involvement in shipbuilding as a result of the pressing demand for new freighters using a traditional, non-strategic material: wood. In an attempt to circumvent the chronic shortage of steel that worsened after the United States entered the war in April 1917, the Imperial Munitions Board commissioned forty-six wooden-hulled freighters. Although this initiative found its most logical home in British Columbia, where the supply of timber and better-equipped yards gave builders a competitive edge, the board also awarded contracts to firms along the St Lawrence River and Great Lakes. Russell formed the Toronto Shipbuilding Company to assist with this program, and leased property on the south side of the Keating Channel. He won contracts for two vessels, and under Russell's guidance some four hundred tradesmen began work on the 2600-tonne vessels in September 1917. Due to difficulties in finding trained workers and sufficient quantities of British Columbia fir (particularly when the Toronto Harbour Commission was competing for the same wood for dock-wall construction; Cousins 1917), Russell struggled to meet production deadlines. The *War Ontario* finally slid down the ways into the Keating Channel on 19 June 1918 and her sister ship, the *War Toronto*, followed four months later. The site was also kept busy with Russell's floating wooden dry dock, which arrived from Wisconsin in July 1917 and became a fixture in the Keating Channel for several decades less than five hundred feet from the site of Coghill's dry dock (*Globe* 1917).

The war further changed the dynamics of the local shipbuilding industry by introducing foreign investment. Christoffer Hannevig was a Norwegian financier and son of a shipbuilder who arrived in New York in 1915 to examine shipping conditions. Anticipating that demand for merchant freighters would outstrip supply due to the high toll exacted by German submarines, he established a ship brokerage firm and procured contracts from Norwegian shipping firms for vessels to be built at shipyards in the United States, including three shipbuilding companies owned by Hannevig in Delaware, Pennsylvania, and New Jersey (*New York Times* 1927, 1921a, 1921b). Hannevig also placed orders with Canadian shipyards in 1916. It is possible that he met with Louis Dahlgren, president of the Thor Iron Works, when Dahlgren visited New York to drum up business after the firm struggled to secure American or Canadian orders, for Thor began applying pressure on the Department of Marine and Fisheries to permit the export of Canadian-built ships to neutral countries such as Norway. The Polson Iron Works submitted similar petitions, and by October 1916 other Canadian shipyards had joined the chorus. The situation presented an attractive opportunity to start steel shipbuilding at several points throughout the country, and to solidify the position of yards already in operation.

The British Admiralty was the primary obstacle to this otherwise promising arrangement. Unable to requisition vessels built for neutrals for the Allied war effort, it convinced the Colonial Office to pressure the Canadian government into building the vessels in their own right. The prime minister, Sir Robert Borden, was not amused. He wired back that Canada had made Britain aware of its ability to build ships and submarines, yet Imperial orders had gone to the United States instead. Canadian orders-in-council were issued in November 1916 to permit Polson and Thor, along with a few other Canadian builders, to export a limited number of hulls for Norwegian registry. While there is truth to the claim by a Norwegian diplomat that orders from his country made Canadian yards well prepared to respond to much larger orders from the Imperial Munitions Board (Royal Norwegian Consul for Canada 1917), this subsequent work may not have been forthcoming had not Canadian builders, led by the two Toronto firms, pressed so hard to create a showdown between Canadian and British leaders over foreign commissions.

Christoffer Hannevig shifted his business strategy of integrated ship brokerage and construction north of the border after his American shipyards were requisitioned by the United States Shipping Board's Emergency Fleet Corporation in August 1917. He purchased the Thor Iron Works from John Russell and, working with capital invested by J.P. Morgan & Co. of New York, formed a new venture called the Dominion Shipbuilding Company (Hannevig also owned the Newfoundland Shipbuilding Company in Harbour Grace). As construction of the harbourhead wall continued east from the Western Channel, Hannevig looked to the Waterfront Plan's industrial reserve at the foot of Bathurst Street as the site for Dominion's shipyard. The six-hectare property was still two-thirds underwater when the twenty-one-year lease was signed in November, providing the Toronto Harbour Commission with an annual rental of $23,000 that offered some return on its investment in waterfront development. The commission undertook to finish reclamation as soon as possible (see figure 4.2).

Additional support was forthcoming in the area of structural expertise, as the commission agreed not only to lay the foundations for the plant, but also to assemble the buildings at cost for labour and materials, plus 20 per cent for office overhead and engineering (Toronto Harbour Commission Investigation 1926). Work progressed in spite of bleak winter conditions, and by May 1918 the hull of the first vessel began to take shape. Another four 2900-tonne freighters soon began to take shape, and it was expected that Dominion's workforce would expand from five hundred to fifteen hundred by the end of July, and to three thousand when construction of the plant was complete (*Toronto World* 1918). Bad weather and the destruction of the Thor Iron Works plant by fire in April 1918 delayed work by several months, but on 26 September 1918 the *St. Mihiel* slid into the harbour.

Shipbuilding's Struggles in the Post-war Period

The Toronto Harbour Commission's close involvement in the affairs of the Dominion Shipbuilding Company addressed city council's desire to stimulate local shipbuilding, an industry that could 'continue building for the quieter ocean commerce of peace' (*Toronto Daily News* 1918: 7). A week after declaration of the armistice, reports of increased payrolls at Dominion Shipbuilding and the Polson Iron Works led one Toronto newspaper to reflect upon the continuing importance of this trade:

> Shipbuilding is one of the fields of industry that can be depended upon to absorb a considerable portion of the labor that is being released from strictly war business. While the shipbuilding industry received its impetus as a result of conditions brought about by the war, prominent Canadian shipbuilders foresee great activities for at least six or eight years, and they are confident that the industry will retain permanently a large place in Canada. (*Globe* 1918b: 11)

But by this time the rules of the industry had changed, and not in

4.2 Reclamation continues east from property of the Dominion Shipbuilding Company at foot of Spadina Avenue, 1919. (Photo courtesy of Toronto Port Authority Archives, PC 1/3/202)

Hannevig's favour. A year earlier, the minister of marine and fisheries, Charles Ballantyne, expressed a reluctance to grant export licences owing to the rapid pace of change in conditions affecting the Canadian shipbuilding industry, and by December 1917 the minister's misgivings had become policy. Ostensibly attributed to a lack of labour and the scarcity of steel for ships' plates, the policy was also a response to growing government concern about the competitive pressures within the nation's shipbuilding industry being exerted by neutral interests at a time when Ballantyne was attempting to launch the Canadian government merchant marine. With the French government offering more per deadweight ton than their own federal government, discontent grew within Canadian shipbuilding circles (*Vancouver Daily Sun* 1918). Ballantyne's policy ensured a lower price and adequate supplies of steel plate for government orders, but was a crippling blow to Toronto's shipbuilding industry and caused considerable concern in other parts of the country that counted on orders from neutral countries to soften the anticipated post-war slump (Conn 1987).

With its berths full with orders from Hannevig covered by the 1916 export licences and freighters ordered by the Imperial Munitions Board, the Polson Iron Works was unable to tender for the merchant marine shipbuilding program. It looked instead to survive on Norwegian orders for ten steel 3600-tonne vessels to be constructed between 1919 and 1921. Ballantyne steadfastly refused to sanction such plans (*Toronto Daily Star* 1919). Dominion Shipbuilding, by contrast, was not an established shipyard when the program was announced, and hence was ineligible to apply. Forced to rely upon the export of vessels for foreign registry to keep his plant going, Hannevig came up with a creative proposal that involved constructing a shipyard in Halifax to build steel and concrete cylindrical barges in exchange for approval to export vessels from the Thor and Dominion yards. Sir Joseph Flavelle, who seemed to respect Hannevig's opinions and bustle, was genuinely impressed by the scheme, but could do little to assist the project. Ballantyne, who occasionally expressed reservations about Hannevig's character to Prime Minister Borden, was not nearly so enthralled (Hannevig 1918a; Ballantyne 1918; Flavelle 1918). The scheme met a quiet end.

Others attempted to rescue the Polson and Dominion Shipbuilding companies, but to no avail. Edmund Bristol, Member of Parliament for Toronto, lobbied hard for Norwegian registry, fearing that if the federal government waited until the war was over, the contracts would go to

British or American yards. Assurances that adequate supplies of steel had been obtained and that labour would be imported from Norway did not strike at the heart of the issue from the government's point of view, and Bristol's proposal made no headway. Tommy Church, the mayor of Toronto, fared better in February 1919 by channelling the ire of all affected parties into a meeting with another Torontonian, Minister of Finance Sir Thomas White, whose tight control over the government's purse strings was sufficiently loosened to allow contracts for two vessels to be given to the Dominion Shipbuilding Company during a supplementary construction program. The government finally allowed Canadian shipbuilders to pursue foreign orders in December 1918, but it was too late. Hannevig predicted in February that the chances of building for foreign registry would be quite limited after the war (Hannevig 1918b), and by preventing Toronto builders from tying up Norwegian and French orders with binding contracts, the federal government had effectively eliminated the chance for these yards to sustain themselves during the difficult years of post-war reconstruction.

In the face of such resistance, an industry employing more than 2500 workers by the end of the war and providing annual wages in excess of $2.35 million came to a halt. John Russell's Toronto Dry Dock Company undertook ship repairs and built small service vessels, but his commercial survival was likely the result of diversification into construction and paving projects. The other yards went into bankruptcy, owing large sums of money. The bankruptcy of the Polson Iron Works in March 1919 meant the loss of an important waterfront industry in operation since 1883, as well as jobs for some 1250 skilled workers. Its last vessel, the freighter *War Halton*, was completed in receivership. The Dominion Shipbuilding Company followed suit on 31 July 1920, when the firm was liquidated, owing the Toronto Harbour Commission almost $103,000 (Toronto Harbour Commission Investigation 1926: n.p.). Christoffer Hannevig was Dominion's largest debtor, owing the company $500,000 with 'no immediate prospect of payment' – particularly after he filed for bankruptcy in 1921 with debts of $8 million (*New York Times* 1921a; *Globe* 1920b). Dominion's last two vessels, meant to save the company's livelihood, were finished using labour from the Collingwood yards, an arrangement that resulted in a bitter dispute between organized labour and the Meighen government when workers were paid less than union scale for their hourly wages (*Globe* 1921a, 1921b, 1920c, and 1920d).

118   Michael Moir

Conclusion

Despite modest beginnings, shipbuilding emerged during the 1890s
as a waterfront industry that offered considerable potential for growth
thanks to the requirements of federal public works undertaken to maintain navigable waterways and the inland navigation companies that
plied these channels and harbours. Toronto's shipwrights turned out a
significant number of passenger and cargo vessels, dredges, car ferries,
cruisers, and steam yachts, craft known for the high quality of design
applied by naval architects Arendt Angstrom and William Redway.
Several have survived as an enduring legacy of their makers' contributions to Canada's maritime heritage. The *Moyie*, restored as a museum
ship on Kootenay Lake in British Columbia, is 'the world's oldest intact
passenger sternwheeler' (Kootenay Lake Historical Society 2008: n.p.).
The steamer *Keenora* sits on a concrete berth at the Marine Museum of
Manitoba after many years of transporting passengers and cargo across
the Lake of the Woods, followed by Lake Winnipeg and the Red River.
The yacht *Wanda*, built by the Polson Iron Works in 1915 for the wife of
Timothy Eaton, has returned to the waters of Lake Muskoka (Wagner-
Chazalon 2007), and the Royal Canadian Yacht Club's graceful tenders
Kwasind and *Hiawatha* and the municipal ferry *Trillium* still traverse To-
ronto harbour. The companies also provided engines, boilers, and machinery used in the construction of factories, public infrastructure such
as the High Level Pumping Station in Toronto's water-supply system,
and Sir Henry Pellatt's Casa Loma.

Despite competition from cheaper foreign builders and no tariff
protection, shipbuilding attracted the attention of municipal officials
and business leaders who saw it as a means to turn the unproductive
marshes of Ashbridge's Bay into a profitable enterprise as early as 1872.
Despite the failure of Alexander Coghill and others to establish a successful dry dock in the wetlands at the mouth of the Don River, the
Polson Iron Works looked to this area for expansion in 1909 in order to
escape the regulatory limits on development along the harbour's north
shore. A crisis in naval supremacy between Great Britain and Germany
that same year sparked a stormy national debate that led to Sir Wilfrid
Laurier's Naval Service Act of 1910. In addition to establishing the Canadian navy, the legislation provided for a small fleet of modern cruisers and destroyers to be built in Canadian shipyards. Borden and his
Conservatives railed against this 'tin pot navy' while in opposition,
but, like Laurier, Borden supported the construction of naval vessels

in Canada instead of the less-expensive yards in Great Britain because of shipbuilding's economic impact, and shored up Canadian builders with civil work after winning the general election in September 1911 (Hadley and Sarty 1991).

The importance of shipbuilding was explored in January 1911 by the *Busy Man's Magazine* (renamed *MacLean's Magazine* two months later). It sought out an expert, 'neither Tory nor Grit, Nationalist nor Colonel Denison' to speak on the importance of shipbuilding 'NOT as to the efficiency of the Canadian navy as a fighting force ... BUT as a great influence on the industrial development of the country' (Nixon 1911: 21). The magazine selected Lewis Nixon, a respected American naval architect, shipbuilding executive, and Tammany Hall boss. After citing the invigorating effect of constructing battleships upon the economic framework of Italy, Germany, Great Britain, and the United States, Nixon explained the industry's impact:

> Shipbuilding calls for almost every line of workmanship, from workers in steel and wood, to painters, decorators and upholsterers; from the manufacture of boilers and engines, to the making of fine instruments. The shipbuilding nation is in the way of becoming a carrier nation – getting the cream of commerce; the fees, I have already said, for transportation, insurance, inspection, and middleman's profits generally. (ibid.: 22–3)

Political debate and journalistic commentary gave shipbuilding a heightened national profile at the same time that the Toronto Board of Trade, municipal officials, railway companies, and others were lobbying for a wholesale reconfiguration of the city's waterfront. The Harbour Commission, born out of the same community of interests that championed shipbuilding, promoted this industry as the vanguard for economically sustainable property development as it began implementation of its Waterfront Plan.

While the tightening of money markets in 1914 had a stultifying effect upon expansion plans of the Polson Iron Works, the heavy loss of merchant tonnage to submarine warfare led to orders from Britain, France, and Norway that resulted in a significant increase in the numbers of yards and workers devoted to shipbuilding in Toronto and elsewhere in North America. The feast, however, was short lived. Peace brought a dramatic reversal of the industry's fortunes; instead of offering employment to redundant munitions workers and returned soldiers, peace meant the closure of shipyards – which only made matters worse. While Toronto's population increased by more than 13 per cent to almost 521,000 between 1916 and 1921, almost 12,000 manufacturing jobs were lost during the same period and unemployment remained a serious issue for the remainder of the decade (Lemon 1985). The demise of shipbuilding also meant a loss of skilled labour and technical expertise from the city, as naval architects, engineers, millwrights, and machinists moved to other Great Lakes ports, particularly in the United States. The situation was by no means restricted to Toronto. More than 23,000 people were employed in Canadian yards in 1919. This workforce fell to 14,847 the following year and then to 3202 as the number of Canadian companies constructing and repairing ships fell from 82 in 1920 to 38 in 1922, the years in which Canadian builders produced the greatest and lowest number of ships between 1901 and the Great Depression (Canada, Dominion Bureau of Statistics 1931, 1925, 1924).

The closures were a serious blow to the Toronto Harbour Commission's plans for the waterfront. By the summer of 1918 most of the reclaimed port lands were devoted to war-related industries that were expected to pay for public works that continued through the war despite pressing difficulties (Moir 1989). The First World War gave hope that this objective would be achieved through leases with the Dominion Shipbuilding Company and possibly the Polson Iron Works, but the federal prohibition on building ships for neutral countries and the glut of commercial tonnage that followed the war added to the commission's debt and seriously undermined its confident prediction that industrial development would pay for a bold program of parks, boulevards, and urban infrastructure. The commission's financial problems were exacerbated by increasingly poor returns on bond issues, questionable business decisions, construction costs that were higher than expected, and the depression that followed the war (O'Mara 1984). Its operations were significantly scaled back during the early 1920s, and by the end of the decade the commission abandoned a long-held principle to lease rather than sell properties to meet financial obligations. By 1929 the commission had sold 29 per cent of its available industrial lands (Desfor et al. 1988). Unable to attract manufacturers to the extent forecast by the Waterfront Plan, the commission opted to use the Port Industrial District for the storage of bulk commodities such as oil and coal (see Prudham et al., this volume; Goldrick and Merrens 1990), uses that did not offer the wide range of well-paying skilled jobs and secondary economic benefits of high-value-added industries such as shipbuilding.

4.3 Launch of the *War Ontario*, Keating Channel, Toronto, 29 June 1918.
(Photo by Arthur Beales; courtesy of Toronto Port Authority Archives, PC
1/1/3061)

The loss of shipbuilding had a less tangible but perhaps equally significant effect upon attitudes towards the Toronto Harbour Commission. Shipbuilding was the only waterfront activity that generated a
strong and memorable connection between industry and the public at
large. Each launch attracted hundreds of spectators to watch tonnes of
steel or wood slide gracefully down the ways. These ceremonies were
extensively reported by the local press, thereby reaching a much larger
audience. When a ship's caulker unexpectedly fell headlong into the
Keating Channel during the launch of the *War Ontario* on 29 June 1918
(see figure 4.3), the chief engineer of the Toronto Shipbuilding Company remarked, 'I think John Russell gave him $10 to jump overboard
ahead of the boat for the benefit of the movies' (*Globe* 1918a: 9).

Such events and ensuing media coverage celebrated the city's industrial progress and its contributions to regional and international commerce. After 1917, frequent launches must have offered confirmation
that the economic sustainability of the Toronto Harbour Commission's

Waterfront Plan of 1912 was a realistic assumption. This connection between the commission's role in urban planning, industrial development, and the general public was gone once the shipyards fell quiet in 1921. The ensuing years brought growing political and public concern over the commission's approach to waterfront development and its apparent lack of accountability, and the optimism that accompanied the sudden rise of shipbuilding during the war was largely forgotten despite a brief revival to produce naval vessels during the next global conflict. Fifty-six minesweepers were built on the site reclaimed for the Dominion Shipbuilding Company, but such work no longer created expectations that shipbuilding would survive the Second World War to drive Toronto's economic growth into the future. Polson's shipyard was buried by dredged sand in the 1920s, and Dominion's buildings were demolished during the 1980s to make way for Harbourfront, a new urban development. Gantry cranes and keel blocks gave way to cooperative housing and condominiums, a testament to the vulnerability of local aspirations and grand schemes to regional, national, and international forces.

5 A Social History of a Changing Environment: The Don River Valley, 1910–1931

JENNIFER BONNELL

> Not far from the spot where, at present, the Don-street bridge crosses the river, on the west side and to the north, lived for a long time a hermit-squatter, named Joseph Tyler ... His abode on the Don was an excavation in the side of the steep hill, a little way above the level of the river bank ... To the south of his cave he cultivated a large garden, and raised among other things, the white sweet edible Indian corn, a novelty here at the time; and very excellent tobacco.
>
> Scadding 1873: 228–9

Henry Scadding's 1873 description of Joseph Tyler's cave is the first detailed record in what would become a long history of homelessness in Toronto's Lower Don River valley. According to Scadding's account, Tyler was an industrious and inventive recluse, a veteran of the American Revolutionary War who manufactured and sold 'pitch and tar' to merchants in town, and ferried the Helliwell brewery's beer in his 'magnificent canoe' when the roads were too muddy to use. He was a puzzling figure – Scadding notes the 'mystery attendant on his choice of life of complete solitude [and] his careful reserve.' His choice of location was equally mysterious: the Lower Don River in Tyler's time (the 1820s and 1830s) was separated from the town of York by the woods of the government reserve, making Tyler a man distinctly on the margins. Whether Tyler chose to live on the Lower Don or was pushed there by circumstance is difficult to determine. Certainly his livelihood of pitch production and pine knot carving would have been facilitated by a location close to the forest, and the river provided easy transportation into town. The uncertainty surrounding Joseph Tyler is emblematic of the history of people on the margins – indeed, the fact that he is named and some details of his life recorded is more than we have for most of the people who found themselves living in the valley, for various reasons, over the last two hundred years.

A connection exists, I suggest, between dominant perceptions of the river valley as a marginal space at the edge of the city and its function as a repository for marginalized people. Toronto is not the only city to witness a connection between ravines or 'low lands' and marginal housing: Kellogg's 1909 *Pittsburgh Survey* reported on 'squatters' and 'disreputable families' living in the polluted area of 'Skunk Hollow,' and Minneapolis's 'Bohemian Flats' shared a similar reputation among nineteenth-century reformers (Kellogg 1914).[1] Certainly, land value and perceptions of risk were at work.[2] Ken Cruikshank and Nancy Bouchier's study of squatters and working-class families in nineteenth-century Hamilton is illustrative in demonstrating the geographic connections between industry, polluted and poorly drained lands, and working-class neighbourhoods (Cruikshank and Bouchier 2004; Bouchier and Cruikshank 2003). Despite substantial work in Canadian historiography on marginalized groups and, in the environmental history literature, on degraded spaces, few studies have examined the links between those places and people relegated to the margins of urban environments. While most studies in the environmental-inequality literature describe the unequal distribution of environmental hazards in racialized or working-class neighbourhoods (see, for example, Platt 2005; Hurley 1995; Bullard 1990), few investigate the congregation of marginalized populations in already degraded spaces or in urban/rural borderlands.[3] Even fewer explore the link between homeless people and degraded environments.[4] How such spaces were constructed as marginal, and the attractions they held for homeless travellers, have yet to receive detailed treatment.

Pointing to this connection between marginality of place and of human populations conjures a number of theoretical pitfalls, not the least of which being charges of environmental determinism. Urban geographers have long attempted to shed the legacy of early-twentieth-century scholars such as Robert Park and Ernest W. Burgess, who applied ideas from the nascent field of ecology to argue that competition for scarce natural resources such as land or water led to the stratification of social groups in different 'niches' through the urban environment. Inasmuch as environment affected behaviour, they concluded, poorer environments produced populations more prone to crime and deviance

(Park 1952; Park et al. 1925). I am not suggesting that environmental factors alone determined the actions of those who sought refuge in the valley. The factors that pulled and pushed people to the valley, and that fuelled corresponding perceptions of marginality, were certainly more varied and more complex. Instead, I seek to draw attention to what emerges from the sources as an indisputably observable phenomenon: the congregation of people widely perceived as 'social undesirables' within what was widely perceived as an undesirable or problematic landscape. In making this connection, I seek to stress that environment *did* play a role in these people's everyday lives: while it was certainly not the only factor drawing them to the valley, the presence of relatively unoccupied land close to the city centre must have presented some degree of attraction to those without regular work or shelter. Other factors, such as the active discouragement of vagrancy in most parts of the city, and the relative absence of policing authority in ravine spaces, likely also played a role in attracting homeless people.

In an attempt to understand better the forces at work in relegating certain populations and places to the margins, I turn to Canadian labour historian Ian McKay's provocative call to re-evaluate the central role of liberalism in shaping Canadian history. As McKay suggests, the extension of a liberal project of rule across early-nineteenth-century Canada created a socio-political landscape of centres and peripheries, insiders and outsiders (2000). 'Centres' in this analogy represent those places and populations in which liberal ideals were effectively taken up, such as the rational street grids of urban centres, the single-family dwelling, the hegemony of the urban (male) middle class; 'peripheries,' by extension, were those places and populations within which aliberal practices persisted, or actively resisted, the rise of a new order: the Canadian north, aboriginal communities, labour unions. As McKay explains, the 'individuals' at the 'conceptual nucleus' of liberalism should be considered not as 'actual living beings' but rather as 'the entity each one of them might, if purified and rationalized, aspire to become' (625). In this way liberalism categorized certain individuals as deficient – among them, 'women, workers, ethnic minorities, and Amerindians' all '[marked] out as "Other"' by the liberal model (626).

What is compelling about McKay's reconnaissance or 're-knowing' of liberalism is its potential to link the processes that marginalized certain populations with similar imperatives at work in classifying difficult or unpredictable environments as marginal or 'waste' spaces. His articulation of liberalism as it was expressed in nineteenth-century Canada emphasizes the simplification of complex systems, the desire to eradicate unpredictability, and the attempt to extend a rational, managerial ethos across territory and populations. Applied to the land, the liberal vision of individuals 'as separate from, and acting upon, the natural world' correspondingly cast environment as property to improve, rationalize, make productive (2000: 631–2). Environments that resisted improvement, that proved somehow difficult to occupy, to make industrious, or to gain value from – mountain-sides and river valleys, deserts and wetlands – were dismissed by this logic as marginal, deviant, uncooperative, wild. That 'peripheral' populations should exist within peripheral environments should not, perhaps, be so surprising. Examples are all around us: the impoverished rural communities of the central Appalachia; the isolated First Nations reserve battling contaminated water and few opportunities; the fishing community pursuing diverse strategies of subsistence on the Atlantic coast. As cultural geographer Rob Shields has observed, social divisions have spatial expression. Places on the margin, in his assessment, become places left behind by the rush of modernity – liminal spaces that invert or actively subvert dominant values of civilization and rationality (Shields 1991). The Don River valley in the late nineteenth and early twentieth centuries, I argue in the discussion that follows, was one of those places.

This chapter draws upon newspaper articles, local histories, historical photographs, and municipal reports to sketch a history of the interactions between people and place in the Don River valley. I have chosen to focus not on the working-class communities that grew up alongside the industrialized areas of the lower valley (south of the forks), but on people who experienced even less security – those who turned to the valley itself for refuge. Throughout the chapter, I return to a central dialectic of perception and experience – the tension between the ways the valley and its inhabitants were perceived by the more privileged residents of the centre and what was happening, as best we can discern from the limited sources that exist, 'on the ground.' Place itself becomes a source in piecing together the experiences of people pushed to the edges of society. The kinds of things people sought in that place, and the opportunities it presented – expected and otherwise – give some sense of the motivations of marginalized groups in choosing the valley over other options for relief housing. I will begin by sketching a brief overview of the factors that relegated an environment once central to the development of the town of York to one that was peripheral and stigmatized by the latter decades of the nineteenth century. From there,

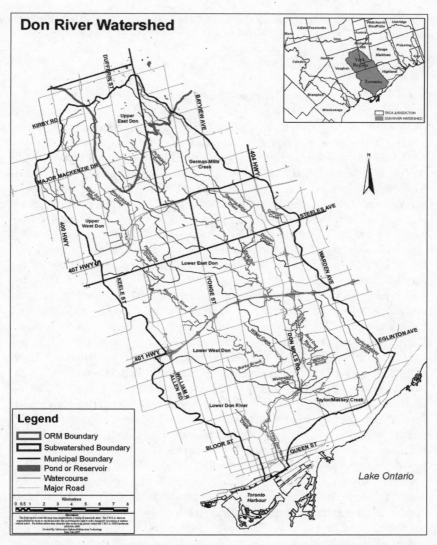

5.1 The Don River Watershed. (Courtesy of Toronto and Region Conservation Authority)

I will turn to the experiences of two groups of people who sought refuge in the valley in the early twentieth century.

A Marginal Environment

For John Graves Simcoe, Upper Canada's first lieutenant governor, the sheltered curve of the east end of Toronto Bay and its tributary streams presented a landscape of possibility. Arriving in the area in the summer of 1793, Simcoe noted the harbour's natural defensibility and its potential to supply the future town of York and its environs with lumber. 'At the Bottom of the Harbour,' he reported to acting colonial administrator Alured Clarke in May 1793, 'there is a Situation admirably adapted for a Naval Arsenal and Dock Yard, and there flows into the Harbour a River [the Don] the Banks of which are covered with excellent Timber' (in Firth 1962: 4). Satisfied with his assessment of the area's potential, he had his surveyor Alexander Aitkin lay out a plot for the future town of York immediately west of the mouth of the Don, at the base of today's Parliament Street. He established a four-hundred-acre reserve for 'government buildings' stretching from the lakeshore north to today's Carlton Street and west of the river to Parliament, and by 1797 the first parliament buildings had been erected near the intersection of today's Parliament and Front Streets (Adam et al. 1885: 211; see figure 5.2). Before returning to England in 1796, Simcoe awarded generous farm lots in the vicinity to military officers and favoured officials within his inner circle. For many grantees, holdings along the Don complemented already valuable properties closer to town. They could dabble with farming along the flats of the river with little pressure to create viable operations. Some, like Simcoe's secretary John Scadding, farmed their holdings with relative success (Robertson 1894: 194–5). Others chose instead to erect lavish suburban mansions on their lands overlooking the valley (Ontario Department of Planning and Development 1950, part 1: 34). This was particularly true west of the river along Yonge and Davenport Streets, where country estates such as Rosedale prevailed until mid-century and beyond. The area around the Lower Don, then, enjoyed a fleeting desirability in the first years of settlement. By the early 1800s, however, development had begun to move north and west from Simcoe's original town plot. Although prominent inhabitants of York continued to speculate in lands abutting the river valley in the 1810s, by 1820 the area had become saddled with an increasingly undesirable reputation (Ganton 1974: 14).

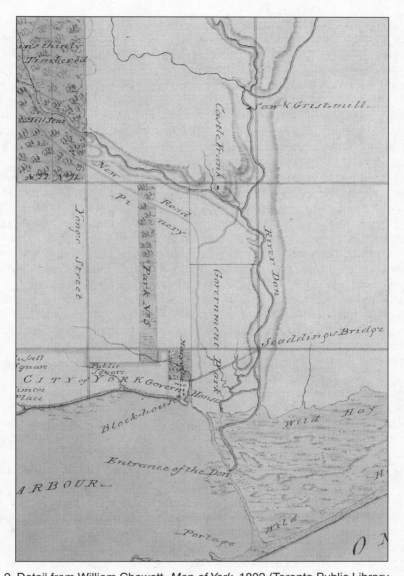

5.2 Detail from William Chewett, *Map of York*, 1802 (Toronto Public Library, MS1889.1.6). Note government reserve (labelled 'Government Park') in centre of map west of Don River and 'Governmt House' (parliament buildings) on lakeshore northwest of the river mouth.

A number of factors worked against the desirability of the lower valley lands in this period. From the earliest days of European settlement, certain problems were especially pronounced in the east end. Most prominent among these was the fever or ague that tormented settler populations each summer. Characterized by alternating symptoms of severe fever and shaking chills, the 'ague' or 'lake fever' was an almost inevitable, if rarely fatal, aspect of life in Upper Canada in the late eighteenth and early nineteenth centuries. Now understood as a strain of malaria (from the eighteenth-century Italian *mal'aria*), a disease spread by the bite of the *Anopheles* mosquito, at the time the ague was thought to result from inhaling 'bad air.' In a letter to a former employer in Quebec City in September 1801, Toronto printer John Bennett wrote: 'I am just recovering from a severe fit of fever and ague which confined me to bed for ten days past – no body can escape it who pretends to live here ... There is a marsh about [half] a mile from where I live from which a thick fog arises every morning – people attribute [the fever] in great measure to that and to the low and uncultivated state of the Country' (in Firth 1962: 242). Gases produced by decomposing organic matter took on the ominous label of 'miasmas' – disease-producing vapours – and the places where such organic matter accumulated, such as swamps and wetlands, became places to fear, avoid, and, best yet, destroy through drainage and fill.

Before the discovery of the malaria parasite in 1880 and subsequent discoveries of mosquitoes as vectors of transmission, place itself bore the mantle of disease risk. Certain environments were considered more 'unhealthy' than others. In 1803, for example, Sir Isaac Brock reported in a letter to military secretary James Green that the soldiers quartered in the Block House at the mouth of the Don were 'falling ill of the Ague and Fever in great numbers,' while the garrison at the west end of town 'continues in perfect health.' The evidence confirmed his suspicions about the environment around the Lower River, '[shewing] plainly that the character given of the situation of the Block House is too well founded' (in Firth 1962: 72). A quarter-century later, petitioners to the Upper Canadian legislature in 1830 stressed the 'inconvenience and unhealthiness' of the site of the recently burned Parliament House, located at the foot of Parliament Street just west of the Don marshes, in their call to reconstruct the Parliament buildings near the lieutenant governor's residence in New Town (west of the original town plot). 'No person having a regard to health would select [the site near the Marsh] for a residence,' they argued; 'the untenanted State of houses adjoining the said Marsh, confirm them in this opinion' (in Firth 1966: 30–1). Ague was not the only disease associated with the marsh; as Jackson shows in this volume, fears of cholera were used to justify extensive improvement plans for the Ashbridge's Bay marsh in the 1890s.

Conevery Bolton Valencius has provided useful context for this notion of 'unhealthy' landscapes in her 2002 monograph *The Health of the Country*. For nineteenth-century Americans, Valencius reminds us, the environment did not stop 'at the seeming boundary of the skin,' but instead, 'the surrounding world seeped into [one's] every pore, creating states of health that were as much environmental as they were personal' (12). She continues:

> Factors of surroundings – the sodden vegetation of local bottomland, the rot and 'scum' atop a nearby stream, the winds that blew over swampland as over soldiers' fortifications – affected the health of environments as they would the health of people within a locale. Place and person were swayed by the same kinds of forces; sloughs and forests underwent the same processes as did lagging recruits and ambitious farmers. (107)

Just as elevated sites with fresh, circulating air were considered salubrious, so low, marshy areas where air and water alike were thought to stagnate were considered insalubrious and malevolent (89–90). Miasmas 'entered the body as breath or fluid, and they operated within it just as they did within terrain. They carried the environment's imbalance, disturbance, or putrefaction into the depths of the body, expressing within the individual the sickly tendencies of the locale' (110–14; see also Melosi 2001, 2000; Tarr 1996). For Brock's soldiers and the petitioners to the Upper Canadian parliament, then, the marshlands around the mouth of the Don were inherently unhealthy. Ironically, despite mistaken theories about the origin of disease, fears of miasma were not entirely misplaced. Brock's observations about the disproportionate frequency of ague among soldiers at the eastern blockhouse corroborate other anecdotal sources in suggesting that malaria cases were more numerous in areas adjacent to the marsh.[5] Indeed, the slow-moving waters of the Don marshes would have provided an excellent breeding ground for mosquitoes, and efforts made to avoid these 'unhealthy places' and to shut out the dangerous 'night air' often had the effect of shutting out mosquitoes as well. (For further discussion on miasma, see Jackson, this volume.)

As the 1830 petition on the location of the parliament buildings suggests, perceptions of unhealthiness also had significant implications for the development of the area. In an 1833 letter to Viscount Goderich, secretary of state for the colonies, Lieutenant Governor John Colborne explained that the westward expansion of the city was the only reasonable option: 'The Eastern part of the Town is affected by the effluvia of the marshes of the Don, and the rapid increase in the population requires that the Town should be extended towards the Westward, the most salubrious and convenient site' (in Firth 1966: 342–3). Toronto did, indeed, 'lean west' in the years that followed, further marginalizing the site of the original town plot near the mouth of the Don. Parliament moved to new and more fashionable quarters in the west end of town (at Front and John Streets) in 1832, escalating with its relocation the desirability of west-end real estate (and the corresponding undesirability of the east end; F.H. Armstrong 1988). When the city incorporated in 1834, the lower river came to represent an official margin, its curving course forming the eastern border of the city between Bloor and Queen Streets. The largely undeveloped area between Parliament Street and the Lower Don fell within the 'City Liberties,' an ambiguous status that meant residents enjoyed neither full city rights and services nor paid full city taxes. Like other suburban areas around the city, development here was slower and more sporadic than in the more desirable and (marginally) better serviced areas of the new centre, and tended to concentrate along central access routes (Ganton 1974: 35).[6] From 1834 until the abolishment of the Liberties in 1859, then, the Lower Don occupied a borderland space within the everyday experience of the city's residents and in the official sphere of city maps and jurisdictional boundaries.

Other factors commingled to cement the area's status as a marginal space. Relatively poor soils, with the exception of the river flats south of Pottery Road, reduced the potential for successful farming initiatives. In an 1811 survey of the former government reserve between Parliament Street and the river, Deputy-Surveyor Samuel Wilmot reported that 'the land consisted of poor thin soil with the timber principally destroyed, but that with good management it might answer for pasture.' The only valuable timber, he continued, 'was close to the lakeshore' (Wilmot 1811). The steep ravine lands of the valley between Bloor and Gerrard streets further limited agricultural potential and complicated access to valley holdings. Unpredictable riparian conditions brought more headaches for landowners. Seasonal floods washed out bridges and roads and occasionally threatened livestock and outbuildings, and

unexpected droughts reduced water flow, threatening mill and agricultural operations alike. For property owners east of the river, the limited
number of bridge crossings over the Don, and the poor quality of those
that did exist, made access to their holdings especially challenging.[7]
These factors added further disincentives to an area already blighted
by perceptions of unhealthiness and distance from the growing commercial and residential core of York. And yet, as much as these considerations played a role in reducing the desirability of lands in and
around the lower valley, particularly for middle- and upper-class buyers, they always existed in tension with pressure in various periods to
expand the city eastward, and with the incentives that came with undesirability: cheaper land prices; lower taxes for property owners; and,
as the century progressed, proximity to industrial employers. As access
improved and population pressures increased throughout the century,
development increased in the area despite associations of risk.

Limited subdivision of the lands surrounding the lower valley took
place in the 1830s and 1840s. As Isobel Ganton found in her detailed
study of changing land ownership in the Lower Don Lands, evident in
this period is a notable shift from the wealthy, prominent citizens who
owned farm lots around the Lower River in the early nineteenth century to an increasing concentration of middle-class and working-class
landowners (Ganton 1974). Proximity to a growing number of industrial employers in the 1860s and 1870s attracted more working-class
residents to neighbourhoods on both sides of the lower river. Clustered
around 'rail yards, noisome factories and packinghouses,' the neighbourhoods around the Lower Don were among several impoverished
working-class districts in the city that, J.M.S. Careless wrote in his
history of nineteenth-century Toronto, emerged 'between high-value
centrally located property and the outlying districts, which became
wealthier enclaves for those who could afford the price of streetcar fare
to work' (1984: 138).[8] An urban borderland had been created. Segre-
gated from the rest of the city by its poverty, its reputedly unhealthy
environment, and its concentration of noxious industries, the area
around the lower river had become, by 1880, a marginal space within
which to isolate the processes of production and waste disposal so vital
to the process of city building. Toronto writer and publisher Graeme
Mercer Adam's description of the area immediately west of the lower
river in 1885 sums up the depth of the area's fall. 'The extreme end of
[the] eastern section [of King Street],' he wrote, 'is a dreary wilderness,
into which no man ever seems to venture except the aborigines, and in

which all the refuse of the city seems to accumulate ... The unsavoury reputation it bears from a sanitary point of view is probably at the bottom of its want of prosperity' (Adam et al. 1885, part 4: 287).

Valley Home: Refuge and Subsistence in an Urban Borderland, 1910–1931

In the first half of the twentieth century, political and economic circumstances around the world resulted in heightened levels of homelessness in cities across Canada. In ways similar to those of the past, but vastly more visible, the Don became a receiving area for those who either could not or chose not to seek out other means of shelter. While the valley remained an area of preference, it was not Tyler's refuge west of the Don bridge that twentieth-century transients chose; instead, they chose areas still capable of providing refuge: the partially wooded flats of the river north of Bloor Street, and secluded copses along the upper branches of the river north of the forks. Indeed, after industrialization and the major engineering projects of the late nineteenth and early twentieth centuries transformed the river south of Gerrard, what remained of the 'rural' in the valley shifted further north.

In the discussion that follows, themes of transience meet with our established themes of centre and periphery, perception and experience. While largely unexplored as a phenomenon in its own right in Canadian historiography, transience was central to Canadian experience in the nineteenth and twentieth centuries. Moving between city and country in pursuit of seasonal labour, moving west in search of access to land and better possibilities, and moving between provinces with disparate employment opportunities are iconic Canadian experiences. And yet, for nineteenth- and early-twentieth-century observers alike, transience was viewed as both an anomaly and a dangerous development. Late-nineteenth-century reformers puzzled over the conundrum of the 'pauperization of the poor' and the need to separate the 'worthy poor' – those willing to work – from those of the 'professional' class, who aimed to take advantage of charitable services. 'Vagrants' almost invariably fell into this latter category; perceived as a sign of declining morality, they were repeatedly singled out as targets for hard labour or restricted assistance.[9] In McKay's terms, an entrenched liberal vision cast vagrants as 'deficient' individuals for their failure to embrace liberal norms of regular waged work and sedentary living. As cities like Toronto struggled with a huge influx of unemployed men in the early 1930s, 'the transient' was again singled out as less deserving of city support than the resident unemployed – a practice that eventually spurred intervention from provincial and federal levels of government in generating make-work projects for unemployed men in remote areas of the country.

Like most marginalized populations, people who sought refuge in the Don valley in different periods are largely absent from the historical record. Census enumerators walked through the neighbourhoods bordering the valley, but didn't enter the wooded areas of the valley to record people living there. City reports on housing and homelessness document city-wide housing crises, particularly in the 1930s and during the post-war boom in the 1940s, but rarely reach the level of specificity needed to trace people living rough in the valley. Policemen did not regularly venture into the valley, except in pursuit of particular suspects. Indeed, it is precisely this absence of scrutiny that may have attracted people to the valley in the first place. As Bouchier and Cruikshank note in their study of working-class residents and squatters in Hamilton's Burlington Bay, 'one of [the community's] attractions was that it was nicely secluded from the gaze of the Harbour Commission and city police authorities that workers on street corners and in busy city taverns often felt' (2003: 22). Despite this relative silence in the official record, public interest in the unfortunate and the alien ensured that some coverage appeared in the newspapers of the day. Two groups of 'undesirables' received significant coverage in Toronto newspapers: Roma immigrants who camped in the valley in the 1910s and 1920s; and the unemployed men who formed a 'hobo jungle' on the flats of the river in 1930 and 1931. Drawing upon a limited record of historical photographs and newspaper articles, I will sketch the movement of people through place, and explore the ways that place – including topography and local resources – provided for and attracted populations with few alternatives.

Roma Travellers, 1910s and 1920s

In their illustrated history of immigration to Toronto in the early twentieth century, Robert Harney and Harold Troper made reference to groups of Roma[10] migrants who carved a space for themselves at the edge of society: 'Moving about in family groups or small "tribes," their wagons or old cars appeared in and around Toronto at certain times of year. The river valleys along the Humber and Don were their favourite

5.3 Roma woman carrying water at camp on Humber River, 12 October 1918.
(John Boyd Sr, City of Toronto Archives, series 393, item 15386)

campsites and those who did not come into the centre of the city to
do business spent their time fishing and making sweet grass and reed
baskets' (1974: 38). As these observations suggest, Toronto's river valleys provided not only refuge from authorities (examples from other
North American cities show that Roma families often faced imprison-
ment or ejection when confronted by local police),[11] but also a source
of sustenance and livelihood. Toronto photographer John Boyd Sr documented the presence of Roma families on the banks of the Humber
River in 1918. His images show women gathering water from the river
and cooking meals on fires fuelled by driftwood from the river banks.
While these images were captured in Toronto's other major river valley,
it is clear from the documentary record that Roma families also camped
along the Don. The images are rich with detail, and provide an excellent companion to the scant textual records available on Roma travellers in the Toronto area in the early twentieth century.

5.4 Roma woman peeling potatoes at camp on Humber River, 12 October 1918. (John Boyd Sr, City of Toronto Archives, series 393, item 15391-1)

An article in the *Toronto Daily Star* on 5 November 1910 described a Roma campsite near the west branch of the Don (at the end of Soudan Avenue, near the intersection of today's Eglinton and Bayview Avenues), noting in patronizing terms its distance from mainstream Canadian experience:

> Tucked away in the bushes around the last bend of a long road to the north of the city, miles from a railroad, and a good walk from any other human habitation, are four little white tents, the dwelling place of the remnants of a gypsy tribe. They have prepared for the winter only by building leaf shelters over the doorways of the tents and there they will stay through storm and sunshine until the wanderlust seizes their gypsy fancies.

At the time, this area of the valley remained rural and largely wooded, with large farms occupying the neighbouring table lands. Not the polluted environment of the lower valley, the area nevertheless occupied a margin in its rurality and its position just outside the city limits. Difficult to harness for productive uses, the valley lands at this time were also largely unoccupied – another draw for travellers seeking sanctuary. Living at the camp 'as one large family,' the reporter noted, 'are four men, three women, three children, two bears, and a baboon.' As best he could observe, the group made a modest income by taking up collections after 'the bear and monkey [gave] exhibitions on the streets' and from fortunes that 'the women of the party tell ... to the unwary.' It seems the reporter was left to draw his own conclusions about the possible relationship between the women and men in the camp, and the purpose of their stay in the area. 'They are not the sociable summer camping party,' he reported with disappointment, 'that their tents might imply'; nor are they 'over fond of stray callers.'

Despite the relative isolation of the camp, local residents – apparently concerned that 'these gypsies might have too many of the story book gypsy characteristics' – attempted 'to show [the Roma] that there were other parts more favorable to their race.' The article doesn't elaborate on the means with which the group was made to feel unwelcome. According to the reporter, the families responded by 'promptly [purchasing]' the property. Having 'shown themselves to be law abiding citizens, and people of wealth,' harassment by neighbours and authorities purportedly ceased. The reporter, however, couldn't resist the speculation that the group would nevertheless 'be off for other parts when the springtime comes around'; with them, he concluded, will go 'the covered wagon and the collapsible stoves, the old hay horse, and the scratching hens that they have taken unto themselves' (*Toronto Daily Star* 1910c). Here is interesting evidence of the 'Other' as a 'doubtful [prospect] for liberal individualism' (McKay 2000: 626). While the purchase of land granted this particular group of Roma some limited respect as 'probationary individuals,' their ethnicity cemented their status as outsiders to the dominant liberal ethos. No further mention of the group appears in the local papers until 4 February 1911, when the *Globe* reported that a 'band of gypsies who have been encamped around Eglinton for some time' was taken in by Dominion Immigration Officers 'preparatory to being deported to the United States.' Apparently the group consisted of 'a number of men, women, and children, four wagons, several horses, and four brown bears.' While it is difficult to be certain if this was the same group described by the *Daily Star* in November, the location 'near Eglinton' suggests so. Area residents had apparently complained of the group's 'persistent begging,' adding to Children's Aid Society reports that children had been observed 'running out in the snow barefooted.'[12]

Ten years later a group of eight 'Serbian gypsy' families occupied a site further upriver, on the west branch of the Don near the intersection of Yonge Street and York Mills Road (*Toronto Daily Star* 1920b). Unlike the 1910 camp, this camp was easily visible from the road. An article in the *Globe* on 1 June 1920 noted that the camp was situated 'not more than one hundred yards from Yonge Street ... so that passing motorists may easily be beguiled to visit their encampment and have their fortunes told' (*Globe* 1920a). The camp's roadside location in the valley provided the dual advantages, the article suggests, of access to the river for cooking, bathing, and drinking water, and access to a source of revenue through roadside sales. Men in the camp apparently worked in the city as chauffeurs and coppersmiths, and supplemented their income with roadside sales of used cars and car parts. As the reporter milled about trying to get an interview with one of the women of the camp, he observed children, apparently 'too numerous to count,' swimming in the Don. They swim with their clothes on, he noted, '[jumping] into the water and then [waiting] for the sun to dry them.' It wasn't long before the camp raised the ire of local residents. Complaints throughout the summer of 1920 about 'the condition of things at the gypsy camp at York Mills bridge' were directed to the county police and health authorities (*Toronto Daily Star* 1920a). The situation was last mentioned in the *Daily Star* on 21 August, when the columnist speculated that 'the gypsies are preparing to move to their winter quarters' (1920c).

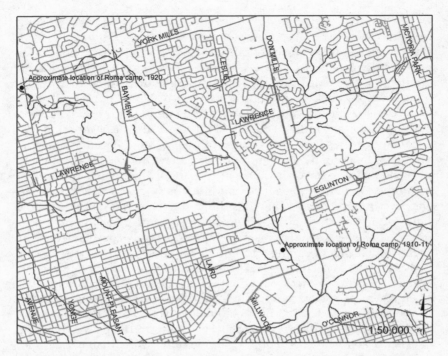

5.5 Approximate locations of two Roma camps along west branch of Upper
Don River, 1910–20. (Map by Jordan Hale)

While the evidence here is sketchy and laced with the prejudices of
its presenters, it nevertheless supports the hypothesis forwarded by
Harney and Troper that Toronto's river valleys provided – temporarily,
at least – refuge and means for subsistence for immigrant families trav-
elling with limited resources. As Boyd's images remind us, the river
valleys provided access to water for drinking, cooking, and bathing, to
driftwood for cooking fires, to fish, and to grasses for basket making.
They also provided a degree of refuge from 'stray callers' and powerful authorities. Some historiographical context on Roma experience
in nineteenth- and twentieth-century North America is useful here. As
Marlene Sway has shown, Roma family groups in the United States and
Canada used nomadism, multiple occupations, and the exploitation of
readily available natural resources as strategies of economic adapta-
tion. Descending in large part from Roma populations who came to

North America during the large immigration of eastern Europeans in the 1880s and 1890s, many Roma groups pursued a nomadic lifestyle due not 'to wanderlust as much as to pressure exerted upon them by … host societies' (Sway 1988: 39, 44). Following occupations that were typically 'seasonal, temporary, marginal, and even precarious,' they moved from place to place and engaged in a number of occupations simultaneously (110). Car repairs and used-car sales, occasional farm labour, scrap-metal recovery, fortune telling, and other forms of entertainment were among the typical overlapping and gendered occupations (Sway 1988; Sutherland 1975).

The use of the natural environment as a means of subsistence and livelihood also has a long tradition in Roma historiography. Sway records the use of fallen branches and scrap wood to produce bowls, spoons, and children's toys, and the collection of holly and heather for seasonal sale in nineteenth-century Europe (1988: 101). Mayall notes the use of grasses and wood from camp locations to manufacture brooms, doormats, baskets, clothes pegs, skewers, and walking sticks in the same period in rural England (1988: 58). As Harney and Troper suggest and Sway confirms, many of these craft occupations were extended to North American environments. The location of Roma camps along the Don in the first decades of the twentieth century may have been due in part, these sources suggest, to access to natural resources. Strategic placement along travel corridors for fortune telling and used-car sales/repair occupations was likely also a significant factor, as the 1920 camp at Yonge and York Mills Road suggests, as was distance from the *gaje*, or non-Roma, population, as both taboo influences on Roma cultural norms and potential sources of threat (Sway 1988; Sutherland 1975).

The 'Hobo Jungle' of 1930 and 1931

Transience in the valley took on much greater visibility during the 1930s, when unemployed men established a large hobo jungle in the flats of the lower valley, north of Bloor Street. Some time in the fall of 1930 a group of transients found refuge in a brick factory in the valley, and rumours began to circulate about the Don valley 'kiln-dwellers.' Some investigative journalism by the left-leaning *Toronto Daily Star* located the camp in early December – the reporter apparently having 'tramped one night almost the full length of the Don valley searching for [the men]' before being tipped off weeks later by a young homeless man who had spent time at the site. 'Last night,' he reported, 'during bitter winds and near-zero [Fahrenheit] weather, forty-two homeless, jobless, and penniless wandering men slept on "hot-flops" in the Don valley yards of the Toronto Brick [Company].' The reporter explained: bricks baked in a series of huge chambers, or kilns, often took up to a week to cool. 'While they are cooling, [the men] climb right inside the kilns, stretch themselves out on the hard, warm bricks and seek the solace of sleep.' How did they come to find shelter in a working brick factory? The reporter was careful to point out that these 'decent and respectable' men were not trespassers:

> These men are not bums. They are not tramps. Nor are they hoboes ... They are residents of the Don valley yards of the Toronto Brick Co. as the invited guests of Frank E. Waterman, general manager of that company, who has not only issued instructions to his staff that the men are to be allowed the privileges of his brick yard, but he has on several occasions stoutly resented the intrusion of policemen and plainclothesmen. (*Toronto Daily Star* 1930: 2)

This emphasis on the men's essential respectability stands in marked contrast to perceptions of the Roma. While concerns about Communist sympathies and anxieties about the presence of 'professional tramps' in the jungle betrayed underlying suspicions about the character of men who had 'let themselves fall' into such circumstances, overall these men received a warmer reception than those identified by their ethnicity and economic practices as hopelessly and permanently depraved.

Based on the documentary evidence that survives, the residents of the Don valley jungle seemed to share an ambiguous relationship with those in the city above them. Frequent references are made in the *Daily Star* coverage of the camp to criticisms and condemnation of the city's charitable institutions. Inhabitants of the camp apparently 'couldn't understand why every restaurant in Toronto didn't let them eat the waste food ... They whole-heartedly doubted that the new Central Bureau of Registration for homeless men would make any difference to their plight' (*Toronto Daily Star* 1930). While institutional responses to Depression-era homelessness and unemployment fell back on earlier approaches – sorting the 'resident' from the 'alien' homeless and focusing support on married rather than single men, the public response to the men in the valley tended to be more generous. As the *Globe* reported in the last days of the camp, '[the men's] self-imposed rigor and independence, their vigorous cry for work and not charity, have appealed to the public imagination. They made good as citizens out of luck' (1931c: 4). Reverend Peter Bryce made numerous visits to the 'jungle' to report on the men's well-being, and church and women's organizations across the city organized donations of food and clothing. In a remarkable document that reinforced – in their own words – representations of the valley residents as 'ordinary citizens down on their luck,' the 'cave and shack dwellers' of the valley scripted a letter of thanks on a scrap of cardboard and posted it at the edge of the valley.

The card, dated 4 August 1931 and signed by eight men, reads as follows:

> To whom it may concern: this is to say that we dwellers of the Don Flats (otherwise known as the 'cave and shack dwellers') do hereby wish to thank all those who have tried to help us out in any way and particularly those kind enough to send any supplies in way of food left over from picnics etc. which might have otherwise gone to waste and we'll be glad to accept in future any kindness that this notice might happen to bring to us. Hoping that things will soon be better we remain thankfully yours.[13]

Public fears about the number of men congregated in the valley also expressed themselves in the local newspapers. Around the same time as the thank-you card was produced, concerns about Communist agitation centred around the Don valley camp led to warnings in the conservative newspapers that 'all drifters should be cleared out of the cities before winter' to stem the possibility of revolution (*Globe* 1931b: 1). The accusations met with vehement indignation from the *Daily Star* and, reputedly, from inhabitants of the valley camp.

Asked why they chose the valley brick works rather than the House of Industry (a shelter for the poor) or one of the city's night missions, one of the men responded, 'We've still got a little pride left' (*Globe* 1931b), adding that they found begging on the streets demeaning. This sentiment was repeated frequently in the *Star*'s coverage of the Don valley camp, and in accounts of hobo jungles in other parts of the country (McCallum 2006; Wade 1997). It was expressed especially clearly in a letter to the editor of the *Daily Star* from an anonymous jungle resident in July 1931. Identifying himself as a First World War veteran who found himself homeless in the same city he had enlisted from years before, he wrote that he was 'of a husky build and suited to manual labor.' 'Before I will accept charity or line up in a bread line,' he continued, 'I offer my services for room or board.' He signed the letter only with his

5.6 Card of thanks, 4 August 1931. (Courtesy of East York Foundation
Collection, Todmorden Mills Museum, City of Toronto)

location: 'Don Valley' (*Toronto Daily Star* 1931b). Another letter to the editor from a resident of the hobo jungle suggested, interestingly, that work could be created for the unemployed men of the valley by creating a project to straighten the river north of Bloor Street and to remove unnecessary weeds and trees from the valley (MacArthur 1931). The project never materialized.

If pride was one reason these men chose the valley, the shrinking availability of other forms of relief was another. A follow-up article in the *Daily Star* on 19 June 1931 counted three hundred men in the valley 'following [the] recent closing of all city missions and shelters, with the exception of the House of Industry.' The brick works population had expanded to one hundred men; an additional two hundred slept 'on the banks of the muggy Don river with the sky as a blanket and the earth as a mattress' (*Toronto Daily Star* 1931a: 1).[14] Later that summer the jungle expanded again, with approximately four hundred men camped along the flats of the Don River. As Reverend Peter Bryce observed in a tour of the valley in August 1931, some men slept in box cars and dugouts; others fashioned 'most ingenious huts' – 'bivouacs of rushes ... bound together by striplings sewn through with thatch' (Bryce 1931: 1).

The river valley provided natural amenities, such as water for drinking, cooking, and bathing, reeds and saplings for hut construction, and driftwood for campfires; it also yielded resources from the history of human settlement in the area. A local dump in the valley north of the Bloor Street Viaduct (the site of today's Chester Springs Marsh) provided a bounty of discarded objects that men used to furnish their makeshift homes: a picture frame, an old trunk, a radio antenna (but no radio), and a semi-functioning kerosene lamp were some of the objects mentioned in Bryce's 1931 report. The most obvious attraction of the Don valley site, however, beyond its proximity to the city centre, were the rail lines that ran through the valley. As former East York mayor True Davidson recalled in her 1976 memoir, 'The jungle became known amongst the fraternity of those riding the rods, and almost every freight that came down the Don brought more inhabitants to the area' (Davidson 1976: 82). As the Depression worsened and ever-increasing numbers of unemployed men from across the country congregated in the valley, mayors from Toronto and East York vowed to crack down on outsiders seeking relief within their city limits. Toronto police vowed to 'watch every freight train' to 'stop transients from forcing themselves on the municipality' (*Globe* 1931b). The coming winter's relief services would be provided to local residents only, and not transients from other areas, the

5.7 Makeshift dwellings in Don valley, 1930–1. (Courtesy of East York Foundation Collection, Todmorden Mills Museum, City of Toronto)

mayors warned. The gap had widened for the men of the hobo camp. No longer the 'respectable men' temporarily 'down on their luck,' the inhabitants of the jungle were portrayed increasingly as an alien threat to the city's stability. In McKay's terms, they had become outsiders to the dominant liberal order, rather than temporary transgressors.

The jungle, it seemed, had to go. In late September 1931 the Province announced that 2500 unemployed men would be drafted from congested Southern Ontario centres for work on the Trans-Canada highway project in Northern Ontario (*Globe* 1931d). Further drafts followed, and by the beginning of October the 'peculiar and varied habitations' of the jungle had been demolished, their residents transferred to northern camps or removed to temporary shelters (*Globe* 1931d: 1). As the *Toronto Daily Star* reported, it seems the men of the Don valley jungle had fared remarkably well for their ordeal: of 213 men examined by medical doctors before joining the first road-building contingent, only three were rejected as unfit for hard labour. No diseases were reported, and no cases of malnutrition – in fact, the incredulous reporter noted, the men on the whole were more likely to be overweight than underweight (Sinclair 1931).

These snapshots provided by newspaper accounts hint at the ways that both Roma families and Depression-era hoboes used the environment around them to enhance what must have been a fairly marginal existence. Both groups, it seems, chose the valley for access to certain amenities, such as water, firewood, and material scavenged from nearby landfill sites. Distance from authorities may also have been important, as the experience of Roma travellers in other parts of North America, and the jungle residents' aversion to institutionalized shelter, suggests. The brick works manager's 'stout resentment' of the intrusion of plainclothesmen also suggests a limited degree of protection afforded to homeless men under his roof. In its role as a semi-rural space on the edge of the city and, in its lower reaches, an industrial and heavily polluted space, the Don River valley became a place on the margins. Devalued by more fortunate inhabitants of the city, it became, as I have argued, a place for people pushed to the edges of society. Despite developments over the last forty years that have seen much of the valley 'revalued' as a recreational landscape, in some respects not much has changed: makeshift tents of the homeless can still be seen on the banks of the river in the lower valley, and as recently as the spring of 2008, the City used the valley as a receptacle for huge amounts of filthy, salt-laced snow from the city's roads.

Conclusion

In its focus on marginal people in a marginal place, this chapter contributes to a growing trend in recent Canadian historiography to draw attention to the structures of power at work in designating people and places within the framework of centres and peripheries – the liberal order framework that Ian McKay outlined so provocatively in his 2000 prospectus in the *Canadian Historical Review*. Drawing from the evidence provided by middle-class perceptions of the marginalized, it seeks to go a step further by shedding light on the lived experience of people 'on the outside' of the liberal project – in this case, those whose 'poverty ... irregular habits, and ... problematic, intermittent relation to the formal market economy, particularly to money and waged work' stood in sharp contrast to liberal values of order, property, and self-control (Sandwell 2003: 447). Assessed as marginal by powerful groups in the urban centre, places like the Don River valley, with its miasmatic lowlands and difficult-to-develop ravine banks, and populations like the Roma and the Depression-era hoboes, were among the casualties of the liberal project of city building in early-twentieth-century Toronto. Here were reputedly unproductive citizens pursuing unorthodox strategies of 'getting by' in a landscape similarly dismissed as unproductive and marginal. As I have attempted to show, the individuals who sought refuge in the wooded areas of the Don valley were resilient, flexible, and creative actors in their own lives. They sought out the valley for the things it offered, as much as for the things they were denied in other parts of the city, and, for limited periods of time at least, it provided the refuge they sought.

NOTES

1 References to Skunk Hollow and the Bohemian Flats were obtained from a conversation initiated in H-Environment's online discussion forum, 21 March 2008.
2 Andrew Hurley (1995), for example, shows how middle-class whites in Gary, Indiana, constructed a 'hierarchy of place' – creating homogeneous neighbourhoods priced out of reach of the poor, while at the same time shielding themselves from environmental hazards.
3 Valerie Kuletz's *The Tainted Desert* (1998) is an exception in its focus on both the marginalization of place and the human populations dependent upon it.

4 Todd McCallum's work (2006, 2004) on Depression-era hoboes in Vancouver describes the establishment of a hobo jungle in a derelict area
of Vancouver's waterfront, but doesn't explore the connection between
marginal space and the marginalized populations that congregated there.
Similarly, Jill Wade's excellent article (1997) on marginal housing in Vancouver describes squatters living on polluted foreshore lands along Bur-
rard Inlet, False Creek, and the Fraser River, but doesn't explore how and
why such places were constructed as marginal. Work on 'marginal places'
in the cultural-geography literature also focuses primarily on the political,
economic, and social factors involved in the marginalization of particular
groups, with little attention to the nature of the environments in which
people find themselves (Ruddick 1996; M.P. Smith 1995; P. Jackson 1993;
Shields 1991).

5 An editorial in the 1853–4 issue of the *Upper Canada Journal of Medical,
Surgical and Physical Science*, for example, in arguing against the siting of
the new Toronto General Hospital in the east end of the city, notes 'plenty
of locations in Toronto' where ague is considerably less prevalent than in
the east end, where 'scarcely a house has been free from its visitation.'

6 The City Liberties stretched east of the river in a thin band from Queen
Street south to the lakeshore and east to the far end of Ashbridge's Bay.
Lands north of Queen, east of the river, fell under the jurisdiction of York
County until the 1880s, when the city began a new round of annexa-
tions. The abolishment of the Liberties in 1859 brought full city rights and
responsibilities to the suburban area west of the Don and east of the river
south of Queen.

7 No bridges existed north of Gerrard in the lower valley, for example, until
the Prince Edward Viaduct was constructed in 1918.

8 Aggregate data from assessment rolls corroborate Careless's conclusions.
Data compiled for the decades between 1870 and 1910 show that property
values within the wards on either side of the river (St David's Ward, parts
of St Lawrence's Ward, and, after 1884, St Matthew's Ward on the east side
of the river) were consistently lower than wards with comparable populations in other parts of the city.

9 James Pitsula discusses these trends as they played out in the reception
of 'tramps' in late-nineteenth-century Toronto. The Associated Charities'
decision in 1881 to implement a 'labour test' whereby recipients of aid
would have to break a quantity of stones or chop kindling before receiving food or shelter was used as a method, Pitsula concludes, of enforcing a
middle-class work ethic 'on a deviating, floating population. It was also an
insidious way of denying the reality of unemployment because the authors

of the labour test assumed that the character defects of the poor, not the unavailability of work, was the central issue' (Pitsula 1980: 132).

10 I have used the word 'Roma' throughout to refer to the diverse group of people who have self-identified in different places and times as the Rom, Romani, or Roma, as 'Travellers' and as 'Gypsies.' Despite contemporary use of the term 'Gypsy' in early-twentieth-century North America, I have avoided use of the term for its derogatory connotations.

11 Lyon (1998) documents the arrest and temporary jailing of male Roma travellers in Peterborough, Ontario, on charges of loitering and obstruction of a public highway. For other examples see Acton (1997) and Sway (1988).

12 Sporadic deportations seemed to continue throughout the 1910s. In his annual report to the Toronto Board of Health, for example, Medical Officer of Health Charles Hastings reports the deportation of a group of Roma he viewed as 'sleeping and living like animals' (Charles Hastings, Annual Report to the Toronto Board of Health, 1914, series 365, Department of Public Health Reports, City of Toronto Archives).

13 Card of Thanks, 4 August 1931, East York Foundation Collection, Todmorden Mills Museum, City of Toronto.

14 Michiel Horn (1984: 12) provides some context for both the heavy burden experienced by Canadian municipalities in providing relief and the attempt to clamp down on assistance to transients in order to force them out of the city and into relief camps.

6 Boundaries and Connectivity: The Lower Don River and Ashbridge's Bay

TENLEY CONWAY

This chapter documents over one hundred years of change in the land-water boundary of the Lower Don River and Ashbridge's Bay, located on the east of Toronto's central waterfront. Many of these changes play out through the alteration of near-shore land cover, the creation of new barriers (e.g., bulkheads, rail lines), and the sharpening of existing boundaries through infill and dredging. The mouth of the Don River is particularly interesting because river corridors and deltas are important zones for the moderation of species, nutrients, and other materials' movement. At the same time, the inherent dynamism of these features is directly at odds with attempts to stabilize waterfronts and waterways in support of the production and transportation of goods.

Waterfronts are shaped by a combination of social and biophysical processes that are regulated, in part, by the physical boundary that exists between the land and water. The shoreline along a lake, river, or other waterbody can be referred to as an 'ecotone,' which Gosz (1991) has defined as a zone of transition between adjacent ecological systems. Ecotones act as permeable membranes, playing a critical role in determining the flow of individuals, nutrients, materials, and disturbances across a landscape (Gosz 1991; Wiens et al. 1985). More than just a boundary between two separate systems, the unique ecological conditions found within land-water ecotones can often support high levels of biological diversity and productivity (Desaigues 1990).

Recent studies have highlighted the importance of understanding past changes in land-water ecotones, with several projects reconstructing historic landscapes along shorelines, coastal wetlands, and river valleys (Van Dyke and Wasson 2005; Oetter et al. 2004; Borde et al. 2003; Collins et al. 2003; Andersen et al. 1996; Kearney et al. 1988). This work has illuminated a dynamic and complex set of socio-ecological inter-actions shaping such boundaries. As Crumley (1994) argues, historical ecology must include an examination of the role of humans because human as well as non-human activities can serve as underlying drivers of landscape form for hundreds to thousands of years (Dupouey et al. 2002). In addition, human-dominated landscapes often follow complex change trajectories that do not represent predictable or linear pathways (Arce-Nazario 2007). These trajectories can only be understood in the context of human management and action.

Currently, many planning discussions surrounding the Toronto wa-terfront are dominated by concepts of integrative ecosystems manage-ment, including increasing human and ecological connectivity within the Lower Don River and former Ashbridge's Bay area. But this was not always the case. For over a century, people actively relocated, stabi-lized, and sharpened the boundary between the land and water, result-ing in reduced biophysical connections across and within the terrestrial and aquatic ecosystems. Documenting these past changes allows for a better understanding of current ecological processes and the challenges associated with realizing future management goals.

Ecotones and Landscape Connectivity

Examining rivers and other waterfronts in the context of ecotones high-lights the unique role they play in regulating landscape flows. While the river's edge represents a boundary between a terrestrial and an aquatic system (Ward et al. 1999), the river itself may also be a bound-ary within a terrestrial landscape that can limit ecological and human flows alike. Some ecotones are defined by an abrupt transition, while others represent a gradient or complex transition zone between sys-tems. Ecotones can be spatially stable over time or highly dynamic in location and width (Risser 1990). In this chapter, 'hard' boundaries or ecotones are defined by physical barriers that make the boundary both abrupt and generally static, while 'soft' boundaries or ecotones describe more gradual transitions zones that vary in location over time. Land-water ecotones can range from very hard, typified by channel-ized rivers whose edges are defined by structural barriers, to the very soft boundaries associated with gradually sloping shorelines composed of loose surface substrate.

In landscapes dominated by human activity, at least two major chang-es tend to occur to riverine ecotones over time. First, existing terrestrial land covers are fragmented as a result of changing waterfront land uses and the creation of transportation and other infrastructure networks across the land-water boundary, greatly increasing the length of terrestrial and aquatic boundary zones (Forman 1995; Loney and Hobbs 1991). Second, the characteristics of these boundaries change. Humans tend to sharpen and linearize ecotones (Correll 1991), while segmenting them by land use or ownership through the use of static barriers (Forman 1995). Thus, land-water boundaries in urban areas tend to harden, rather than existing as temporally and spatially dynamic gradients. These changes lead to an alteration of pre-existing biophysical and human flows (Harris and Scheck 1991), while at the same time enabling new ones (Bennett 1991).

Ecotone characteristics also influence landscape connectivity since the characteristics and abundance of boundaries determine the degree of connectedness among features in a landscape. Landscape connectivity is an inherently spatial concept that focuses on the ability of material (species, nutrients, energy, etc.) to move across the landscape (Turner et al. 2001). If a landscape is highly connected, there may be a larger usable habitat area for organisms, with increased movement between resource patches, and/or greater material flows. A less-connected landscape impacts individual organisms' access to resources, metapopulation dynamics, and material flows (Forman 1995; Miller and Harris 1977).

There are two components to landscape connectivity: 'structural connectivity' and 'functional connectivity' (Tischendorf and Fahrig 2000). 'Structural connectivity' refers to the composition and configuration of habitat and other relevant features on the landscape (Griffith et al. 2000), while 'functional connectivity' reflects an individual organism's ability to move across the landscape (Wiens et al. 1997). Thus, the functional connectivity of a landscape for a given organism depends on characteristics of the organism itself and the structural connectivity of the landscape at a particular spatial scale.

As a result of the scale- and organism-specific nature of connectivity, some ecologists argue that examining functional connectivity should always take precedence over structural connectivity (Moilanen and Hanski 2001; Tischendorf and Fahrig 2000). However, this is not always feasible when multiple organisms or components of the landscape are considered. Thus, when one is examining a landscape from an ecological planning perspective, as opposed to focusing on the management of one species or material type, structural connectivity of green space is usually emphasized (Conway 2006; Perlman and Milder 2005). While high structural connectivity does not guarantee high functional connectivity for all organisms, this is more likely than in landscapes with very low structural connectivity. As such, structural landscape connectivity primarily will be examined in this chapter.

Rivers and other water bodies can play complex roles in governing landscape connectivity within urban areas: they can create barriers to terrestrial flows, yet support high levels of movement within the river itself and along its banks, which is often the only remaining vegetated corridor in an urbanized context (Puth and Wilson 2001).

In addition to supporting landscape connectivity, most river systems represent highly connected networks along a number of other dimensions (May 2006). Hydrologists describe the lateral connectivity of rivers as exchanges across the land-water boundary, and their longitudinal connectivity as exchanges within the river system itself (Naiman and Bilby 1998). A river prone to flooding has a high level of functional connectivity, with such events facilitating movement between the land and water, and down the river (Pringle 2003). From an economic perspective, rivers can have high structural connectivity, as a result of shipping channels, piers, and other infrastructure that facilitate movement within the river and across the land-water boundary, as well as high functional connectivity due to economic ties with distant ports (May 2006). May (2006) also notes that urban rivers can create connections between people and natural processes that are otherwise hidden in built environments.

It is important to remember, however, that the multiple forms of connectivity associated with land-water ecotones are often at odds with one another. For example, the hardening of an urban waterfront to support economic connections usually occurs at the expense of biophysical flows and people's ability to connect with the natural system.

Study Area

The study area encompasses the Lower Don River, starting just south of the Bloor Viaduct, and the full extent of the former Ashbridge's Bay area (figure 6.1). This area is of particular interest because several current management efforts are attempting to soften the ecotone, reversing nearly a century of activities that create a predominantly hard land-water boundary (see Desfor and Bonnell, this volume).

The Lower Don River valley was created with the retreat of Glacial Lake Iroquois to the present boundary of Lake Ontario. Prior to human alteration, several smaller streams flowed into the lower portion of the

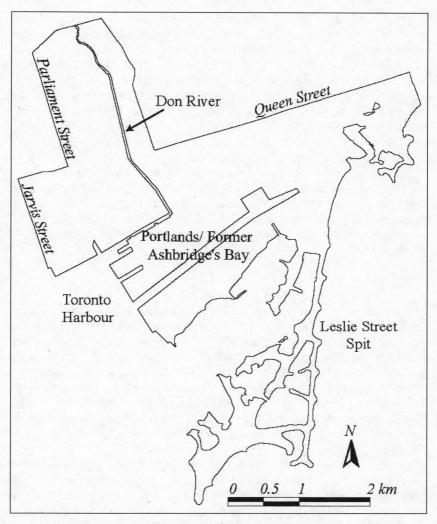

6.1 Study area of boundaries and connectivity analysis, Toronto. (Map by author)

river. Historically, this stretch of river was narrower than today, and rather sluggish, dropping only 0.4 metres over its last three kilometres (Task Force to Bring Back the Don 1991). There is also evidence of regular flood events, which have continued to the present.

Until the start of the twentieth century, the Don River flowed into Ashbridge's Bay, approximately 560 hectares of marshland that was separated from Lake Ontario by a long sand bar along its south-eastern edge. The river deposited significant amounts of silt and other material into the marshland (Desfor and Keil 2000), but by the early nineteenth century raw sewage and other refuse was also freely flowing out of the river's mouth (Fairfield 1998; see also Moir, chapter 1, and Desfor et al., this volume). West of the Don lay the sandy shoreline of Lake Ontario, punctuated by several small streams. There is evidence that this beach had been eroding since at least early settlement (McIlwraith 1991). In the 1830s, active dredging of the harbour began to build up land along the lakeshore, sharpening the boundary with the lake. As the original town settlement grew eastward towards the Don, the soft shoreline was eventually replaced with a wall. By the late 1850s, a hardened shoreline stretched from the central waterfront nearly to the Don River (McIlwraith 1991).

Methods

Historic maps and air photos, from 1851 through 2002, were examined for the Lower Don River and Ashbridge's Bay, including the Port Industrial District and Leslie Street Spit (figure 6.1). Use of these sources supports the detailed study of urban landscapes (Small 2001; McPherson 1998) over longer time periods than satellite or other remotely sensed imagery (Arce-Nazario 2007). Dates were chosen from available material based on key events in the history of the study area (table 6.1). The 1851 map does not include the entire study area, but represents an important snapshot of the mouth of the Don River before the complete hardening of Toronto's shoreline.

Digital land-use and land-cover maps that highlight land-water boundaries were derived from the original maps and photos. Aerial photographs from 1954 and 2002 already existed in a digital format. Paper maps and photographs were obtained for the other dates and converted to a digital format. All digital images were projected to a common map projection (Universal Transverse Mercator) using an existing-road data layer as reference. This enabled the overlay of maps from different dates, as well as a comparative analysis of land use/land cover areas and boundary lengths. In several cases, multiple air photos were needed to cover the study area. To keep images a reasonable size, these photos were not digitally stitched together, but were retained as

Table 6.1
Sources of information used to create land use / land cover maps

Year	Title	Publisher	Original material	Notes
1851	Topographical plan of the City of Toronto, in the Province of Canada, from actual survey by J. Stoughton Dennis, Provincial Land Surveyor	H. Scobie	Paper map	Drawn by Sandford A. Fleming; dedicated to mayor, alderman, and commonality of the City of Toronto; original paper map 60 × 81 cm
1902	Plan of the City of Toronto	City Engineering Office, Toronto	Paper map	Original paper map, 45 × 89 cm
1916	Map of Greater Toronto and Suburbs	The Map Company, Toronto	Paper map	Original paper map, 50 × 73 cm
1954	Black and white air photo	Energy, Mines and Resources Canada	Paper photographs	Received scanned copy; 2.5 metre resolution
1974	Black and white air photo	City of Toronto	Paper photographs	Created digital version; original paper resolution 1:5000
1992	Colour air photo	The Airborne Sensing Corporation	Paper photographs	Created digital version; original paper resolution 1:5000
2002	Digital colour orthophoto	J.D. Barnes First Base Solutions	Digital	20 cm resolution

separate tiles, with efforts made to ensure alignment between tiles. A head's-up digitizing approach was then used to identify land use, land cover, and land-water boundaries in each image. Head's-up digitizing is a standard image interpretation method, where the analyst traces the boundary of relevant features on the digital image.

The classification scheme in the analysis is a modification of Anderson et al.'s (1976; table 6.2), a standard land use/land cover classification scheme that is often adopted for urban mapping. The classification

Table 6.2
Mixed land use / land cover classification scheme

Land use / land cover Level 1 – broad	Land use / land cover Level 2 – specific
Built	Industrial Other built (i.e., res., comm.)
Transportation	Rail line Highways and major roads Bridge
Undeveloped	Vegetated land (i.e., parks, marshes, unused) Bare
Water	River Stream Harbour Keating Channel Shipping Channel Lake

used in this analysis primarily differs from Anderson et al.'s by separating transportation corridors from other urban uses, and by identifying vegetated and bare land on sites not actively used for transport, industrial, residential, or commercial purposes.

These modifications help to highlight the development of the extensive transportation system and the status of abandoned urban areas. Determining when industrial or other land uses on a site have been halted is difficult from air photos. As a result, undeveloped land is limited to sites without buildings or other major infrastructure, and may underestimate the true amount of 'unused' land. In addition, land used to store coal and other bulk material was considered industrial. Within the undeveloped class, bare land cover includes exposed soil as well as sand located along soft shorelines, while vegetation incorporates grass, shrubs, and trees.

From the classified maps, the total area of specific land uses and land covers was determined. The length of the Don River and shoreline were also calculated for each date. This information was used to illustrate changes in land-water boundaries and connectivity.

It is important to remember that there are some limitations to using historic maps and air photos in such an analysis. All photos and maps represent a snapshot in time. The photos were taken at different times

Table 6.3
Length of land-water boundaries in study area, in kilometres

Year	Don River*	Don River w/ Keating Channel	Total land-water boundary	Total hard boundary	Total soft boundary
1854	5.7	–	N/A	N/A	N/A
1902	3.8	–	26.0	5.2	20.8
1916	3.6	–	24.6	5.1	19.5
1954	3.1	3.9	17.8	11.6	6.2
1974	3.1	3.9	33.4	11.1	22.3
1992	3.1	3.9	46.8	12.7	34.1
2002	3.1	3.9	46.9	12.4	34.5

*When two outlets existed, the longest route is reported.

of the year, and as a result, slight changes in conditions may exist because of seasonal fluxes rather than longer-term trends. However, the magnitude of the changes in the location of the Don and creation of new land greatly outweighs any differences associated with seasonal fluctuations or specific storm events. The use of the early maps is a bit more problematic for two reasons. First, the maps tend to show a clear distinction between land and water. This does not adequately represent the marshy nature of Ashbridge's Bay, with the frequent changes in water level that likely occurred. Second, the maps may not reflect conditions on the ground so much as what the mapmaker or intended audience hoped to be there. Thus, there may be too great an emphasis on dry land and open water in Ashbridge's Bay. Also, there is evidence that maps of the waterfront during the nineteenth century tended to exaggerate the amount of infill that actually occurred (McIlwraith 1991). Given these caveats, however, deriving information from a combination of map and air photos can provide a rich historical land use/land cover record (Skånes 1997).

Changes in the Lower Don River and Ashbridge's Bay

Similar to the situation in other land-water ecotones, increasing human activity in the study area along the Don River and Ashbridge's Bay has altered the location, length, and conditions of the boundary (table 6.3). Since the 1850s, the Lower Don River has been reduced in length by almost 50 per cent owing to the straightening of the channel and ma-

Table 6.4
Percent of land under different land usee / land covers in study area*

| Year | % Built | Undeveloped | | Total land area (ha) |
		% Bare	% Vegetated	
1902	65			784
1916	73			771
1954	80			1077
1974	70	20	10	1195
1992	68	7	25	1310
2002	63	5	32	1330

*Only those years where full maps were available are included. For early years, undeveloped land was not given a level 2 classification due to data resolution issues.

jor changes made to the location of the river mouth. The Lower Don is also wider and deeper, as a result of continued dredging activities (Task Force to Bring Back the Don 1991). At the same time, analysis of the classified maps suggests that the land-water boundary in the rest of the study area almost doubled in length during the study period. This, however, was not a linear increase; rather, the land-water edge captured by the historic map analysis shows an initial shortening, followed by a sustained period of edge creation.

Major changes were also seen on the land in terms of the extent of urban activities and location and characteristics of undeveloped areas (figures 6.2–6.8; table 6.4). Not surprisingly, all types of urban land uses increased through the 1950s. However, the percentage of the study area used for urban purposes starts to decrease in the 1970s as a result of the creation of new land in the form of the Leslie Street Spit as well as the abandonment of existing industrial areas. The following sections discuss the analysis of land use/land cover and boundaries for each classified map in more detail, situating the conditions represented by the map in the context of relevant policies for the period.

1851 Map: Pre-industrialization

The classified map from 1851 highlights the formidable boundary the Don River created at the time. To the west was a continuous grid of streets and increasing number of buildings – including the Gooderham and Worts distillery at the mouth of the Don and several smaller saw-

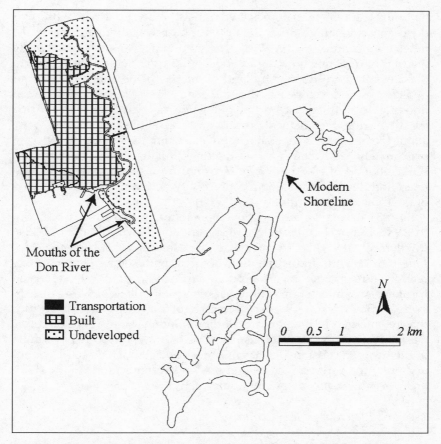

6.2 Mixed land use / land cover classification, 1851. Modern shoreline is
shown to highlight smaller extent of this map as compared to other dates.
(Map by author)

mills and grist mills in the river valley (McIlwraith 1991), but to the
east of the Don, urban activities were nearly non-existent (figure 6.2).
There were also few crossings over the river, suggesting the river acted
as a barrier to the movement of people and goods overland, even as it
facilitated the movement of goods along its lower stretch.

   The Don River's pathway is shown as relatively sinuous, cutting
across the northern edge of Ashbridge's Bay before emptying into the

harbour. The 1851 map depicts two outlets to the Don River, while evidence exists to suggest that the upper mouth was dredged during the nineteenth century (Seton 1998). The map, however, does not capture the highly dynamic boundary between the river, which was prone to flood events, and the marshy land of the bay. Thus, much of the land depicted as undeveloped in the 1851 map likely experienced seasonal flooding. In addition, the portion of the bay that was open water varied greatly during the nineteenth century as a result of storms: in 1852 only about 150 hectares of vegetated 'land' existed in the bay, but in 1910 approximately 525 hectares were present (Whillans 1998). This indicates the likelihood of a soft edge, not evident from the map, which facilitated high levels of functional connectivity between the lower reaches of the river and Ashbridge's Bay.

By 1851, several waterfront development plans had already been put forth, including Bonnycastle's 1834 plan and Howard's plan of 1846 (McIlwraith 1991). These early plans focused on supporting the shipping industry and industrial development, with some mention of recreational green space to garner public support, a pattern often repeated in later plans. Interestingly, Bonnycastle's plan called for filling in Ashbridge's Bay (Desfor 1988; see Moir, chapter 1, this volume), an idea that re-emerged in the Toronto Harbour Commission's 1912 plan (see Desfor et al., this volume). These early plans, however, were never fully implemented. Thus, in 1851 there is not yet a completely hard boundary along the harbour's edge, and the land-water ecotone in the study area was minimally altered by human activity.

1902 and 1916 Maps: Early Planning

By 1902, the Don River was no longer a boundary to human activities, with urban land uses extending well east of the river (figure 6.3). The 1902 map also shows an increase in the number of crossings over the river, including a rail line that was completed along the lake shorefront in the 1850s (McIlwraith 1991). In addition, the Don River valley had become a major transportation corridor: in 1902 a rail line was built on the eastern edge of the valley and major streets line the valley's edge.

Urban expansion, including increasing transportation connectivity across and within the river corridor in support of those land uses, was achieved, in part, by the straightening and channelization of the Lower Don in 1886 (Desfor and Keil 2000; see also Desfor and Bonnell, this volume). This reduced the dynamism of the river's path, creating dry land

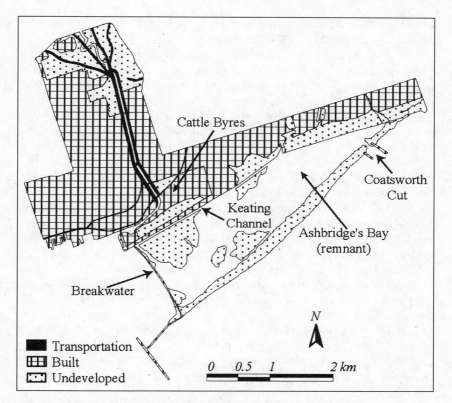

6.3 Mixed land use / land cover classification, 1902. (Map by author)

out of the marshy flood plain. At the same time, several small tributaries were buried. The modification of this river system likely resulted in the loss of many species that thrived in the dynamic flood plains and shallow pools along the Lower Don.

These changes to the Don River valley occurred after the hardening of the lakeshore in the 1860s (McIlwraith 1991), and at the same time as the construction of a breakwater between Ashbridge's Bay and the harbour. An increase in industrial activity in the river valley, as well as several cattle byres just north of the bay, meant that significant levels of industrial and agricultural wastes were flowing into the marshland. An opening in the south-eastern end of the Bay, known as Coatsworth Cut, was created earlier to help flush pollutants out of the bay while allowing freshwater to enter (see Moir, chapter 1, this volume). The goal of the breakwater was to keep pollutants, silt, and other material from floating into the harbour (Desfor 1988).

The hardening of the ecotone was continued under the 1882 Keating Plan. The plan called for the creation of a deep channel along the northern edge of Ashbridge's Bay and a modification in the course of the Don River to flow directly into the new channel (Desfor 1988; see Moir, chapter 1, this volume). Very quickly, the first portion of the Keating Channel was dredged, from the breakwater eastward, as is evident in the 1902 map.

The goal of the Keating Plan was to create more dry land in support of industrial development, provide deep-water access to that land, and minimize impacts on bridges and other infrastructure from floods. By 1902, the land-water boundaries in the study area were drastically altered to increase economic flows on land and water routes at the expense of biophysical flows. In particular, there was a reduction in lateral hydrological connections along the Lower Don, while Ashbridge's Bay was now disconnected from the river and harbour. This disconnect likely modified nutrient flows into the bay, as well as water levels, stressing plants and other species and possibly altering the composition of species present.

A major waterfront development plan was adopted in 1912, which guided activities on the waterfront for several decades (see Desfor et al., this volume). The 1916 map depicts conditions just after adoption of this transformative plan (figure 6.4). Since 1902, the second step of the Keating Plan was completed, connecting the mouth of the Don River with the Keating Channel, which created a ninety-degree turn in the flow of the river. However, the 1916 map indicates that the dredged channel was no longer separated from open water in the bay, suggesting water still flowed between the Don River and Ashbridge's Bay. Overall, the amount of green space is reduced between the two maps. However, this may be more an issue of depiction rather than actual change, reflecting a desire to create solid land and deep water out of the marshland. There is some evidence that water levels in Ashbridge's Bay may have actually gone down during this time, due to the redirection of the Don River, and that vegetated land had been increasing for several decades (Whillans 1998).

1954 Map: The Filling of Ashbridge's Bay

The adoption of the 1912 waterfront plan established the framework for the parallel activities of infill and dredging to create a deep-water

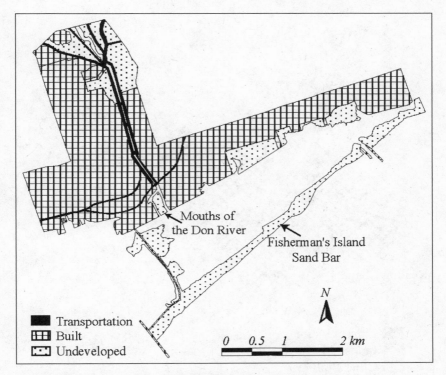

6.4 Mixed land use / land cover classification, 1916. (Map by author)

port. The Toronto Harbour Commission, which implemented the plan, was primarily a development agency with the power to buy, sell, and expropriate land (Merrens 1988; see Desfor et al., this volume). The discussions that preceded the formation of the commission were often over greater connectivity between the city and deep water for the transportation of goods (Desfor and Vesalon 2008; Desfor et al. this volume), without consideration of the ecological effects of sharpening the boundary.

The dramatic changes that occurred under the commission's authority are evident when one compares the 1916 map with the 1954 map (figure 6.5), the latter of which represents the nearly full implementation of the 1912 plan. By 1954, almost all of Ashbridge's Bay had been filled to support industrial and shipping activities, except for a deep-water shipping channel that was built as part of the new Port Industrial

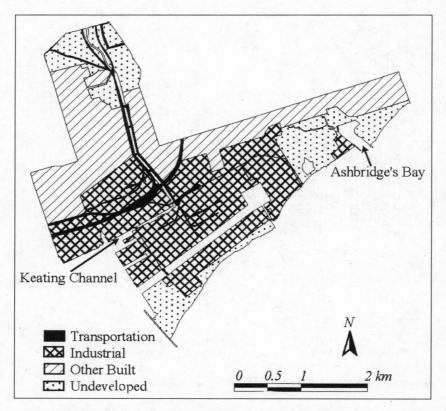

Keating Channel

Ashbridge's Bay

N

■ Transportation
⊠ Industrial
▨ Other Built
▥ Undeveloped

0   0.5   1   2 km

6.5 Mixed land use / land cover classification, 1954. (Map by author)

District. The infill activity eliminated existing habitat in Ashbridge's Bay, significantly marginalizing all species found at this site.

However, after the infill was complete, new factories did not locate on these lands quite as expected (see Moir, chapter 4, and Desfor et al., this volume). In 1933 the commission reported that forty firms had established in the Port Industrial District (Lemon 1990), but it is clear from the original 1954 air photo that most industrial areas were used for bulk storage (figure 6.5). One of the only undeveloped areas in 1954 was the south-eastern edge of Ashbridge's Bay. The initial 1912 plan depicts this strip as parkland. Steps taken in the late 1940s enabled the commission to create an outer harbour here, but no action around such development occurred until the 1960s (Merrens 1988). Thus, in 1954, this isolated piece of green space existed in an unmanaged state.

While not explicitly developed as parkland, that stretch of land and a small area around the remnant Ashbridge's Bay represented the only portions of the Lake Ontario boundary in the study area with a soft shoreline. In all, the length of hard shoreline more than doubled owing to the filling of the original Ashbridge's Bay, meeting an explicit goal of the 1912 plan to increase dock capacity in support of additional economic connections. But these changes likely further halted the exchange of biological material between the land and the water as well as recreational opportunities associated with the bay. Terrestrial and aquatic species that existed in these areas likely represent a transformed species assemblage, with reduced richness as a result of the restriction in biological material flows to these locations.

1974 Map: Starting the Outer Harbour

Following the creation of the Port Industrial District, two major activities had an impact on boundaries and connectivity around the mouth of the Don. The first was the planning for an outer harbour. In 1967, the regional Metropolitan Toronto (Metro) government produced a new plan for its eighty kilometres of shoreline. The Metro plan represented a major deviation from previous ones, as it highlighted the need for recreational green space, with an explicit goal to reconnect people to the waterfront (Metropolitan Toronto Planning Board and Metropolitan Council 1967). However, protection of ecological systems was still largely overlooked. The Metro plan also emphasized continued economic development along the central waterfront, under the control of the Toronto Harbour Commission, through the creation of an outer harbour and protective headlands.

The Toronto Harbour Commission had discussed creating an outer harbour, located on the undeveloped tip of land along the south-eastern edge of the Port Industrial District, as early as the 1920s (Merrens 1988). The construction of the protective headlands actually began in 1965, and the Harbour Commission's 1970 annual report identified the construction of the outer harbour and protective headlands as extremely important (Toronto Harbour Commissioners 1970). Thus, while the broader Metro waterfront development plan represents a new vision of an urban waterfront with significant green-space connectivity for recreational purposes, activities near the Don River still focused on de-

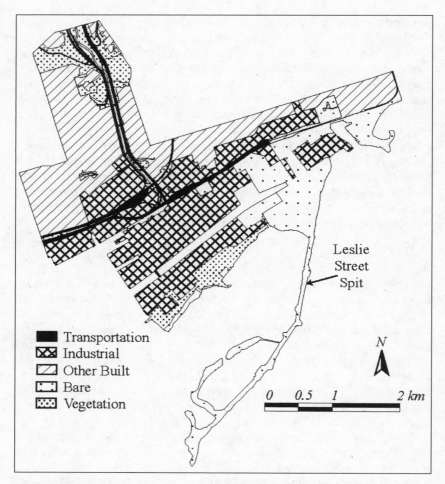

6.6 Mixed land use / land cover classification, 1974. (Map by author)

veloping greater connectivity between the industrial harbour and inter-national shipping activity.

The 1974 map shows that the infill activities of the commission had added over one hundred hectares of new land since 1954 (figure 6.6). This created approximately sixteen kilometres of relatively soft shore-line along the five-kilometre 'spine' of the protected headlands, now known as the Leslie Street Spit. Except for continual dumping, all other activities were prohibited on the Spit until 1973. By 1974 several species had opportunistically colonized the spine, creating a very sparse cover of vegetation that supported an increasing number of birds and other species (Carley 1998).

While plans had been formalized to create an outer harbour in 1967, it was clear by then that additional capacity was not needed (Merrens 1988). The 1974 map indicates that land used for industrial purposes shrunk by 80 per cent in comparison to 1954, creating a highly connected swath of unused land along the outer edge of the Port Industrial District through to the Leslie Street Spit. However, these lands were covered by sparse ruderal vegetation as a result of economic trends and land abandonment rather than a purposeful 'greening.'

The second major change occurring after 1954 is related to transportation connectivity. Construction of the Gardiner Expressway, running just north of the Lake Ontario shoreline, began in 1955. By the late 1960s, the Gardiner connected to the newly constructed Don Valley Parkway, which runs along the existing rail line on the eastern edge of the river valley. Thus, while the 1967 plan sought to increase access to the waterfront through support of local green space and recreational opportunities, it was adopted following a period where connectivity between the city and shoreline was further limited at the expense of a more highly connected regional transportation network.

1992 and 2002 Maps: Turning Back

Starting in 1973, dumping of silt dredged from both the harbour and Keating Channel onto the Leslie Street Spit greatly expanded the size of the headland (Toronto and Region Conservation Authority 2008), creating more opportunities for vegetation to colonize the site. The continued reduction of industrial activity within the Port Industrial District also led to more vegetation establishing in this area. Thus, the area of vegetated land in the Port Industrial District increased by 52 per cent between 1974 and 1992 (compare figures 6.6 and 6.7). It should be emphasized that much of the increase in green space resulted from opportunistic colonization rather than active management.

Starting in the late 1960s, the Toronto Harbour Commission and later the Toronto Regional Conservation Authority sought to develop the Leslie Street Spit. In 1976 the Metropolitan Toronto Regional Conservation Authority presented a plan to build marinas, hotels, amusement

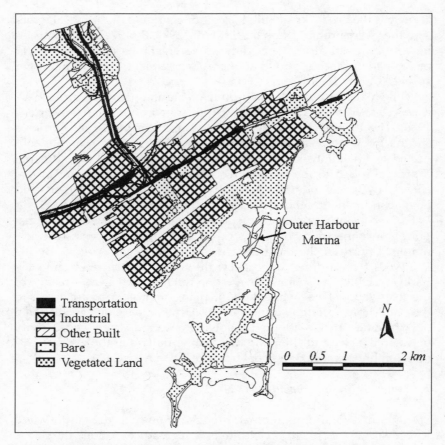

6.7 Mixed land use / land cover classification, 1992. (Map by author)

parks, and other infrastructure-intensive recreational activities on the spit (Carley 1998). The plan envisioned potential benefits to the port lands, with the possibility that recreational facilities would attract infrastructure to the port area (Port Industry Task Force 1975). However, these plans were not widely supported by the public, who had been granted limited access to the spit since 1973 and who recognized the ecological value of the site. Thus, many years passed as various stakeholders debated the future of the spit, while the spit itself continued to support higher levels of biodiversity as a result of colonization and successional processes (Foster and Sandberg 2004).

Successful establishment of many of the species on the Leslie Street Spit highlights the functional connections that existed between the spit and other localities that served as source populations, even as the spit and lower port lands remained geographically isolated green space. For example, several species of water birds established colonies on the spit as early as 1979 (Ontario Ministry of Natural Resources 2006). Some mammal, amphibian, and reptile inhabitants may have existed in remnant patches along the port lands through the mid-twentieth century (Peuramaki 1998), enabling their quick expansion on to the spit. The establishment of these populations and their associated food webs created functional connections between the terrestrial and aquatic systems.

A turning point in the management of the Toronto waterfront came in 1995, with the adoption of a management plan for the Leslie Street Spit that privileged the ecology of the system over economic development in the area. The plan was a result of discussion among several stakeholders, who had been debating development plans since the 1970s (Foster and Sandberg 2004; Kavanagh 1989; Kehm 1989). As a result of the plan's adoption, numerous trees, shrubs, and other forms of vegetation have been planted in the upland and wetland habitats of the spit, near-shore habitats were constructed, and to date little further infrastructure for recreation or other activities has been allowed. At the same time, dumping of dredged materials still occurs along the southeastern portion of the spit.

At the same time that the amount of vegetated cover was increasing on the spit, the Task Force to Bring Back the Don was beginning to work to restore the Don watershed. Having been permanently established in 1990, the group's ultimate goal was to restore the watershed's ecology while creating access opportunities for humans along the river that were consistent with natural functions (Task Force to Bring Back the Don 1991). By 2002, thousands of trees and shrubs had been planted in the valley, regular volunteer clean-up days were held, and pedestrian access had been improved along the Lower Don River (City of Toronto n.d.a). Several restoration projects along the unchannelized portion of the Lower Don had also taken place, most notably the 1996 re-naturalization of the Chester Marsh, a former landfill, at the north end of the study area (City of Toronto n.d.b). The result of these projects has been greater landscape connectivity between the land and the water within the river corridor and increased opportunity for connections between people and the natural functions of the river. But an examination of the 2002 map (figure 6.8) shows that significant barriers still limit biophysi-

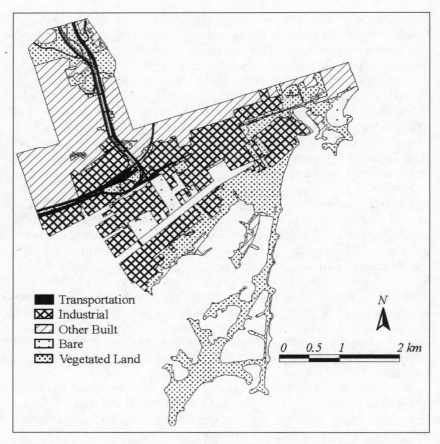

6.8 Mixed land use / land cover classification, 2002. (Map by author)

cal flows between land and water, most notably the intensely used land that surrounds much of the channelized Lower Don, and the physical barriers that separate the Don River from the former site of Ashbridge's Bay.

Conclusions

Over the last century, the land-water boundary zone along the Lower Don River and Ashbridge's Bay has undergone major changes in length, location, and characteristics. This zone is an example of a location in which a few actions significantly altered ecological conditions, with economic connectivity across land and water increasing at the expense of the biophysical system's connectivity. Thus, we see the sharpening of the land-water boundary through infill, channelization, bulkhead creation, and dredging, which eliminated near-shore environments that benefited from and regulated flows across the ecotone.

A slight return to a more highly connected landscape, from a biophysical perspective, has occurred over the last few decades. However, this trend is not a result of purposeful greening. For example, an ecologically grounded plan for the Leslie Street Spit was adopted only after numerous birds, mammals, amphibians, and other species managed to colonize and establish linkages between the terrestrial and aquatic systems. Such unexpected occurrences highlight the potential for functional ecological connections to occur even within isolated green space and other unconnected sites, which have the ability to support colonization.

While not explicitly examined in this research, the flora and fauna have likely been radically altered as a result of the changes in the ecotone. The channelization of the Don River eliminated the ecosystems that existed in the slow-moving shallows of the river. The hardening of the broader ecotone and infill of Ashbridge's Bay removed a significant stretch of land that would have regularly flooded, due to seasonal fluxes or storm events, eliminating the vegetation that thrives in such dynamic locations. Finally, urbanization along the lake shoreline and Don River have impacted hydrological flows and water chemistry in and around the Lower Don (Helfield and Diamond 1997), further marginalizing the historic aquatic-species assemblage.

The creation of the Leslie Street Spit has no doubt supported an increase in species richness, but this strip of land and the related landwater boundary are not a replica of the earlier ecotone. As a result, the flora and fauna found there today should not be considered synonymous with the nineteenth-century composition, but rather an alternative (although partially overlapping) assemblage of species in place of the long marginalized historic biota.

A major limiter in the restoration of the land-water ecotone today is the channelization of the Lower Don. Discussions to re-naturalize the river's mouth, after it was disconnected from Ashbridge's Bay more than a century ago, have occurred for more than a decade (see Desfor and Bonnell, this volume). Naturalization would likely create a softer shoreline, reducing the physical barriers that currently dominate the ecotone. However, it is important to remember that a soft boundary is not necessarily a dynamic one. Dynamism in the form of flood events that temporarily, and even permanently, alter the location of the boundary is crucial for the exchange of material across the zone (Naiman and Décamps 1997). Additional management challenges associated with a naturalized mouth may also exist as a result of lateral connectivity between the river and watershed. Helfield and Diamond (1997) note that the highly urbanized region above the mouth may contribute more flow volume and pollutants than the flood plain can assimilate. Thus, re-naturalization of the mouth of the Don must consider the nature of connections between the land and river throughout the watershed.

This chapter has documented changes to an urban waterfront ecotone. For over one hundred years, tensions have existed among multiple forms of connectivity defined along ecological, hydrological, and economic dimensions. In the study area, a century of physical change supported an industrial waterfront highly connected to international shipping routes, national rail lines, and regional highways. Ensuing alteration of the land-water boundary increased economic flows, but did so at the expense of biophysical connections and recreational opportunities. In the last few decades there has been a reversal of this trend, with landscape connectivity increasing across underutilized sites and newly created land that serendipitously has created new recreational opportunities within the ecotone. Over the coming years, the tension among an inherently dynamic boundary zone, static physical infrastructure, and the multiple dimensions of connectivity will likely continue to shape and reshape the Lower Don River and Ashbridge's Bay.

7 Networks of Power: Toronto's Waterfront Energy Systems from 1840 to 1970

SCOTT PRUDHAM, GUNTER GAD, AND
RICHARD ANDERSON

> Urban networks in the contemporary city are largely hidden, opaque, invisible, disappearing underground, locked into pipes, cables, conduits, tubes, passages and electronic waves. It is exactly this hidden form that renders the tense relationship between nature and the city blurred, that contributes to severing the process of social transformation of nature from the process of urbanization. Perhaps more importantly, the hidden flows and their technological framing render occult the social relations and power mechanisms that are scripted in and enacted through these flows.
>
> Kaika and Swyngedouw 2000: 121

Modernity, Urban Infrastructure, and Socionatural Networks

In the nineteenth and twentieth centuries, complex networks of extraction, transformation, and circulation provided the growing city of Toronto with crucial material inputs – including water, energy, and building materials – required for urban and industrial expansion. These networked linkages were more, however, than mere provisioning systems. Rather, they also 'hybridized' nature and the city in the urban landscape and in the urban consciousness. The 1911 lighting of Toronto's city hall with hydroelectric power generated over 150 kilometres away at Niagara Falls serves as a prime example (Careless 1984). This moment not only consolidated connections between the growing city and its hinterland, but also galvanized the dream image of a modern city forged from the fusion of nature and the urban.

Erik Swyngedouw (1996), in attempting to theorize a political ecology of urbanization, coined the term 'cyborg urbanization' to refer to the distinct ways in which the growth and development of cities draws on metabolic relations between ostensibly distinct social and natural processes, fusing them in networked relations of production, circulation, and use with definite implications for the spatial form and political experience of the cityscape. In similar fashion, Matthew Gandy develops a perspective on socio-technological networks involved in the extraction, processing, distribution, and delivery of water and other forms of nature as processes foundational to the modern city (primarily in reference to Paris and New York – see 2005, 2002, 1999). For Gandy these processes have constituted urban modernity via the production of distinctly modern forms of urban spatial networks (e.g., water, sewage, and energy systems) that have not only produced and sustained the social and physical spaces of cities, but have also given them meaning in the fusion of nature and the urban.[1]

And yet, these networked provisioning systems tended to elicit profound ambivalence. Drawing from Gandy's work on New York (2002), nineteenth-century development of the city's water-supply infrastructure – most notably in the form of the Croton Aqueduct – was certainly propelled and proudly signified by a distinctly Promethean impulse whose hallmarks were the conquest and rationalization of nature and space. And yet, while some features of the system boldly proclaimed a muscular modernity, great efforts were devoted elsewhere to obscuring it from view, particularly those facets deemed ugly, distasteful, or otherwise undesirable (e.g., sanitary sewers and the like). In this manner, for Gandy, nineteenth-century New York water infrastructure both celebrated a new urban synthesis of nature and culture and yet paradoxically retrenched cleavages between the city and its hinterland. Kaika (2005) makes similar observations with regard to modern water infrastructure in Athens, Greece, noting that the movement of water through space via highly invisible networks from hinterland to tap helped domestic water take on simultaneously a mundane and yet mystical character. For Toronto, direct parallels may be drawn in considering the juxtaposition of the celebrated art deco Harris filtration plant in the city's east waterfront area with the otherwise largely hidden network of connections linking taps and tubs with water intake deep beneath the surface of Lake Ontario.[2]

Efforts to actively disclose and obscure the socio-technical networks at the heart of cyborg urbanization help to give specific material shape and cultural meaning to the particular spatial arrangements or 'spatial fixes' (Jessop 2006; Schoenberger 2004; Harvey 1989b, 1982) that enable commodities – including raw and refined material inputs – to circulate through urban spaces.[3] In this chapter, our goal is to examine the role of energy networks and infrastructure in the emergence of Toronto as a leading (and eventually the leading) Canadian city and, in particular, to focus on Toronto's waterfront in this respect. We examine the city's central waterfront as a space shaped by networked relations of energy provisioning which acted as a fix of sorts for the movement of energy commodities through space, not least via the establishment of energy infrastructures for storage, conversion, and movement. Our focus on the production of Toronto's waterfront spaces as they were implicated in the urban metabolism of energy provisioning is inspired by scholarship examining the role of metabolic relations between town and country in the historical geography of capitalist urbanization in general terms (e.g., Gandy 2005, 2002, 1999; Kaika 2005; Kaika and Swyngedouw 2000; Cronon 1991), but also by a desire to elucidate in particular the dynamics and implications of emerging, modern, and largely fossil-hydrocarbon fuel systems.

A focus on energy systems is clearly pertinent to the environmental history and political ecology of cities, not least because of the central role played by high-quality and relatively cheap (largely fossil) fuels in the historical geography of capitalist modernity (Clark and York 2005; Altvater 1993). For some time now, expert and lay speculation has centred on whether or not the age of oil – and to some extent that of fossil fuels more generally – has passed its apogee. And while approximately 80 per cent of the world's primary energy still comes from fossil fuels, the age of cheap available energy may well be past (Holdren 1992).[4] If so, among the myriad implications is a need to understand energy systems as constitutive elements of experienced and inherited historical geographies, urban and otherwise. In short, what is required is attention to the particular hows and whys of energy systems and their social and environmental geographies (Huber 2009a, 2009b; Zalik 2008; S. Watts 2006; M. Watts 2003), including in an urban context.

In looking at the nexus of energy systems and Toronto's urban waterfront over the period from about 1840 to 1970, we draw inspiration in particular from the work of Debeir et al. (1991). In their largely overlooked book *In the Servitude of Power*, Debeir et al. call for a broad historical political economy and ecology of energy systems and energy transitions in order to understand the role of energy supply and energy conversion in capitalist modernity. This includes focus on the ways in which social and thermodynamic notions of *power* give shape to energy systems. Eschewing a crude materialist or economic determinism, we nevertheless insist that the material properties (and what might in retrospect be called the 'materialities' more generally) of energy sources and energy conversion be factored into analyses of how and why energy systems (including primary fuels, conversion and distribution technologies, end-use social demands, as well as controls and constraints on energy provisioning) arise, and how and why transitions from one energy system to another take place. We adopt some of the conceptualization and terminology deployed by Debeir et al., including their emphasis on interconnected, networked elements of energy systems (not merely primary fuels) and the various energy converters and energy carriers linking upstream appropriation of fuels to end uses via complex chains of physical and social connection and transformation.

Explicit conceptualization of the *geography* of energy systems is for the most part absent in Debeir et al., and yet a geography of energy systems is clearly implicit. This is not least because a focus on energy systems clearly points to cities. Growing cities typically need increasing inputs of all kinds, including water, food, and energy. The 'energy problem' has proved to be a central bottleneck for urban development at particular junctures as well as a source of complex and geographically uneven social, technical, and organizational transformations caught up in the transition from one energy system to another.[5] Wood shortage in pre-industrial London constitutes a well-known and intriguing example. Widespread deforestation along navigable rivers in southern England led to the shipment of 'sea coal' from Newcastle to London as early as the twelfth century (Cipolla 1993), and certainly long before the onset of industrialism on a wide scale. Likewise, a major seventeenth-century fuel-wood crisis in England led to dramatic increases in coal shipments to London from the Newcastle area and the institutionalization of an elaborate water-based coal transport and trading system, including distribution via canals (see Cowen 2008; Velkar 2006; Cipolla 1993; Flinn 1984).

In Toronto, the energy problem took on particular dimensions shaped by the exhaustion of nearby fuel-wood supplies after the middle of the nineteenth century, as we discuss below. This problem was met not only by substituting coal as a primary fuel, but also by the emergence of oil and the development of long-distance electricity distribution from remote hydroelectric sites. Examining Toronto's energy transitions after about 1840, and in keeping with the focus of this collection on Toronto's waterfront, we pay particular attention to the city's lakeshore as an energy hub situated within more far-flung relationships in the city's energy supply networks. This is no mere incidental focus. Rather, Toronto's waterfront acted as a key node in the city's energy conversion and delivery systems leading up to and following the turn of the twentieth century. In particular, the waterfront emerged as an important space of flows for energy supplies coincident with the transition from wood to coal as a primary fuel. And yet the development of this role was never linear or pre-given. Toronto's waterfront instead occupied a shifting place within the city's evolving energy networks shaped by three dynamic and sometimes contradictory influences: (1) the primary fuel in question; (2) the dominant mode of transportation and distribution, particularly with regard to water-borne shipping versus the railroad; and (3) the spatial pattern of end-use demands for energy and attendant modes of distribution within the city itself.

And yet, throughout, we note the role of substantial portions of Toronto's waterfront as sacrificial or purgatorial spaces, more suggestive of places forgotten and forsaken than of markers of industrial triumph, necessary but in many ways invisible or overlooked facets of the networked delivery of newfound potencies in the fossil age. This haunting, spectral landscape, more conduit than location per se serves as both contrast and backdrop for more contemporary efforts to resuscitate and integrate Toronto's waterfront more directly into the social life and spaces of the city. It also stands in marked contrast to urban waterfronts in cities such as Detroit, Pittsburgh, and even nearby Hamilton, as well as with the ambitions and boosterish proclamations of the 1912 Harbour Commission spearheading the creation of Toronto's Port Industrial District (see Desfor et al., this volume). This contrast speaks to several facets of the role and character of Toronto's waterfront. First, it is testimony to the waterfront as a space of flows for energy and other inputs to the city as much or more than as a space of industrial agglomeration per se. It also speaks to the character of Toronto as an urban agglomeration with a *metropolitan* economy (Green 1991: 9) whose industrial might was always balanced by a strong tertiary sector, especially through the presence of trade, finance, government, and a range of high-order services. Toronto's manufacturing was also biased towards more finished products rather than towards 'heavy industry.' Moreover, all branches of manufacturing tended to be quite spatially dispersed (Gad 2004, 1994; Lemon 1990). Finally, the contrast highlights the aforementioned ambivalence of socio-natural networks linking the country and the city in urban modernity. If the delivery of high-quality energy to Toronto was welcomed as a defining feature of modern urban life (as it unquestionably was), then the relegation of coal piles, oil storage tanks, and large, dirty energy conversion and distribution infrastructure to the waterfront bear witness to the highly *fetishized* manner in which energy was received.

Toronto's Emerging Energy System and the Nineteenth-Century Waterfront

Until the 1840s, the urban settlement called York and then Toronto relied largely on wood as a primary fuel for heating and cooking. This is true not only of residential energy requirements, but also of those of simple manufacturing processes, including baking, brewing, and tanning. Wood was complemented by wax and tallow candles and by 'sperm oil' (from whales, including sperm whales), used for lighting in homes and shops. Fuel wood, especially high-value and energy-dense hardwoods such as white oak, hickory, or ironwood, came largely from the mixed Carolinian forests along the shores of Lake Ontario to the east and west of the city, shipped by schooners into Toronto.

Toronto, however, like London, England much earlier, began to outstrip its nearby wood supplies as it grew, experiencing increasingly acute fuel-wood shortages between the 1840s and 1860s. The cordwood crisis of the late 1860s, in particular, propelled wood supply networks further and further afield. Increasingly, wood was supplied to the city from upper New York State via ships on the return journey across Lake Ontario from grain deliveries in the United States (*Globe* 1847a; *British Colonist* 1843). In addition, both the Toronto municipal and Ontario provincial governments intervened to assist private railway entrepreneurs to establish two new railroads – the Toronto and Nipissing Railway and the Toronto, Bruce and Grey Railway – with specific mandates to transport cordwood to Toronto from as far as 150 to 200 kilometres to the north-east and north-west, tapping into mixed forest and agricultural lands stretching from the Kawartha Lakes to Lake Huron and the Bruce Peninsula.

But while an expanding radius of supply networks fed wood into the city, the shortage also helped precipitate Toronto's first significant energy transition, that from wood to coal. Coal first appeared in Toronto in the 1830s as a curiosity and luxury item. However, in the 1840s the establishment of the first coal-gas plant signalled the arrival of coal in Toronto as a significant primary fuel. Coal soon became widely used

in Toronto in all sectors of the economy as a direct fuel source, including in households. In addition, it became an important primary energy
source used as the basis for energy conversion, including into deriva-
tives or secondary energy such as 'coal gas' or 'town gas,' and later as
a fuel for firing boilers and driving steam turbines in electricity generation. Coal-gas consumption was kick-started by its first use in Toronto
street lighting in 1842, spreading to more widespread use in lighting
shops, factories, and homes.[6] Gradually, gaslight and later electric light
displaced oil lamps, especially kerosene lamps.

The transition to coal was enabled in significant measure by the combination of rising fuel-wood prices and falling transportation costs for
coal shipped to the city by both rail and water. As uses for coal grew,
total shipments to Toronto increased, reaching 100,000 tons per annum
by the 1870s. A renewed fuel-wood crisis in the early 1880s led to deepening coal dependence as the railroad companies also began switching
their train engines to coal. By 1891, annual coal shipments to Toronto
had reached almost 500,000 tons. Coal became the city's primary fuel
of choice, with consumption passing two million tons per year by the
early 1920s (see table 7.1).

Toronto's primary supplier of coal during this period was Pennsylvania, in the form of both anthracite coal (more popular for domestic
use) and bituminous coal (preferred for use in powering trains, but also
in brick making). Both kinds of coal were shipped to Toronto increasingly by rail, with water-borne coal declining as a percentage of all coal
shipped to the city from half in the 1880s to less than 5 per cent by
the early 1920s. Some appreciable amount of coal was also shipped to
Toronto from Wales, very likely via cargo ships coming up the St Lawrence River.[7]

Whether coal arrived by rail or by water, Toronto's waterfront played
a key role in the coal energy system. Not only did the coal arriving by
ship come to the waterfront; so too did much of the coal arriving directly by rail. This reflects the role of the central waterfront as an important
conduit, staging area, and break of bulk point for railroad lines coming
into and out of the city, and as a hub for the distribution of coal arriving
by both rail *and* ship throughout the city more generally. Business ad-
vertisements and insurance plans of the 1880s and 1890s, for example,
show coal trains along the Esplanade in the corridor of land located
between the lake and the city across the foot of the central city (see
figure 7.1). Ample evidence from the early twentieth century points to
railway spur lines or 'sidings' leading into most coal and wood yards

Table 7.1
Coal receipts in Toronto by water and rail, selected years 1886–1933 (1000 tons)*

Year	Water		Rail		Total
	1000 tons	%	1000 tons	%	
1880	–	0.5	–	50.0	–
1886	119	31.9	254	68.1	373
1891	163	33.9	317	66.2	479
1896	153	25.4	449	74.6	602
1901	184	23.4	602	76.6	786
1906	162	13.9	1005	86.1	1167
1912	122	6.7	1700	93.3	1822
1921	79	3.3	2321	96.7	2400
1926	129	5.1	2396	94.9	2525
1931	560	22.7	1909	77.3	2469
1933	1326	54.1	1126	45.9	2452

*Presumably short tons of 2000 pounds, or one short ton = 0.907 metric tons.

Sources: For 1880, Annual Report 1934, Toronto Harbour Commissioners, 39; for 1886–1906, Mellen 1974, 261, based on Reports of the Harbour Commission; for 1912–34, Annual Reports of the Toronto Harbour Commissioners / Harbour Masters Reports, with summary table for 1926–33 in 1934 Annual Report, 39.

along both sides of the bundle of main-line tracks on the Esplanade. These sidings provided links from the railroad to storage yards used as distribution nodes for delivering fuel to the city more widely, as well as to more proximate energy conversion facilities relying on wood and then coal as a primary fuel – including, for example, coal-gas production and electricity generation.

The structure of this distribution system for coal was very much built upon the prior wood energy system, so much so that most coal dealers listed in business directories, insurance plans, and other records from the period appear as integrated or combined wood and coal dealers. These dealers proliferated after 1870 (see table 7.2) in the form of a network of yards distributed about the city, largely linked via rail lines to the waterfront and, in particular, to the eastern central waterfront. Between the 1840s and 1880s shipments of wood and coal arrived at various locations along the waterfront between Bathurst Street in the west and Parliament Street in the east. In 1856 there were nine important coal and wood dealers on the waterfront; by 1881 there were seventeen.

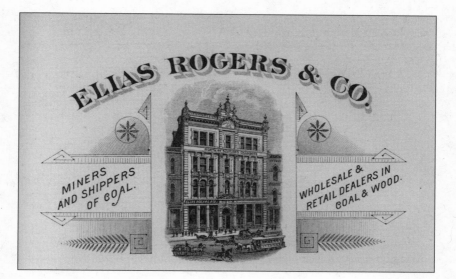

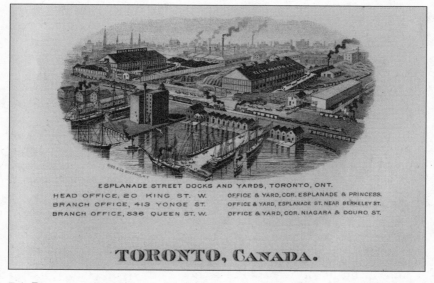

7.1 Representations of a coal and wood dealer, Elias Rogers and Co., 1885.

Table 7.2
Coal and wood dealers in Toronto, 1856–1928

Year	Firms	Locations				
		Waterfront yards				
		East	West	Other yards	Offices	Total
1856	12	6	3	3	0	12
1861	15	7	0	8	0	15
1867	13	8	3	3	0	14
1871	19	7	4	8	1	20
1875	63	12	5	49	3	69
1881	66	13	4	57	8	82
1891	97	7	2	70	24	103
1914	78	9	4	108	ca. 50	171
1928	123	7	2	167	ca. 50	226

Source: Compiled by G. Gad from *Toronto City Directories, 1856–1928*. Toronto: Might
Directory Co., Murray Printing Co.

By 1881 numerous large coal and wood dealers had become established, with about six to ten of these large firms emerging as the dominant players or 'majors' in the Toronto coal and wood trade. By 1880–1 these firms had made a considerable impact on waterfront land use. The wood and coal yards of the majors were particularly important in this respect, with waterfront or docks-area yards ranging from 2000 to nearly 10,000 square metres by 1900 (see figures 7.2 and 7.3). To put this in perspective, very few waterfront manufacturing establishments were of anything approaching this size at the time. The 1885 portrayal of the Elias Rogers Company in figure 7.1, for example, shows a coal train going right into the coal yard north of the Esplanade, while also depicting coal trains on the main railway tracks along the waterfront (Mulvaney 1885). The Patrick Burns company, with its major coal yard at Front Street and Bathurst (somewhat removed from the docks) claimed that it received wood by rail and coal by both rail and water (ibid., vol. 2). Since there is no evidence that Burns had storage space at the nearby Queen's Wharf, coal arriving by ship was probably carted to the huge Burns yard over a distance of about 500 metres shortly after being unloaded from the boats.

And yet, the majors were multi-locational firms typically with a head or principal order office in the central business district, complemented

7.2 Conger Coal Company docks on the south side of Esplanade, just east of the foot of Church Street, 1890. At the far end the steel frame 'coal hoists' mark the mooring points for ships. From the hoists, 'elevated trams' lead to the coal shed and to coal piles near the Esplanade side of the dockyard. (From G. Mercer Adam, *Old Toronto and New* [Toronto: Mail Printing Co., 1891], 169)

by a series of branch order offices, with a central large coal and wood yard at the waterfront docks, and a series of smaller yards located across the city. Most of these smaller yards were situated at strategic locations where railway lines intersected with arterial roads such as Yonge, Bathurst, Queen, and Gerrard Streets (see, for example, figure 7.1) Again, a look at individual businesses can be instructive. The afore-mentioned business of Patrick Burns, established in 1856, was by 1885 handling 150,000 tons of coal per year and 35,000 cords of wood while employing 300 people (making the firm one of the larger employers in the city at the time). Burns moved coal and wood from various yards to locations throughout the city by means of 150 to 200 teams using horse-drawn wagons (Mulvaney 1885, vol. 2). Other majors include the

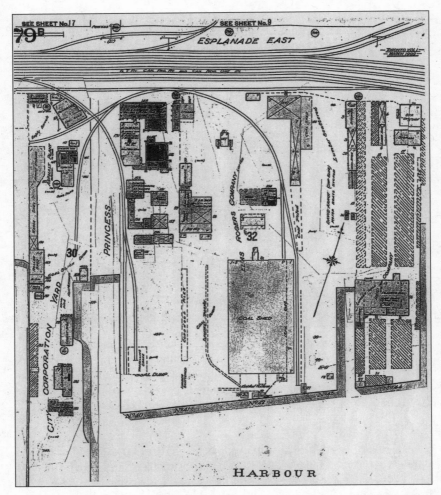

7.3 Elias Rogers and Co. yard on wharfs 41 and 42. (From Goad's Atlas, 1914)

Elias Rogers Company, the P.D. Conger Company (in later years the Conger Lehigh Co.), the Ontario Coal Company, and the Milnes Company (for brief company histories and illustrations of dock yards, see Adam 1891).

Away from the waterfront, coal and wood yards were of course much smaller, typically on the order of approximately six hundred square metres. Already by 1880, dealers and their branch yards were scattered all over the city, by 1890 appearing in some of the older suburbs, including for example in West Toronto Junction. One outstanding example is a coal and wood yard north-west of the Keele-Dundas intersection evident on the 1890 insurance plan. This establishment with a large coal shed was flanked on two sides by railway sidings that brought coal from the nearby Canadian Pacific Railway line into the shed. The operation was typical of the smaller yards distributed throughout the city, most located in emerging high-density areas not far from retail and service sub-centres in the city with connections to the waterfront hub, and yet also typically (and predictably) well removed and hidden from the more upper- and professional-class neighbourhoods of the day.

Apart from the wood and coal distribution network, energy 'converters' also emerged to form an important part of the city's energy system and waterfront land-use complex. Perhaps the earliest and for a long time the most significant waterfront energy converter was the Consumers' Gas Company. A predecessor firm established the first coal-gas plant in Toronto in 1841, as noted above, based on a franchise from the City of Toronto for street lighting and using land at the water's edge south of Front Street between Sherbourne and Princess Streets along the east waterfront. In 1848 the company became Consumers' Gas and built a new coal gasification facility in the block bounded by Parliament, Mill, Cherry, and Front Streets (just north of the Gooderham and Worts distillery; see Swift 1991). Over time the gas plant spread over several adjacent blocks of land to become a significant presence helping to shape the emerging waterfront energy complex.

Yet the list of significant waterfront energy conversion sites also includes the aforementioned Gooderham and Worts Distillery, arguably the only truly industrial-scale operation serving as an anchor tenant along the east-central urban waterfront. As a very capital-intensive operation whose processes required considerable heat and also internal distribution of grains and liquids, the distillery was a ferocious consumer of wood and coal. Not only was the distillery a major energy consumer; the Gooderham family were also the major business interest behind the Toronto and Nipissing Railway, thus helping to give particular shape to this part of the city's broader energy system and reinforcing the spatial agglomeration of energy-conversion, energy-storage, and energy-distribution infrastructure along the waterfront.

The city's waterworks also had its principal pumping station on a wharf at the foot of John Street on the west-central waterfront. In the last two decades of the nineteenth century, this facility had one of the biggest steam-engine installations in the city and was one of Toronto's largest coal consumers. Insurance plans clearly show the coal storage areas on the wharf, and in many depictions of the city at the time the plume of smoke from the waterworks pumping station is clearly evident.

In addition, the Toronto Electric Light Company (TELCo) became an important waterfront energy converter, obtaining a franchise from the City of Toronto to provide electric street lighting in the 1880s, successfully displacing Consumers' Gas in this respect. By 1883 TELCo had built an electricity generating station located along Toronto's central-eastern waterfront at the foot of Scott Street (Stamp 1991). This plant was also largely powered by coal, first brought to the generating station by rail and from 1898 onward by ship (*Globe* 1899a). Again, insurance plans from 1890 and 1914 indicate large coal piles and a range of structures for the handling of coal where land and water came together. Toronto's streetcar company (strangely named the Toronto Railway Company) also became a major source of electricity generated at a thermal power plant. The company built a substantial electric power plant on the east side of Frederick Street between Front Street and the Esplanade in the early 1890s. The plant was marked by a towering smoke stack rising 250 feet, or 76 metres, above the surrounding areas, reputedly the third highest in North America at the turn of the century (*Globe* 1894d, 1892b).

Toronto's Diversifying Energy System and the Waterfront into the Twentieth Century

Coal was unquestionably the primary fuel of the late nineteenth century in Toronto, particularly for commercial and industrial processes. However, the arrival of kerosene (primarily used for lighting as a replacement for sperm oil) shortly after the development of Canada's first commercial oil wells near Petrolia, Ontario, in the late 1850s and early 1860s marked the commencement of Toronto's reliance on refined petroleum products as a source of primary energy.[8] Where the kerosene used in Toronto during the latter nineteenth century was actually refined is not entirely clear, though there were certainly oil refineries in the city. But these were few in comparison to the emerging refinery complex closer to the oil wells in the Sarnia region, and it is highly likely that early refineries in the city were engaged in producing lubricating oils for machinery. All the cartographic footprints we have seen in documents from the period indicate very small refineries and few storage tanks of any size. There were two of these small establishments on the eastern waterfront around Sherbourne Street and another two on the west bank of the Don River between Gerrard and Queen Streets. Consumers' Gas records also indicate that by 1879 the company had diversified from coal as a primary fuel and was receiving petroleum shipped by rail cars from oil wells in southwestern Ontario to its gas plant on Toronto's waterfront (see Tucker 1948; and also Goad 1884, sheet 11, with entry 'Making Gas from Petroleum'). In 1909, Consumers' Gas opened an additional plant east of the Don River between Eastern Avenue and the new Keating Street, relying on petroleum shipped by rail from the Sarnia area in specialized tanker cars (Tucker 1948). Detailed maps show railway spur lines entering the gas plant's grounds, with some of the spur lines going straight to large oil storage tanks and others to coal unloading facilities.

The character and scale of Toronto's oil energy system changed in 1906, however, with the construction of the British American Oil Company refinery for the production of gasoline, other fuels, and lubricating oils on recently reclaimed land at the mouth of the Don River.[9] Toronto Harbor Commission records indicate that the crude oil used in this facility was shipped to Toronto by rail until the 1930s, reinforcing again the role of the waterfront as a transportation, storage, and conversion hub for energy flows into and within Toronto. By the mid-1930s however, crude oil from wells in Oklahoma and Texas appears to have been arriving by ship via ocean tanker to Montreal and then on to Toronto in tankers designed for the Great Lakes (Middleton 1934).

While coal and oil became increasingly important primary fuels whose conversion and distribution systems created appreciable spatial footprints along the waterfront in the late nineteenth and early twentieth centuries, electricity also emerged as an important source of secondary energy around the same period, also with significant infrastructure in the central waterfront. Electricity was first introduced to Toronto in the 1880s, and until 1910 was generated almost exclusively for lighting and mechanical processes from coal, possibly complemented by some use of petroleum as a primary fuel for powering steam engines.[10] But electricity's role in Toronto's energy mix was qualitatively transformed with the construction of long-distance transmission lines connecting hydroelectric generation at Niagara Falls to the city, highlighted and celebrated by the 1911 lighting of city hall with

Niagara power (supplemented in the 1920s by hydropower from the Ottawa and Gatineau valleys). Gradually, cheap and reliable hydropower displaced the less-centralized, on-site generation of electricity from coal and petroleum sources. TELCo, for instance, was taken over by the government-owned Ontario Hydro-Electric Power Commission (known later simply as Ontario Hydro) in the 1920s, with HEPCO assuming control of the former TELCo generating station on Toronto's waterfront. Later in the decade, the power plant was largely demolished to make way for the railway viaduct, signalling an important shift for the eastern central waterfront.

The Evolution of Waterfront Energy Networks before and after the 1912 Waterfront Plan

Beginning in the 1880s, land use along Toronto's waterfront, including the footprint of energy-related infrastructure, began to change significantly. While the Front/Bathurst Street cluster of energy dealers remained, the most central part of the waterfront district did not. The large Robert Hay furniture factory – formerly Jacques and Hay – which had dominated the west-central waterfront relocated to a new site far from the water's edge, while the Canadian Pacific Railway expanded to occupy more and more of the city's west-central waterfront land. While the CPR swallowed up lands including those formerly used by the Hay factory, two of the largest coal and wood dealers also had to relocate, moving to waterfront sites east of Yonge Street. A major fire in 1904 finished the remaining manufacturers and wholesale establishments in the district, with the result that almost all of the west-central waterfront (that is, immediately west of Yonge Street) became dedicated to railways infrastructure, anchored by the site of the new Union Station, officially opened in 1931.

The result was a trend, already evident by 1890, towards agglomeration of interlinked energy, transportation, and manufacturing land uses along the central waterfront to the east of Yonge Street. Using a crude land-use classification system and drawing on a variety of plans and inventories of the day (compiled from data for 1889, 1890, and 1891), table 7.3 provides a portrait of these land uses broken down into three sub-zones of the eastern waterfront for 1890 (see also figure 7.4). In aggregate, we estimate that energy networks and infrastructure alone[11] occupied about 22 per cent of the waterfront area stretching from Yonge Street in the west to the Don River in the east, third behind transporta-

Table 7.3
East Bayfront land use, 1890

| Land use | Sub-areas | | | |
	Central (Yonge to George)	Intermediate (George to Parliament)	Fringe (Parliament to Cherry)	Total
Energy	38,572 m^2 25.7%	30,757 m^2 24.6%	20,387 m^2 16.2%	89,716 m^2 22.4%
Transportation	60,524 m^2 40.4%	46,120 m^2 36.9%	16,802 m^2 13.4%	123,446 m^2 30.8%
Manufacturing	16,685 m^2 11.1%	32,192 m^2 25.8%	60,195 m^2 47.9%	109,072 m^2 27.2%
Commercial	30,676 m^2 20.5%	0 0.0%	0 0.0%	30,672 m^2 7.9%
Residential	0 0.0%	3675 m^2 2.9%	25,132 m^2 20.0%	28,807 m^2 7.2%
Other/vacant	3382 m^2 2.2%	12,212 m^2 9.8%	3163 m^2 2.5%	18,757 m^2 4.7%
All uses	149,838 m^2 100%	124,957 m^2 100%	125,680 m^2 100%	400,475 m^2 100%

tion-related land uses (some of which, it must be said, was also essential to energy provisioning) and manufacturing.

Spatial disaggregation of these data, however, allows us to see how energy-related infrastructure had clustered prior to completion of the Ashbridge's Bay infill and the realization of the 1912 Waterfront Plan. This provides a baseline for comparison after the east waterfront was reconfigured. Table 7.3 shows that exclusively energy-related land uses were most important in the areas closest to downtown, that is, from Yonge to George Streets and from George to Parliament Streets. So too for transportation-related land uses. These patterns reflect the importance of central locations along the waterfront for delivery and storage at or near the aforementioned major energy users and converters, but also for distribution throughout the city along established transportation routes.

The spatial pattern and overall significance of energy-related land uses changed again, however, moving forward into the twentieth century, shaped significantly by the channelization of the Don River, the construction of the Keating Channel, and the completion of the To-

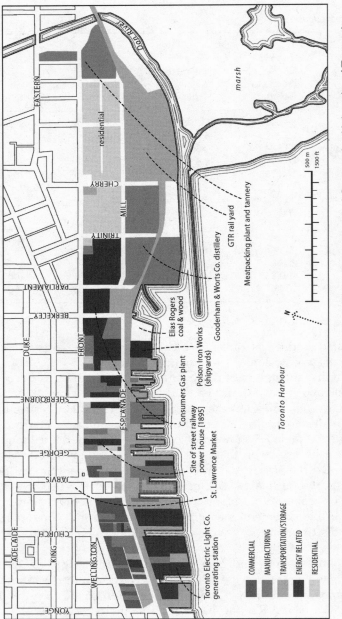

COMMERCIAL
MANUFACTURING
TRANSPORTATION/STORAGE
ENERGY RELATED
RESIDENTIAL

EASTERN

residential

CHERRY

MILL

TRINITY

marsh

Don River

GTR rail yard

Meatpacking plant and tannery

Gooderham & Worts Co. distillery

PARLIAMENT

BERKELEY

DUKE

FRONT

ESPLANADE

Elias Rogers coal & wood

Consumers Gas plant

Polson Iron Works (shipyards)

SHERBOURNE

GEORGE

JARVIS

Site of street railway power house [1895]

St. Lawrence Market

ADELAIDE

CHURCH

KING

WELLINGTON

YONGE

Toronto Electric Light Co. generating station

Toronto Harbour

N

500 m
1500 ft

7.4 Land use on the eastern waterfront, 1890. (Map by Mark Fram, Department of Geography, University of Toronto)

ronto Port Industrial District, or port lands. Initially, between 1890 and 1914, energy-related uses increased their hold on the east-central waterfront. Manufacturing also gained, influenced most by the dramatic water-ward expansion of the Polson Iron Works, which increased its shipbuilding facility by extending a substantial pier further into the harbour. Polson became the largest single lot occupant, with about 26,000 square metres in 1914; and while clearly a manufacturing facility, the Polson site, like Gooderham and Worts to the east, epitomized the often interlinked character of energy, transportation, and manufacturing, in this case driven by a voracious appetite for coal in its production. The TELCo generating plant was also enlarged at this time, with its power plant occupying about 24,000 square metres. Of the next eight largest lot occupants, seven were coal yards (including one coal and ice dealer) and the other the western outlier of the gas works.

After the First World War, the energy-waterfront complex shifted east as a result of both push and pull factors. The lots of the largest land-users were becoming bigger and bigger, leading to considerable congestion in the east-central area and pushing development further to the east. At the same time, the 1912 Waterfront Plan and the policy of railway grade separation made it impossible to land coal or even to bring it to the central waterfront by rail.[12] The role of the east-central waterfront as an energy conversion and distribution hub for the city was further eroded by collapse of the Polson Iron Works after the First World War (as the result of a loss of shipbuilding contracts; see Moir, chapter 4, this volume), and by the conversion and downgrading of the former TELCo generator to a transformer station in 1922. Only Consumers' Gas remained as a vestige of the earlier energy complex along Toronto's more central waterfront.

By contrast, land was opening up for energy-related development further to the east. A key influence came in the form of the Port Industrial District, planned in 1912 and slowly constructed over the next twenty years. This major initiative, promoted by a coalition of Toronto's economic and political elites and coordinated under the auspices of the Toronto Harbour Commission (see Desfor et al., this volume), opened up land around the newly configured mouth of the Don River, with north-western portions of this decidedly produced space ready for occupancy before the end of the war. Among the first occupants was an electric-arc-furnace steel plant. The plant did not prove economically viable, however, and soon after the war the site became host to Toronto's second large oil refinery, operated by the McColl-Frontenac Oil

Company. Plant B of Consumers' Gas was built in 1909 on land to the east of the Don River, while a new BA oil refinery went in just to the north of the still new Keating Channel. At roughly 125,000 and 75,000 square metres respectively, these facilities anchored an energy cluster forming around the emerging, planned spaces of the east waterfront at the mouth of the Don River. Four coal yards were established by 1928, followed by more in the 1930s, accompanied by oil- and gasoline-tank farms. By 1939 (according to the 1940 City Directory), there were twenty-four coal and ice dealer establishments, one oil refinery, and seven oil storage establishments in the port lands, which had become, essentially, one large energy storage and supply centre.

The colonization of the new port lands as an energy hub, more of a staging area for energy provisioning than for industrial activities per se, was in many ways propelled by the resurgence of water-borne coal deliveries to Toronto's waterfront. With the opening of the Welland Canal in 1931, larger and more economically efficient carriers capable of transporting five to ten thousand tons of coal could travel between Lake Erie and Lake Ontario. In Toronto, these ships were offloaded at the new harbour facilities constructed as part of the Port Industrial District project. And yet, the port lands facilities and coal docks were more remote from the central city than the coal docks and yards of the old east-central waterfront. Thus, critical to the emergence of the port lands as an integral part of Toronto's energy system was the emergence of the motorized truck as a more flexible and eventually dominant carrier of coal and petroleum products for distribution throughout the city.

By 1949, we estimate that two-thirds of the two-square-kilometre area of the port lands were serving energy-related uses (see figure 7.5). Primary users were the oil companies, who occupied nearly 68 hectares or 35 per cent of the port lands, followed closely by 17 coal yards and one ice dealer accounting for just less than one-third of the area. The apex of the port lands as Toronto's waterfront energy-provisioning hub may well have been the construction of the coal-fired Richard L. Hearn thermal generating station in the 1950s. During its first phase of operation the plant had a capacity of 188 MW, expanded to 1.2 GW by 1961 and consuming approximately three million tons of coal per year. In 1971, just beyond the end date of this chapter, the entire generating station switched to natural gas as a fuel for generating electricity, although four units retained the option to burn coal.

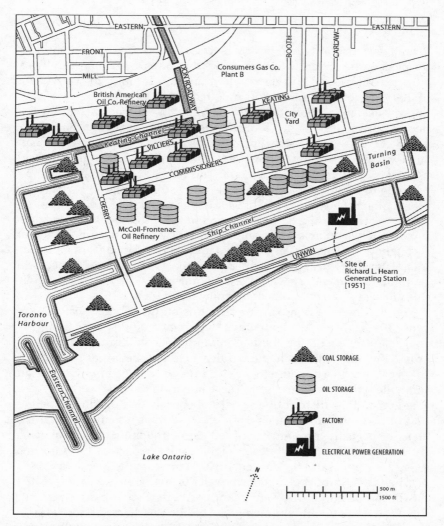

7.5 Major land uses in the Port Industrial District, 1949. (Map by Mark Fram, Department of Geography, University of Toronto)

Conclusion

If the construction of the Hearn Electric Generating Station signified the peak of the eastern waterfront and port lands as an energy delivery, storage, conversion, and distribution hub for Toronto, the conversion of the plant to a natural-gas-burning facility in 1971, largely as a result of protests over air pollution, also highlighted another turn. In the two decades before this conversion, one after another, coal yards had closed across the waterfront as coal declined as a primary fuel. In 1954, Consumers' Gas shut down its two plants on the old east-central waterfront as well as one on Eastern Avenue. The city's two oil refineries, both near the mouth of the Don, were also laid still, displaced by lake-side plants along the waterfronts of Mississauga, Oakville, and Burlington to the west. Natural gas, the third fuel in the fossil revolution, became more widely available in Toronto, arriving by pipeline and distributed throughout the city via an extensive underground grid from a massive inland terminal near the northern boundary of the city. Henceforth, more than ever, energy would come almost magically by nearly invisible means into homes, offices, hospitals, and universities.

The decline of Toronto's waterfront as an urban energy hub in recent decades bears all the hallmarks of a changing spatial fix for the movement of energy (and other) commodities within the urban landscape. Key elements of the new order included the larger refineries to the west; a modern road network and the urban hegemony of the automobile (particularly trucks in this context) in the post–Second World War era; and the distribution of natural gas via long-distance pipelines and buried intra-urban lines. Though fossil fuels remain dominant, in some respects the prominence of refined petroleum and natural gas in the later fossil era constitutes as significant a departure from the coal energy system as did the coal energy system from the wood-based system before it.[13] And true to the character of spatial fixes, each transition has been constituted by significantly different spatial arrangements. Put another way, and reinforcing one of our key themes, energy transitions are also geographical transitions, in this case reworking the urban landscape and in particular giving shape to the production of space along Toronto's waterfront.

And yet, there are important continuities here in thinking about the broader cultural politics of space and nature under the influence of cyborg urbanization. Contemporary pressures to redevelop Toronto's waterfront are propelled in no small measure by changing sensibilities about urban sustainability, nominally green amenities and lifestyles (increasingly for affluent and middle-class residents living in larger numbers along the water's edge), coincident with a revaluation of waterfront land as residential and commercial real estate, itself a form of spatial fix. Waterfront redevelopment is a complex material and semiotic process. And yet the material bases of emerging waterfront lifestyles and amenities continue to come via complex urban socio-technical provisioning systems for water, food, materials, and, of course, energy. And though energy must be provided to shops, dance clubs, condominiums, streetcars, and the like, it does so in ever less visible and increasingly taken-for-granted ways.

The almost magical appearance of contemporary energy for myriad uses enables the mystification and fetishization of energy, powerful cultural processes seemingly only disrupted by the emergence of global climate change as perhaps the most important issue of the day. This points to a paradox of technological modernity highlighted by the work of Gandy, Kaika, Swyngedouw, and others. Huge amounts of social labour and capital are invested in sustaining urban life, and yet, equally, these investments tend towards making less visible the necessary provisioning systems. If and when works of engineering are celebrated, it is typically in spectacular fashion and in ways that help to reinforce the magical illusion of emancipation. Toronto's waterfront, by acting as a central delivery, storage, conversion, and distribution hub for energy between about 1840 and 1970, was in this respect a central spatial technology of cyborg urbanization, a hybrid liminal space between land and water, city and country, culture and nature, mediating between energy uses (and users) on the one hand and energy provisioning on the other. Never really host to the large industrial agglomerations typical of more truly industrial waterfront cities, and cut off from much of the social life of the city, Toronto's waterfront in this sense epitomized and embodied the ambivalence directed at modern socio-technological networks. And though the waterfront is now becoming more an amenity space, its past begs that we ask what has *really* changed.

NOTES

1 It bears noting that our terminology and conceptualization of the con-
   joined production of space and nature here draws not only from Harvey
   (1989b, 1982) and Lefebvre (1991) but also centrally from Neil Smith (2008,

1996) and his insistence on understanding the inter-twined production of space and the production of nature as received material and ideological geographies of capitalism. For an extraordinarily lucid discussion of modernization as an active fusion of nature and society in historical-geographical materialism, see Swyngedouw 1999.

2 Indeed, Kaika and Swyngedouw (2000) reference passages describing the Harris filtration plant in Michael Ondaatje's *In the Skin of a Lion*, a novel which also traces some of the social and cultural ambiguity of such modernist projects by exploring the role of immigrant labour and racialized class conflict in their construction.

3 Harvey's (1989b, 1982) notion of the spatial fix and the spatio-temporal fix is a broad, multifaceted one (see Jessop 2006 for a critical review). We invoke specifically his attempt to capture how social capital is sunk into relatively long-lived investments in an urban context. Schoenberger describes this facet of the idea as 'the creation of an expanded and improved built environment – investment in the whole suite of physical installations that sustain and enhance the system's ability to create wealth. This includes, for example, transportation networks, water supply, waste disposal systems, communications systems and the like. The beauty of this form of the spatial fix is that it is so intensely grounded' (2004, 429).

4 We agree with Holdren and others in emphasizing that while absolute physical quantities of fossil energy sources may not be exhausted anytime soon, the increasing social, environmental, and technical costs of exploiting these resources into the future has effectively brought to an end the era when sufficient, high-quality energy from fossils can be assumed.

5 We do not posit that a singular energy problem has confronted and does confront all cities across historical time and geographical space. In fact, quite the opposite. Different cities with different socio-technical characteristics induce their own distinct energy problems, albeit often embedded within broader institutional and technological contexts or chains of causation. In fact, the most pressing dimension of energy problems does not always pertain to mobilizing sufficient fuels per se; instead, as is the case in many contemporary cities, more pressing issues may arise around the environmental and human health consequences of particular energy-using and energy-converting technologies (e.g., urban smog from internal combustion engines).

6 Coal gas was extracted by baking coal in a retort or oven without oxygen at temperatures of about one thousand degrees Celsius. The extracted gas was collected in gas holders or 'gasometers' and then distributed throughout the city by an underground network of pipes. In the coal-gas

energy cycle, coal served a dual purpose. First, it contained the primary energy source extracted in the form of volatile gases, but also, second, coal provided the process heat to drive the gases out. In 1841 a Montreal-based company was franchised by city council to provide Toronto with gas street lights. The first gas plant was built in 1841, and in 1842 the gaslights were in use (Swift 1991).

7 From table 7.1 it is also evident that the delivery of coal by ship experienced a renaissance both in absolute quantity and in its share of modal split compared to rail shipments after 1931. This would seemingly correspond most directly with the opening of the Welland Canal, which allowed faster and more efficient shipping via Lake Erie into Lake Ontario, but also with the opening of new quays and storage areas in the newly manufactured industrial waterfront spaces including and surrounding the Keating Channel.

8 For an account of the role of kerosene in displacing whale oil in lamps and in kick-starting the age of oil more generally, see Yergin 1991.

9 The actual site of this refinery north of the Keating Channel and just east of Cherry Street was obliterated by the construction of the Gardiner Expressway and the multi-lane Lakeshore Boulevard in the 1960s.

10 For example, the Canada Foundry generated electricity on its factory site at Lansdowne and Davenport, and the 1914 insurance plan showing the Christie Brown biscuit factory bears the inscription 'electricity generated on premises.' The Eaton Department Store and factory complex at Queen and Yonge also had its own generating facilities (see Stamp 1991).

11 That is, facilities primarily or exclusively dedicated to energy delivery, storage, and conversion. This includes coal and wood yards or docks (but not lumber dealers), ice dealers and ice houses, gas works and thermal electricity generation, and a few fairly small oil refineries or oil merchants. We realize, however, that this classification underestimates the importance of energy provisioning as an influence on emerging urban waterfront spaces in so much as transportation, energy, and manufacturing were interlinked through energy provisioning via the role of transportation networks in distributing energy to and throughout the city, on the one hand, and the energy-intensive demands of manufacturing facilities. We attempt to address this in the text by referring more generally to the clustering of energy, transportation, and manufacturing land uses in particular configurations.

12 By 1930, new land created south of the old docks and the new railway viaduct cut off the central city from the water. The construction of the railway viaduct was ordered by the federal government's Board of Railway

Commissioners to achieve grade separation between the railway and street
traffic. The viaduct became a major physical barrier between businesses,
especially the coal dealers, and the edge of the water, where vessels could
land coal and wood (see Stinson and Moir 1991; Lemon 1985).

13 It should be said that some characterize the era of wood as the era of mus-
cle power (human and animal) as well (for discussion see Huber 2009a).

PART TWO

Shaping the Post-Industrial Waterfront

8 Creating an Environment for Change: The 'Ecosystem Approach' and the Olympics on Toronto's Waterfront

JENNEFER LAIDLEY

Waterfront Planning in Toronto: Contradictions and Connections

Between the late 1980s and the early 2000s, the focus of Toronto's waterfront planning activity and the rationale for its development underwent a significant shift, from the 'ecosystem approach' recommended by the Royal Commission on the Future of Toronto's Waterfront to a 'global imperative' approach being pursued by Waterfront Toronto, a public development corporation originally named the Toronto Waterfront Revitalization Corporation (TWRC).[1] While on the surface these two approaches to waterfront development seem incongruous, the analysis presented in this chapter demonstrates their deep political and economic connections in a period of transition from an industrial to a post-industrial waterfront; that is, the ways in which nature–society relationships were constructed to function in support of waterfront development during this time.

In 1992, the royal commission[2] released its final report, entitled *Regeneration*, which was heralded as a new era of environmentally based planning for Toronto's waterfront and the ecosystem of which it is a part. The 'ecosystem approach,' as it was called, promised to bring together in one development model 'the long-term promise of a healthy environment, economic recovery and sustainability, and maintaining a livable community' (Royal Commission on the Future of the Toronto Waterfront 1992: 16–17). Ecosystem planning, it was said, produces 'more effective and creative solutions' than traditional planning owing to its concentration on understanding the interactions in ecosystems, its long-term view of change, its focus on diversity, heritage, environmental capacity, and flexibility, and its inclusionary mode of decision making (77–81). Founded on the notion that 'everything is connected to everything else' (Royal Commission on the Future of the Toronto Waterfront 1990: 17), the ecosystem approach recognized connections between human activity and the natural world and the various impacts of environmental health and degradation on economic and social activity. Only through a reconfiguration of waterfront planning and development from within the intersection of environment, economy, and community, the ecosystem approach proclaimed, could the vision be found to 'restore the health and usefulness of the waterfront' (83).

The approach quickly gained currency. It was described in the media as 'very heady stuff' (Valpy 1990), and 'the wave of the future' (Toronto Harbour Commissioners 1992: 4), a revolutionary 'greenprint' (J. Armstrong 1992) praised by environmentalists, academics, politicians, and pundits alike. The ecosystem approach was said to have become a requisite part of contemporary municipal planning efforts in Toronto (Suzuki 1992), to signal 'the emergence of an innovative approach to waterfront planning and policymaking' that 'placed urban waterfront planning in the novel context of environmental sustainability' (Goldrick and Merrens 1996: 219–20), and, indeed, is still hailed by some as an 'exemplary' example of environmental planning (Hodge 2003: 263; Hodge and Robinson 2001: 222–5).

Within ten years, however, a new approach to waterfront planning and development had gained ascendancy. In November 1999, the federal, provincial, and municipal governments announced an unprecedented cooperative plan to redevelop forty-six kilometres of Toronto's waterfront and, within one year, publicly committed to a $1.5 billion investment in infrastructure that would spark a 'virtuous cycle,' attracting billions in private investment from the companies and people fuelling key sectors of the global economy, thereby creating jobs and, ultimately, the tax revenues necessary to fund public services (City of Toronto 1999a: 7). To oversee this new vision, the three levels of government joined forces to create the TWRC, a nominally public body whose planning and implementation work is driven by its private-sector board, management team, and consultants. The TWRC's first plan for waterfront development, its *Development Plan and Business Strategy*, identified the same problems – and, indeed, proposed many of the same solutions – as the royal commission. However, the new vision it embodied was predominantly focused on the economic benefits of waterfront development. More importantly, however, it positioned waterfront development as a competitive necessity, in the context of twenty-first-century global economic restructuring, for the economies of Toronto, its surrounding urban region, and the country as a whole (Toronto Waterfront Revitalization Corporation 2002). For Toronto to compete globally, this new vision suggested, the waterfront must be developed in particular ways that accommodate the needs and desires of the global economy.

This chapter argues that the roots of the current global vision for the waterfront can be found in the royal commission's 'ecosystem approach' to waterfront development. Through the commission's work, an environmental approach to development was popularized that not only allowed a variety of actors working in concert to contain political and economic struggle by resolving long-standing institutional and political problems, but also gave rise to a particular configuration of ideological and economic imperatives driving the revitalization of Toronto's central waterfront. As such, Toronto's waterfront is one of the crucial sites of a 'metabolic metropolitics' (Keil and Boudreau 2006) that has seen a significant neoliberalization of urban policy intertwined with the institutionalization of ecological concerns. Perhaps paradoxically, at the same time that urban entrepreneurialism and competitiveness took firm root in Toronto (Kipfer and Keil 2002), an increasingly environmentally focused politics has fundamentally shaped the city's political and policy terrain (Keil and Boudreau 2006; Desfor and Keil 2004). Indeed, as 'urban development processes have become increasingly associated with ecological concerns' (Desfor and Keil 2004, xii), a 'green consensus' was built in Toronto that saw the city's future as fundamentally dependent on an ecological/developmental nexus (Keil and Boudreau 2006).

Drawing from the literature connecting the politics of nature to urban development processes (see, for example, Swyngedouw et al. 2005; Desfor and Keil 2004; While et al. 2004; Keil and Graham 1998), this chapter explores the construction of this green consensus in Toronto from a historical perspective. I contend that waterfront planning activity in Toronto between the late 1980s and the early 2000s – the period in which both an intense neoliberalization of the city's urban policy (Kipfer and Keil 2002) and the 'ecosystem approach' to waterfront planning occurred – was a major contributor to achieving this consensus.

Moreover, I argue that the ecosystem approach was instrumental in resolving three historic problems that had hampered Toronto's ability to reconfigure its waterfront for the twenty-first century. As such, it may be the case that Toronto's green consensus, insofar as it relates to the politics of development, may have been achieved not as a result of Toronto's conservative elites leaving their 'environmental flank unprotected from a surging environmental activism' (Keil and Boudreau 2006: 41), but rather through their explicit incorporation of environmental concerns into a growth-oriented and spatially ordered prescription for the city. In many ways, therefore, the argument in this chapter is analogous to that of While et al. (2004), who propose that contemporary political economic and ecological crises are, in part and temporarily, resolved through a 'sustainability fix.' According to this proposal, the selective incorporation of environmental goals into the active remaking of urban areas has become a significant basis for urban entrepreneurialism and, thus, further processes of urbanization. In Toronto, the ecosystem approach was a highly effective strategy through which seemingly antagonistic ideological and material logics of global urban competition and environmentalism were reconciled, opening up the conceptual, political, and physical space necessary to allow for a post-industrial, globally focused spatial fix.

My research approach draws from media reports, City of Toronto council minutes, federal and provincial legislative debates, and a wide range of planning and policy documents from all four levels of government. I also examined reports of the royal commission, conducted interviews with some of the key players of the period, and reviewed scholarly literature about development politics in Toronto, environmental politics in Ontario, and waterfront development and Olympic Games research worldwide.

While 'urban development processes have become increasingly associated with ecological concerns' (Desfor and Keil 2004: xii), the literature critically examining the pitfalls of ecological modernization has demonstrated that such 'win-win' approaches to urban problems subsume environmental issues under neoliberalized concerns of 'efficiency, competitiveness, marketability, flexibility and development' (Keil and Desfor 2003: 1). The following narrative illustrates the microprocesses through which the royal commission, and its successor agencies the Waterfront Regeneration Trust (the Trust) and the TWRC, have acted as key agents of ecological modernization in Toronto, and highlights the ways in which recent locally focused political struggles and economic activities, embedded within an environmental approach to urban planning and development, have influenced the processes of urban change.

Waterfront Development Struggles in Context

By the late 1960s, with deindustrialization, industrial outmigration, and containerization on the rise, Toronto's central waterfront (see map A) became a 'terrain of availability' (Greenberg 1996) with only a remnant of its historic industrial and port-related functions. In the ensuing two decades, the waterfront was the site of a fractious debate over which institutions of government should have primary control over planning and development, which land uses should be allowed to dominate, and what degree and type of access the public should have to both waterfront lands and the water itself. The development politics of the period can thus be characterized as being deeply concerned with three primary issues: jurisdictional gridlock, industrial zoning, and the management of private versus public interests.

First, a patchwork quilt of government agencies, departments, and bodies with overlapping and sometimes conflicting mandates held a variety of jurisdictional claims to waterfront lands. The Toronto Harbour Commissioners (THC), a federal agency constituted in 1911 as an industrial development and port-minding body, claimed jurisdictional supremacy. However, a plethora of agencies, departments, and special-purpose bodies of all four levels of government (municipal, regional, provincial, and federal) held some measure of responsibility over waterfront-related issues. The tension around these competing responsibilities resulted in a state of 'jurisdictional gridlock' that was often blamed for continuing indecision, delays, and a lack of coherent development planning (Desfor 1993).

Second, despite industry's continuing decline, much of the waterfront remained exclusively zoned for industrial and port-related uses. The land-use policies of both the City of Toronto and the Metropolitan Toronto regional government staunchly supported the retention of industrial jobs and defended the role of industry in the city's economy. However, major mixed-use projects on parts of the waterfront demonstrated the growing economic potential of non-industrial uses. Vacant waterfront sites became increasingly seen as economic opportunities for the development industry, and the benefits of increasing tax revenues became increasingly difficult for local governments to ignore. In addition, a bid for the 1996 Olympic Games proposed opening up the eastern waterfront to sport and residential uses. While the bid ultimately failed, it added much to the debate over the appropriate use of waterfront lands. Moreover, public demand mounted for recreational access, and public dismay over the shape and form of mixed-use projects led to calls for firmer development guidelines, height and density restrictions, and more open space (Greenberg 1996).

Third, the public increasingly expressed concern about what could be characterized as the privatization of the waterfront. Publicly held lands on the western waterfront were being privately developed for what were seen as 'mainly luxury' condominium units and retail uses (Crook 1983: 6). The seeming exclusivity of these developments ran directly counter to the widely acknowledged need for affordable housing in the city, and to calls for increased public waterfront access. Private residential developments on waterfront land contributed to the sense that private profit-taking was being privileged over the public interest.[3] As the first interim report of the royal commission stated, the public expressed considerable 'dismay and anger' that 'at the moment their waterfront was reappearing, it was being lost again. That instead of being joined to it, they were being further separated from it. That instead of being opened up, the waterfront was being walled off' (Royal Commission on the Future of the Toronto Waterfront 1989b: 9–10). The disjuncture between the public's interest in waterfront accessibility and affordability and the condoning of high-cost private development by the THC and the City was a matter of intense public debate. Other levels of the Canadian state were also making a shift towards market-based governance and a neoliberalization of public policy. Driven by fiscal concerns, provincial policy increasingly positioned publicly owned waterfront lands as an economic rather than environmental or recreational resource (Ontario 1996a). Federally, the 1984 election saw the Progressive Conservative party win the largest parliamentary majority in Canadian history, indicating a significant shift towards privatization, program rationalization, and less government intervention in the economy (Savoie 1994: 89). Indeed, that government's 1987 report on federal lands was critical of agencies such as the THC, concluding that 'the federal government's legitimate constitutional responsibilities did not include being in the "land business"' (Desfor 1993: 174; McLaughlin 1987). By the mid-1980s, Toronto's waterfront had become a territorial, economic, and political battleground. Action was required to resolve jurisdictional problems, competing land-use visions, and concerns about waterfront privatization, and to quell the chorus of widespread and increasingly vocal public discontent.

The Royal Commission: A Mandate for Change

In 1988, the federal government responded by creating the royal commission, giving it a broad mandate to 'inquire into and to make recommendations regarding the future of the Toronto Waterfront' (Royal Commission on the Future of the Toronto Waterfront 1989b: v). Former Toronto mayor David Crombie, whose involvement in Toronto's civic reform movement of the late 1960s and early 1970s had given him a reputation as an advocate for 'reasonable' development, was appointed sole commissioner. The commission's mandate indicated that jurisdictional and land-use issues would be major areas of consideration, and that creating agreement around waterfront development was a primary goal. And while the mandate of the commission did not explicitly include examining the role of private interests in waterfront development, Crombie declared early on that resolution of waterfront problems hinged on 'the willingness of public authorities and private interests to recognize the needs of others and the value of concerted action' (Toronto Harbour Commissioners 1989: 2). An environmental focus was also written into the commission's mandate and, while not initially central, the environment would rapidly become key to its work.

The Ecosystem Approach: Creating an Environment for Development

The first year of the commission's mandate was largely devoted to addressing jurisdictional infighting; however, its hearings on these issues were dominated by environmental concerns: 'almost everyone urged the Commission to spend more time on environmental matters and to view the Commission's mandate through the prism of environmental responsibility' (Royal Commission on the Future of the Toronto Waterfront 1989b: 12). Indeed, a 1989 poll showed that the environment was Canadians' top concern (Adams and Neuman 2006). Although essentially a footnote, the commission's 1989 *Interim Report* recommended the creation of a 'green strategy' for the entire watershed in order to protect the environment while promoting development (Royal Commission on the Future of the Toronto Waterfront 1989b: 195; see Goldrick and Merrens 1996). One short year later, however, the environment had become the dominant theme and experts in many environmental fields had been contracted as advisers to the commission. By the time of the commission's second report in 1990, the initially peripheral 'green strategy' had become the foundational paradigm for the commission, which it called an 'ecosystem approach' to waterfront planning.

The commission's ecosystem approach focused on appreciating 'links and relationships' and preserving 'the integrity, quality, productivity, dignity, and well-being of the ecosystem,' emphasizing the notion that 'everything is connected to everything else' (Barrett 1991: 37; Royal Commission on the Future of the Toronto Waterfront 1990: 17). Cities, it proposed, should be understood as natural ecosystems within which environmental, economic, and community concerns are interrelated and mutually constitutive. Waterfront-related studies and plans, therefore, should 'be undertaken in an integrated way, examining the links among economic, social, and environmental matters' (Royal Commission on the Future of the Toronto Waterfront 1992: 34).

It is significant that the commission's adoption of the ecosystem approach occurred during a period of intense public interest in environmental issues. This period has been characterized as a second 'green wave' in Canada that peaked in 1989 and saw both an increase in public stewardship activity and an intense level of public pressure directed at governments, which in response enacted a variety of new policy directions and strengthened environmental legislation, programs, and enforcement (McKenzie 2002; Krajnc 2000; Hartmann 1999). The commission's emphasis on environmentalism can be seen as a similar response. The ecosystem approach was a strategy that as much responded to public sentiment as led it, serving to generate support for waterfront development among a broad constituency – including environmentalists, a group traditionally opposed to the imperatives and consequences of growth. Key to the approach was the notion that 'a good quality of life and economic development cannot be sustained in an ecologically deteriorating environment' (Royal Commission on the Future of the Toronto Waterfront 1990: 156). The health of the environment was positioned as a functional prerequisite to economic growth, and environmental regeneration became a primary rationale for waterfront development.

As McKenzie shows, the second wave of environmentalism took a conciliatory approach to capital, actively pursuing concepts such as 'market-based incentive, demand side management, technological optimism, non-adversarial dialogue, and regulatory flexibility' (2002: 65). As such, the environment/development nexus of the ecosystem approach dovetailed well with prevailing sentiments. The ecosystem approach was thus able to address much more than the environmental concerns implied by its name. Harvey notes that 'the contemporary battleground over words like "nature" and "environment" is a leading edge of political conflict' because these words 'convey a commonality and universality of concern that can all too easily be captured by particularist politics' (1996b: 118). In this case, however, the universality of the ecosystem approach helped to quell political conflict, giving all concerned an acceptable and defensible foundation upon which to pursue their various interests. Indeed, a large part of the commission's success lay in the ability of both the term and the approach to encompass a range of meanings. And under the aegis of the ecosystem approach, the commission took a number of steps which brought a measure of resolution to the three primary issues in the development politics of the period, which together were effectively preventing a politically acceptable, publicly supported, and coordinated plan for waterfront redevelopment.

Moving Towards Resolution: The Ecosystem Approach and Jurisdictional Gridlock

The commission's initial steps towards resolving gridlock lay in ending the THC's hold over waterfront development. As a consequence of the THC's inability to both fully develop the industrial potential of its lands and protect the lands from environmental degradation, the commission insisted that the agency's development powers be separated from its port-management role. Following heated battles (Desfor 1993), action was taken which restricted the THC's mandate to port-related functions, reduced the port itself from 486 hectares to approximately 40, and transferred the remaining land from the THC to an economic development corporation of the City of Toronto.

Second, the commission created a new model for decision making, one that would better accommodate the forms and processes of nature. The commission stated that an ecosystem approach required recognizing that 'ecological processes ... rarely conform to political boundaries, such as city limits' (Royal Commission on the Future of the Toronto Waterfront 1992: 41). Planning would thus have to be 'based on [much larger] natural geographic units – such as watersheds – rather than on political boundaries' (Royal Commission on the Future of the Toronto Waterfront 1990: 20). The ecosystem approach thus expanded the territorial purchase of Toronto's waterfront, increasing the scope and scale of the issues and jurisdictions involved and subsuming urban political boundaries under a larger geopolitical unit, the watershed. This green rescaling of the waterfront not only widened Crombie's own base of influence, but also focused the various political jurisdictions away from turf wars and onto both larger and, given the environmental tenor of the times, more politically expedient concerns.

The commission thus subsequently adopted a 'stakeholder roundtable' model, based on the broader conceptual territory of the ecosystem approach. The roundtable model was perhaps the commission's greatest strength, both in terms of addressing jurisdictional gridlock as well as in forging a new consensus around waterfront development. Indeed, the commission's work groups, committees, and public consultations brought together 'agencies, organizations, levels of government, and individuals – in some cases, those that had never worked with or even met each other before' (Royal Commission on the Future of the Toronto Waterfront 1992: 46) – from a wide range of fields and interests, both public and private. This broad inclusivity – coupled with the politically powerful environmentalism reflected in the ecosystem approach – assisted in galvanizing support for waterfront development from all levels of government as well as many other groups and sectors.

The Ecosystem Approach and Industrial Zoning

The convergence of economy and environment in the ecosystem approach facilitated consideration of a broad range of waterfront land uses, which were deemed necessary for achieving both economic and social sustainability. A variety of the commission's stakeholder roundtables explicitly challenged local industrial retention policies as constituting an inadequate use of the land's inherent value, and proposed opening up the waterfront to a variety of uses, most particularly the increasingly lucrative mixed-use model. Residential development on the waterfront was thus rationalized as a defence of the environment. The commission noted that suburbanization had resulted in a host of environmental and quality-of-life problems, such as increased smog and commuting times, fossil-fuel consumption, and the loss of natural areas and farmland. Increasing residential density on the waterfront was thus deemed vital to improving environmental quality in the entire region (Royal Commission on the Future of the Toronto Waterfront 1992: 320), and thus the ecosystem approach allowed waterfront development to be reconceived as a response to environmental problems.

Improving environmental well-being was also the justification for allowing and promoting new types of industrial activity on the waterfront. In defence of industrial employment and in response to the growth of new economic sectors, the commission saw the waterfront as a site for 'second-generation industry,' which it lauded as more flexible, globally competitive, and 'green' (Royal Commission on the Future of the Toronto Waterfront 1989b: 114; 1989c: 89). The commission urged that emerging industries 'geared to environmental protection and improvement' be encouraged to locate on the waterfront (115). Environmental degradation was perceived to hold the potential for economic benefit, allowing new industries 'to profit – quite literally – from past mistakes' (Royal Commission on the Future of the Toronto Waterfront 1990: 142).

The ecosystem approach also helped to undermine the exclusivity of industrial zoning by allowing for recreational opportunities and better public access. In doing so, the commission recommended the creation of a Waterfront Trail across the entire length of the waterfront which would not only provide further opportunities for water's-edge uses, but would also connect existing recreational and cultural facilities and green spaces (Reid et al. 1989). The trail was also, however, the main feature of a system of 'green infrastructure' that would act as a catalyst 'for urban redevelopment, prompting private investment in adjacent areas' (Royal Commission on the Future of the Toronto Waterfront 1992: 186). Thus, the trail was a multidimensional strategy which combined environmental concerns with the provision of recreational uses and private-sector involvement.

As a foundation for development, 'green infrastructure' also included remediation of the waterfront's soil and groundwater contamination and resolution of the flooding threat from the nearby Don River. These remnants of earlier modes of development, in which polluting land was an acceptable externality and channelizing the river created territorial certainty, were portrayed by the commission as direct impediments to new – and increasingly indispensable – land uses. Highlighting environmental problems was thus a crucial step in undermining industrial zoning, and so the term 'green infrastructure' came to mean not only a system of parks and open spaces, but also environmental remediation and a process of engineered 'renaturalization.'

The commission's recommendations for new land uses resulted in many legislative changes to the industrial zoning regime. The City of Toronto's Official Plan of 1992 opened a large section of the waterfront to residential and mixed-use development, parks, and public facilities. Industrial retention on the Port Industrial District was maintained, although 'new and relocating high employment industries' were permitted, as well as parks and recreational uses, habitat protection, retail uses, and a 'water's edge promenade' to increase 'the attractiveness' of the area 'to the public and to industry' (City of Toronto 1994: s. 14.35–40; 1992: s. 14.33–8).

The Private Sector and the Ecosystem Approach

The ecosystem approach allowed the commission to consolidate an acceptable role for the private sector in waterfront development in two ways. First, the need for 'green infrastructure' under prevailing conditions of public fiscal restraint necessitated finding 'new and innovative financing techniques' (Royal Commission on the Future of the Toronto Waterfront 1989c: 124), opening the door to private-sector investment. Second, the rescaling of the physical and conceptual territory of the waterfront – from waterfront lands to the entire bioregion, and from the political arena to 'the interactions among ecological, social, economic, and political systems within the bioregion' (Royal Commission on the Future of the Toronto Waterfront 1990: 46) – allowed the commission to accede to the increasingly common ideological position that the public sector was ineffective, inefficient, and incapable of resolving pressing issues. The involvement of the private sector, which would supply 'enterprise, initiative, and capability for investment and creativity' (Royal Commission on the Future of the Toronto Waterfront 1992: 309), was required.

The stakeholder roundtable model was also a major avenue through which private-sector interests were welcomed and privileged. Based on the egalitarian premise that 'all partners should be at the table when plans are being made for the waterfront' (Barrett 1991: 104), the model suffered from a democratic deficit in that – like many other development planning processes – it did not recognize, accommodate, or attempt to ameliorate differential power relations (see Flyvbjerg 2002; Neuman 2000; Yiftachel 1999; Friedmann 1998; Harvey 1996a; Checkoway 1994 for criticisms of such approaches).

A New Vehicle for Change: The Waterfront Regeneration Trust

As the commission's mandate ended in 1992, the provincial government created a new agency, the Waterfront Regeneration Trust (the Trust), to facilitate the commission's implementation strategy. Also headed by David Crombie, the Trust explicitly adopted the commission's ecosystem approach in all aspects of its work (Barrett 2000). While the Trust's activities during its seven-year public mandate[4] are too numerous to recount here in any detail, it is sufficient to highlight some aspects of its considerable influence over reshaping waterfront relations to address jurisdictional gridlock, industrial zoning, and public–private relations.

The Trust was constituted specifically as a coordinating body, and was given the ability to negotiate with other levels of government over waterfront-development planning and projects (Goldrick and Merrens 1996: 227; Ontario 1992). As such, it provided a specifically tailored institutional response to the problems standing in the way of waterfront development. Its continued use of the stakeholder roundtable model for decision making resulted in a number of jointly financed and managed development agreements between various waterfront municipalities and the provincial government, and between various combinations of community-based groups, corporations, organizations, and public agencies. This was particularly true in its facilitation of construction of the Waterfront Trail, which became a catalytic 'clothesline' on which development projects were hung, and a physical and political incentive around which governments, community members, businesses, and groups and organizations of a variety of descriptions could coalesce in support of a common, nominally 'green' goal. As such, the Trust acted in many ways as a new model for jurisdictional cooperation, pursuing a strategy of 'progressive incrementalism' to creatively accommodate and facilitate a spatial response to economic change.

The Trust also actively took steps to promote a wide variety of land uses for the waterfront and, through a succession of reports, workshops, consultations, and planning processes, consolidated the acceptability of ending industrial zoning. The Trust promoted residential, 'new industry' and parks and public-space uses as being necessary 'to achieve [a] vision of the waterfront of the future' (Waterfront Regeneration Trust 1995a: 74) that was strategically tinted a distinct shade of green. Dense residential developments were deemed necessary to alleviate urban sprawl. 'Green enterprises' were necessary to create supposedly nonpolluting jobs. Parks and recreational space would facilitate tourism, as well as improved environmental quality and habitat restoration. The waterfront of the future would be a place to 'live, work, and play' with economic development – now declared an environmental panacea – given priority.

Just as important were the new technological and regulatory solutions proposed by the Trust to resolve soil and groundwater contamination (see Lu and Desfor, this volume) and the flooding threat, allowing new land uses to be seen as both economically possible and politically acceptable. In sum, the Trust's work encouraged 'green' flexibility and entrepreneurialism, demonstrating that 'the goals of economic renewal, community well being and environmental health can be combined to promote redevelopment and job creation' (Waterfront Regeneration Trust 1995b: i). Before long, the dominance of industrial zoning on the waterfront came to an end, and a new era begin wherein the City of Toronto became an active promoter of more lucrative and competitively advantageous uses.

While the Trust continued to include the private sector in its planning processes and consultations, perhaps its most important contribution to transforming public–private relations on the waterfront came through a reconfiguration of these sectors' respective roles in infrastructure financing. Public-sector investment in 'green infrastructure' such as parks and habitat restoration could provide environmental benefits but, more important, was seen as strategic for encouraging private-sector investment in development. And with environmental contamination a limiting factor, the City's long-entrenched 'polluter pays' principle (Waterfront Regeneration Trust 1993: 59) was undermined through the strategic use of nature as a public economic good. Creating society's wealth in the past through industrial production had compromised nature's health, the Trust stated. But improving nature's health would be required to continue to create societal prosperity into the future. Since all of society would benefit, the Trust argued, it would only be 'fair' for investor liability and private capital's environmental externalities to be paid for by government (79).

Not only did the Trust emphasize the importance of providing private economic opportunities through public investment in environmental improvement, its work also revealed a growing concern with reconfiguring waterfront lands to meet the imperatives of the global economy. Reports called on governments to recognize the geographic consequences of global economic restructuring and to reconfigure the waterfront in ways that would allow it 'to play its constructive role in positioning the Toronto region for the 21st century' (Waterfront Regeneration Trust 1993: 5–6). Developing the waterfront became an instrument for participation in and the furtherance of the global imperative. Reconciling jurisdictional authority, reconfiguring land use, and realigning public–private relations increasingly became the means by which the waterfront would be made to both respond to and foster the global economy's reach.

Overall, the Waterfront Trust's mandate can be characterized as the period within which the imperatives of the economy, and particularly those of the global economy, eclipsed the environmentalism of the ecosystem approach (see Keil and Desfor 2003; Keil and Graham 1998). But constructing the green infrastructure necessary to facilitate development was prohibitively expensive, and the Waterfront Trail was proving insufficient to mobilize funding for a comprehensive transformation of the waterfront. Crombie and other principals of the Trust determined that a larger-scale project would be necessary. They made a conscious decision to 'go big' and launched another bid to host an Olympic Games.

Going Big: A Mega-Green Waterfront

Having learned from the Trust's ecosystem approach–based successes, the Trust began a series of one-on-one and small group discussions with a wide range of groups to identify and address their concerns, at least one year before news of the proposed bid for the 2008 Summer Olympics became public. This multi-sectoral, community-based strategy, which the 1996 bid eschewed, secured much-needed support from across a wide range of sectors. In addition, a set of 'Olympic Principles' – required by city council in return for its endorsement and financial support (City of Toronto 2000a) – promised a plethora of social benefits to various local communities and organizations.

By the late 1990s, political conditions across all scales of the Canadian state had shifted such that the focus on fiscal efficiency, program rationalization, and debt reduction was joined by a growing preoccupation with improving economic integration at the global scale (Macdonald 1997). Public-private partnerships had become the answer to supposed government inefficiency, the promotion of sectoral agglomeration was gaining steam, and cities were increasingly recognized as primary generators of new economic activity (Bradford 2003). The City of Toronto's

Economic Development Strategy, adopted in July 2000, insisted that, to successfully compete with other cities, Toronto should adopt such neo-liberal tools as 'innovative new financing instruments,' 'harnessing the power of public, private and voluntary sector partnerships,' and adopting 'new roles in economic development' such as 'entrepreneurship' and 'risk financing' (City of Toronto 2000e: 6, 20–1). Toronto was poised to be recognized as the province's and the nation's economic engine in the new global economy.

The promise of a 'world class' event like the Olympic Games was thus a draw for governments increasingly focusing their policies around global interurban competitiveness, and rescaled the issues to help resolve jurisdictional fragmentation. This mega-event strategy also became the consolidating moment for the mixed land-use plans that had already been made by the commission and the Trust. The bid would prove to be the last step in the long process of changing waterfront zoning regulations to allow for twenty-first-century economic uses.

In November 1999, Canadian prime minister Jean Chrétien, Ontario premier Mike Harris, and Toronto mayor Mel Lastman gathered on the waterfront to announce 'a grand, 10-year plan for massive redevelopment of the city's 46-kilometre waterfront' (Moloney and DeMara 1999). The plan recommended an integrated program of green infrastructure elements, including a 'greenway' along the entire waterfront, renaturalizing the mouth of the Don River, making the waterfront an 'area that nurtures wildlife, restores and creates natural habitats, and provides water that is clean and healthy' (City of Toronto 1999a: 5), as well as public amenities such as 'bandshells, a new aquarium, a new museum,' affordable housing, and a 'home for Toronto's ... leading-edge environmental industries' (17). Provision of these green infrastructural elements was portrayed as the catalyst of an economic renaissance, and the 'spectacular' places and spaces that would be built on the waterfront would 'create the synergies that will draw even more jobs and investment to Toronto' and 'add to Toronto's allure as a tourist destination' (3, 21). Toronto was exhorted to respond to the exigencies of the global economy, and a revitalized waterfront became the optimal location to engage the 'highly competitive world where entrepreneurs, skilled workers and innovative companies gravitate to cities that offer the best quality of life' (3).

While the waterfront development plan was perhaps disingenuously positioned not as foundational to the Olympic bid but rather as a distinct project 'big enough to embrace' an Olympic Games (City of Toronto 1999a: 3), the report made clear their interrelated political economy. The provision of green infrastructure held the potential to provide for the requirements of both the Olympic bid as well as future development. But since the International Olympic Committee's financing rules required longer-lasting, city-building expenditures to be financed by 'the public authorities or the private sector' (International Olympic Committee 2000), the massive costs of 'green infrastructure' would have to be met elsewhere. In a ground-breaking statement, the report pledged public-sector funds to create these new opportunities for land-based capital accumulation:

> Strategic public investment in cleaning up contaminated sites and improving public spaces, primes the pump and creates new opportunities for investment. It creates a 'virtuous cycle' in which new business generates more property taxes, more property taxes lead to better public facilities, better public facilities attract more investment and more investment creates more jobs. (City of Toronto 1999a: 7)

Not only did the public assumption of such investment allow the private sector to evade responsibility for the massive costs of remediation, it also transformed a Keynesian-based rationale for public-sector spending into support for 'trickle-down' economic and social policy.

The lines between TO-Bid, the private corporation which took over promotion of the Olympic bid from the Trust, and the three levels of government began to blur. TO-Bid recruited Robert Fung, a successful investment banker, corporate financier, mining company director, and long-time friend of the prime minister, to assist in creating both the Olympic and waterfront-development budgets. Simultaneously, Mayor Lastman announced that Fung had been appointed to head a 'citizen task force' (Moloney and DeMara 1999) that would report to council on project costs, timing, and 'opportunities for government and private sector involvement' (City of Toronto 1999b). The Fung task force was made up almost exclusively of private-sector businesspeople, many of whom were directly connected to the Olympic bid. Although it held no public consultations, the task force sought the advice of senior real estate and finance executives, corporate strategists, and urban design, engineering, and production consultants (Toronto Waterfront Revitalization Task Force 2000). In early 2000, the task force produced its report, which outlined a three-part 'strategic business plan' for waterfront development.

The task force's 'development concept' provided for all the new land uses that had gained popular approval through the ecosystem approach. The 'financial concept' called on governments to provide much of the $5.2 billion investment necessary to accommodate the project's infrastructural and environmental remediation needs. And the 'operational concept' provided a market-focused institutional remedy to the problem of jurisdiction, calling for the creation of a 'development corporation' that would 'operate in a business model' offering 'investors or partners a greatly simplified planning process' with an 'efficient and action-orientated' governance structure (Toronto Waterfront Revitalization Task Force 2000: 61). The task force report thus consolidated the work of the royal commission and the Waterfront Trust in a development model which incorporated the operational practices of the private sector, functioning in accord with the logic of capital.

The task force report was subsequently approved by council (City of Toronto 2000d) and, in October 2000, Chrétien, Harris, and Lastman converged once again on the waterfront to announce a joint investment of $1.5 billion in 'major infrastructure development; a thorough environmental clean-up of the area; and the creation of green spaces at key points along the waterfront' (Ontario 2000). The Olympic bid thus not only transformed government policy in favour of waterfront development, as the Trust had desired, it also forced governments to finance environmental remediation and infrastructure provision. This was one of the main focuses of the Olympic effort from the beginning, not only because of the longer-term benefits to development interests, but also, more strategically in the short term, because environmental initiatives were one of the International Olympic Committee's three Olympic 'pillars,' along with sport and culture.

The politics of the Olympic bid thus saw two mutually reinforcing, scaled strategies at play. The global event promised the potential for economic and political benefit for all levels of government, and government investment in the waterfront's local green infrastructure made the globally focused Olympic bid palatable for local politicians and residents. As such, a 'Green Olympics,' as the 2008 bid became known, was a forceful strategy to facilitate waterfront development. In Toronto, as in many other cities, the mega-event strategy both consolidated the growth coalition and operationalized its ambitions, permitting 'the powerful interests in cities to attach their agendas to the Olympic process, creating the perfect policy mechanism for ensuring a growth agenda' (Andranovich et al. 2001: 127). But in Toronto, this policy mechanism was decidedly green, an outgrowth of the royal commission's ecosystem approach to waterfront development.

The October 2000 announcement also committed governments to the task force's corporate development model. Council voted to support the creation of the TWRC, the vehicle through which public-sector financing could be taken off the books of the Olympic bid. At the same time, the Fung task force report was being 'translated' into the City's *Central Waterfront Secondary Plan* by many of the same planners, urban designers, and urban strategists who had consulted on the task force (Urban Strategies 2005: n.p.). Thus, the plan for the Olympics, which the task force was in effect intended to produce, also became the City's waterfront plan. The roles of the public and private sectors in planning for and developing the waterfront became deeply intertwined.

The Olympic bid and its waterfront plan was the vehicle through which Toronto could be repositioned on the global stage and thus become a 'world class' city. Policy and legislative documents resulting from the Olympic bid's work made explicit comparisons between Toronto and other international cities, such as London, Barcelona, Baltimore, and New York, which were said to be 'reaping the benefits' (Moloney and DeMara 1999) of their own waterfront development initiatives. While many of these cities have experienced negative social, environmental, and economic impacts resulting from these projects (Moulaert et al. 2003; Basset et al. 2002; Sandercock and Dovey 2002; Swyngedouw et al. 2002; Florio and Brownill 2000), the economic benefits to business, the catalytic 'sparking' of external investment, the improvement of urban aesthetics, the luring of well-heeled tourist dollars, and the construction of a cosmopolitan, vibrant, and urbane aura that were said to have arisen from their reconfigured waterfronts were lauded as models for Toronto. The answer to Toronto's long-standing waterfront problem was to build 'the greatest waterfront in the world' (City of Toronto 2000b) based on speculative investment in green infrastructure.

With the hyperbolic rhetoric at a fever pitch, in July 2001 the International Olympic Committee announced that Beijing, and not Toronto, would host the 2008 Olympics. Despite this loss and despite many ensuing hurdles, the vision for waterfront revitalization that arose from the Olympic bid continues to be pursued.

Conclusions: A New Waterfront Development Paradigm

This chapter illustrates one episode in the ongoing coupling of nature and society in the politics of urban development in Toronto. While I do not want to imply an instrumentalist correlation between the activities of the royal commission and the formation of the TWRC, this chapter highlights the significant notion that the variety of activities undertaken under particular local conditions and influenced by extra-local economic and political transitions are important in the construction of the urban landscape, and in particular the capitalist urban landscape. In so doing, this chapter demonstrates that 'what is happening along the urban waterfront is a reflection of changes in the city itself and, more importantly, of the changing political economy in which the city is located' (Desfor et al. 1989: 499).

The analysis presented in this chapter suggests two primary conclusions. First, while the environment/development conflation demonstrated in the 'ecosystem approach' promises to improve environmental conditions on the waterfront, it also promises to transform its frontier-like terrain of availability into a beachhead of possibility for large-scale capital investment. The 'ecosystem approach' to planning, a powerful paradigm in which a variety of conflicting groups, ideological positions, political imperatives, environmental concerns, and social values were reconciled, resolved a variety of historic problems that were impeding the progress of waterfront development. The wide-ranging consultations that both led to and followed from its adoption were instrumental in creating support for growth and significantly improved the conditions within which waterfront development could support the accumulation of capital, providing the political climate necessary for continued growth under changing macro-economic conditions. And while development was effectively stalled for many years pending completion of the work of the royal commission, its longer-term transformation of the legislative and conceptual context necessary for development provided the conditions within which a larger-scale transformation – currently being pursued by the TWRC – could become possible.

Second, the prevalence of extra-governmental bodies and processes in the reconfiguration of the legislative conditions under which large-scale, globally focused waterfront development could be undertaken in Toronto demonstrates not only the institutional flexibility accompanying the ecosystem approach, but also the increasingly secondary role that urban planning has played in encouraging waterfront change. Indeed, as is demonstrated in the TO-Bid/City planning exercise, the City of Toronto's planning function has largely become reactive rather than proactive, and largely responsive to the vagaries and desires of private interests.

Goldrick and Merrens note that, despite its 'bioregional rhetoric' (1996: 237), the royal commission did not, in fact, adequately address the promise of the ecosystem approach, but instead settled for a variety of institutional reforms that were unable to achieve its own stated goals. As the events of this period have demonstrated, however, the ecosystem approach and the method by which it was operationalized by the commission and successive bodies – that is, as a conceptual device and political tool – facilitated the formation of a new waterfront development paradigm that explicitly incorporated environmental concerns into its prescriptions for economic growth while restructuring the processes and power relations of waterfront planning in a manner that privileged private interests. As such, the ecosystem approach of the Royal Commission on the Future of the Toronto Waterfront can be understood as a very successful means through which the seemingly contradictory concerns embodied in waterfront development were made to conform, providing the political economic and discursive basis for a 'sustainability fix' necessary to facilitate further economic growth on new frontiers of urbanization.

NOTES

1 While other chapters in this volume use the name Waterfront Toronto, 'TWRC' will be used throughout this chapter to signify this corporation, as the name change occurred after the period described in this chapter.

2 A royal commission is the highest level of government inquiry at the federal level of the Canadian state. Recommendations made by a royal commission are not, however, binding on government. The shortened forms 'royal commission' or 'the commission' will be used throughout this chapter.

3 In this instance, the highly problematic term 'public interest' was defined in terms of accessibility to publicly owned lands that had long been unavailable for public use. And indeed, while private interests had long been involved in guiding public planning for the waterfront (Desfor 1993), it appeared that city hall increasingly favoured market imperatives.

4 The Waterfront Regeneration Trust acted as a public agency between 1992 and 1999 and was converted thereafter, through a privatization effort undertaken by the Mike Harris Conservative provincial government, into a non-profit, non-governmental agency.

9 From Harbour Commission to Port Authority: Institutionalizing the Federal Government's Role in Waterfront Development

CHRISTOPHER SANDERSON AND PIERRE FILION

For more than a century, Canada's federal government has been a key player in the development of Toronto's waterfront. The extent of its waterfront landholdings and its ability to establish organizations with legislated authority and financial resources have made the federal government particularly influential, but in complex and often enigmatic ways. This chapter explores the role of the federal government in the planning and development of Toronto's waterfront. Between 1911 and 1999, the federally incorporated Toronto Harbour Commission (THC) dominated port and harbour operations and waterfront land-development activities. However, 1999 saw the dismantling of this once-commanding corporation, and its resurrection in a new guise as the Toronto Port Authority (TPA). This transformation represents an institutional compromise between, on the one hand, intense objections both to the dominance of a federally constituted body on Toronto's waterfront and to its planning and development consequences, and, on the other hand, the federal government's commitment to maintaining a presence on the waterfront. In the current period of heightened interest in and concern over federal engagement in municipal issues, the chapter provides an overview of the practice of inter-jurisdictional planning as well as a caution to those who underestimate the impact of organizational structures on planning outcomes.

A central theme of this chapter is how transitions in urban spatial functions are mediated by actors, agencies, and governments operating at various scales. In the case of Toronto's waterfront, this transition was closely associated with the move from an industrial to a post-industrial economy. As in many other cities across North America, much of the urban waterfront's industrial function became redundant, opening possibilities for alternative uses. Our investigation of the politics of this transition recognizes the importance of nature–society relationships; as Harvey reminds us, 'socio-political arguments are not ecologically neutral' (Harvey 1996a: 182). But since ecological arguments are similarly not politically neutral (see Desfor et al., this volume), we focus on the conflicts arising from the differing agendas of these mediating bodies and their respective interests in the waterfront – and especially the unique role of the federal government in these conflicts.

This chapter draws on the work of an ongoing research project on the development of the Toronto waterfront. Documents covering decades of planning were supplemented by newspaper content analysis and seventeen in-depth interviews. Two thousand *Globe and Mail* and *Toronto Star* articles covering a forty-year period were consulted. While newspapers are obviously not free from bias, they are well suited to the reconstruction of historical events, such as the protracted waterfront planning and redevelopment process, that are marked by repeated debates and controversies. Interviews with members of Parliament, heads of development agencies and urban planners, which concentrated on policy making, intergovernmental relations, social forces, and policy evaluation, added to these sources of information. The chapter provides a narrative of selective interventions by the federal government as they relate to the transition from the THC to the TPA as well as the intersection of federal port policy with local planning. Outcomes of this process and lessons for federal–municipal relations are provided in a concluding discussion.

The case presented here concerns a federal corporation, the THC (1911–99), and the transition of this organization to the TPA (1999–present). The federal government has indeed played a special role in Toronto, adopting legislation that established both the THC and the TPA. Further, it created the Royal Commission on the Future of the Toronto Waterfront in 1988 to inquire into how conflicts among federal agencies and local planning authorities could be resolved (Royal Commission on the Future of the Toronto Waterfront 1992). As underscored by the commission, federal–municipal relations relating to the Port of Toronto and waterfront development have historically been enmeshed in tangles of conflict.

To understand the role of the federal government on Toronto's waterfront, we briefly introduce federal responsibilities as they relate both to Canadian cities in general and to the Port of Toronto more specifically. We then examine the activities of the THC along with many of the conflicts in which this organization was embroiled. The establishment and recommendations of a royal commission about the future of the THC are then considered, and we explain why they led to additional conflict. In the course of the tumult, a local federal member of Parliament surprised City of Toronto councillors by succeeding in having the Port of Toronto designated a port of national significance under the newly created Canada Marine Act. The justification for this legislation and its impact for ports such as Toronto's are considered, and the statements of supporters of a reconstituted port authority in Toronto are used to explain how and why the THC was dismantled.

A discussion of an organizational transformation of federal–urban relations concludes the chapter. Though the federal government does not have the same authority for making land-use decisions as provincial and municipal governments, it often holds the resources and authority to move projects forward. In the case of the THC and the transition to the TPA, we see a history of selective intervention on the part of the federal government which contributes to many of the organizational tensions between other organizations and levels of government. Federal intervention to create the TPA did not resolve outstanding land-use and planning considerations. Like several other critiques of federal intervention in urban affairs, we believe a more collaborative and coordinated planning mode would be of benefit.

Federal–Municipal Relations, the Toronto Harbour Commission, and Its Conflicts

Limited formal policy coordination exists between the federal government and cities, even though federal policy has an impact on virtually every aspect of urban life – for example, in the areas of housing, transportation, the environment, immigration, and infrastructure (Sutcliffe 2007; Bradford 2005; Courchene 2005; Donald 2005; Magnusson 2005; Tindal and Tindal 2004). Despite the range and importance of their spheres of intervention, in land use planning for example, municipalities are constitutionally mere creatures of the provinces. There is thus an absence of formal connection between the municipal and federal levels. Still, this does not prevent interactions between municipalities and the federal government. Significant public and academic attention has been paid over the last decade to these interrelations and the constitutional status of local governments, in what is referred to as the 'new deal' for cities (Sancton 2006). Started as a series of campaigns emphasizing the unique role of cities in a federal system, the 'new deal' for cities became a public and policy discussion which culminated in a federal program called the 'new deal for communities' (see Donald 2005 for a good synopsis). The cities of Vancouver, Calgary, Winnipeg, Toronto, and Montreal engaged in a campaign to bring attention to their special urban challenges. Other organizations have also engaged in the debate, including the Canada West Foundation, the Canadian Urban Institute, the Federation of Canadian Municipalities, and the TD Bank (ibid.). These perspectives encouraged a diversity of interpretations of municipal governance, including suggestions for redrawing constitutional responsibilities, increasing power and autonomy for large cities, coordinating federal–local relations, and allocating a greater proportion of tax revenues to urban areas in recognition of their special place in knowledge-based economies. However, by most accounts, there is 'little evidence of a coherent agenda' regarding federal interventions in urban affairs (Courchene 2005: 31), and federal activities are 'little informed by a place-sensitive perspective' (Bradford 2005: 13).

The Toronto Harbour Commission within a System of Canadian Ports

The federal government has jurisdiction over the regulation of Canada's navigable waterways and ports. Until the introduction of the Canada Marine Act in 1997, there was considerable diversity in the port management structures at work in Canada (Ircha 1999). Most of Canada's major ports operated under the mandate of the Canada Ports Corporation, and many of its regional ports were the responsibility of Transport Canada Public Harbours and Ports. The Harbour Commissions Act of 1965 regulated a small number of ports that were administered by harbour commissions, which provided a high level of financial and political autonomy to boards constituted of stakeholders nominated by the transport minister and municipal councils (Ircha 1993).

The THC was somewhat of an anomaly. It was one of only two harbour commissions not regulated through the Harbour Commissions Act, and it was given unique powers by the federal government, including the ability to raise funds, reclaim and develop real estate, and the right to expropriate (Canada 1911). Perhaps its most unusual feature was that, despite being a corporation of the federal government, a majority of the members of its board of directors were appointed by the City of Toronto.

The federal government's primary interest in the THC was focused on its port-related operations, and it paid little heed to the THC's selling of real estate assets to pull itself out of debt, though this increasingly brought the organization into conflict with City of Toronto councillors, planners, and citizens. In the words of a former THC chairperson:

> From the Feds this was seen as the Port of Toronto operation ... There was no interference. There was no dialogue, really. The only dialogue I ever had was attending a seminar or get-together of authorities from ports throughout Canada. Certainly, there was no pressure put on us. I had no separate meetings with any representative from the government or any request that I conduct myself in a certain manner. (Interview 2007c)

Conflict and the Toronto Harbour Commission

The THC and the City of Toronto and its citizens have a long and tumultuous history, as the THC's development role and its aggressive land-development program was a source of conflict. For example, Harbour Square, a hotel and high-end residential complex on THC land on the central waterfront, was criticized for creating a private enclave for the affluent that walled off public access to the waterfront (Greenberg 1996; Goldrick and Merrens 1990). The project provoked just one of the conflicts over land sales by the THC, whose decision-makers faced heavy criticism for insensitivity to emerging waterfront redevelopment concepts, aggressive land development proposals, incompatible land uses, and alleged impropriety. First, the THC's construction of the Outer Harbour Headlands (commonly known as the Leslie Street Spit) was highly contentious, as its lakefilling activities were taking place in a part of the lake over which it had no jurisdiction. In addition, the THC's dredging and land-reclamation activities on the spit aroused the ire of environmentalists, boaters, waterfront residents, and heritage associations (Hartmann 1999; Royal Commission on the Future of the Toronto Waterfront 1990).

Second, in the mid-1970s the THC was embroiled in many conflicts related to the Bold Concept, its major scheme for redevelopment of the central waterfront. The plan called for a major reorientation of waterfront functions, including filling in major portions of the Outer Harbour and the creation of a Harbour City neighbourhood for some 40,000 new residents. The plan also proposed moving the Toronto Island Airport (later renamed the Toronto City Centre Airport) east to the Leslie Street

Spit. Elements of the plan, such as Harbour City, were pursued by the provincial government and involved such figures as Jane Jacobs and Eberhard Zeidler in the design of the proposed community (Craig, Zeidler and Strong, Architects 1970). As discussed elsewhere, however, the plan to relocate the existing airport raised citizen opposition to proposed flight paths over the quickly gentrifying Beaches neighbourhood (Hodge 1972). The provincial government ultimately abandoned the proposed relocation of the airport, effectively blocking some of the more ambitious elements of the Bold Concept.

Third, the THC generated significant controversy as a result of its plans to expand the Toronto City Centre Airport at its existing location. A tripartite agreement signed in 1983 between Transport Canada, the THC, and the City of Toronto put limits on airport activity and expansion (for example, through noise restrictions and forbidding both the commercial use of jets and the construction of a fixed link across the western channel to the airport). Proposals that required an amendment to the agreement polarized opinion between strong supporters and strong opponents of the central waterfront airport (Royal Commission on the Future of the Toronto Waterfront 1989d). The Toronto Board of Trade underscored the value of the downtown airport's convenient service for business and government travellers to major US and Canadian destinations (J. Armstrong 1993b). However, many local residents and environmental groups objected to the air and noise pollution arising from the airport and its perceived incompatibility with the growing number of post-industrial uses on the waterfront, especially with the presence of nearby condominium developments (Community AIR 2007).

Fourth, by the late 1980s, the THC came under criticism for its development tactics. The THC's approach to land sales and development was to sell land on a piecemeal basis to cover its operating expenses. Following a series of real-estate deals, a former Toronto city planning commissioner concluded that the THC had become a serious impediment to coordinated redevelopment of the waterfront (McLaughlin 1987).

Fifth, the THC was challenged for alleged improprieties in the 1986 sale of Marine Terminal 27 at the foot of Yonge Street (Interview 2007b). In June of 1987, and in connection with the Marine Terminal 27 debacle, Toronto City Council sought to regain control of the THC's policy agenda by nominating councillors to the board rather than private citizens (see Desfor et al., this volume), citing the need for greater accountability and coordination of development strategies (Monsebraaten 1987). As a result, although city council rejected calls to impeach the sitting THC board of directors, their terms were not renewed and the City resolved to appoint only councillors from then on (ibid.).

These many concerns, from the expansion of the outer harbour headlands to aspects of the Bold Concept, to proposals for an airport expansion, all raised sustained criticism of the THC. In addition, the THC's piecemeal development strategy was also a concern to some City planning officials. Alleged impropriety at the THC brought attention to the organization's activities, and added fuel to these long-standing concerns.

The Royal Commission and Its Recommendations for the Toronto Harbour Commission

The federal government established a royal commission in 1988 to inquire into the future of Toronto's waterfront under the direction of a single commissioner, David Crombie, who had been a member of Parliament and former mayor of Toronto. The royal commission was mandated to explore possibilities for waterfront development and to build inter-jurisdictional consensus for its recommendations (Royal Commission on the Future of the Toronto Waterfront 1990: 3). Support for the royal commission was enhanced when the Province of Ontario used its land-use planning powers to declare a provincial interest and effectively froze development on the Toronto waterfront. A year after the initiation of the federal royal commission, the Province of Ontario appointed Crombie to also oversee its interests, making the Royal Commission on the Future of the Toronto Waterfront only the second dual federal-provincial commission convened in Canada's history (Royal Commission on the Future of the Toronto Waterfront 1992).

The future of the Port of Toronto was explicitly dealt with in a royal commission report entitled *Persistence and Change: Waterfront Issues and the Board of Toronto Harbour Commissioners*, which focused on the role of the Toronto port and the institutional mandate of the THC. The report found that although the THC had been established as a port-minding and industrial development corporation, many of its more recent land-development projects had little to do with the port's role as a transportation hub, but rather were more relevant to the city's emerging post-industrial economy (Royal Commission on the Future of the Toronto Waterfront 1989d: 47). These projects were especially problematic because of the complex relationship among multiple jurisdictions involved in waterfront matters and the consistent inability of the THC to negotiate adequately with these parties (ibid.: 50). In its first interim report, the royal commission criticized the THC's development approaches. It recommended that the THC be limited to its port, marine, and airport functions, and that its remaining land holdings be transferred to an agency of the City of Toronto (Royal Commission on the Future of the Toronto Waterfront 1989b).

The issue of the Toronto Island Airport was addressed in a report on the airport's future and the first *Interim Report* (Royal Commission on the Future of the Toronto Waterfront 1989b, 1989a). The royal commission looked at the airport's expected profitability and the community costs that would accrue were it to be closed. On the one hand, the commission wanted to avoid the cost and environmental consequences of an expanded airport, but on the other hand, it also wanted to keep the airport in operation because of its use by downtown business people. Its final recommendation was that the airport should remain, because closing it would create undue hardship for its users, operators, and surrounding commercial interests, but that it should be maintained at its existing scale, becoming cleaner and quieter and more sensitive to the needs of its users (Royal Commission on the Future of the Toronto Waterfront 1989c). The operating conditions imposed by the 1983 tripartite agreement were to remain unchanged.

Failed Development and Transitioning the THC

Although the royal commission promoted consensus building among major intergovernmental agencies on the waterfront, it nevertheless took the strong position in its recommendations that radical changes to the THC were required. After the publication of the commission's interim report, forging a consensus over these recommendations seemed unlikely. Much of the waterfront had been under consideration for redevelopment since the 1960s and the royal commission presented its recommendations for the Harbour Commission in 1989. But a consensus between the City of Toronto and the federal government over what to do with the THC, its port and industrial landholdings, and its management of the airport was still elusive by the mid-1990s. This state of affairs seems to support the finding of Gordon (1997b) that Toronto is distinguished among international waterfront redevelopments by its exceptional delays from project initiation to plan approval. We suggest that a complex pattern of relations between numerous factors was at play, including the following five:

Environmental Challenges: Many of the sites on the waterfront are badly polluted from industrial activities and, at the time, considerable uncertainty existed over the regulatory procedures and technologies necessary to clean up these sites, the liabilities associated with remediation, and the extent of accompanying costs and risks, making full-scale remediation prohibitively burdensome (see Lu and Desfor, this volume; Desfor and Keil 2004; De Sousa 2003). One major project called Ataratiri was abandoned by the provincial government when the expense associated with extensive soil remediation became known. Much of the THC's lands were similarly polluted.

Fiscal Collapse: The recession of the early 1990s and the effects of the Canada-US Free Trade Agreement hit Toronto especially hard. Many head offices located in Toronto were eliminated to avoid redundancy between US and Canadian markets. Toronto grew less in the early 1990s than most major US cities, and downtown commercial development suffered disproportionately (City of Toronto 2006; Ontario 1996b). Waterfront redevelopment projects were tied to volatile property markets, which suffered badly in the early 1990s as Toronto entered its worst property-market collapse since the Great Depression. Major post-industrial projects on waterfront lands owned by the province and the railway companies (and by extension the federal government in the case of Canadian National railway land) were abandoned. These same economic conditions similarly compromised the THC's pursuit of its post-industrial developments on sites across the Toronto waterfront.

Strength of Civic Politics: Toronto has not experienced the extent of urban regime politics witnessed in many US cities. An absence of business activism may be partially responsible for this state of affairs. Another possible factor is the shifting attitude of the City of Toronto towards development (Donald 2002; Lemon 1996). In the early 1990s, however, Toronto's inner-city oppositional politics coalesced around the conflict between reformers, a group of councillors who first appeared on council in the late 1960s, and a pro-development old guard (Magnusson 1983; Lorimer 1972; J. Sewell 1971). Though considered 'antidevelopment' by some, the reformers were not so much opposed to development as supportive of regulations favouring 'human scale' development and the quality of public space, and providing controls on height and design as well as the affordability of housing (Ley 1996; Caulfield 1994). Reform politics was diverse, bringing mainstream residents together with more radical elements.

Under these political circumstances, an enduring consensus regarding the future of the THC would have required an exceptional compromise that would satisfy multiple claims on renewed public spending and the space of the waterfront. Instead, Toronto politics became more oppositional at the end of the 1980s in reaction to federal housing and social welfare reforms, as well as to the City's market-oriented regeneration strategies at a time of a massive shortage of affordable housing. A major waterfront project, Harbourfront, was restructured following considerable controversy about profits from real estate development being used to fund cultural programs. The prospect of the 1996 Olympic Summer Games also faced stiff opposition. The 'Bread Not Circuses' campaign, citing a failure of many previous Olympic Games to deliver on promises of housing and employment, helped undermine the Olympic bid (Filion 2001). Under these political circumstances, it proved difficult to develop an enduring consensus over the future of the THC.

Diffusion of Political Power: Toronto has had exceptional delays in developing a consensus about, as well as in project implementation for, its waterfront, which must be understood, at least in part, as due to the diffusion of political power on Toronto City Council. Unlike in some American cities where development authorities were effectively controlled through the mayor's office (Gordon 1997b), or in the City of Vancouver where council elections are held at large (Friedmann 2005), the THC was subject to the political machinations of ward-based politics on Toronto City Council. As several of our interviewees explained, Toronto city councillors on the board of the THC took positions that contradicted the intention of the Toronto mayor and the majority of city councillors, impeding decision making regarding the THC.

One example of such a delay occurred during the City's consideration of a land-transfer and operating subsidy between the THC and the City-controlled Toronto Economic Development Corporation (TEDCO). The required level of subsidy to be paid to the THC by the City was in dispute, and a large minority on council protested that a higher subsidy should be paid (Tasse 2006). Councillors Walker, Ellis, and Adams were part of a minority on council that opposed the City proposal and, as the City's three appointees to the five-member board of the THC, refused to take direction from city council (J. Armstrong 1993a). After considerable delay, council removed the three councillors from the board and replaced them with City bureaucrats in an effort to restructure the organization.

While centralization of authority is not necessary for decision making or implementation, the protracted decision making surrounding the future of the THC must be understood in the context of diffuse power in city council. Council made the majority of appointments to the board of the THC, and should easily have been able to set its reforms for the organization. However, it proved difficult to achieve a consensus within a fractious and shifting city council regarding the future of the THC.

Selective Intervention of the Federal Government: The federal government has often been the wild card in Toronto waterfront-redevelopment efforts. Land-use planning is not a constitutional responsibility of the federal government, yet the federal government has become engaged in urban planning issues at different times (Leo 2006, 1996). It often uses arm's-length development agencies to pursue its own objectives, which may conflict with local land-use planning expectations. In the present case, however, the federal government's jurisdictional predilections were centred on port functions rather than on urban development, leading it to be more concerned about maintaining the THC's port operations than about the inappropriateness of the THC's post-industrial land development (Interview 2007c; Royal Commission on the Future of the Toronto Waterfront 1989d). But the royal commission had recommended that the THC's port operations and airport management be separated from its land development activities, which it had come to rely upon as a source of income. The federal government took no action.

Toronto council subsequently took matters into its own hands by imposing the royal commission's recommendations. With city councillors ousted and city staff appointed, the City used its majority on the board to force the THC to accept land and financial arrangements (J. Armstrong 1994). To make matters worse for the THC, when the federal government did act, it acted on its fiscal agenda, removing its subsidy to the airport ferry (as did the provincial government). This added to operational difficulties at the City Centre Airport and disrupted the financial expectations upon which the royal commission had based its recommendations for the future of the airport. The result of the federal government's selective intervention on the waterfront was continued uncertainty about the future of the THC.

Transitioning the THC

By the mid-1990s, both the City and the federal government were taking actions that made it appear likely that the THC would not continue
in its then current form. City council approved a series of motions, including one that directed its representatives on the THC board to cut
the THC's workforce in half, and requested that the federal government
give full control of the THC to the City. Council also proposed privatizing the Outer Harbour Marina, closing one of the marine terminals, and
transferring the THC's World Trade Centre office complex to the Metro
Toronto Board of Trade (J. Armstrong 1994).

At the federal level, the Progressive Conservative government accepted in principle the recommendations of the royal commission and
engaged in discussions about the land transfer with the City of Toronto.
However, agreement on all aspects of the royal commission's recommendations about the THC could not be reached before 1993, when the
government changed after a federal election (Tasse 2006). Meanwhile,
Toronto City Council continued to control the THC through the use of
its majority on the board of directors and limited its ability to pursue its
operations. Those supportive of the THC, such as Councillor Joy, spoke
of an intentional strategy to impoverish the THC and limit its operations (Canada 1997).

In 1995, the federal Liberal government introduced the National
Marine Policy, which appeared to resolve the organizational future of
the THC. The federal government began to divest itself of small ports
through the Federal Real Property Act and the Surplus Crown Assets
Act (Canada 1998b). At the same time, it was in deliberations on a new
Canada Marine Act that would convert Canadian ports of national significance (in terms of trade and financial self-sufficiency) into federal
port authorities. The management of all other ports was to be handed
over to local authorities (Canada 1998c). The Port of Toronto, however,
had previously been identified as being involved primarily in regional
trade (Booz et al. 1992; Royal Commission on the Future of the Toronto
Waterfront 1989d), owing in large part to the inability of the St Lawrence Seaway to accommodate the large containerized cargo ships tra-
versing international waters. Indeed, by 1990, less than 3 per cent of
ships transporting dry goods could negotiate the St Lawrence Seaway
(Booz et al. 1992: III-3). Similarly, the THC had a history of financial
problems, which were compounded by the loss of revenues from its

landholdings and airport subsidies (Canada 1996). The regional nature of trade and financial difficulties at the Port of Toronto appeared to make it an excellent candidate for divestiture to the City.

Establishing the Toronto Port Authority

The question of whether the Port of Toronto should become a federal port authority under the Canada Marine Act was extremely controversial, becoming a major issue for Toronto City Council. According to the submissions of some city councillors to a senate committee and reports in local newspapers, council believed that Toronto would not be added to the list of new port authorities (Canada 1997b; Vienneau and Moloney 1997) largely because the Toronto port was of regional rather than national significance. Yet on 14 April 1997, Dennis Mills, the member of Parliament for Broadview-Greenwood, stood in the House of Commons during second reading of the Canada Marine Act to propose the addition of the Port of Toronto to the list of nationally significant ports. This amendment was accepted by Parliament (Tasse 2006).

This surprising turn of events gave rise to a federal inquiry into the process by which this policy change took place, which can itself be interpreted in many ways. First, those opposing Toronto's inclusion perceived it as a federal ploy to raise the government's profile in Toronto in an election year, undermining the rational policy-making process intended under the Canada Marine Act (Barber 1997; Interview 2007d). Second, there is evidence that some of the actors involved in creating the TPA, such as Harold Peerenboom and Dennis Mills, had ambitions for more robust federal engagement on the Toronto waterfront. In particular, Peerenboom, a federal appointee to the THC, wanted the federal government to take back the lands transferred to TEDCO, and consolidate Harbourfront, the CN Tower, and the railway lands under a single development agency that would 'speak for all the citizens of this country, not just the citizens of Toronto' (Barber 1996). He believed that city council had strategized to 'rape and pillage the THC assets and treasury' (Canada 1998a) and that the creation of the TPA would force city council to negotiate a settlement allowing for the continued operation of the port authority.

For his part, Dennis Mills, a former vice-president of Magna International and then-Liberal member of Parliament, had made several unsolicited private and public proposals for the redevelopment of the waterfront at regular intervals over a twenty-year period (Spears 1994; Daw 1986). He voiced his support in the House of Commons for federal intervention on Toronto's waterfront and told news reporters that 'there is a strong view that the government of Canada must support [the Port of] Toronto in a more vigorous way and have a stronger presence' (Vienneau and Moloney 1997).

Others had different views. A federal official explains why the addition of the Port of Toronto had his support:

> There's no question that the Port Authority was done … for two reasons. One is what I would call … expanding the federal presence which was what Mills was more concerned about. I was concerned about that, but what drove it for me was that I would consider the public policy goal of using water transportation much more effectively. As I said earlier, this is Canada's largest city, and I thought it could make a go of things. So, I had no problem at all with what they wanted to do. (Interview 2007e)

But the Liberal caucus itself may have had other intentions. As Peerenboom explained to the senate, the Liberal caucus determined to include the TPA under the Canada Marine Act: 'I approached Members of Parliament, Dennis Mills and Tony Ianno, and I met with the Toronto caucus at the CN Tower. They demonstrated their leadership, and had the gumption to have Toronto designated a port authority, thereby reaffirming the Government of Canada's commitment to the renewal of the Toronto economy. That is how it got in' (Canada 1998a).

In creating the Toronto Port Authority, the federal government was assured that its appointees would hold an overwhelming majority on the board of directors. This change in accountability removed the prospect of Toronto City Council attempting to set the agenda for the TPA. It also allowed the board of the TPA to seek legal action against the City without deference to council, avoiding the conflict inherent in a city councillor or representative having to vote on a motion to launch such legal action. However, the hasty addition of the Port of Toronto to the list of nationally significant ports posed one significant problem: it simply did not fit the criteria.

According to the Canada Marine Act, port authorities can be incorporated if the minister of transport believes that the port '(a) is, and is likely to remain, financially self-sufficient; (b) is of strategic significance to Canada's trade; (c) is linked to a major rail line or a major highway infrastructure; and (d) has diversified traffic' (Canada 1998c). As part of the introduction of the Canada Marine Act, a review was conducted of ports across Canada to determine their appropriateness for inclusion under the act. The review concluded that the THC did not raise enough revenues to be considered self-sufficient, and relied on a subsidy from the City of Toronto that could be withdrawn if municipal priorities changed (Canada 1996). As discussed, the Port of Toronto had difficulty maintaining fiscal solvency and its operations appeared to be regional in scale. Its activity had remained far below levels reached in the 1960s and earlier, and the majority of its business centred around aggregate, cement, asphalt, and salt (Mariport Group 1999). Nevertheless, a federal official was able to explain how the port had failed the test and how the issue was dealt with and resolved:

> It wasn't included in the legislation because the BMO Nesbitt Burns study on Port viability done on each of the Harbour Commissions demonstrated that financially there wasn't a case for a viable port. Part of the problem had to do with the issue of the airport and its drain on the revenues. I think in terms of the port being the port, it did break even. Anyways, ... officials [were told], 'Listen, get someone, let's have another go at this. See if we get creative, see if when certain things are done, this could make a profit.' So they came back with a positive answer. (Interview 2007e)

On 8 June 1999, the minister of transport established the TPA, which replaced the THC and became a federal arm's-length agency. The TPA does not take direction from Transport Canada and the Financial Administration Act does not apply (Tasse 2006). The City of Toronto no longer appoints a majority of board members and no politician or civil servant can sit on the board. Instead, of the nine board members,[1] one is appointed by the provincial government, one by the City, one by the federal transport minister, and the remaining six by the transport minister in consultation with stakeholders from the port, airport, and recreational facilities under the mandate of the TPA (*Canada Gazette* 2008).

But the TPA did not become the agency that its proponents had envisioned; it is a minor actor on Toronto's waterfront. Its operations are restricted to overseeing the port, the Outer Harbour Marina, and the inner harbour as well as managing the City Centre Airport. Its ability to borrow is limited. It does not have powers of expropriation and its letters patently, rule out involvement in such projects as industrial parks or entertainment and casino facilities (Tasse 2006; *Canada Gazette* 2004,

1999). Nevertheless, as we will see, the contestation around its creation has become a source of lingering conflict.

Conflict and the New Toronto Port Authority

From the time of its establishment, the Toronto Port Authority was embroiled in a variety of intertwined conflicts with the City of Toronto. First, the TPA took legal action against the City, seeking compensation for the transfer of revenue-generating lands away from its predecessor, the THC. The TPA delivered a $1 billion lawsuit to the City in 2001. TPA officials claimed that the City had acted illegally by using its majority on the THC's board to transfer its lands to TEDCO, alleging that the directors had violated their sworn duty to represent the interests of the THC (Monsebraaten 2001).

Second, in order to improve access to the City Centre Airport and thereby increase flights and revenue, the TPA continued to pursue its proposal to build a bridge across the Western Gap. During the early 1990s recession, City Express, a major commuter airline at the island airport, declared bankruptcy, leading to much lower volumes at the airport (Sypher-Mueller International 2001). The creation of a bridge to the airport came to be seen as a way of renewing activity at the airport. This strategy, however, required an amendment to the 1983 tripartite agreement between the TPA, the City of Toronto, and the federal government, which forbade the construction of a fixed link (Canada 1983).

At the same time, the TPA accepted a proposal from Robert Deluce, a long-time airline executive, for a new regional airline at the airport. The proposal gained a great deal of support from Bombardier Corporation, its Toronto employees, and their union, the Canadian Auto Workers, as the new airline would use Toronto-built Bombardier turboprop planes. Plans for the airport also enjoyed the support of the council of the newly amalgamated City of Toronto, which was dominated by suburban representation.[2] Mayor Mel Lastman supported the bridge proposal, as had the old City's reformist mayor Barbara Hall. But what differentiated the two on this issue was that the amalgamated council was less encumbered by the need to be responsive to inner-city reformist politics and thus could be more forceful in its support of the bridge.

Though technically the resolution of the lawsuit, the bridge proposal, and the upstart airline company were separate issues, opponents of the airport perceived them as a concerted attempt to force an expanded airport on downtown residents, with the City left to foot the bill (Community AIR 2007). These issues, along with the federal government's imposition of the TPA on the city, conjured up a long history of conflicts over development issues, which detractors of the bridge skilfully used to attack the proposal. What is more, inner-city residents had been angered by the forced amalgamation of Metropolitan Toronto and the resulting dominance on council of pro-development and anti-tax suburban interests. Plans for the bridge became a flashpoint. Perhaps most important, areas adjacent to the airport had become thriving middle- and upper-income residential and commercial districts. The prospect of expanded airport traffic raised the ire of local residents, who were skilled at organizing and ultimately successful in building a broad coalition of an eclectic mix of interest groups, including environmentalists, academics, boaters, and artists. But a city council dominated by suburban interests was not convinced by the airport opponents' views. The City and the TPA settled the lawsuit and signed off on construction of the bridge. The federal government abided by the decision of council and ratified an amendment to the 1983 tripartite agreement permitting the construction of the bridge.

But controversy surrounding the bridge continued, and the airport became an issue in the 2003 municipal election. Toronto councillor David Miller differentiated himself from other mayoralty candidates by opposing the bridge and pledging to stop construction without cost to the City. The bridge became the foremost issue of the municipal campaign (Walkom 2003). Miller won the election and used his political legitimacy to pressure the federal government to reinstate the ban on a bridge to the airport. This strategy would allow the City to avoid assuming the liability towards the TPA and airline operators that it would have had if it had simply withdrawn its approval (Harding 2004). After negotiations, the federal government acquiesced and paid $35 million to the Port Authority (Lewington 2005; Safieddine and James 2005).

The controversy surrounding these events led the federal Conservative government to undertake a review of the Port Authority's operations. The report of this review, released in October 2006, found no fault with the process by which the TPA had been included in the Canada Marine Act and endorsed its continued operation, although it did suggest that the TPA take a more open and conciliatory approach to those affected by its actions (Tasse 2006). With regard to the issue of process, the report stated that the minister of transport must be satisfied that a port meets the criteria for inclusion in the Canada Marine Act. Since the minister had indeed approved the addition of the Port of Toronto to the list of nationally significant ports, and since parliament had endorsed this decision, the report considered the matter closed.

Making Sense of Organizational Transformation

Our discussion has situated the transformation of the THC into the TPA at the intersection of three dimensions: the transition from an industrial to a post-industrial urban economy, organizational conflict, and the important role played by influential individuals.

The move to post-industrialism, which is exemplified by the decline in shipping volume at the Port of Toronto, provides the background against which much of our narrative of the Toronto waterfront's institutional change unfolds. Of the different parts of cities, perhaps none felt post-industrial transition with as much intensity as waterfronts. A combination of technological change, in the form of containerization, and the spatial consequences of economic restructuring had a devastating impact on waterfronts, because these areas had historically been the locations of heavy industry. Waterfronts soon found it difficult to compete with suburban industrial locations and, as the post-industrial transition progressed, proved especially appealing to a growing share of the population seeking urban lifestyles rich in culture and entertainment. As other authors in this volume have mentioned, the waterfront opened up as a 'terrain of availability,' bringing opportunities for residential-, entertainment-, and tourism-oriented development (Greenberg 1996).What makes the case of the THC unique is its endurance and its commitment to its port and industrial functions despite significant financial impediments and political pressure for change (Desfor 1993).

Organizational conflict is the second dimension of the transformation. Our narrative has illustrated how interagency power relations are shaped in large part by organizational arrangements and constitutionally defined hierarchies. We have seen that the City of Toronto successfully used its majority on the THC's board to take possession of waterfront land. Later, the City invoked public opinion (and thus its electoral weight) to convince the federal government to cancel the bridge to the City Centre Airport and compensate the TPA. But the City of Toronto's positions on waterfront issues shifted, in contrast with the consistency of THC and TPA policies. This difference reflects the difference between the City's broad and diversified jurisdictions and sensitivity to political pressure, and the narrow responsibilities of both the

THC and TPA, as well as their absence of electoral accountability. The attitude of the City towards THC and TPA initiatives varied according to the changing dominance of either pro-development or reformist caucuses on council.

The federal and provincial governments are also sensitive to public opinion about the waterfront, but for them the political imperative to respond to such pressures is less than it is for the City of Toronto. Urban-land-use planning issues do not predominate among senior government responsibilities, and indeed are totally absent from federal jurisdiction. For these governments, the electoral impact of local mobilization is diluted by much larger constituencies than those of municipal governments. These circumstances explain the limited emphasis on land-use planning in the mandate of the THC and TPA and the episodic (some would say opportunistic) federal response to political pressures about the waterfront.

Another aspect of organizational conflict concerns the almost mystical power of the THC. Several of our interviewees emphasized that those appointed to the THC's board of directors would subsume the interests of the organizations from which they were appointed to those of the THC. We have noted several occasions when appointees to the THC became advocates for its operation even when this conflicted directly with their roles in other organizations. There was thus a powerful inner coherence to the THC, which explains its endurance and the ongoing pursuit of its organizational objectives in the face of intense pressure for change, which largely originated from the City. The THC endured despite increasing objections to its approach to redevelopment, not simply because it held a strong organizational imperative, but also because of the presence of factors impeding transition; as discussed, environmental challenges, fiscal crisis, strong civic politics, weak political leadership, and unpredictable federal intervention all help to explain how the THC could exist for so long.

With its limited finances, the TPA has more narrowly focused objectives than those of the THC. The likelihood for its board members to have conflicting loyalties is much less than that of the THC, as the large majority of appointments on the TPA board is made by the federal, rather than City, government. Nonetheless, unresolved conflict remains. As discussed above, the City Centre Airport continues to be an object of contention for Toronto City Council, waterfront residents, and anti-airport groups. But some of the broader concerns over land use no longer apply to the TPA, as much of the THC's land is now under the control of the City of Toronto and a new development agency, Waterfront Toronto.

If organizations have played a key role on the Toronto waterfront, so did certain influential individuals who have significantly altered the course of events (on relations between structures and individuals see W.H. Sewell 1992; Giddens 1984). By formulating new visions for the waterfront, coalescing opposition to prevailing approaches, and being instrumental in setting up new organizations, some individuals played a catalytic role in the evolution of the waterfront. Three such individuals stand out in our narrative. David Crombie contributed to the formulation and dissemination of an environmental and post-industrial vision of the waterfront that was in direct opposition to then prevailing land-use designations (see Laidley, this volume). The report of the royal commission he chaired made a powerful case for a restructuring of the THC and the transferring and reuse of its lands, which took place in the 1990s and 2000s. Another influential actor was David Miller, who focused his mayoralty campaign on objections to construction of the bridge to the City Centre Airport and who then persuaded the federal government to ratify the City of Toronto's decision and pay compensation to injured parties. Finally, there was Dennis Mills who, in defiance of the criteria set to define ports of national significance, lobbied for the inclusion of the Port of Toronto under the Canada Marine Act. He thus ensured the establishment of the TPA and, thereby, an enduring federal presence on the waterfront.

We conclude this discussion with a consideration of lessons for planning in a federal-urban context. The first and most obvious lesson is that despite the absence of formal federal responsibilities for land-use planning, federal–urban relations can have a major impact on urban planning and development. The THC had an anomalous position, as it was not included in reforms to Canada's port management system during the twentieth century. This arrangement was not addressed for many years, despite the THC's contentious activities. Even after a major inquiry into the future of the Toronto waterfront, the municipal and federal governments were unable to work out a mutually agreeable solution for the THC. While federal-municipal conflict is certainly nothing new, the endurance of this matter is truly remarkable and has had a major impact on the future of Toronto's waterfront.

Second, this case may serve as a warning to those who might attempt to modify organizational arrangements without due consideration of their impacts. A federal policy process for creating port authorities was introduced in the Canada Marine Act. But the imposition of a port authority that struggled to meet the conditions of the legislation resulted in an agency that needed to impose its development agenda to meet its financial obligations.

Third, a more collaborative and coherently planned approach to intergovernmental relations could be of benefit. This case is consistent with the observations of others regarding federal intervention in urban affairs throughout Canada and, specifically, Toronto's waterfront (Courchene 2005; Bradford 2005; Desfor et al. 1989). Namely, federal intervention in urban affairs is unpredictable, and in relation to the Toronto waterfront, the federal government has intervened selectively. These interventions have not always been in accord with local considerations, and have come without the kinds of planning and coordination necessary to drive proposals for urban development that are large scale, consistent with an overall vision of the waterfront, and respectful of public opinion. While the federal role is not considered the sole determinant of proposals presented here, the acceptance of a more collaborative mode of planning may have made a difference and may serve as an example for future interventions.

NOTES

1 In 2008, an internal dispute divided the board of directors of the TPA. The minister of transport subsequently modified the letters patent of the TPA, expanding the number of directors from seven to nine (*Canada Gazette* 2008). Other port authorities have seven directors.
2 The governing provincial Progressive Conservative Party amalgamated the Metro Toronto region into a mega-city effective 1 January 1998, which diluted local Toronto representation. Under amalgamation, the former central city now holds a minority of representatives on the new mega-city council.

10 Cleaning Up on the Waterfront: Development of Contaminated Sites

HON Q. LU[1] AND GENE DESFOR

In 1989, the Ontario Ministry of Environment[2] published its first guide-lines for cleaning up contaminated sites in the province. The publica-tion of these guidelines marked the provincial government's entrance into a new policy area with links to a web of complex socio-ecological development issues. Though the guidelines were aimed at regulating social practices, they had to contend not only with political and eco-nomic pressures from place entrepreneurs (Molotch 1976), but also with a range of poorly understood ecological relationships and incomplete evidence about how soil and groundwater contaminants affect hu-man and environmental health. Land developers, city planners, public health officials, and financial institutions and their lawyers all quickly realized that the province's 1989 *Guideline for the Decommissioning and Clean up of Sites in Ontario* was largely inadequate for resolving difficul-ties associated with interrelated ecological and societal relationships so prevalent in the cleaning up of contaminated urban sites. Critics of the policy claimed that the *Guideline* increased development costs by plac-ing 'unreasonable' and uncertain standards on clean-up procedures and imposing long delays on approval processes. Perhaps even more important, investors and lending institutions were alarmed by court decisions that signalled they could be liable for clean-up costs simply by participating in land-development project management.

The intensity of opposition and a crash in real estate markets made it clear to provincial officials that the government's clean-up policy needed to be overhauled. In July 1992, the ministry signalled that it was going to embark on a process that would create more flexibility in regulating clean-up practices. After only two years, an interim proposal was put into use. By 1996, the ministry had released the new *Guideline for Use at Contaminated Sites in Ontario.*

The 1989 guidelines focused on ensuring an 'environmentally accept-able' clean-up, but the 1996 version overlaid these environmental health issues with greater attention to clean-up costs, financial liabilities, and other economic considerations. The newer policy does not abandon ecological and human health in favour of growth and development. Rather, it re-articulates the link between the economy and the environ-ment and affirms a belief that win-win solutions emerge from integrat-ing economic growth with a restoration of ecological health (National Round Table on the Environment and the Economy 2003). The series of rapid changes to provincial clean-up policy began during an economic downturn and a precipitous fall in real estate values. But managing de-cline includes preparation for the next growth cycle. And these policy changes should be understood in the context of preparation for that next round of economic growth (Desfor and Keil 2004, 1999).

In this chapter, we seek to better understand the formation of new in-stitutional arrangements and regulatory roles that began as possibilities for a new wave of waterfront development started to become apparent. Planning for that new wave of development meant preparing to estab-lish a regulatory system with more clarity about site remediation and regulatory oversight practices. The localized structure of compliance that public- and private-sector actors eventually adopted – as discussed in the chapter – is situated within Ontario's overall framework for re-mediation of contaminated sites and overcomes jurisdictional overlaps, fragmented land ownership, financing barriers, a web of environmen-tal liability regimes, and uncoordinated design, planning, and envi-ronmental engineering approaches to redevelopment (De Sousa 2001, 2000).

We focus on the ways quasi-public government organizations forged collaborative relations and new institutional arrangements to deal with a shifting terrain of scientific knowledge of contamination and con-tested soil clean-up practices. As community, environmental, and other civil-society organizations increased their awareness of the health and ecological problems emanating from contaminated sites, governments have had to confront past corporate and unregulated land development practices that enabled such contamination to take place. Government's conventional role has been to promote and facilitate the cleaning up of contaminated sites by the private sector. In many cases it has sought to facilitate the emergence of win-win solutions by leveraging its financial resources, legal authority, and regulatory powers associated with de-velopment costs and environmental risks. Recent environmental policy and practices have tended to blur distinctions between the public and private realms as governance regimes incorporate greater influence from non-state actors. As we discuss, the case of Toronto Economic Development Corporation's (TEDCO) port lands illuminates the way a public-private partnership was established to deal with complex urban ecological problems arising from the cleaning up of contaminated sites.

TEDCO, a quasi-public urban development corporation, was established in 1986 as a wholly owned municipal company, but with a mandate to operate at arm's length from the City. TEDCO was intended to support job creation and economic development by facilitating the expansion, retention, and attraction of businesses, as well as assisting in the development and implementation of the City's economic development strategy (Woods Gordon 1994). It was an example of a state-sponsored urban development corporation established to enable cities to play a more interventionist and entrepreneurial role in planning economic growth. In addition, urban development corporations have tended to mediate influences of globalized market forces and increase community participation in economic growth (Harvey 1989a). TEDCO was founded to provide such entrepreneurial functions for the city and to operate within a web of local enterprises and international markets, financial institutions, labour markets, and capital flows.

The particular geographical focus of this chapter is Toronto's port lands, an area of approximately four hundred hectares, much of which came under TEDCO's management. The Toronto Harbour Commission (THC) had regulated port and harbour operations and owned and managed the port lands for much of the twentieth century. However, through a series of intricate and highly contested manoeuvres (the tangled and contentious process by which this happened is beyond the scope of this chapter; see Desfor 1993), a significant amount of the THC's management, development, and land holdings on the waterfront were transferred to TEDCO in the early 1990s (City of Toronto 1991). Two large properties were transferred to TEDCO in 1992, and subsequently it acquired two other large sites owned by Imperial Oil Limited following the decommissioning of its fuel terminals. Much of TEDCO's newly acquired land was severely contaminated from a long legacy of industrial activity and production practices that paid little attention to air, soil, and groundwater pollution.

As it acquired title to the waterfront lands, TEDCO sought to assemble a corporate capacity to deal with complex environmental planning processes required to return these lands to productive use. During the past two decades and in conjunction with other public- and private-sector organizations in Toronto, TEDCO worked to redefine a number of regulatory roles and establish new institutional arrangements for proceeding with the revitalization of its contaminated land holdings.

Before presenting TEDCO's initiative for a new regulatory procedure, we briefly discuss three topics that set the stage for understanding our case: (1) the condition of the soil and groundwater in the port lands; (2) the emergence of risk assessment and management as an array of social and scientific methods for dealing with the uncertainty of hazardous situations; and (3) Ontario's regulatory approach for cleaning up contaminated sites.

Soil and Groundwater Contamination in the Port Lands

Soil and groundwater contamination in the port lands has been documented in a systematic way since at least the early 1980s (TEDCO 1997; Munson 1990). This documentation was initially done by the Toronto Harbour Commission, as the principal landowner or property manager, and as clean-up processes were being contemplated as a condition for subsequent development projects. Although describing contaminant conditions in detail is well beyond the scope of this chapter, we summarize the types of contaminants currently known to be present on the port lands as an indication of the extent of the clean-up problem.

Contamination in the port lands originates primarily from three sources: industrial and storage activities, dumping of waste materials, and fill used in constructing the port lands. These contaminants are inclined to be concentrated at relatively shallow depths due to the high water table and tend to consist of one or more of the following:

– heavy metals (e.g., copper, lead, zinc, and arsenic) from coal storage, fuel additives, heavy manufacturing, and imported fill material from industrial sources;
– non-metal inorganic compounds from salt storage and usage;
– petroleum hydrocarbons from refining, fuel terminal operations, and onsite use and disposal of fuels and lubricants;
– volatile organic compounds from gasoline storage and usage, waste solvent recycling, and disposal and manufacturing activities; and
– semi-volatile polycyclic aromatic hydrocarbons associated with mid- to high-molecular-weight petroleum hydrocarbons and coal and coal by-products (TEDCO 2001).

As the contaminated condition of the soil and groundwater became better understood and as a new wave of waterfront development began to give rise to a demand for these port lands, governments at various levels were asked to determine the extent to which polluted sites were 'safe' for reuse. The public wanted more knowledge about health problems that could arise from exposure to contaminated soil and groundwater. Health officials wanted to know 'how clean is clean.' And developers and financiers wanted more certainty about the liabilities to which they would be exposed if they participated in development projects on such land. Risk assessment and management became a way to deal with these issues.

Risk Assessment and Management as an Emergent Public Discourse

By the 1980s, scholars were commenting on the pervasive risks that had become part of everyday life in advanced technological societies. Ulrich Beck's notion of a 'risk society' (1992) noted that people regardless of their social class were experiencing unprecedented risks brought on by the very industrial and technological innovations they pursued in order to create opportunities for new wealth accumulation. The disasters of Bhopal, Chernobyl, Love Canal, and Port Hope, radium contamination on McClure Crescent in Toronto, and more recently the spread of infectious diseases, are all environmental crises introduced by technological societies that have sought to define new relations with nature.

In response to this set of massive societal problems, a new discipline called risk assessment and management was unleashed as a way to officiate over decision-making processes that required consideration of a vast array of technological and environmental data and ecological relationships. Supporters of the new discipline indicated they wanted to supply decision-makers and the public with objective information obtained through scientific processes and expressed largely in quantitative form. Quantitative models were developed that simulated relationships among a set of variables and predicted statistical probabilities for various outcomes. Objective information from such modelling exercises would counter the 'irrationalities' of political decision making. Experts would then be able to identify an 'acceptable' exposure to risk and steps could be taken to achieve an outcome with that exposure level. The Ontario Ministry of the Environment refers to risk assessment as 'the technical, scientific assessment of the nature and magnitude of risk [that] uses a factual base to define the health effects of exposure of individuals or populations to hazardous contaminants and situations' (Ontario Ministry of the Environment 1996).

Within the last several decades, the discourse of risk assessment and management has come to dominate many policy-making processes. Investments in medical research, security plans, transportation facilities, emergency management systems, public health measures, financial planning, and food security are all immersed in the discourse of risk assessment. And the cleaning up of contaminated sites is no exception. At the centre of such methods is the estimation of liability, within a risk-managed regime, that would be associated with managing or discharging new development projects and lands uses. Defining and managing environmental liability required not only scientific or technological knowledge so that redevelopment could be completed at a lower cost, but also a discourse that advocated a public policy for urgently cleaning up contaminated sites.

Ontario's Regulatory Approach and the Guidelines

Ontario's regulatory system for cleaning up contaminated sites does not require strict adherence to federal or provincial remediation statutes or regulations. Rather the Ontario Ministry of the Environment (MOE) has set administrative practices or guidelines, which allows for flexibility and interpretation of the extent of clean-up programs in two principal ways. First, clean-up programs differ depending on the intended future land use of the site, whether or not the groundwater resource in the area is being used for potable water supply purposes, and the proponents' willingness and ability to retain contaminants on site that would be subject to the provisions of a risk management program.

Second, landowners and municipalities can decide for themselves 'how clean is clean' by choosing from three different types of clean-up criteria: background levels; generic criteria; or site-specific risk-based criteria. Regardless of the category chosen, the onus is on the proponent to demonstrate to the MOE that human and environmental health have been adequately protected and can be maintained at each site in perpetuity. From 1996 to 2001, the MOE set the maximum allowable levels on more than 117 specific chemicals that might be contained in the soil or infiltrate groundwater.

As the *Guideline* noted, environmental clean-ups other than full-scale remediation to meet background or generic levels are permitted, and these are to be based on site-specific risk assessment methods. Site-specific risk assessment generally involves four steps: first, identification and evaluation of the type of hazards in the contaminated soil and water; second, selection of 'contaminants of concern'; third, characterization of human and ecological 'receptors'; and fourth, identification of pathways by which the contaminants affect the receptors. Based on information collected in these steps, simulation models are formulated that estimate the risks associated with each specified land-use activity. Estimated risk levels are calculated assuming that development and land use considerations proceed without extensive excavation, limited onsite or offsite treatment, and disposal of contaminated soil into licensed landfill facilities. Landowners and regulatory authorities must agree on 'acceptable' levels of risk, and, based on these levels, management procedures are then formulated to make sure these levels are not exceeded.

Risk management may involve the use of 'control measures' that are intended to ensure that opportunities for exposure to contaminants, and thus risks, are reduced to acceptable levels (as determined by a landowner's risk tolerance) for the specific activities proposed for the site. These control measures may be engineered or administrative. Engineered controls include procedures such as capping contaminated soil with clean fill, and the partial removal of polluted soil or groundwater. Administrative controls include, for example, the registration of a document on the land ownership title that indicates existing conditions of the site, establishing an active site-monitoring program, and financial assurances that a program of mitigation will be maintained.

As part of the 1996 regulatory changes, Ontario's government delegated responsibility for overseeing the clean-up of contaminated sites to municipalities and the private sector, and relies on an interesting combination of 'defensible scientific knowledge' and market forces to clean up legacies from an earlier industrial era. Such an approach meant that the decentralized work of actually cleaning up the sites was left largely within private and local hands: the provincial government was not directly involved with cleaning up contaminated sites or their redevelopment, unless legal compliance or adverse impacts were identified by the general public or other institutions, and that rarely happened. Private or public landowners were to clean up their sites as integral aspects of development processes – the province seems to have taken this direction because it feared incurring liability if it were to be directly involved in the clean-up. Although the studies used to assess risks underwent peer review by private engineering companies and periodic audits are performed for quality assurance, there was very little oversight by the province during implementation. Consequently, successful clean-up relied heavily on the integrity of the private sector to deliver on its environmental commitments for the protection of public goods such as community health and ecological integrity.

In sum, the application of risk management procedures by the Ontario government to contaminated sites does not permit wholesale discharge of environmental liabilities, but it does expedite the development of contaminated sites at significantly lower costs and within a much shorter time frame than would otherwise be the case.

TEDCO's Initial Initiatives to Secure Agreement on Clean-up Procedures

Following the transfer of the THC's port lands in the early 1990s, TEDCO faced a major challenge in reaching an agreement with the Province and the City for comprehensively cleaning up contaminated sites. It required concurrence on ways to work through myriad highly contested and largely intractable socio-ecological problems, including an uncertain regulatory environment, ambiguous liability risks, limited 'defensible scientific knowledge' about soil and groundwater contaminants, and a largely indeterminate understanding of the effects of soil contaminants on public health. But the potential benefits of achieving such an agreement were substantial for TEDCO, the City, the MOE, and private-sector developers.

The City of Toronto began transferring waterfront properties from the Toronto Harbour Commission to TEDCO, and TEDCO initiated a series of due-diligence exercises, which included an array of extensive environmental site assessments. The assessments involved detailed property inspections and incorporated the findings of a number of environmental investigations and studies previously conducted by the THC and by current or former tenants. TEDCO carried out supplementary investigations on several problematic properties for which there was little or no information available, and it then estimated clean-up costs to meet the MOE's generic criteria for industrial or commercial activities (MOE 1996). A key component of each assessment was determining whether any lands posed a significant or immediate exposure concern to tenants, the general public, and the overall environment.

In 1992, TEDCO began its first site decommissioning at 75 Commissioners Street in the port lands. Its experiences during this exercise were important influences on further initiatives. TEDCO soon discovered extensive groundwater contamination on the site, but its groundwater recovery program was not effective because the specific sources of contamination could not be verified. Given the high water table (as the lands are so close to Lake Ontario), it was felt that a groundwater pumping program might draw more contaminants onto the site. At the same time, preparations were getting under way for the redevelopment of Shell Canada's site at 500 Commissioners Street. The relocation of Toronto Hydro's management and training offices, however, was also entangled in complications from trying to determine co-mingling responsibilities.

As the 1992 decommissioning exercises proceeded, TEDCO's staff was able to construct a model for estimating preliminary risk tolerances and liabilities with the information it was gathering. With information from this model, TEDCO's environmental managers and city and provincial officials quickly recognized that the then current regulatory framework was not effective in guiding real estate investment decisions. While TEDCO soon realized that a different approach to remediation was needed, provincial regulators needed to be convinced.

Conventional engineering solutions (e.g., digging and dumping or the removal of soil and groundwater) would not be effective for two main reasons. First, standard clean-up procedures, done on a site-by-site basis, did not take into consideration unusually complex contamination co-mingling that had no regard for property boundaries. Second, the migration and co-mingling of contaminants from various adjacent sites prevented measurement of the discrete point sources of these contaminants. Based on these difficulties, TEDCO realized that site-by-site clean-up procedures as contemplated in the extant MOE policy frameworks would not be effective – that is, effective from neither a health perspective nor a corporate standpoint.

TEDCO understood that it needed to redevelop the newly acquired lands under its management in a timely way to secure its corporate future. To do so, TEDCO decided to pursue two corporate strategies to deal more effectively with an uncertain regulatory environment. First, it decided to enlarge its organizational capacity and strengthen its co-alition-building opportunities, so that it might build working relationships with development corporations, community and environmental groups, and government agencies interested in the cleaning up of contaminated waterfront sites. With this enlarged organizational capacity and with the help of the Waterfront Regeneration Trust (a provincial body that emerged from the Royal Commission on the Future of the Toronto Waterfront with responsibilities for facilitating waterfront revitalization; see Laidley, this volume), TEDCO embarked on a series of initiatives to advise the major waterfront 'actors' on the changing regulatory environment and help them define and clarify their roles and responsibilities in clean-up processes.

Second, TEDCO, as the principal landowner on the waterfront, constructed a comprehensive archive of information on environmental conditions in the waterfront area and possible liabilities associated with those conditions. Armed with this database, it commissioned a comprehensive liability evaluation, which was necessary to estimate preliminary clean-up costs for planning purposes and negotiate private-sector real estate transactions. The port lands had been zoned primarily for industrial and commercial purposes, but developers (as well as the City and the Province) were interested in promoting land uses more in tune with an emerging urban lifestyle, and the extensive database was useful for analysing the financial implications of residential, parkland, and mixed-use developments.

Thus, TEDCO looked to seize the moment of an uncertain and confusing regulatory environment so that it would be in a better position to realize the financial potential of its waterfront lands and secure its institutional future by developing its underutilized and contaminated sites more quickly at lower cost, and avoid overburdening itself with resource-consuming liabilities.

The Environmental Management Strategy (EMS) for the Port Lands

By the end of 1992, TEDCO understood that to develop its port lands in a timely fashion it needed to establish a new and comprehensive regulatory arrangement – its Environmental Management Strategy (EMS). TEDCO decided, by the mid-1990s, to organize a number of preliminary discussions with the district office of the MOE to see if would be possible to agree on a new regulatory paradigm. A new land-management paradigm would take into consideration complexities in clean-up procedures stemming from a host of both historical and contemporary circumstances, including the history of landfilling that had begun in the early part of the twentieth century; the varied activities of former tenants; the effects of property subdivision and consolidation; the fragmented ownership of public and private lands; the characteristics of a contemporary urban economy; the scarcity of resources available for site clean-up; and the relative ease with which contaminants could move among sites due to the high groundwater level.

During its discussions with the MOE, TEDCO pointed to its considerable land holdings, the difficulties in cleaning up waterfront sites, and its mandate to pursue development strategies that were in accord with the public interest. In response to these arguments, the MOE agreed to consider developing a cooperative environmental planning and management program. It also agreed that TEDCO had an important public role to play in this program and recognized that both organizations shared similar mandates to maintain or enhance the public good (City of Toronto 1997b).

In 1996, following four years of investigations and intense negotiations, TEDCO was in a position to commit itself to undertake an area-wide soil and groundwater strategy (the EMS) in partnership with the MOE and City of Toronto. In light of preliminary agreements with the MOE, TEDCO thought it was appropriate to organize discussions involving a large number of parties interested in waterfront development. One of the key steps in organizing these discussions was the establishment of a steering committee of the EMS.

The steering committee played a critical role in the process of achieving a long-term agreement. The interjurisdictional committee, comprising representatives from TEDCO, the City of Toronto, the MOE, port area land owners (Imperial Oil, Shell Canada Ltd, Sunoco), and the financial community (Canadian Imperial Bank of Commerce), met on a regular basis to review current development activities and openly discuss various problems. The committee was a space for members to discuss substantive issues without adhering to their public- or private-sector affiliations, and where cross-sectoral support for a long-term agreement on the EMS was anchored. An example of an essential achievement reached in these discussions was a commitment to re-balance informational asymmetries around contaminated sites within the banking and financial-investment community. Such information sharing contributed to the establishment of stronger alliances and mutual trust among committee members, as well as the participation of private-sector financing in waterfront projects (National Roundtable on the Environment and the Economy 1997). Disparate actors, who had been wary of sharing information, found a space that allowed them to discuss common difficulties and identify mutual interests leading to pragmatic alliances for resolving previously intractable issues, such as cross-contamination of groundwater.

The Waterfront Regeneration Trust played an important role in the successes achieved by the steering committee. Trust representatives took on dual roles: they were both facilitators of discussions and an 'actor' or interested party. In its facilitator role, the Trust sought to build consensus among private-sector representatives and city and provincial politicians by seeking a common understanding of issues. And as an interested party, it sought to take advantage of its expertise with the regulatory complexities of soil and groundwater contamination and succeeded in securing a number of consulting contracts. Representatives of the Trust sought not only to facilitate discussions among the group of disparate representatives, but also to impart its knowledge to government officials – particularly representatives from city hall – in three main areas: first, the complexities of clean-up procedures; second, a need to have greater public knowledge of and debates on contamination issues; and third, the legitmacy of private-sector influence within a provincial environmental regulatory strategy. Through quiet but persistent efforts, the Trust gained support with city staff who, in turn, made it clear to city politicians that they needed to gain support from the provincial government. In particular, city politicians were convinced to lobby provincial representatives to allow the private sector greater influence on environmental regulatory procedures. They argued that the private sector (who were key investors in TEDCO's proposed development schemes) should be able to obtain regulatory forbearance, which would allow them to develop more flexible remediation programs based on risk-management approaches (Pukonnen 1998; City of Toronto 1997b).

These discussions produced agreements on many aspects of the EMS. TEDCO committed itself to undertake an area-wide clean-up strategy. The MOE concurred that an overall agreement for cleaning up contamined waterfront sites was required, and that such an agreement should include new regulatory principles, one of which focused on who should have authority as a regulator. In conventional governmental frameworks, public agencies tend to have sole regulatory authority. But, because of the complex circumstances involved with cleaning up waterfront sites and because TEDCO was a quasi-public corporation, the MOE was willing to consider allowing TEDCO to have three main regulatory responsibilities. First, it would regularly monitor and report on soil and groundwater conditions. Second, it would undertake appropriate follow-up studies to evaluate potential environmental concerns on its properties. And third, it would develop and implement remedial or mitigative programs for projects that negatively impacted human health and the environment (City of Toronto 1997b).

In recognition of these new responsibilities, the MOE would exercise forbearance in issuing Ministerial Orders to clean up TEDCO sites[3] (City of Toronto 1997b). TEDCO would *not* be required to implement remedial work orders on the sites it had acquired from the THC or as a condition of interim site development work. But the MOE did require TEDCO to put in place and maintain a comprehensive environmental management program, which considered emerging development projects. TEDCO also saw a need to facilitate redevelopment of its lands in an orderly manner and to develop and manage a framework to address regional groundwater contamination issues in a comprehensive yet cost-effective manner (City of Toronto 1997b).

Fundamental to this procedure was the MOE's agreement that the port lands (figure 10.1) would be regarded as *one* contiguous holding, rather than being dealt with on a site-by-site basis. This would provide flexibility and relief to the extant regulatory regime, which sought compliance at each individual site's boundaries. The MOE also agreed that soil and groundwater contamination on TEDCO's lands did not pose a significant or imminent concern to human health or the environment as long as proper management procedures remained in place (TEDCO 1997). It agreed to this assessment because it accepted the findings from TEDCO's environmental site evaluations, which were completed as part of the THC land-transfer process. Thus, an agreement was constructed which provided a way for proceeding with port lands clean-up projects that provides for new regulatory roles. The EMS was formally incorporated into a Memorandum of Understanding (MOU), thereby setting the stage for the devolution of regulatory roles to quasi-public local and private actors on the waterfront. And the MOU could be seen as a means by which the three signatories could gain access to assistance and knowledge in attempting to fulfil their own corporate objectives.

The MOU and Downloading of State Functions through the Formation of New Administrative Partnerships

In October 1997, TEDCO, the City of Toronto, and the Ontario Ministry of the Environment signed a Memorandum of Understanding that established an 'environmental road map for the assessment and restoration of soil and ground water conditions based on the specific biophysical conditions of the area and intended land use' (TEDCO 1997: 40). It is based on a new relationship between the province's regulator and the regulated, provides greater autonomy to city organizations, and redefines levels of regulatory certainty for all parties by clarifying

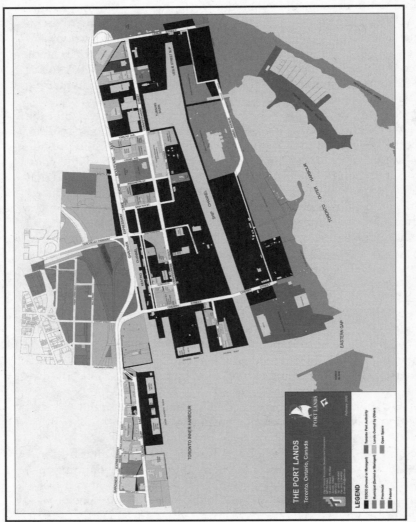

10.1 Toronto's Port Lands. Parcels in black define the lands considered to be one contiguous holding by the Ontario Ministry of Environment for cleaning up soil and groundwater contamination. (Courtesy of Toronto Port Lands Company)

approval processes and minimizing confusion about overlapping municipal and provincial regulatory jurisdictions.

The MOU has two main components: an area-wide monitoring program and an individual site compliance-management program. The area-wide monitoring program includes procedures for defining the way land management should be undertaken, sharing confidential environmental information among signatories to the MOU, regularly reviewing and discussing environmental activities in the port lands, and coordinating communications with the public. The site-specific compliance program stipulates how individual sites will be cleaned up in accord with risk assessment methods. According to the MOU, developers would no longer have to negotiate and navigate between two levels of government, but would deal directly with TEDCO in order to gain better facilitation through the environmental approvals process.

The purposes of the MOU are threefold. First, it meets the MOE's requirement that TEDCO have in place a soil and groundwater management strategy for its properties in the port lands. Second, it describes the basis for that strategy (e.g., clean-up may be managed at a scale larger than individual sites) and formalizes the roles and responsibilities of the three parties to the agreement (that is, a framework for the devolution of provincial and municipal responsibilities to a quasi-public corporation). And third, it provides a technical and policy basis from which site-specific agreements between TEDCO, the MOE, and a proponent of a development project may be established (City of Toronto 1997b).

The MOU was important for the corporate future of TEDCO because it permitted the corporation and its private-sector tenants (present and future) to formulate businesslike decision-making frameworks based on a risk management approach, with full disclosure of information-sharing transactions, and thereby allowing for risk transfer arrangements between consenting interested parties. A key aspect of the MOU was the removal of conventional provincial and municipal regulatory responsibilities, and this change was central to the social construction of a new terrain of institutional engagement on Toronto's waterfront.

The MOU embodies a move towards governance arrangements in which the roles of regulator and regulated are blurred, and in which place entrepreneurs have revamped regulatory, economic, and science-based practices with the aim of creating an avenue for attracting new capital. The devolution of regulatory authority to quasi-public corporations, such as TEDCO, institutionalizes a framework that gives priority to the more pragmatic realities of remediation and redevelopment with an overarching goal of encouraging new private-sector capital investment.

Central to the MOU are mechanisms that transfer environmental liability. These mechanisms are intended to provide public-sector indemnification to private interests for their past mistakes, and to modify fundamentally the 'polluter pays' principle. According to these mechanisms, liabilities associated with risks from soil or groundwater contaminants are transferred by indemnifying one party in exchange for regulatory immunity. This procedure requires the indemnified party to carefully fulfil its contractual obligations and the other party to grant forbearance. Here we see a shift of regulatory oversight from the government to quasi-private corporations. This process creatively restructures liability maps, and it may provide some breathing room from environmental compliance that could eventually lead both public and private organizations to achieve their interests.

The shifting terrain of regulatory oversight provides an opportunity for new institutional actors to emerge and renegotiate conventional regulatory roles. By moving such roles towards a more local and devolved structure of compliance, municipal and provincial institutions tend to become irrelevant and primarily helpful in maintaining the façade of a regulator.

Conclusions

In this chapter, we have sought to illuminate the ways a quasi-public corporation, public officials, and the private sector came together in the formation of new institutional arrangements for cleaning up Toronto's port lands. In the early 1990s, Toronto's real estate market was experiencing a serious decline, but plans for renewed growth were being put in place, and contaminated lands on the waterfront were a 'terrain of availability' (Greenberg 1996). But the 'rules of engagement' needed to be clarified, procedures for redevelopment expedited, risk liabilities controlled, and, of course, public health assured. New institutional arrangements for dealing with these socio-ecological issues were agreed upon when a Memorandum of Understanding was signed by the Ontario Ministry of the Environment, the City of Toronto, and TEDCO in October 1997.

From our analysis we draw four conclusions. First, new institutional arrangements emerged from highly contested processes for environmental regulation that provided flexible procedures for cleaning up waterfront sites. These new arrangements, or what might be called flexible urban governance (Desfor and Jørgensen 2004), expedited continued development of waterfront properties and secured the corporate interests of many of the involved parties, at least temporarily. The institutionalization of such a flexible urban governance regime reminds us of experiences in other urban centres. In those cases, an ensemble of individuals and organizations constructed networks of flexible relations that integrated a particular urban area with a broader regime of post-Fordist economic accumulation (Desfor and Jørgensen 2004; Lauria 1997; Swyngedouw 1997; Jessop 1995). In much the same way, the discussions and negotiations that took place among the various public-, private-, and quasi-public-sector actors prepared the ground for redevelopment that would enmesh Toronto's economy with globalization processes. Redevelopment of the waterfront was seen to benefit the City, the private sector, and the environment. Such benefits were said to include less sprawling spatial patterns of development, reduced transportation requirements, increased tax revenues, job creation, effective use of municipal infrastructure, opportunities for wealth accumulation, and an improved position for TEDCO's self-financing requirements.

Second, a quasi-public corporation was successful in championing a redefinition of environmental regulatory procedures, which contributed to redevelopment of contaminated waterfront properties. TEDCO had corporate feet in both the public and private sectors and a capacity for understanding both regulatory and market mechanisms, which were essential for dealing with the complexities of real estate development in central city areas.[4] The emergence of a quasi-public corporation may be helpful in resolving tensions in public-private development arrangements.

Third, the case examined in this chapter provides an important example of the devolution of public-sector regulatory authority to the private sector and the transference of risk liabilities from the private sector to the public sector. The Environmental Management Strategy for the port lands has operated for more than a decade in cleaning up contaminated sites on Toronto's waterfront. The rapidity of economic change brought on by global economic restructuring and its consequent deindustrialization of many urban centres, including Toronto, is closely associated with neoliberal governance structures, including altered public–private relationships and governmental regulatory responsibilities. Our case documents a take-over of traditional regulatory roles by the private sector.

Finally, the environmental history of industrialization on Toronto's waterfront and its production of contaminated landscapes (i.e., the port lands) have made it necessary for contemporary institutions to deal with legacies originating with private market mechanisms and past government policies. In this poorly conceptualized and inadequately regulated policy area, nature and society, as well as governance structures, are currently being reconstituted to respond to a desperate situation. The formation of the Environmental Management Strategy for the port lands constructed a framework for liability transfer from the private sector towards the public sector, marking a departure from state-led applications of regulation. In this remapping of policy, a polluter still pays, but has more options to control the process by which the scope and magnitude of their pollution impacts are estimated. With its array of sophisticated quantitative tools, environmental risk management has been accepted as a way to enable the shifting of liability responsibilities from the private to the public sphere. And in this complex and uncertain regulatory nexus, inter-jurisdictional partnerships have resolved the regulatory problems associated with a particularly intractable socio-ecological problem, the cleaning up of contaminated sites on the highly contested terrain of Toronto's waterfront.

NOTES

1 Hon Lu was Manager of Urban Environmental Services and Planning with TEDCO. Some of the information in this chapter stems from his first-hand knowledge.
2 The Ontario Ministry of the Environment was also known as the Ontario Ministry of the Environment and Energy during this period, but we use the shorter name throughout the chapter to avoid confusion.
3 Such discretionary forbearance is allowed under a director's authority within the context of the Ontario Environmental Protection Act (Ontario 1990).
4 We note with some irony that, despite TEDCO's apparent success in championing these new environmental regulatory arrangements, the City of Toronto restructured this quasi-public corporation, and as of 28 October 2008 it was reorganized into two separate corporations, Build Toronto and Invest Toronto. TEDCO will still continue to exist as a corporate entity, but has been reduced to being a land-leasing company (Toronto Port Lands Company).

11 Who's in Charge? Jurisdictional Gridlock and the Genesis of Waterfront Toronto

GABRIEL EIDELMAN

> One couldn't help but wonder, who's in charge? Is it the [Toronto Waterfront Revitalization Corporation], the landowners, the City, Province, nobody, everybody?
>
> Hume 2007: 24

The evolution of Toronto's waterfront is rooted in a history of jurisdictional disputes. When the Royal Commission on the Future of the Toronto Waterfront began its inquiry in 1988, upwards of one hundred departments, agencies, boards, and other special-purpose bodies, spanning all levels of government, reportedly held some jurisdiction over waterfront lands (Royal Commission on the Future of the Toronto Waterfront 1992: xxi). Although that number has since diminished, bureaucratic battles between the City, the Province, and the federal government have been considered the 'one insurmountable obstacle' impeding large-scale redevelopment along Toronto's shoreline (*The Economist* 2006: 50).

The formation of the Toronto Waterfront Revitalization Corporation (TWRC) in 2001 (since renamed Waterfront Toronto) – a joint federal, provincial, and municipal enterprise created to serve as the lead waterfront development agency – was intended, at least in part, to break through such jurisdictional gridlock by consolidating control over waterfront planning, coordination, and implementation under one roof.[1] Modelled on similar administrative entities established in various US and European cities over the past two decades, this 'small, efficient, action-oriented' urban development corporation was expected to integrate each level of government's diverse, and often conflicting, urban agendas into a single shared policy program (Toronto Waterfront Revitalization Task Force 2000: 4). While progress towards this goal remains nebulous, it is clear that the genesis of the TWRC as an institutional 'champion' of waterfront redevelopment signals the re-emergence of a corporate model of waterfront governance in Toronto, albeit in new form.

This chapter is an attempt to understand the evolution and ramifications of this governance experiment by examining the nature and extent of the political paralysis that still dominates Toronto's waterfront development. These jurisdictional hurdles, reinforced by decades of delay and disagreement, deserve our attention, in large part because they point to competing interests with different visions of society's relationships with nature that have both driven and thwarted processes of waterfront change. While this chapter is primarily an analysis of the political aspects of recent waterfront change, I am mindful that urban development, particularly at the waterfront, is very much an intermingling of socio-ecological processes, and even more so that all political projects are also environmental projects (Swyngedouw 2007). I am therefore motivated to ask three deceptively simple questions about waterfront development: Who is in charge? Why? And why does it matter?

I begin this chapter by mapping the jurisdictional landscape that precipitated the creation of the TWRC, and that continues to influence waterfront planning and policy processes today. I then proceed to explain the context in which this new governance model has emerged, drawing on various literatures in the fields of public policy and administration. Finally, I conclude by considering what this next phase in the history of waterfront governance in Toronto might entail with regard to notions of democratic responsiveness, public accountability, and political legitimacy.

Diagnosis: Gridlock

The final report of the Royal Commission on the Future of the Toronto Waterfront is a lengthy document, covering everything from ecosystem planning to the health of urban watersheds. Yet in summarizing the extent of the institutional inertia plaguing Toronto's waterfront, Commissioner David Crombie needed few words. According to Crombie, 'Jurisdictional gridlock throughout this region is the single biggest obstacle to its environmental (and economic) regeneration' (Royal Commission on the Future of the Toronto Waterfront 1992: xxii). Others, particularly in the media, have been less diplomatic in their assessments. Waterfront authorities of all stripes have consistently been chastised for engaging in a 'childish but dangerous game' (Pigg 1989: A17) characterized by 'political pettiness of the worst sort' (Hume 2005b: B3). As one editorial described it, the pattern is frustratingly simple: 'Queen's Park rages against Ottawa, which rails against the province, and Toronto is caught [somewhere] in the middle' (*Toronto Star* 2000).

On closer inspection, however, the political barriers stalling large-scale redevelopment along Toronto's shore are far more complicated, rooted, I believe, in three fundamental obstacles. The first pertains to the fact that public administration of the waterfront is shared across all three levels of government. On paper, jurisdictional responsibilities are relatively straightforward: federal powers pertain exclusively to port operations and shipping (seaports and airports), fisheries, Canada-US boundary issues, and aboriginal affairs; provincial responsibilities include regional transportation, natural resources, and housing; while land-use planning and local infrastructure fall under the purview of the City of Toronto. In practice, however, it is not always apparent where federal, provincial, or municipal jurisdiction begins or ends.

Indeed, to trace the patterns of government interaction is nothing less than 'a labyrinthine exercise' (Tunbridge 1988: 78). Responsibility for environmental matters, for example, such as environmental assessments and pollution regulation, are, to a greater or lesser extent, the joint responsibility of both the federal and provincial governments. The province also holds *de facto* veto power over land use thanks to its constitutional authority over municipal affairs. And housing and community development issues are rarely decided on without input from municipal governments.

Jurisdictional tensions also exist *within* each level of government, as administrative responsibility for waterfront development, and urban affairs more generally, seldom fall within the realm of one ministry or department. Nowhere is this more apparent than at the federal level, where the demise of the Ministry of State for Urban Affairs in the late 1970s fractured ministerial interest in urban redevelopment initiatives, leaving Toronto's waterfront to be punted between a host of departments and agencies. For example, before the City decided to bid for the 2008 Olympic Summer Games, responsibility for waterfront development rested with Public Works and Government Services Canada as the designated custodian of federal properties along Toronto's shoreline. As waterfront and Olympic planning intensified, however, federal leadership quickly shifted to the Privy Council Office, and even the Prime Minister's Office, owing to the political sensitivity of the file.

Since losing the Games, ministerial responsibility has followed Toronto's regional representative in cabinet, regardless of the respective portfolios. From 2001 to 2003, under Prime Minister Chrétien, responsibility rested with David Collenette, minister of transport. Under the Martin government, from 2003 to 2006, it moved to Joe Volpe, originally as minister of human resources and skills development, and later as minister of citizenship and immigration. After Prime Minister Harper's election victory in January 2006, the waterfront file landed on the desk of John Baird, first as president of the Treasury Board (and minister responsible for Ontario), and subsequently as minister of the environment. As I write this (April 2009), ministerial responsibility has shifted once again, resting with Jim Flaherty, minister of finance. With each move across departments comes a new waterfront secretariat and with it a highly unstable bureaucratic environment.

The second obstacle, paradoxically, is that a large proportion of waterfront land remains in public hands. Approximately 40 per cent of land in the East Bayfront area is publicly owned, a number that rises to 80 per cent in the Port Industrial District, and virtually 100 per cent in the West Don Lands (Toronto Waterfront Revitalization Task Force 2000: 17). But these assets are fragmented across a hodgepodge of public agencies, corporations, and authorities – some, such as the Canada Lands Company (federal), and even the Liquor Control Board of Ontario, that have little or no interest in the long-term development of Toronto's waterfront apart from the prospective benefits of increased land values.

As noted, the Crombie commission identified anywhere from forty-seven to over one hundred institutional actors with some claim to jurisdiction over waterfront lands.[2] Based on its recommendations, as well as controversial municipal restructuring efforts during the late 1990s, many of these organizations have either been consolidated or dissolved. In all, the number of organizational interests has at least been halved. Still, the jurisdictional landscape remains daunting. More than twenty federal, provincial, and municipal departments, agencies, and secretariats currently correspond with Waterfront Toronto on an almost daily basis (see figure 11.1).

Such institutional interdependence underpins the third major obstacle, namely, the rigidity of political institutions themselves. Once established, institutions tend to persist over time. The Toronto Harbour

GOVERNMENT OF CANADA

Department of Finance**
Environment Canada
Fisheries and Oceans Canada

Cdn. Environmental Assessment Agency
Toronto Port Authority (TPA)
Harbourfront Corporation

GOVERNMENT OF ONTARIO

Min. of Energy and Infrastructure**
Min. of Economic Development
Min. of Tourism
Min. of Environment
Min. of Training, Colleges, and Universities
Min. of Municipal Affairs and Housing

Ontario Realty Corporation
Ontario Power Generation (OPG)

Intergovernmental
Steering
Committee

WATERFRONT
TORONTO

Toronto and
Region Conservation
Authority (TRCA)

CITY OF TORONTO

Waterfront Secretariat
City Council

Toronto Economic Development Corp. (TEDCO)
Toronto Transit Commission (TTC)
Toronto Community Housing Corp. (TCHC)

**Denotes respective
waterfront secretariat

11.1 Federal, provincial, and municipal departments and agencies actively involved in waterfront planning and/or development, December 2008. (Diagram by author)

Commission, for instance, remained actively involved in waterfront development from its creation in 1911 until its eventual restructuring/reinvention as the Toronto Port Authority in 1999. As policymakers and interested groups coalesce around prevailing institutional frameworks, policy generally proceeds along increasingly irreversible paths. Pierson (2000), among others, refers to this phenomenon as path dependence, whereby the prospects of reversing course diminish as the administrative, financial, and political costs involved in switching increase over time. Only certain fateful events or 'critical junctures' have the potential to disrupt this self-reinforcing process.

In the Toronto case, the city's bid to host the 2008 Olympics is often singled out as just such a catalyst (see Laidley, this volume). The prospect of holding a high-profile international event along the city's shoreline is said to have injected all three levels of government with an unparalleled sense of urgency surrounding waterfront redevelopment, culminating in the establishment of the Toronto Waterfront Revitalization Corporation. This, however, is only part of the story. With the loss of the Games to Beijing, and with relatively little to show in terms of on-the-ground progress, it remains unclear whether a wholly new course has been taken. As will be discussed, the governance of Toronto's waterfront is, to a large degree, still plagued by institutional resistance to change.

In sum, the high degree of bureaucratic gridlock along Toronto's waterfront can be attributed to three interconnected factors: the legislative distribution of constitutional powers relating to waterfront resources (both land and water); the geographic distribution of land ownership among different levels of government (and their agencies); and the rigid institutional legacies that have historically defined political interaction between governmental units. Taken together, these elements have worked to create a political and bureaucratic climate historically averse to integrated decision making and coordinated waterfront planning. The Toronto Waterfront Revitalization Corporation was conceived as an institutional remedy for these administrative and jurisdictional hurdles.

Treatment: An Urban Development Corporation

Understanding the political context that precipitated the formation of the TWRC, and the new governance model it represents, is crucial when considering its longer-term implications, both for resolving gridlock as well as a host of other issues. This section therefore lays out the decisions and events, in some cases going back to the 1980s, that led to the TWRC's creation, including the circumstances in which these decisions were made, before reviewing its functions, composition, and powers.

The Concept

On 19 October 2000, with television cameras rolling, the City of Toronto, the Province of Ontario, and the Government of Canada committed $1.5 billion over a fifteen-year period to establish the Toronto Waterfront Revitalization Initiative. The funding package, to be evenly shared between the three levels of government for the purposes of infrastructure development and environmental remediation, was announced as a response to the final report of the Toronto Waterfront Revitalization Task Force. Headed by Robert Fung, a well-connected financier and investment banker, and supported by a self-described 'small team of business-focused individuals with a strong civic commitment' (Toronto Waterfront Revitalization Task Force 2000: 10), the task force was brought together by Prime Minister Chretien, Premier Harris, and Mayor Lastman in November 1999 to develop a strategic business plan for Toronto waterfront redevelopment compatible with the city's Olympic ambitions. The final report, released in March 2000, called for a $12 billion, twenty-five-year overhaul of the Lake Ontario shoreline.

The plan's 'operational concept,' laid out in just two of the report's seventy pages, outlined the organizational structure, objectives, and intergovernmental relationships deemed necessary to ensure the implementation of the task force's master vision. It called for waterfront authority to be consolidated within a single entity empowered with a clear mandate to oversee all planning and implementation procedures. As stated in the report, 'That entity must be a Corporation with its own legal persona,' a single-purpose development corporation that 'would act in a business-like way but possess key government powers for catalysing development,' such as the power to sell, lease, or mortgage land assets, and raise its own revenues (Toronto Waterfront Revitalization Task Force 2000: 61).

These arguments are reminiscent of those surrounding the establishment of the Toronto Harbour Commission (THC) in the early 1900s. Created in 1911, the THC operated as a corporate body with extensive powers 'to acquire, expropriate, hold, sell, lease and otherwise dispose of such real estate ... as it may be deemed necessary or desirable for the development, improvement, maintenance and protection of the harbour' (Canada 1911). But it is unlikely that Fung had the THC in mind. The THC's initial mandate, after all, was to transform Toronto's waterfront, largely via systematic lakefilling, into a major industrial port (see Desfor et al., this volume).

The task force's affinity for a corporate governance structure was, rather, chiefly inspired by the 'success' of more recent waterfront redevelopment projects undertaken in various international cities, including London, New York, Barcelona, Shanghai, and Sydney. In each case, the task force noted, waterfront authority was concentrated in the hands of an urban development corporation (UDC). UDCs are public agencies that possess extensive governmental authority, yet operate in a manner similar to private firms. Unlike the majority of public corporations, however, their purpose is to encourage private-sector real estate investment, not deliver public goods or services. Ideally, this is accomplished by consolidating land ownership and regulatory operations within a single corporate entity, which helps streamline bureaucratic processes and therefore entice private developers to invest in a designated urban area.

Former Ontario premier David Peterson had hinted that an umbrella organization akin to a UDC might be necessary to rationalize waterfront development back in the late 1980s (Walker 1987). But at the time, the royal commission rejected such proposals on the grounds that the 'issues are too complex, cut across too many boundaries, [and] involve too many scales and levels ... [to] be left in one pair or even in several sets of hands' (Royal Commission on the Future of the Toronto Waterfront 1992: 460). For Commissioner Crombie, coordination required more robust channels of communication among governmental partners, not centralization. The royal commission therefore recommended the creation of a coordinating agency as a mechanism to facilitate cooperation across the three levels of government.

Figure 11.2 presents the distinguishing features of a coordinating-agency-based and a UDC-based governance model in diagram form. In the conventional model of waterfront development, described here as 'independent government action,' each level of government pursues its own waterfront projects in isolation. The coordinating-agency model, by contrast, creates a forum for intergovernmental collaboration through which public and private partners can coordinate action. It operates as a power broker, an intermediary through which governments can integrate their priorities and implementation plans, albeit with no legal decision-making authority. The Waterfront Regeneration Trust is the closest Toronto has come to witnessing this governance model.[3]

The UDC model, on the other hand, sees governments either transfer or cede temporary control of public lands to the central development corporation. The corporation then coordinates, manages, and executes development projects according to a master plan agreed upon by its government shareholders. As an ideal type, the urban development corporation therefore offers a fully consolidated model of waterfront governance. In practice, however, such consolidation is rarely consistent. Experience in the United Kingdom, for example, reveals that no two UDCs are built alike (see Imrie and Thomas 1999). Each develops a unique range of formal (i.e., institutional) and informal linkages across social and political groups, and each pursues different policy objectives (e.g., land acquisition, economic development, social inclusiveness, etc.) subject to evolving local conditions. As will be discussed later, this generates important questions surrounding notions of democratic responsiveness, public accountability, and political legitimacy.

Two marquee projects referenced by the Fung report have come to exemplify the benefits and pitfalls of urban development corporations: London's Docklands and New York's Battery Park City. The London Docklands Development Corporation (LDDC), the first UDC in the United Kingdom, was established in 1981. The LDDC served as the flagship of Thatcherite urban policy, which privileged market-led economic growth over the perceived inefficiencies of local government, until its dissolution in 1998. Its primary objective was to stimulate private-sector investment in various 'underused' and 'derelict' lands in London's east side. And it did, producing 3500 hectares of redeveloped land, 40,000 housing units, and £14 billion of private-sector investment (Imrie and Thomas 1999: 25). But its sole emphasis on property development, not social welfare or democratic engagement, left the corporation's legacy (and that of the twelve other development corporations established across the UK during the 1980s and 1990s) shrouded in controversy. To its critics, the corporation not only undermined the legitimacy of local officials and community-based planning and broke down conventional accountability structures; it symbolized the neoliberal demolition of the welfare state (Brownill 1990).

In a similar vein, the Battery Park City Authority (BPCA) was created by the State of New York in 1969 to oversee the development of a thirty-seven-hectare site (roughly the same size as Toronto's West Don Lands) located at the southwestern tip of Manhattan, in New York City. Like the LDDC, the BPCA's primary mandate was to entice private-sector developers to the area by offering various tax abatement and advantageous lease arrangements. Unlike the Docklands project, however, Battery Park City was built on empty landfill excavated during the construction of the World Trade Center, meaning that the city could build new housing without displacing existing communities. But what was originally planned as a self-financing low- and middle-income community in the heart of downtown eventually evolved into what one observer describes as an 'overwhelmingly wealthy, white enclave in an otherwise diverse city' (Kohn 2004: 154). While such criticism may be overstated – a substantial portion of revenues generated by the BPCA have been funnelled into affordable housing projects in other New York

11.2 Diagram of three possible waterfront governance models. (Adapted from Mercer Consulting [2004], appendix D)

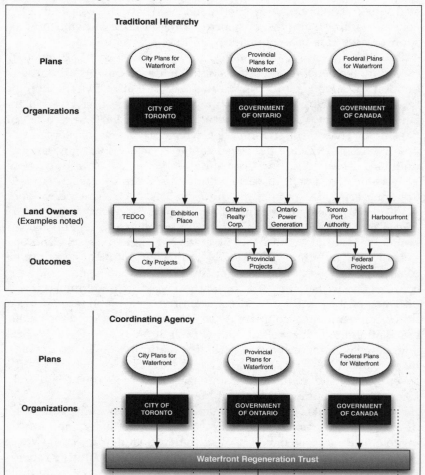

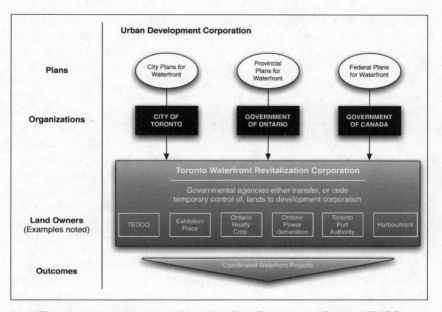

Note: Though I include the names of the Waterfront Regeneration Trust and TWRC to illustrate the application of each model to the Toronto context, in reality, neither agency fully attains these ideal forms. The Waterfront Regeneration Trust, for example, was not intended to coordinate all projects along the waterfront. Although the Trust served as an intermediary through which governments could integrate ecosystem planning into project plans, its primary objective was rather to encourage the development of a greenway along the north shore of Lake Ontario, known as the Waterfront Trail.

neighbourhoods, such as the Bronx and Harlem, largely at the request of community leaders representing those groups originally meant to move into the area – the BPCA's corporate structure generally discouraged public input and democratic engagement, particularly during the initial planning phases (Gordon 1997a; Fainstein 1994).

The lessons from these experiences were not thoroughly considered by the Fung task force. No comprehensive case studies were ever commissioned, as the task force had only several months to complete its report. Instead, recommendations were primarily based on the personal experiences of the report's authors, including but not limited to one of the group's key advisers, urban designer Tony Coombes, who was heavily involved in both London's Canary Wharf and New York's Battery Park City developments, among other international projects

(Coombes 2009). As a result, despite acknowledging Toronto's situation as 'distinct in a number of respects' (Toronto Waterfront Revitalization Task Force 2000: 16), the report never made clear exactly how these international experiences might be adapted to the Toronto context. Their successful 'translation' was taken as given.

The Context

How, then, might we explain why the UDC model gained so much traction among policy-makers? Some have pointed to the power of neoliberal political and economic forces as a structural explanation (Lehrer and Laidley 2008; Kipfer and Keil 2002). These authors draw a link between the centralization of waterfront authority within a single corporate entity and the strategic importance of the Toronto waterfront as a site for capital accumulation and economic growth. I do not deny the analytic power of this explanation, nor the economic pressures it details. Instead, I wish to highlight the influence of three related ideational and institutional shifts that developed in parallel with (and often as a result of) these structural forces, which have garnered substantial attention in the fields of political science, public policy, and public administration in recent years. I contend that these shifts helped create a decision-making environment particularly sympathetic to the UDC approach.

The first concerns a shift in policy style from government to governance – that is, from a traditional understanding of politics and policy making centred on political leaders, government agencies, and bureaucracies, to one that acknowledges the role of businesses, social groups, and citizens with whom governments relate and interact on a daily basis (Stren and Polese 2000). For a variety of reasons – whether because of fiscal challenges, democratic pressures, or otherwise – governments no longer maintain the same ability to independently carry out their policy programs without the help of non-governmental partners. Translated to the realm of urban policy, and urban waterfronts in particular, this notion of governance 'encompasses the view that local authorities today have to co-exist and collaborate with a much wider network of agencies and interest groups than in the past' (Bassett et al. 2002: 1757).

The TWRC as proposed in the Fung report reflects this outlook in that a defining element of its organizational mandate, eventually enshrined in legislation, was to encourage private-sector involvement in waterfront governance in the form of 'public-private partnerships' (Ontario 2002: sec. 3.1.3; Toronto Waterfront Revitalization Task Force 2000: 64). Indeed, the original $1.5 billion funding package (since adjusted to $1.8 billion based on land sales) announced by the three levels of government in 1999 is still considered by the corporation as merely the first instalment of an estimated $4.3 billion in public infrastructure improvements meant to attract another $13 billion of private-sector investment (Oliver Wyman–Delta Organization & Leadership 2007: 73).[4] Accordingly, the corporation has also consistently made clear its commitment to a stakeholder-based approach to waterfront decision making, whereby government, community, and private-sector 'partners' are expected to collaborate together in the design and implementation of waterfront initiatives (Waterfront Toronto 2007a; see Toronto Waterfront Revitalization Corporation 2005a: 3).

The second shift concerns the ascendancy of New Public Management (NPM) principles in the practice of public administration. New Public Management is a management philosophy that maintains that certain public services are provided most efficiently when government organizations operate in a more businesslike manner (Osborne and Gaebler 1992). Although in theory this approach allows public officials the flexibility to achieve policy objectives in more innovative and cost-effective ways, results on the ground have been mixed (see McLaughlin, Osborne, and Ferlie 2002). Nevertheless, the NPM paradigm is now broadly accepted as standard practice in many countries, including much of Europe and Australasia (OECD 1995; Kettl 2000). Here in Canada, its implementation has been less pronounced (Aucoin 1995). But the principles themselves have still 'profoundly altered' processes of public administration, including the flattening of traditional bureaucratic hierarchies as well as the encouragement of horizontal collaboration and creative risk taking among public servants (Young and Leuprecht 2004: 11).

The TWRC, and the UDC model more generally, is in many respects an institutional by-product of the NPM blueprint. Premised on the benefits of a streamlined bureaucracy, the TWRC was envisioned as an organizational mechanism designed to achieve its service-delivery goals according to a corporate logic of efficiency and competition. It relies heavily on outside consultants, utilizes performance-based operational guidelines, and pays considerable attention to issues of branding and strategic communications (see Waterfront Toronto 2008b). It is also subject to periodic 'value for money' audits (e.g., Oliver Wyman–Delta Organization & Leadership 2007; Mercer Delta Consulting 2004)

– standard practice in the corporate world. In many respects, these managerial features are not unique to the TWRC. As mentioned, the Toronto Harbour Commission was originally designed with similar organizational features, as are hundreds of public corporations currently operating across Canada. Yet few of these entities were established with the specific aim, as the NPM paradigm encourages, of leveraging public assets and/or public funds from multiple levels of government through a corporate mechanism in order to stimulate private service delivery – in this case, real estate development.

The third shift concerns the evolution of multilevel governance processes. As a federal state, Canada has a long history of multilevel arrangements among governments. But the contemporary concept of multilevel governance as discussed in the public policy literature goes beyond traditional federal–provincial relations. Initially developed in the context of European integration, multilevel governance refers to the emerging reality that political power has become increasingly fragmented across different scales, or levels, of jurisdictional control (Hooghe and Marks 2003). In the Canadian context, this is most apparent in terms of the gradual inclusion of municipalities, long regarded as constitutional 'creatures' of the provinces, in many areas of policy making (Andrew et al. 2003). It is also observable in the institutional mechanisms through which governments now engage in policy making. For as policy problems grow more complex, traditional mechanisms for intergovernmental coordination (i.e., top-down, hierarchical relations) have given way to more collaborative approaches based on negotiation and shared responsibility and, more important, an awareness that different scales of policy engagement are needed to generate locally appropriate policy outcomes – what Canadian scholars have referred to as 'place-based' public policy (Bradford 2005) or 'deep' federalism (Leo 2006).

As a joint federal, provincial, and municipal venture, the TWRC qualifies as an invention of such multilevel arrangements. Unlike the original UDCs installed in the United Kingdom under the Thatcher regime, which used the constitutional authority of the national government over local affairs to run roughshod over municipal/community interests, the TWRC was explicitly envisioned as a tri-level initiative between three equal government partners. Indeed, the City of Toronto, which has historically held little direct control over waterfront development, bought into the UDC model from the outset (see City of Toronto 2000c).

All in all, one might characterize the policy environment within which the TWRC was established as particularly amenable to the type of UDC-based governance model proposed in the Fung report. The details of how this concept would be implemented, however, were not straightforward. When it came time to put such plans into action, the real-world politics of intergovernmental relations in Canada prevented these ideas from reaching complete fruition. The story of how this came to be remains something of a mystery.

The Compromises

It was not until December 2002, some eighteen months after the TWRC was first announced, that its enabling provincial legislation, the Toronto Waterfront Revitalization Corporation Act, was passed into law. As passed, the act formally mandates the TWRC to enhance 'the economic, social, and cultural value of the land in the designated waterfront area … in a fiscally and environmentally responsible manner' (Ontario 2002: sec. 3.1.1).[5] But it does so without granting the TWRC sufficient powers to fulfil such a mandate. Although it supplies the TWRC with the legal autonomy of a private corporation under the Business Corporation Act, it also prohibits the corporation from acting as a legal agent of any level of government. The TWRC therefore cannot mortgage assets, form subsidiaries, acquire land, raise revenue, or borrow money without the express consent of all three governments. This point cannot be overemphasized. In stark contrast to other UDCs, the TWRC's role is limited to preparing and overseeing the implementation of waterfront precinct plans, business plans, phasing strategies, marketing campaigns, developer proposals, and environmental remediation efforts along the waterfront – no more, no less.

By preventing the TWRC from expropriating land, mortgaging assets, and borrowing money, the act deliberately undermines its capacity to act as a 'master developer' over waterfront lands. This is evident in terms of both the TWRC's fiscal autonomy (the power to generate its own revenue) and, to a lesser degree, its administrative autonomy (the power to determine its own organizational objectives and priorities). From a fiscal perspective, the agency is funded via contribution agreements negotiated by the three levels of government on a project-by-project basis,[6] leaving the TWRC financially vulnerable to bureaucratic delays. Such was the case in early 2004, when the TWRC reportedly teetered on the brink of bankruptcy thanks to an apparent dispute between the federal and municipal governments over construction costs (Lewington 2004; James 2004). From an administrative perspective, the TWRC must manoeuvre within a bureaucratic landscape that could change at any moment, whether by election and a resulting switch in government or the shuffling of political portfolios across ministries, departments, and secretariats.

Subsequent due-diligence reviews have produced numerous suggestions to strengthen the TWRC's operational and financial capacities, including streamlining intergovernmental approval processes for contribution and indemnification agreements, and establishing a predictable, long-term funding model (see Oliver Wyman–Delta Organization & Leadership 2007; Mercer Delta Consulting 2004). Save for a legislative amendment which grants the mayor an automatic seat on the board of directors (see Ontario 2005a: sched. 23), little has come from these proposals. The federal and provincial governments have consistently resisted efforts to confer additional powers on the TWRC. The Government of Canada did not even respond to the first governance review conducted in 2004 (Oliver Wyman–Delta Organization & Leadership 2007: 18). And while the City has since endorsed the 'empowered corporation' model for the TWRC as originally envisioned by Fung and his task force – even recommending that it be transformed into a wholly owned municipal corporation (Toronto City Council 2004: 27) – it has steadfastly refused to give up responsibility for planning approvals.

Despite these structural limitations, the TWRC has managed to make partial gains in terms of land ownership and control. In September 2005, a memorandum of understanding was reached between the TWRC, the Ontario Ministry of Public Infrastructure Renewal, and the Ontario Realty Corporation, transferring provincial lands in the West Don Lands development into the TWRC's hands. A similar memorandum was signed in February 2006 between the TWRC, the City, and the Toronto Economic Development Corporation (TEDCO) regarding the East Bayfront and Port Industrial District areas. Both MOUs confirmed the TWRC's role as the lead planning and coordinating body responsible for waterfront lands. Yet they still include several ambiguities and exemptions, making it difficult to gauge the full scope of the TWRC's political influence.[7]

The key conclusion in all this is that the initial concept for the TWRC envisioned in the Fung report never fully materialized. Major components of the original plan, such as a guaranteed funding model and powers of expropriation, were never conferred on the corporation. The politics underlying this decision remain cloudy. One might surmise that the other levels of government – particularly the Province, which under the Harris regime had passed the bill to establish the Corporation – were uncomfortable with handing over so much control over valuable waterfront assets to a relatively untested, quasi-independent body. But beyond speculation, there has been little if any work conducted investigating the political motivations and interests that went into drafting of the bill. As such, we are left with as many questions as answers – no more so than in terms of the impact that the Corporation's governance model will have over time.

Side Effects: Unknown?

Toronto has a long history of experimenting with special-purpose bodies involved in waterfront development.[8] As noted, the Toronto Harbour Commission, for instance, operated as something of a hybrid development corporation, combining the infrastructure and investment functions of a state agency with the real estate management functions of a private corporation (Desfor 1993). More recently, the municipally owned Toronto Economic Development Corporation, incorporated under the provincial Business Corporations Act in 1986, owned significant waterfront land holdings and was a political mainstay of waterfront development until its dissolution in December 2008.

The TWRC, however, represents a new beast altogether. Unlike TEDCO, which was responsible to only one level of government (accountability of the Toronto Harbour Commission was problematic; see Desfor et al., this volume), the TWRC must answer to three political masters at once. Currently, only one other urban redevelopment project in Canada, Winnipeg's Forks development, is subject to the same level of tripartite involvement (see Leo and Pyl 2007).[9] The balancing act involved in navigating this relationship complicates the pursuit of its development goals. For in any large-scale development process, there is an 'inherent tension between the desire to create an efficient special authority empowered to face new challenges and produce results, and the commitment to democratize the planning process, ensuring that all stakeholders have a voice' (Greenberg 1996: 216). The following section examines the ramifications of this tension with respect to issues of democratic responsiveness, public accountability, and political legitimacy.

Democratic Responsiveness

When political scientists speak of democratic responsiveness, they generally refer to how often government policies are consistent with public opinion, as measured via public opinion polling (e.g., Petry 1999). Here, I use the term responsiveness in a more general sense. I focus less on the extent to which waterfront policy corresponds with specific measures of public opinion than on the degree to which the TWRC has shown a willingness to respond to the demands of the community that it serves. In this regard, concerns have been raised that the TWRC, like the LDDC and the BPCA before it – agencies that, at least at their outset, tended to disregard local interests (Gordon 1997a; Fainstein 1994) – is too insulated from public scrutiny to engage in meaningful consultation with members of the local community (Desfor and Keil 2004; see also Desfor and Jørgensen 2004; Swyngedouw et al. 2002).

As a special-purpose body burdened by an unrelenting pressure to demonstrate progress on the ground – its primary purpose, after all, is to actually develop the waterfront, not just plan for it – the TWRC will always run up against the temptation to charge ahead with only limited public engagement. Generally speaking, however, the public consultation strategy carried out by the TWRC is a far cry from the closed-door, elite-only approach originally presented by Fung and his associates and, to a lesser extent, those documented across Europe. Certainly, there remain various groups, such as members of neighbouring low-income communities, that are left underrepresented in the many public forums and design charrettes conducted by the TWRC. But on the whole, relative to recent practice, the TWRC's numerous consultations have been far more inclusive.

Given its fiscal vulnerabilities, a case could actually be made that the TWRC has a vested interest in strengthening its consultation efforts even further. For without backing from the local community, and the political will that comes with such support, the TWRC may not be able to convince government partners to extend its funding beyond 2014, the provisional end date approved in its long-term business plan. Whether this will necessarily translate into better-quality consultations, however defined, or a greater number of consultations, is difficult to predict. But public consultation in one form or another will likely remain a central motivation for the TWRC over the long term.

A separate concern on the topic of responsiveness centres on the ever-present threat that senior governments might be inclined to utilize the TWRC to marginalize municipal authority over waterfront planning, as was the case early on in the UK experience. It could be argued, for example, that the TWRC effectively cements the powers of the federal and provincial governments in a policy area that should principally rest with city hall. One need not look any further than the constant political gamesmanship surrounding the Toronto Port Authority (TPA) as a case in point (see Sanderson and Filion, this volume).[10] Preliminary evidence, however, does not support this conclusion. Indeed, the TWRC may even represent one of the first formal institutions to offer the City a level playing field from which to participate in intergovernmental negotiations. Governed by three *equal* government partners, each with an equal financial stake in the long-term project, the TWRC is hardly in a position to cater to the demands of one government over another.

Public Accountability

In terms of accountability, the forecast is less promising. By accountability, I refer to the means by which an individual or organization can be called to account for their actions (Mulgan 2000). The consolidation of waterfront authority in the hands of the TWRC would seem to offer certain advantages along these lines, at least from the perspective of the individual citizen. Rather than guess about whom to contact with questions or, for that matter, whom to blame when things go wrong, Torontonians are now generally able to point to one central agency. In reality, however, the actual lines of accountability remain blurred. In the end, the corporation is directly accountable only to its board of directors – and by association, its government shareholders – *not* the general public.

Paradoxically, one could argue that this is actually a strength of the UDC model. The TWRC must report to all three levels of government, thus providing a significant check on its authority. Each level of government, for example, effectively holds veto power in the allocation of funds and other planning decisions. But this is the case only if we accept that board members consciously vote in the interests of the body that appointed them – a situation, ironically, that challenges the TWRC's quasi-independent status. Nowhere in the TWRC's enabling legislation, by-laws, or conflict-of-interest procedures is this responsibility confirmed or even discussed. As it stands, one is left to assume that each member simply 'knows' what is expected of them.

The accountability structure becomes even less clear when we look beyond the TWRC to the relations between the three levels of government. The role of the Intergovernmental Steering Committee (IGSC), established as part of the initial $1.5 billion investment committed by three levels of government in October 2000, is a case in point. Comprising various senior management (i.e., deputy- and assistant-deputy-minister–level) officials from each level of government, the IGSC was ostensibly created to serve as the principal forum for intergovernmental negotiations concerning contribution agreements, the selection of funding criteria and priority projects, as well as the long-term structure of the TWRC (Human Resources and Social Development Canada 2005). Yet its actual role and responsibilities remain ambiguous and ill defined. The IGSC functions without any explicit or transparent operational guidelines, and its meetings are held on an infrequent basis. What's more, when the IGSC does meet, the TWRC is formally shut out of the proceedings. Two separate external audits have confirmed these concerns (Oliver Wyman–Delta Organization & Leadership 2007; Mercer Delta Consulting 2004).

For its part, the TWRC deserves credit for making available a considerable amount of materials on its website. But again, it is not obligated to do so. As a corporate entity registered under the Ontario Business Corporations Act, the TWRC is not subject to provincial freedom-of-information legislation normally applicable to government agencies. In other words, there is limited legal recourse to ensure that the TWRC will always follow through on its stated commitment to openness and transparency (see Waterfront Toronto 2007b). As the TWRC transitions to the implementation phase of its redevelopment plan, which includes the purchase and sale of extensive areas of privately and publicly held lands, issues of accessibility and accountability will surely escalate.

Political Legitimacy

Finally, a brief word regarding notions of legitimacy. Skogstad reminds us that political legitimacy 'has both an input and output component. Political authority enjoys input legitimacy when individuals believe that those who make legally enforceable decisions have a right to do so' (2003: 956). In a democratic system such as ours, the mechanisms through which issues of democratic responsiveness and public accountability are addressed, as noted above, are matters of input legitimacy. Open debate, public consultations, conflict-of-interest policies, access-to-information requirements – these are the input-related instruments that confer legitimacy in public authorities. As noted, the TWRC has made important strides in these regards, while still leaving plenty of room for improvement.

When it comes to the overall goal of redeveloping Toronto's waterfront, however, it must be emphasized that success will largely be measured in terms of output legitimacy; that is, 'when the outputs of governing – public policies and other decisions – meet social standards of acceptability and appropriateness' (Skogstad 2003: 956). Here, debate centres not only on how waterfront development might best be achieved, but on whether it can be achieved at all. For, rightly or wrongly, there is a sense among many Torontonians (see, for example, Hume 2005a) that their waterfront is not what it could be, that change is necessary. Although this volume provides a compelling counter-narrative, demonstrating that change has *always* been a part of Toronto's waterfront history, such impressions are not likely to fade any time soon. If the TWRC – now Waterfront Toronto – can somehow break through the jurisdictional gridlock that has plagued development over the past half-century, it is not unreasonable to suggest that it will reap the benefits of considerable political legitimacy. Exactly what these benefits might entail is difficult to forecast – legitimacy can be exploited for various purposes. I simply note that one should be careful not to underestimate their motivating potential.

Conclusion

This chapter began with the premise that the formation of the Toronto Waterfront Revitalization Corporation in 2001 signalled the return of a corporate model of waterfront governance in Toronto. To better understand the causes and consequences of this change, I proceeded to ask three basic questions: Who is in charge? Why? And why does it matter?

My answers to these questions led me, first, to explore the nature and extent of jurisdictional gridlock that precipitated the creation of the TWRC. I concluded that the high degree of gridlock complicating redevelopment efforts is attributable to three important factors: the distribution of *power* across levels of government; the distribution of *land* across associated government agencies; and the path-dependent nature of institutional change.

I then proceeded to review the political pretext that led to the formation of a UDC-based governance model as well as the specific functions, composition, and powers of the TWRC. In sum, the 'operational concept' outlined in the Fung report was inspired by various high-profile international projects that were consistent with prevailing trends in the field of public policy and administration, such as the proliferation of New Public Management principles and innovations in multilevel governance. The plan, however, was never fully operationalized. The TWRC (now Waterfront Toronto) remains handcuffed by the limitations of its statutory powers. The streamlining of regulatory and financial considerations has indeed moved ahead, but not without complicated intergovernmental negotiation, most of it taking place behind closed doors.

Finally, I considered the implications of this governance model with regard to questions of democratic responsiveness, public accountability, and political legitimacy. Despite the temptation to demonstrate results as quickly as possible, the TWRC's vulnerable fiscal situation suggests that the prospects for meaningful public consultation remain favourable; continued public support will be critical to demonstrating the TWRC's value to government shareholders over the long term. As plans move towards the implementation phase, however, weaknesses inherent in Waterfront Toronto's accountability structures, typified by the rather mysterious role of the Intergovernmental Steering Committee, may undermine such responsiveness. It is questionable, for instance, whether Waterfront Toronto can maintain its commitment to openness and transparency while expediting the sale of land assets for private development. How it manages this balancing act will dictate the corporation's perceived legitimacy as it moves forward.

In all, what emerges is a picture of waterfront governance as complex as it is intriguing. The deliberate consolidation of waterfront authority within a single development corporation has helped simplify previous policy processes while establishing a new set of political obstacles. Jurisdictional gridlock still dominates discussions of waterfront development in Toronto, but on different terms than before. The return of a corporate governance model to the development of Toronto's socio-ecological shoreline therefore provides fertile ground for further research exploring the network of actors, interests, and institutions involved in waterfront development, specifically, as well as the broader practice of urban politics and policy in Canada.

NOTES

1 For the sake of clarity, I generally refer to Waterfront Toronto as the TWRC throughout the chapter.

2 The exact number of relevant organizations is difficult to verify. Desfor (1993: 175), for example, suggests that 47 boards, agencies, and special-purpose bodies were identified during the royal commission's work. The preface to the final report, on the other hand, notes more than 100 organizational actors somehow involved (Royal Commission on the Future of the Toronto Waterfront 1992: xxi). By the concluding chapter, this estimate was narrowed down to 'more than 75 by the Royal Commission's count' (ibid.: 457).

3 It is important to note that although the Waterfront Regeneration Trust succeeded in helping governments integrate ecosystem planning into their project plans, it was never expected to coordinate *all* development along the waterfront. Its primary goal was instead to encourage the development of a greenway along the north shore of Lake Ontario, known as the Waterfront Trail. Accordingly, the Trust does not completely satisfy the coordinating-agency model.

4 This figure is based on the most recent formal audit of the TWRC's finances, completed in June 2007. Earlier estimates outlined in the 2000 Fung report projected a total investment in the order of $12 billion, with approximately $5 billion coming from public-sector spending on infrastructure, and $7 billion from private-sector investments (Toronto Waterfront Revitalization Task Force 2000: 5). As of September 2008, there are indications that escalating construction costs have already forced the TWRC to reassess its long-term priority projects in light of formidable fiscal uncertainties. Recent estimates presented to the board of directors suggest that the final cost of the projects initiated since 2001 will likely rise to $3.6 billion, well above the original $1.5 billion total pledged as seed capital in 1999 (see Moloney 2008; Waterfront Toronto 2008c).

5 The 'designated waterfront area' refers primary to lands encompassing the Central Waterfront Area, extending from Dowling Avenue in the west to Coxwell Avenue in the east, including the East Bayfront, West Don Lands, and Port Industrial District. See Ontario Regulations 200/03 and 79/04 for a complete listing.

6 As of October 2008, 34 contribution agreements have been approved, totalling over $650 million (Waterfront Toronto 2008a: 44).

7 The MOU signed by TWRC, the City, and TEDCO, for example, partially insulates certain TEDCO properties from TWRC authority. TEDCO's 'project lands,' such as the Filmport development, are a case in point: It is unclear how the recent break-up of TEDCO into two separate agencies, Build Toronto and Invest Toronto, might impact these arrangements.

8 I use the general term special-purpose bodies to describe any type of agency, board, or commission that is (1) either wholly or partially owned

by government(s), (2) established to pursue public objectives or perform specific government-like functions, and (3) operates with a certain degree of operational autonomy, including the use of businesslike administrative guidelines. See Richmond and Siegel (1994) and Mitchell (1999) for a more comprehensive account of related organizational forms in Canada and the United States, respectively.

9 Launched in 1986, the Forks Renewal Corporation was tasked with redeveloping a former CN rail yard located where the Assiniboine flows into the Red River. Now operating under the auspices of the Forks North Portage Partnership, the Forks is governed by a board of directors with equal representation from all three levels of government. It manages roughly $90 million of land assets (Treasury Board Secretariat 2007: 115), a portfolio similar to that controlled by Waterfront Toronto as of 2008 (Waterfront Toronto 2008a).

10 As I write this, the federal government has appointed two extra members to the Toronto Port Authority board of directors, ostensibly as a means to exert greater influence over the future of the controversial Toronto Island Airport (Wingrove 2009).

12 Public-Private Sector Alliances in Sustainable Waterfront Revitalization: Policy, Planning, and Design in the West Don Lands

SUSANNAH BUNCE

Sustainable revitalization is now a commonplace policy and planning strategy for new urban redevelopment initiatives in cities across Europe and North America. With the popularity of urban and regional growth management concepts such as smart growth planning, built-form practices of urban intensification and compact city development, and emphases on in-fill buildings and brownfield regeneration, the focus of urban policy has now shifted towards the implementation of these planning and redevelopment approaches. Recent research on sustainable urban revitalization practices suggests increasingly concerted public-sector emphases on achieving an 'end product' of sustainability in cities through the implementation of specific planning, design, and development directives created at different and intersected scales of policy formulation (Raco 2007, 2005; While et al. 2004). Research on sustainable urban revitalization practices has also shown increasingly sophisticated connections between multi-scalar urban sustainability policy and the implementation of policy directives by private-sector urban planners and residential developers in relation to processes such as gentrification and political-ecological change at the city scale (Bunce 2009; Cidell 2009; Dale and Newman 2009; Moore and Bunce 2009; Davidson 2006; Davidson and Lees 2005). These arrangements point to a process of 'property-led revitalization' or 'bricks and mortar regeneration' (Shaw and Robinson 1998), with private-sector residential developers taking the lead in implementing urban revitalization policy with the insertion of sustainability objectives.

The plans for redeveloping Toronto's waterfront into a constellation of sustainable residential and commercial neighbourhoods provide a local example of the complex associations between public-sector urban

sustainability policy and private-sector-implemented urban revitalization through new high-density residential and commercial development or the practice of urban intensification. Here, government and
other public-sector agencies liaise with private-sector actors to fulfil the
objectives of urban intensification. The construction of the new communities is to be done by private-sector developers in compliance with
the directives of public sustainability policy. The emphasis on urban
intensification as a built-form practice for fostering sustainability reflects the increasingly popular urban policy model of the 'compact city.'
Normative descriptions of the benefits of compact cities suggest that,
'in compact cities travel distances are reduced, thus fuel emissions are
lessened, rural land is saved from development, local facilities are supported and local areas become more autonomous' (Williams et al. 1996:
83). Thomas and Cousins (1996) note that the sustainability advantages
of compact cities are generally considered to be 'less car dependency,
low emissions, reduced energy consumption, better public transportation services, increased overall accessibility, the reuse of infrastructure
and previously developed land, the rejuvenation of existing urban areas and urban vitality, a high quality of life, the preservation of green
space, and a milieu for enhanced business and trading activities' (56).
As Burton, Williams, and Jenks (1996) observe, 'The compact city has
been advocated by many as the most sustainable form of development'
(231). The creation of compact urban spaces through urban intensification connects with the policy delivery of the 'public good' of sustainability, yet it also links with private developers' interest in the creation
of new real estate enterprises, particularly in areas such as central-city
waterfront districts.

This chapter[1] discusses the public/private-sector alliances that have
been developed between Waterfront Toronto,[2] the publicly funded
urban development corporation responsible for managing Toronto's
waterfront development process, and private-sector developers in the
implementation of policy, planning, and design strategies. Waterfront
Toronto's primary sustainability policy, the *Sustainability Framework*,
first created in 2004, is the document that guides the implementation
of sustainability objectives, and suggests how private developers are
to implement sustainability targets, specifically through Leadership in
Energy and Environmental Design (LEED) ratings. The policy definition of sustainability that is put forward by Waterfront Toronto derives
from the overarching and unspecific 'three pillar' model of sustain-

ability – a balance and interrelationship between economic development objectives, social development goals, and ecological protection. In
administrative discussions regarding policy implementation, sustainability is chiefly defined in terms of the development of new mixed-
use, high-density residential and commercial neighbourhoods that can
attain LEED certification. This chapter explores public/private-sector
alliances in the implementation of Waterfront Toronto's sustainability,
land use planning, and urban design policies through an analysis of
the formulation of urban intensification plans and sustainable design
techniques for the West Don Lands area of the waterfront. The study
of the West Don Lands demonstrates close and compatible associations
between the sustainability policy objectives of Waterfront Toronto and
the development interests of private real estate developers in the creation of a new waterfront neighbourhood.

Planning Sustainable Revitalization in the West Don Lands

The West Don Lands site is located to the west of the Don River and
north of Lake Shore Boulevard and the Gardiner Expressway. The land
is owned by the provincial government's landholding agency, the Ontario Realty Corporation, and co-managed by the Province of Ontario's
Ministry of Public Infrastructure Renewal. The planning and redevelopment process for this site is managed by Waterfront Toronto through
a recent legal memorandum of understanding with the provincial government.[3] Waterfront Toronto's vision for these lands is the creation
of a high-density master planned sustainable community with both
residential and commercial uses and LEED[4] Gold sustainable building
design.

The West Don Lands site provides an example of context-specific
planning, design, and development strategies and, further, of the con-
vergences between sustainable policy formulation and private-sector
development interests in Waterfront Toronto's planning and redevelopment process. Waterfront Toronto emphasizes linking its sustainability
objectives with a vision of planning and market-oriented land development. The connection of sustainable urban planning and land development is posited as a 'win-win-win' situation for Waterfront Toronto, the
central waterfront, and the City of Toronto. In this sense, it is assumed
that a successful linking of sustainability objectives with planning and
market-oriented land development will achieve an end goal of sustain-

ability that will have wide-reaching impacts across many territorial scales. Waterfront Toronto states that,

> most importantly, however, the West Don Lands [plan] is inherently sustainable in terms of land utilization and achieving smart growth principles: reducing the risk of natural hazards through flood proofing controls; re-mediating brownfields within the City [sic] core; reducing the need to develop agricultural and environmentally-sensitive land outside the City; increasing the supply of affordable housing; reducing air pollution associated with commuting; making public transit, cycling, and walking the primary modes of transportation; efficiently using existing infrastructure; increasing the amount of park land and community services; increasing economic development opportunities; demonstrating the feasibility of green buildings. (Toronto Waterfront Revitalization Corporation 2005c: 35)

Relating these objectives to multi-scalar government policies, Waterfront Toronto suggests that 'these benefits will contribute greatly to helping achieve the City's vision for a Clean and Green waterfront, to furthering the Province of Ontario's Smart Growth initiative, and to assisting the federal government meet its Kyoto Protocol targets' (ibid.).

Waterfront Toronto's sustainable planning and development activity in the West Don Lands is based upon a history of public discussions about the future of land development on this site. The West Don Lands area has been the subject of several planning visions for redevelopment over the past decade, with the first plan for residential redevelopment of the area being the Ataratiri plan. Ataratiri was formulated in 1990 following the provincial government's expropriation of the land in 1988 for the purpose of developing a new residential community with affordable housing.[5] After the provincial government's redevelopment initiative was halted during the planning phase, a subsequent provincial government strategy aimed to sell a portion of the West Don Lands to a private-sector harness racing company. This plan was stopped with pressure from a citizens group, the West Don Lands Committee (WDLC). In 1999, the same group worked with public-sector representatives to revisit plans for the residential and commercial redevelopment of the area, and to envision the area as a proposed site for the Olympic media village as part of Toronto's 2008 Summer Olympics bid plans. The outcome of this process influenced Waterfront Toronto's current plans for a new master planned community in the West Don Lands consisting of four smaller neighbourhood units, River Square, Mill Street, Don River Park, and Front Street, and one park district, Don River Park.

Waterfront Toronto is responsible for financing, coordinating, and supervising the planning process for the West Don Lands site and preparing strategies for the transfer of public land to private developers. The land development process will be orchestrated by private-sector development firms with the guidance of Waterfront Toronto following land sales. Waterfront Toronto estimates that it will have to subsidize part of the land price to encourage the private sector to develop land in accordance with Waterfront Toronto's sustainability specifications (Interview 2006). Land parcels within the West Don Lands site are to be sold to private developers at or above current market rates for residential and commercial land in Toronto's downtown core. There is also an expectation of higher building costs for developers owing to the premiums attached to sustainable building materials and design features.

Waterfront Toronto's plans for the West Don Lands specifically illustrate how publicly formulated sustainability policy is integrated into revitalization planning and design strategies that are to be implemented eventually by private-sector actors. The plans connect a range of policies that integrate the objectives of sustainability into the planning, design, and redevelopment process. Neighbourhood characteristics, design, building heights, and densities are prescribed by Waterfront Toronto in the *West Don Lands Precinct Plan* (TWRC 2005c) and the *West Don Lands Block Plan and Design Guidelines* (TWRC 2006b), two 'guidebooks' for developers that provide a framework for the aesthetic character and form of development. The planning details in these documents are augmented by sustainable building-design specifications, guided by LEED Gold rating requirements, found in the *Performance Specifications for Green Building Initiative for West Don Lands* (TWRC 2006a) ('green design guidelines') and the overarching 'three pillar' vision for waterfront sustainability found in the *Sustainability Framework* (TWRC 2005b). A majority of these documents were formulated by private-sector planning and design firms contracted by Waterfront Toronto between 2003 and 2006. The *West Don Lands Precinct Plan*, for example, was coordinated by Waterfront Toronto planning project managers Urban Strategies Ltd, with planning and design work led by a Pittsburgh-based firm, Urban Design Associates, with the assistance of Toronto-located planning, environmental engineering, and design consulting firms Joe Lobko Architects, du Toit Allsop Hillier, LEA Consulting, Earth Tech, and GHK International.

In the context of the West Don Lands, the integration of sustainable planning concepts and sustainable design specifications are supported by both public- and private-sector planners, designers, architects, and other public-sector officials involved in planning and design. The following sections explore how Waterfront Toronto's sustainability vision is integrated into planning policy and sustainable design strategies for the West Don Lands, formulated with an aim of alleviating planning and development constrictions for private-sector actors.

Precinct Planning Policy and Sustainability

Urban intensification is emphasized in the precinct plan for the West Don Lands as a planning and development practice for the achievement of sustainability objectives. The precinct plan emphasizes a high-density neighbourhood with both commercial and residential land uses and is complemented by directives for LEED Gold building design, pedestrian walkways, bicycle paths, and publicly provided neighbourhood services such as daycare spaces, an elementary school, and a recreation centre. The introduction of the precinct planning concept to Waterfront Toronto's planning process is compatible with its vision of sustainable planning, design, and redevelopment. The idea of using precinct planning as a strategy for the development of new waterfront neighbourhoods was first initiated by Toronto-based urban planning and design consultants Michael Kirkland, Tony Coombes, and Joe Berridge during the formulation of the City of Toronto's *Making Waves* plan in the early 2000s (Interview 2005b). The concept of the precinct plan originates in British town planning and was first introduced in Patrick Abercrombie's plan for the County of London in 1943. The intention of a precinct area was to provide quiet areas for social activity and 'seclude an area for a particular purpose such as shopping, university, or civic precinct, or to protect an area from undesirable intrusions, such as through traffic, with parts exclusively for pedestrians' (Whittick 1974: 845). Waterfront Toronto's introduction of the precinct planning model to Toronto's waterfront planning and development process is conceptually interesting because of its association with the idea of community seclusion from vehicular traffic – an important component of Waterfront Toronto's sustainability vision for the waterfront. The use of precinct planning is also a novelty within Toronto's municipal planning structure through its formation of an additional level in the planning process that lies between secondary

12.1 Design renderings of mixed residential and commercial West Don Lands neighbourhoods. (From West Don Lands Block Plan and Design Guidelines [TWRC 2006b]; courtesy of Waterfront Toronto)

plans ascribed through the provincial Planning Act,[6] and narrower specific site plans.[7]

Waterfront Toronto suggests that the introduction of precinct planning was intended to diminish the 'red tape' of the municipal planning approvals process (Interview 2005c). An intention of the precinct planning concept is to provide private-sector developers with a guidebook to the aesthetic character of central waterfront neighbourhoods in the form of an 'unofficial' planning policy. Waterfront Toronto's precinct plan acts as an umbrella for another 'unofficial' document, the *West Don Lands Block Plan and Design Guidelines* (2006b), prepared for Waterfront Toronto by private-sector urban design consultants Urban Design Associates. The document prescribes detailed guidelines for the development process through the outline of building specifications such as building-envelope density, building setbacks, quantity of residential units and commercial units, and site allocations, such as for parking spaces, recreational parks, and community services. Such planning components are typically found in municipal secondary plans, but in the context of the West Don Lands they are placed in policy documents that do not have a formal connection to provincial planning legislation and, as a result, do not have legislative accountability. In order to create a legal framework for planning in the West Don Lands, Waterfront Toronto, in conjunction with the City of Toronto's Waterfront Secretariat, have created new zoning by-laws for the West Don Lands.[8] The zoning by-laws, rather than the usual secondary plan, serve as the planning documents that provide regulations and accountability as per the requirements of the provincial planning legislation. Waterfront Toronto states that 'the Precinct Plans are intended to outline development principles and guidelines at a level of detail not possible within the broader Secondary Plan. The intent is that these principles and guidelines form the bridge that allows the city to move from Official Plan policies to Zoning by-law provisions' (TWRC 2006b: 4). As a result, Waterfront Toronto by-passes the traditional directives found at the secondary plan scale and creates a new and direct connection between the Official Plan for Toronto and detailed by-laws for the West Don Lands precinct planning area.

To augment these documents, the *Performance Specifications for Green Building Initiative for West Don Lands* policy ('green design guidelines') (TWRC 2006a), written for Waterfront Toronto by Toronto-based environmental engineering firm Halsall Associates, details the implementation of targets from the *Sustainability Framework*. The policy outlines the LEED rating system and strategies for how Waterfront Toronto will provide assistance for private developers to build in accordance with LEED Gold specifications. While the zoning by-laws for the West Don Lands prescribe building height and setback specifications for specific areas of the precinct, private developer commitment to LEED Gold sustainable design requirements will be sought by Waterfront Toronto during the development 'call for proposals' process and at the point of public land sale.

Although the precinct plan for the West Don Lands adds another scale to the municipal planning process, Waterfront Toronto suggests that the changes allow for a smoother planning process and provide more certainty for private-sector developers (Interview 2007a). Waterfront Toronto will provide their guidelines directly to the private developers in order to decrease administrative negotiations between developers and the municipal planning department. Through adherence to specific details pertaining to the built form of each precinct section and the sustainable design specifications, developers will commit to the planning and design vision for the precinct and acquire rezoning from Waterfront Toronto in advance of the land sale and development process. As a result, the only municipal consent that private developers will need to obtain following land purchase will be site plan approval and a building permit. The intention is to soften the terrain of planning and development in the West Don Lands in order to entice private-sector interest (Interview 2005b). As John Campbell, Waterfront Toronto's chief executive officer, suggests, 'We want to give the developers a lot more certainty … We want the bids [from private developers] to come back after zoning is locked up. We're going to be quite aggressive in what we're asking for so we want to be really credible – to say [to developers] "We've got the zoning." If we went out there with none of that in place, it just wouldn't look credible' (Interview 2006). Through the formulation and provision of planning policies, planning approvals, and sustainable design guidelines before construction occurs in the West Don Lands, Waterfront Toronto provides a tabula rasa of land primed for private-sector development alongside prescriptive visions for neighbourhood sustainability to be implemented by private developers.

Built-Form Intensification and the West Don Lands

Built-form intensification is envisioned by Waterfront Toronto as a method for creating and achieving sustainability, yet it is also viewed as a way to encourage private-sector interest in land development. Creating a high level of neighbourhood density in the West Don Lands through the intensification of both human activity and built form[9] allows Waterfront Toronto to highlight the future financial benefits of intensified land use in the neighbourhood. The built form strategy for intensification in the West Don Lands centres on a plan of twenty-four residential and commercial development blocks. These development blocks are sited on land that is currently publicly owned, but Waterfront Toronto has also created plans for two blocks on another two parcels of privately owned land. Waterfront Toronto defines a development block as 'land defined for private development, not its adjacent public or publicly-accessible open space' (TWRC 2006b: 36). The blocks are all located within what are called 'character areas' (Toronto Waterfront Revitalization Corporation 2006b: 4), four neighbourhoods within the larger West Don Lands neighbourhood. In addition to the blocks, there are nine open-space areas consisting of classical square and triangle 'parkettes' and green pedestrian mews, with the proposed Don River Park serving as the largest area of green space on the eastern edge of the West Don Lands.

Apart from one complete residential development block, the blocks consist of a mix of residential and commercial uses. The development blocks are proposed to be at a high density and different height scales, with the average building at eight to ten storeys in the form of an eight-storey apartment block with a two-storey step back at the top (TWRC 2006b). The proposed building setback from the lot line is an average of two to three metres (ibid.). While specific densities are not inscribed in the precinct plan or the urban design guidelines, the TWRC provides approximations of the density and form of the development blocks in order to offer private developers a means of understanding development yields from each block.

In a synthesis of the proposed new population and building mass estimations in the West Don Lands, Waterfront Toronto is proposing 5560 new residential units, with a forecasted population of 11,000 new residents. Residential and commercial building development will cover 96 of the 232 hectares of the neighbourhood, with 105 hectares marked for the development of streets, parks, and rail-line easements[10] (TWRC 2006b). At the scale of the development blocks, the TWRC has estimated an average of 90 square metres per unit (968.4 square feet per unit), less than 90 square metres per unit for the 25 per cent classified as affordable housing units, and 15 square metres (161 square feet) per parking space. In total, the mass for residential buildings in the West Don Lands is proposed at 511,760 gross square metres (GSM) (or 73,693,440 square metres) and for non-residential buildings at 73,990 GSM (10,654,560 square metres) (TWRC 2006b: 63). The expected average ratio of new resident to floor space in the residential units is one to 45 square metres (484 square feet),[11] with an average of 1.98 persons per residential unit (synthesized from data found in TWRC 2006b). Overall, Waterfront Toronto's estimations show a high density of built-form space and level of residential population with the provision of small residential units geared to one or two persons.

These approximations allow Waterfront Toronto to provide their expectations for built form and population density to private developers in order to gauge the prospective quantity of residential and commercial units. With Waterfront Toronto doing this strategic work in advance of development, developers are provided with the estimations needed to evaluate the type of necessary development financing, the potential cost of housing, and eventual housing type that will be provided. While these remain only guidelines for development, Waterfront Toronto is requesting that developers specify how they will be addressing density guidelines in their development proposals. Waterfront Toronto will also be integrating height specifications into the public land-sale agreements (Interview 2007a). In terms of height limitations on buildings, a Waterfront Toronto official suggests that they will be 'playing hardball at land transfer' (Interview 2005b) by writing these limitations into the formal land-sale agreement. The inscription of height limits into official land-sale documents will be done in order to prohibit developers from requesting height variances from the municipal planning department following land purchase.[12]

With the absence of density specifications, municipal bonusing procedures for increased densities will not be applied to private developers, despite being a popular method for financing public infrastructure with urban municipal governments facing reduced operating budgets.[13] Instead, Waterfront Toronto notes that 'it all comes out of the land price. Developers will pay good money for land when they don't have to be subject to bonusing. It's a public job to create public spaces' (Interview 2005b). In this way, a mutually beneficial situation is suggested for Waterfront Toronto and private-sector developers wherein private developers will avoid the upfront financial costs of applying for density increases and facing municipal bonusing practices and, conversely, the revenues generated from the sale of public land to private developers at market rates will finance the future provision of public infrastructure on the waterfront by the City of Toronto government and Waterfront Toronto.

Waterfront Toronto makes a connection between urban intensification as a sustainable urban practice and the financial benefits of denser developments for private developers. The corporation notes that 'sustainable urban revitalization is about reducing sprawl, increasing density, increasing quality of life, [and] bringing housing into the inner core' (Interview 2006). Increased densities are expected to stimulate commercial services as well as the provision of public infrastructure. The financial benefits of higher densities within a single area for private developers are, most simply, an increased consumer market as well as increases of building mass for the provision of market-oriented residential and commercial units specifically in the form of multi-storey buildings. The creation of high densities in the West Don Lands carries another mutually beneficial situation for both Waterfront Toronto's policy directives and the interests of private developers: the achievement of Waterfront Toronto's goal of creating sustainable urban form in the West Don Lands and private-sector development objectives of maximizing real estate profits.

Sustainable Design and the West Don Lands

The design character of a high-density, mixed residential and commercial sustainable community in the West Don Lands is considered by Waterfront Toronto to be a core component of its institutional mission for making the waterfront a 'national and global model for sustainability' (Toronto Waterfront Revitalization Corporation 2006a: 35). Waterfront Toronto conceptualizes design as the connection between sustainable technologies – such as solar and green roofs, sustainable construction materials, district energy provision, and rainwater collection – and the architectural character of buildings. Waterfront Toronto also understands sustainable design as a way to create added financial value and uniqueness in new residential and commercial developments. Jointly, the specifications for sustainable design and the vision for the architectural character found in Waterfront Toronto's urban design and green design guidelines present an 'up-scale' aesthetic character for eventual development in the West Don Lands. Waterfront Toronto's guidelines also provide assurances and specifications for developers as to how to accurately implement this vision through an integrated design process. The integrated design process is defined as a 'formalized process that encourages developer/design teams to work collaboratively to: set targets, share knowledge, and test design ideas for success, early in the design process' (ibid.: 2). Here, developers who formulate bids for development must outline their plans for addressing the urban-design and green-design guidelines, and be aware of the importance that Waterfront Toronto places on 'good and unique design' (TWRC 2006a: 2).

The design plans for the West Don Lands, in keeping with the notion of a 'secluded' precinct area removed from the congestion of vehicular traffic, are internally focused, with the proposed development blocks arranged in an inward-facing, north/south-oriented pattern. The streets connect the blocks together in a grid pattern, with the arterial east/west streets linking with the Don River Park located at the eastern edge of the precinct area. The urban design guidelines state that 'this precinct is designed with small blocks and many streets to create a pedestrian-friendly neighbourhood with a rich diversity of public space' (TWRC 2006b: 6). The building designs are provided through architectural renderings found in the urban design guidelines, with four proposed building types – townhouses, small apartments, large apartments, and towers (ibid.: 30). The urban design guidelines suggest the construction of eight condominium towers, to be located at the inside edges of the West Don Lands. These towers are to be narrow, with a limitation of tower floor plates at a maximum of 800 square metres (8608 square feet), and an average height of fourteen storeys. The tallest towers in the area, at twenty-four storeys, will be located at the northeastern boundary of the neighbourhood and on the southern edge in close proximity to the proposed district energy plant (ibid.).

The LEED Gold rating requirements for the West Don Lands and additional sustainability requirements outlined in the *Sustainability Framework* are synthesized and articulated in the green design guidelines. Through these guidelines Waterfront Toronto proposes to 'motivate developers to adopt new approaches to building more sustainable buildings; set requirements that, while requiring changes to existing practices, are economically viable in the market; and result in a development that reflects the TWRC's financial, societal and environmental drivers for sustainability' (TWRC 2006a: 1). In creating the green design guidelines, Waterfront Toronto intends to provide more certainty for developers in building according to LEED Gold specifications. Following consultations with invited private developers in 2005,[14] the corporation established specific principles for the achievement of targets by developers. These principles include the provision of 'first-in incentives,' such as professional expertise and marketing assistance, for the developers who will be first to purchase public land. The incentives are intended to mitigate the concerns of private developers about the potential construction premiums that are often attached to building with sustainable design. Waterfront Toronto states that 'getting into the precinct early will carry reduced risk since the TWRC is providing process and technical support to early entrants into the West Don Lands, [and the] TWRC marketing efforts will support the developer's marketing [of sustainability] and further enhance the market differentiation sought' (TWRC 2006a: 2). Waterfront Toronto's proposed 'integrated design process' will hire professional experts in sustainable design to guide and work in accordance with developers for the duration of the construction process.

The provision of professional advice in the construction process suggests a continued amicable relationship between Waterfront Toronto and private-sector developers in the implementation of sustainable design policy even following the sale of publicly owned land. The attention and support that Waterfront Toronto is providing to private developers in the implementation of green design specifications illustrates the integral role of sustainable design in the eventual provision of market-oriented residential and commercial buildings in the West Don Lands. With these practices, publicly formulated sustainable design policy becomes entwined with the profit-making objectives of private-sector, market-oriented land development on the waterfront.

Conclusion

The compatibility of Waterfront Toronto's sustainable revitalization policies with the interests of private developers highlights a planning and redevelopment process that is well orchestrated and mutually beneficial for both public- and private-sector interests. The alteration of traditional municipal planning practices to connect with the objectives of Waterfront Toronto's precinct planning process emphasizes the creation of planning techniques that encourage private development companies to invest in waterfront development and foster a more comfortable partnership between the public-sector institution and private developers in the planning and design of the West Don Lands. The high densities and block plans for the proposed neighbourhood show a reliance by Waterfront Toronto on intensification as a sustainable urban planning strategy, in terms of both higher-density buildings and a high-density neighbourhood population. The intensification plans create a quid pro quo arrangement with private developers. Developers will receive more certainty of garnering financial gains from the sale of small and numerous market-oriented residential and commercial units and Waterfront Toronto will rely on the profits from public land sales in order to fund public infrastructure projects, such as recreational parks and community centres, in the West Don Lands.

Waterfront Toronto's sustainable design vision for the West Don Lands is presented in both the urban-design and green-design guideline policies for the precinct. With the assistance of an integrated design team of consultants provided by Waterfront Toronto, private developers are expected to build according to LEED Gold design specifications. The establishment of the integrated design process is intended to provide more certainty for private developers through the provision of design and professional expertise that will guide construction in the neighbourhood.

These practices show close and comfortable associations between public policy developed for sustainable urban revitalization on Toronto's waterfront and the implementation of these policy directives by private-sector developers. The careful construction of a mutually agreeable partnership between Waterfront Toronto and private developers for the residential and commercial redevelopment of the West Don Lands suggests the emergence of a new mode for implementing urban sustainability objectives in Toronto. The formulation of waterfront sustainability policy intended for the 'public good' and its eventual implementation by private-sector developers for profit-making purposes emphasizes the increasingly nuanced public/private-sector connections in sustainable revitalization as an urban redevelopment agenda.

The focus on the private-sector provision of market-rate-sustainable housing points to the inevitable problems that this model raises for achieving social equity in relation to access to sustainable housing in the West Don Lands. With the policy emphasis and planning, design, and development strategies focused on the construction of market-oriented housing, the application of sustainability objectives will be geared towards affluent homeowners rather than individuals and families in need of affordable housing. The current global financial context and its resultant impact on real estate development in cities raises another problem regarding a close and comfortable alliance between

Waterfront Toronto and private-sector actors. Reliance on private developers to implement sustainability policy is subject to the vulnerabilities of the real estate market and, as a result, plans and development strategies such as those for the West Don Lands hinge on the interest, financial ability, and availability of developers. Paradoxically – given these contexts – policies, plans, and designs for waterfront sustainability become 'unsustainable' as a result of a focus on a gentrified vision of sustainability in waterfront residential development (Bunce 2009), real estate market vulnerability, and over-reliance on private-sector actors.

NOTES

1 The findings detailed in this chapter are part of doctoral dissertation research conducted between 2004 and 2007.
2 Waterfront Toronto is equally funded to the sum of $1.5 billion by the governments of Canada, the Province of Ontario, and the City of Toronto. The Toronto Waterfront Revitalization Corporation (TWRC), formed in 2002, changed its name to Waterfront Toronto in 2007. This chapter will refer to the TWRC as Waterfront Toronto, although the policy documents that are referred to were authored under the auspices of the TWRC.
3 A Memorandum of Understanding (MOU) was signed between the Ministry of Public Infrastructure Renewal, the Ontario Realty Corporation, and the TWRC pertaining to the West Don Lands (WDL) on 9 September 2005. This document 'defines the TWRC's role as Master Developer in the WDL … project' (Ontario 2005b: 3), and gives the Ontario Realty Corporation responsibility for flood protection implementation, soil and groundwater remediation, and risk assessments in accordance with the Environmental Protection Act. The MOU gives the TWRC responsibility for coordinating these efforts, producing all planning and design documents, and coordinating all future land sale arrangements between the Ministry of Public Infrastructure Renewal and the land purchaser (Ontario 2005b).
4 LEED is the most recognized system of sustainable building rating in North America, and has been adopted by municipal governments for use in public buildings in Chicago, Seattle, and Vancouver (TWRC 2006a: 4). In the LEED credit system, to achieve LEED Gold accreditation, a building must receive 39 out of 70 credits based upon specific sustainability targets. LEED accreditation can only be received following the construction of a building and once it has been inspected by an arm's-length, LEED-accredited professional such as a structural engineer. The Canada Green Building

Council (CaGBC) currently administers the accreditation process for LEED buildings in Canada.

5 The Ataratiri Plan was instigated by the Liberal provincial government in 1988 and was designed to establish 7000 units of public-sector affordable housing. A site plan was created in 1990 for the City of Toronto's housing department, by private-sector planning and design firm The Kirkland Partnership, that envisioned a block planned, high-density residential community. This plan was based on the Toronto Olympic Commitment plan, established for Toronto's unsuccessful 1996 Olympic bid, for the creation of 2500 units of new housing as part of a proposed Olympic media village. The provincial government stopped the planning process in 1992 after much public critique over the estimated public-sector cost of soil remediation in the area (Olds 1998; Pelango 1992). The planning vision for the site was subsequently delivered to the Toronto Waterfront Regeneration Trust to be incorporated into a report proposal for residential redevelopment. It was also integrated into the municipal secondary plan in 1994 and revisited by Toronto's 2008 Olympic bid team in its planning process (Interview 2005b).

6 The *Province of Ontario Planning Act* specifies that municipalities must have an official plan with corresponding secondary plans. Secondary plans are neighbourhood-oriented and provide area-specific requirements on issues such as zoning provisions, building densities and height limits, signage, and parking. As secondary plans specify neighbourhood-level municipal by-laws and are a component of official plans, they act as enforceable documents.

7 Under the auspices of the Planning Act, site plans are prepared by the landowner and/or developer and submitted to the municipal government for approved correspondence with secondary plan requirements.

8 A zoning by-law for the first phase of development in the West Don Lands was approved by the City of Toronto in July 2006.

9 Williams et al. (1996) succinctly define intensification as both the increase in human activities within an already existing urban area and the reuse of existing buildings and increased building densities.

10 The remaining 9 hectares consist of existing buildings, with 5 hectares marked for a proposed school site.

11 This estimation is based on a sum of expected residents divided by a multiplication of estimated residential units and estimated average floor space of the units in square metres.

12 As land sales have not yet been formalized, it is difficult to assess whether the articulation of height requirements into a land-sale agreement is pos-

sible and to ascertain in what legal forum this would then be challenged if a minor variance application was submitted by a developer or owner.

13 In accordance with section 37, Increased Density Provision By-laws, of the provincial Planning Act, the municipal government can request the provision of public services such as parks, community centres, and day-care centres, or 'cash-in-lieu' from private developers in return for increased development densities. This specification permits municipalities to leverage funds for public services from private developers.

14 The selected developers represented a range of large condominium development companies such as the Shane Baghai Group, a luxury condominium development corporation, Minto Inc., Tridel Inc., and the Daniel Corporation, as well as a specialized sustainable design company, Windmill Developments (TWRC 2006a: G3).

13 Socio-ecological Change in the Nineteenth and Twenty-first Centuries: The Lower Don River

GENE DESFOR AND JENNIFER BONNELL

On 2 February 2007, Waterfront Toronto, the city's lead waterfront development corporation, announced an international design competition intended to secure a world-class plan for developing forty hectares of land at the mouth of the Don River. The task given to firms selected for the competition was an ambitious one: they were to envision the 're-naturalizing' and revitalization of an area that has been marginalized for years. Waterfront Toronto had called for a plan for the Lower Don Lands that would establish a 'common vision for this area' and would construct an 'iconic landscape' to bring new urban life to the area (Waterfront Toronto 2007a: 7).[1] The initiative of Waterfront Toronto to re-invent the mouth of the Don River marks a major reversal in changes to the Don that began in the late nineteenth century. It is part of an ongoing process aimed at re-imagining, reconfiguring, and reshaping a problematic area of the waterfront.

It is particularly appropriate that the final chapter in this volume focuses on a comparison between contemporary plans for 're-naturalization' of the Don River and the changes made to the river in the late nineteenth century. The volume begins with chapters that discuss the ways Toronto's waterfront was transformed in conjunction with an industrially oriented era of development and ends with discussions of the more recent wave of development. This chapter uses the particular case of the Don River to compare the ways that socio-ecological changes in the two periods were similar and different. Late-nineteenth-century city builders constructed plans for the Don that spoke ambivalently of nature both as exalted and outside the bounds of human control, but also as requiring improvement as the key to unlocking its productive capacity in support of urban growth. In contrast, contemporary plans for transforming the Don use language and images that emphasize sustainability, recognize the importance of promoting and maintaining healthy urban ecosystems, and expound ecological modernization's 'win-win' solutions for both the economy and the environment (for more on ecological modernization see Desfor and Keil 2004; Gibbs 2000; Hajer 1995). The socio-ecological transformations of the Don differ dramatically in their form – the first a straightening and encapsulation of the river; the more recent an attempt at re-naturalizing, or 'undoing' the effects of those earlier alterations. They share similarities, however, in that they both linked nature with urbanization.

The late-nineteenth-century project of straightening the Don was primarily linked, we suggest, with industrialization of the city. In contrast, the more recent plans for re-naturalization were established by and support a knowledge-based economic mode of development. By the mid- and late twentieth century, as global economic restructuring was taking hold, industry moved out of or closed down on the central waterfront and left behind landscapes of little consequence for Toronto's emerging economy. The 'industrialized' Don needed reinvention to be relevant for a new urban-space economy. Waterfront Toronto's initiatives for the Lower Don Lands, and in particular for the Don River, are essential aspects of this reinvention process.

The winner of Waterfront Toronto's international design competition was a consortium headed by Michael Van Valkenburgh, professor of landscape architecture at the Harvard Graduate School of Design. The interdisciplinary planning team used what it called ecological and sustainable strategies to 're-integrate strategically important post-industrial landscapes while reframing their interactions with the natural environment' (American Society of Landscape Architects 2008). The Michael Van Valkenburgh & Associates (MVVA) proposal has won a number of prizes that commend it not only for its urban design but also for articulating new relationships between nature and urban development. The American Society of Landscape Architects presented it with its 2008 Award of Honor, celebrating the way it 'heralds a new relationship between the urban and the natural' and praising the plan for its reinvention of the Don River 'as an agent of urbanism' (ibid.). The plan also received the Best Futuristic Design Award at the 2009 Building Exchange Conference in Hamburg, Germany, where an international panel noted its contribution to sustainability, efficiency, and 'collaboration with the built environment' (CNW 2009).

Central to the MVVA proposal is the creation of a new type of terri-

13.1 'Urban Estuary,' from the plan for the Lower Don Valley by Michael Van Valkenburgh and Associates, 2010. (Courtesy of Waterfront Toronto)

tory – an 'urban estuary.' According to the plan (see figure 13.1), this new territory is to be constructed so that 'the city, lake and river interact in a dynamic and balanced relationship,' becoming 'a place of exchange, where urban and natural systems intermingle' (2007: 42). The MVVA's urban estuary extends the conventional geologic definition of an estuary as a partly enclosed coastal body of water into which flow one or more rivers or streams. The urban estuary becomes a metaphor for the coming together of two disparate systems – the urban and the natural – which overlap and interact with each other but maintain their distinct identities. We, however, prefer a conceptualization of 'urban' and 'natural' in which they are not seen to be in opposition, as though they are separate worlds. Rather, 'urban' and 'natural' are fused together as a dense network of interwoven human, biophysical, cultural, discursive, spatial, and, of course, material processes (Swyngedouw 2004). In this conceptualization, David Harvey's contention that there is nothing especially unnatural about New York City (1996a) becomes clear. We suggest that MVVA's proposed urban estuary should be understood as a hybrid landscape, or what Swyngedouw calls 'socio-nature' (1996: 68). For us, socio-nature is a concept that indicates a deep intertwining of biophysical and societal networks that are effectively inseparable.

Socio-natures and Urbanization

In this section, we briefly explore relationships between socio-natures and urbanization. By this we mean our interest in both societal relationships *with* nature, as well as societal transformations *of* 'nature' into commodities, infrastructure, and urban form itself.

Cities have been the centres of civilization and modernization for centuries. 'Modern' urban planners, engineers, politicians, and other place entrepreneurs (Molotch 1976) have consistently had prominent positions in discursive and material processes involved with the transformation of cities (see Moir, chapter 1, this volume). And city builders subscribing to modernity's principles have taken their cues from the virtues of civilization that stress reason, progress, and profitability. In the Western world, modernity's approach to urbanization has been largely based on the notion that progress could be achieved through the logic of the Enlightenment and scientific procedures (see, for example, Kaika 2005; Harvey 1996a). The Enlightenment rests on an ideology wherein the logic of scientific experimentation leads to new knowledge about a nature that is largely divorced from human systems. With such knowledge, society is able to dominate this external nature through control and manipulation (Leiss 1974). Plans for the design, use, and signification of cities have drawn on this ideological frame, envisioning societal institutions and organizations that have an ability to transform nature into new urban spaces. But the transformation of nature into urban spaces has been based on partial or imperfect knowledge of a complex array of biophysical and social processes – that is, knowledge of both the purportedly distinct biophysical and social processes and the interrelationships between these worlds is fragmentary and, in important instances, oversimplified. In such cases, the production of new socio-natures has tended to lead to many unpredictable results and unintended consequences. Though modernity portrays a rationalized, predictable, and controllable nature, history is replete with examples of catastrophes resulting from city building predicated on human domination of a well-behaved nature.

The last few decades have witnessed the emergence of a substantial political ecology literature that has revisited modernist approaches to an external nature (Davis 2001; Herzogenrath 2001; Wallerstein 2000; Cronon 1996; Harvey 1996a). Fundamental to this multidisciplinary literature is a rejection of the centuries-old divide that left nature and society as distinct entities. At the urban level, this literature has tended to focus on both conceptual and empirical analyses of the production of urban environments that situate the particularities of change within a broader context of critical social theory (see Keil 2005, 2003). These approaches conceptualize biophysical and social processes within a tightly woven network through which urban spaces are shaped. For example, Heynen et al. note that the 'environment combines socio-physical constructions that are actively and historically produced, both in terms of social content and physical-environmental qualities' (2006: 11). A central aspect of the 'social content' necessary for the production of built environments is political decision making. Consequently, the unravelling of political processes embedded within 'the construction of socio-physical constructions' is central to understanding urban change.

Matthew Gandy's work is at the forefront of this urban-oriented political ecology literature, and his analyses have helped inform our conceptualization of the roles of socio-nature in urbanization process-es. His work on infrastructure development in New York City (2002) emphasizes both the material and ideological bases for nature–society relations in city building, arguing that society manipulates biophysical nature as a precondition for urban life. Gandy's exploration of water as it flows through urban spaces highlights the multiple and complex roles that socio-nature plays in city building. 'Nature is built into the fabric of the city,' he writes, 'not just as a material element in urban space, but also as a commodity that is integral to the abstract dynamics of capital accumulation' (2004: 1025). For Gandy, 'metropolitan natures' – water systems, highways, parks – are produced not only through networks that bring together raw materials from far-off places, but also through ideologies that support city life. Such metropolitan natures – or, in our terms, socio-natures – provide a concrete conceptualization of the ways that cities are produced through integrated and largely inseparable forms of human and non-human natures at various scales.

In our historical comparison of socio-ecological change along the Don River, socio-natures influence urban growth or decline in four specific ways. First, they underpin urban growth or decline as imbricated components of physical form; second, they are centrally involved with ongoing biophysical processes, such as, in our case, flooding and siltation; third, they are a key aspect of political processes that influence the conditions and institutions of urban-development policy formation; and, fourth, they alter spatial relations in the city – by, for example, making some areas more desirable, and consequently marketable, as accessibility is increased to 'nature,' employment centres, recreational spaces, and 'healthy ecological systems.'

The Don Improvement Project, 1886–1891

By the 1870s the Lower Don River had become befouled by munici-pal and industrial wastes and was widely recognized as a menace to public health. Years of waste and sewage disposal by local industries and municipal authorities, combined with changes in the river's hy-drology caused by deforestation, soil erosion, and water diversion for agricultural and industrial purposes, contributed to highly polluted conditions in the slow-moving, serpentine reaches of the lower river and the massive reach of marshlands at its mouth. As one area resident commented in a letter to the daily *Globe* in 1874, 'The water and marsh [at the mouth] of the Don continues to be filled with a foul combination of [wastes] ... so that whenever the wind sets to a particular quarter, and agitates the water, the result is [an] abominable smell ... injuri-ous to the comfort [and] the health of all within its reach' (*Globe* 1874: 2). From the perspective of ship captains and harbour officials, even more significant than the problem of filth and disease was the costly and pernicious problem of siltation. Each spring, harbour-minding of-ficials cursed the river for depositing large quantities of silt and detritus in Toronto Harbour, creating hazards for shipping traffic (Eads 1882; Tully 1872). Damage to property caused by seasonal flooding presented yet another complaint that area landowners and civic representatives directed at the river.

In response to these problematic 'natural' processes, civic politicians sought to alter the river and thereby produce a new form of socio-na-ture that would serve the city's urbanization interests. They forwarded a plan in the early 1880s to 'widen, deepen, and straighten' the Lower Don River in accordance with four central objectives: (1) to improve the sanitary condition of the area; (2) to make the Don a navigable stream for large vessels; (3) to accommodate rail traffic into the City; and (4) to create new lands for industrial purposes (City of Toronto 1889).

For residents of Toronto's east end, the idea of the improvement project conjured images of prosperity and revitalization for an area that had long been relegated to the margins of the city. Throughout the early 1880s, they petitioned council to take action to implement this ambitious river-improvement scheme. At a public meeting to discuss the project in October 1881, for example, landowner J.P. Doel 'pleaded on behalf of the health of the neighbourhood and city for the straightening and deepening of the Don,' imagining a future where the Don would become 'the great shipping centre for Toronto' (*Globe* 1881a: 7). Alderman Thomas Davies, who owned a manufacturing firm along the river, expressed the vision of area residents in his submission to the City's Committee on Works in early January 1882:

> This great scheme ... will afford sites and facilities for all kinds of manufacturing enterprises, coal yards, lumber yards, and many factories we may not now think of, the establishment of which will most assuredly go far towards making Toronto, what I believe it is destined to become, a great manufacturing as well as a business centre ... The miasmatic atmosphere with which this locality is too often troubled will be dispelled and the healthfulness greatly increased. Freshets and ice-jams will be things of the past, and the current in the River unobstructed. (City of Toronto 1881a: 888–90)

Visions for the Don River also appeared in real estate broadsides for the period, which referred potential east-end buyers to the proximity of the improvement project and its potential to 'materially advance the value of surrounding districts.' As one 1887 advertisement read, 'That hitherto despised stream' would soon become 'the commercial shipping centre of Toronto, not only for lake and river, but for railway commerce as well' (Armstrong and Cook 1887). The improvements, in sum, would turn a stigmatized and peripheral area into a productive district of the city, producing profits for the City and local landowners alike.

While area landowners and industrialists sought to remove the uncertainty and unhealthiness of their surroundings, city council members saw the improvement as an opportunity to augment paltry assessment revenues and to address flooding and health concerns that carried the threat of litigation. In early February 1880, Toronto City Council resolved to form a special committee to report 'upon the state and condition of the Don River ... from a sanitary point of view' and to develop a scheme to abate the nuisance. Alderman Davies, a vocal proponent of the Don improvement plan, argued that 'every manufactory brings with it assessable property, and when numbers of them are located on the River, it will become a paying work and a profitable undertaking to the City' (City of Toronto 1881a: 7).

Little action seems to have followed from this resolution until five years later, when the Canadian Pacific Railway Company finally propelled the project out of council chambers. In the spring of 1886, the railway, which had attempted since 1881 to connect their east–west lines with Toronto, succeeded in winning the support of City officials to create an eastern entrance to the city along the west bank of the Don Improvement (Mellen 1974). The powerful railway company did much to secure project fortunes, and in March 1886 the Don Improvement Act was passed by the provincial legislature, empowering the City to borrow funds and expropriate lands to complete the improvement works.[2]

Work began in the fall of 1886, but the completion of the Don Improvement Project was anything but straightforward. The magnitude and ambitiousness of the project were soon apparent in a series of unforeseen problems and associated setbacks. Problems with contractors, disputes with area residents and industrialists, protracted negotiations with the railway companies, and unanticipated problems with the biophysical elements of the site all contributed to delay the project's progress and increase the amount of funds required (for a complete history see Bonnell 2010).

Before ending our discussion of the improvement project, we want to briefly focus on that section of the river that connected directly to Toronto Bay – for it is this section more than any other that has given rise to both historical and contemporary calls for change. Work on this section began in September 1908 and, by mid-July 1909, the river had been diverted from its curving westerly course into Toronto Bay to run instead directly south to meet up with an outlet known as Keating's Channel. Final adjustments to the mouth of the river occurred within the context of the newly incorporated Toronto Harbour Commission's (THC) 1912 Waterfront Plan. Under the leadership of THC chief engineer E.L. Cousins, a series of studies through 1912 presented different alternatives for the creation of new industrial land within the Ashbridge's Bay marsh. The THC decided that the river would curve southwest, then south to meet with a widened and reinforced Keating Channel before entering the harbour. Objections by the British American Oil Company, whose property lay along the line of the proposed diversion, led to the final amendment in the long history of plans to alter the river mouth. Rather than curving through British American Oil's property, the river would continue straight south to connect at a right angle with Keating Channel – the same jarring alignment that persists today.[3]

Re-naturalizing the Don in the Twenty-First Century

Our more recent history of the Don River examines attempts to undo the 'improvement' to the river that took place during the late nineteenth century. We start by highlighting the major elements in MVVA's winning submission for the Lower Don Lands and then look back to its antecedents and influences in an attempt to understand better why, within the relatively short historical span of a hundred years, such an apparently radical reversal is being pursued.

According to MVVA, its plan makes the site more natural, creating the potential for new networks of biophysical relationships within a more complex river mouth. The three most prominent features in the MVVA proposal, from our perspective, are the reconfiguration of the mouth of the river, the creation of new parkland, and the construction of five mixed-used neighbourhoods (see figure 13.1). The plan shifts the river's mouth so that it winds south of its current right-angle turn at the Keating Channel and then empties into the harbour. It envisions a curvilinear river with multiple outlets to the lake – the main flow emptying into the harbour after moving south of the Keating Channel and winding its way through the port lands. MVVA underscores the naturalization aspects of its plan for the mouth of the river. However, we believe that the naturalized Don River should be understood as a new form of socio-nature that unites various biophysical functions (e.g., flood protection) and has the social purpose of producing waterfront property and residential neighbourhoods supporting urban development.

Surrounding the river, a newly created landscape is to be devoted to parkland – the second prominent feature of the plan. This new parkland serves to bring together a more naturalized river mouth, a floodway, and new neighbourhoods into a single landscape 'that supports and becomes the generator of new urban life' (MVVA 2007: 6). The parkland is intended to simultaneously provide a central design feature and serve a key ecological function; that is, according to the plan, the 'central parkland … by virtue of its size, scale, and complexity, is able to take on river-mouth hydraulics while providing habitation and recreation … "Naturalization of the mouth of the river" is not a token gesture but a sustainable urban estuary in the functional and social sense' (ibid.: 10).

While the primary focus for the estuarine functions of the reconfigured river is to provide protection against flooding, its new entranceway will, without a doubt, provide a splendid view of the harbour and central waterfront. Five mixed-used neighbourhoods, the third major element of the plan, integrate the urban with the natural to take advantage of the amenities afforded by these harbour views, a closeness to 'nature,' and a central waterfront location. Land values around the river mouth and other sites at the water's edge will be very high, we expect, and are thus likely to spark struggles to use some of the parkland for residential or commercial development.

Though MVVA's ambitious vision for the area has strikingly innovative and creative elements, it builds on ideas and plans suggested earlier by the city's activist movements concerned with conservation and civic environmentalism. Many activists have taken their inspiration from Elizabeth Simcoe, the wife of Lieutenant Governor John Graves Simcoe, whose paintings and descriptions of the valley in the late eighteenth century, with its clouds of passenger pigeons, majestic pine groves, and salmon-filled waters, remind us that the river was once at the heart of a thriving ecosystem. Conservationist Charles Sauriol (1904–95) is perhaps the best representative of this conservation legacy. Between 1927 and 1968, Sauriol and his family spent each summer in a rustic cottage in the valley. It was here that Sauriol wrote his 1981 book *Remembering the Don*, which has become a classic for conservation-oriented activists and civic environmentalists concerned with the Don Valley. In 1947 Sauriol co-founded the Don Valley Conservation Association (DVCA), which worked to protect valley resources and educate the public about the need for conservation. Nature walks and annual tree planting days helped inform the public about a threatened wilderness at their doorsteps, and the first ever Paddle the Don event, organized by the DVCA in 1949, encouraged Toronto residents to see the valley as a place for fun and recreation. A champion of the Don throughout his life, Sauriol's skill as a fundraiser and his unwavering dedication to conservation proved instrumental in protecting portions of the valley from development in the 1960s and 1970s.

Civic activism around the river valley received a boost from an unlikely source in October 1954, when Hurricane Hazel dumped 285 millimetres of rain in the Toronto area, washing out bridges and roads across the city and taking eighty-one lives in the space of forty-eight hours. In Toronto alone, over 1800 people were left homeless. Reactions to this storm marked a turning point in mid- and late-twentieth-century regulation of the city's river systems. As the city recovered during the winter of 1954–5, it did so with a new awareness of the power of biophysical processes and the significance of valley lands as natural drainage channels for flood waters. In 1957, four Toronto-area conservation authorities, including the Don Valley Conservation Authority, amalgamated to form the Metropolitan Toronto and Region Conservation Authority (MTRCA, now called the Toronto and Region Conservation Authority, or TRCA), which allowed for greater coordination among jurisdictions in regulating the use of valley lands. Multiple levels of government recognized the need to protect large sections of central Toronto from flooding, and development plans were put on hold until these problems were overcome.

Hurricane Hazel also prompted a broader grassroots response to environmental degradation in the city. Inspired by the activism of the late 1960s, a new generation of environmental activists began organizing to find more sustaining solutions to ecological problems. These efforts came to fruition in 1989 when a group of city residents and politicians established a citizen-driven body to advise city council on restoration initiatives for the Don River (Desfor and Keil 2004). The Task Force to Bring Back the Don has become the central body for activating change and has taken the lead in creative thinking in three main areas of responsibility: community organization; knowledge development and educational projects about the Don; and political advocacy. It has sponsored clean-up days, tree plantings, community stewardship programs, boating on the Don, walks along the Don, and fundraising events. And it was instrumental in getting funding and approvals for the production of the Chester Spring Marsh, a groundbreaking project aimed at re-naturalizing a wetland in the Lower Don Valley and thereby reorienting important societal relations with urban biophysical processes.

The task force, situated both inside and outside of City government, seeks to go beyond balancing the interests of 'nature' and the economy; its approach to ecological change is grounded in a new relationship between society and nature. In the case of Chester Springs Marsh, the restored wetland provides habitat (shelter, food, and a breeding ground) for wildlife in the city; helps to regulate the quantity and quality of water in the river; and removes harmful pollutants and contaminants from the environment (City of Toronto 2010). Here we have an example of how ecological and human health are woven together into a integrated network of socio-ecological relationships.

The task force's approach and actions are similar to those of other North American activist groups. Comparisons can be made, for example, to citizen-led initiatives to restore the Los Angeles River, which have recently resulted in the adoption of a River Revitalization Master Plan to transform a thirty-two-mile stretch of the river into an 'urban greenway.' Lewis MacAdams, poet and founder of the Friends of the

Los Angeles River, reputedly asked the river 'if it minded being saved. "The river did not say no," MacAdams recalled, "so I decided to go ahead"' (Coburn 1994: 50). In a similar way in Toronto, the Task Force to Bring Back the Don looked to the river itself as a source of inspiration. The MVVA consulting team appropriated this discourse when it wrote that it approached the design competition with two initial questions: 'Where does the mouth of the Don River want to be?' and 'What form can it give the city?' (MVVA 2007: 7). Here we have both an international planning team and a poet-activist from Los Angeles articulating the agency of rivers, and seeking guidance from those rivers instead of seeking to guide them.

Plans for the Lower Don Lands continue to change despite Waterfront Toronto's international competition and award-winning plan. In late 2008, Waterfront Toronto seemed to have shifted course by delaying implementation of its plans for the Lower Don Lands. This decision was connected not only to current political and economic situations (that is, a Conservative federal government with no elected representatives from Toronto, and the most serious economic recession since the Great Depression), but also to a proposal to, once again, link the future of the Lower Don Lands to a major international sporting event (see Laidley, this volume) – this time the 2015 Pan Am Games. The Lower Don Lands is being planned as the site for a number of athletic facilities for these games and the West Don Lands, the adjoining neighbourhood, is scheduled to be the home of the Athletes' Village. In addition, Waterfront Toronto announced on 19 May 2009 that Bill Clinton's Climate Initiative and the US Green Building Council's Climate Positive Development Program have selected the Lower Don Lands as one of sixteen global urban projects they will support in helping to demonstrate that cities can grow in ways that are 'climate positive' (Waterfront Toronto, n.d.) Thus, at the time of writing, plans for transforming the Lower Don Lands continue to evolve and move opportunistically forward.

A Comparison of Nineteenth- and Twenty-First-Century River Transformations

As noted at the outset of this chapter, we are interested in comparing planning for new forms of socio-natures in city-building projects during the current period with those of the nineteenth century. Such a comparison will enable us to begin to unravel the complex nature–society relations embedded in hybrid landscapes and better understand the production of new forms of socio-nature, including the unearthing of the ideology and politics that are integral to constituting those landscapes. We recognize, as do Waterfront Toronto and the Toronto and Region Conservation Authority, that the MVVA plan represents only a starting point, and will not necessarily be implemented as presented in the international competition. Nevertheless, we believe that comparing the MVVA plan with those of the nineteenth century provides insight into both continuing and changing societal relationships with nature.

We have identified four categories through which plans and planning link socio-natures to urban development and use these categories as the basis for our comparison. That is, we compare the ways the two plans represent socio-nature's relationship with (1) changing land uses, their spatial organization, and the production of new territories; (2) altering biophysical processes; (3) increasing accessibility to the city; and (4) building new understandings of 'nature' and 'the urban' and competitive city processes.

Changing Land Uses, Their Spatial Organization, and the Production of New Territories

In both the nineteenth and twenty-first centuries, city planning has been centrally concerned with the production of new socio-natures. Supporters of the nineteenth-century Don River improvements sought to alter the then existing land uses and create new territory. Straightening the river would primarily benefit the railway companies by providing new space for the laying of tracks into and out of the city; filled land along the former meandering river channel would also create sites for rail-side industry. And for several aldermen with manufacturing firms along the river, the relocation of the river channel would extend their property and increase its value through proximity to the railway. Railway interests largely shaped the Don Improvement Project, shifting the emphasis from the development of a navigable shipping corridor to a rail and road corridor, from the river itself to the space alongside it.

A straightened river was also seen as a benefit to adjacent neighbourhoods, transforming a stigmatized and peripheral area into a productive district of the city. Adjacent neighbourhoods would benefit through economic growth and better health, and the City and local landowners would gain from increased land values. As noted by Alderman Davies in 1882, the Don Improvement Project would 'make [the area] as it ought to be – as healthy as any other part of the City' (City of Toronto

1881b). And as real estate developers enthused, improvements would dramatically increase property values in the area, making it 'the most desirable and valuable part of the whole city' (ibid.).

The MVVA plan, in contrast, frames its land-use changes within an overarching concept of an urban estuary. This new kind of urban space radically transforms the notion of an estuary as a mixed land-water territory that provides myriad essential biophysical functions for sustaining aquatic and land-based ecological networks. MVVA's new notion of an urban estuary foresees a highly desirable place not only for plants and animals and the exchange of nutrients, minerals, and so on, but also for human developments having abundant interactions with the environment, adjacent neighbourhoods, and other areas of the city. Its highly permeable land-water boundaries envision places for enormous social and economic exchanges as well as biophysical ones.

Complementing the area's estuarial exchange value, the MVVA plan aims to integrate what had been considered marginal and underutilized lands into an active and thriving urban space. This new space is intended to meet Toronto's contemporary needs, and to create a landscape for twenty-first-century urban life that supports the city's competitive position with other global cities. The plan conceives of the Lower Don Lands as a landscape for upwardly mobile members of the new knowledge economy, discarding in the process its reputation as a 'waste space' for noxious materials, marginalized people, and disreputable activities (see Bonnell, this volume). The new location for the river mouth will '[reassert] the presence of the river in the city' (MVVA 2007: 11), creating the attraction of 'urban nature' that provides a respite from the everyday tensions of high-powered city life situated just steps away in the financial district and creative-economy zones. And its development strategy for this new zone of opportunity is based on leveraging the attractive powers (i.e., marketability) of a more 'natural' river mouth, substantial parkland, improved transportation facilities, and a central city location all framed within an urban-estuary concept.

A comparison between this dimension of the nineteenth- and twenty-first-century plans suggests important similarities and differences in the portrayal of nature–society relations. Both plans present an instrumental approach to an external nature – that is, a belief in society's ability to manipulate nature to meet its needs. Society did undertake and currently proposes to manipulate nature through the production of a new landscape as a way to integrate a marginal area into active city life. And both plans propose to use nature to support economic development. While nineteenth-century plans intended to transform nature for the use of manufacturing enterprises and coal and lumber yards – that is, making the area an industrial centre – current plans are designed to produce new forms of socio-nature that preclude industrial activities. These plans aim to support an economy dominated by knowledge-producing and information-processing enterprises, by constructing a profitable landscape of mixed office, residential, and recreational uses.

Altering Biophysical Processes

The primary biophysical process addressed by both the plans is flooding. Although major variations in river flow have resulted from 'natural' processes largely unrelated to societal activities, urbanization has long been linked to increased risks of flooding through the replacement of porous surfaces with pavement, and associated increases in the rate of surface run-off. And of course, building in a flood plain increases the risk of damage to property and person. In the nineteenth century, attention focused more on damage caused by annual spring freshets, while concerns in contemporary plans are discussed in terms of a major 'once in a century' storm such as Hurricane Hazel.

Proponents of the nineteenth-century plan predicted that 'freshets and ice-jams will be things of the past' following the completion of the improvement project (City of Toronto 1881a: 888–90). A new form of socio-nature would create infrastructure to move water and ice from spring breakups out of the area more quickly and thus reduce damage from flooding.

The MVVA plan speaks to flood control in two ways. First, it incorporates a berm constructed as part of the Don River Park into its plan, thereby simultaneously reducing liabilities associated with building in a flood plain and creating opportunities for urban growth and development (see Introduction, this volume). The 7.3-hectare berm is fundamentally a flood protection device, a mound of earth that raises the ground level above predicted flood-water levels from a once-in-a-century storm. With the berm in place, constraints on building within the Regulatory Floodplain west and north of the Don River can be removed (Waterfront Toronto n.d.c.: n.p.). The berm, itself a special and quite technically sophisticated form of socio-nature, functions to make possible development on 210 hectares of central-city land, and also serves as parkland with an 'urban meadow' (ibid.). Second, the MVVA plan proposes to reduce the risk of flooding by constructing a floodway with multiple paths by which the river will be able to reach the lake, and through the inclusion of marsh features to absorb and filter seasonal floodwaters. The plan 'proposes a braided system of water channels cut to different depths to accept and deliver varying volumes of water, from low to moderate to severe flood events' (MVVA 2007: 36). Thus, MVVA's multi-tasking socio-nature intends not only to reduce the risks from flooding but also to make possible urban expansion with new neighbourhoods and recreational opportunities all working together in support of twenty-first-century urban lifestyles. As the proposal states, 'the bold new park [the urban estuary] at the centre of our scheme consolidates the program of a naturalized river mouth, floodway, recreational park, and neighbourhood icon into a single and complex central landscape that supports and becomes the generator of new urban life' (ibid.: 6).

The production and removal of sediment in the river is another process addressed by both the nineteenth- and twentieth-century plans, and has long been recognized as a contentious problem by harbour-minding bodies and conservation authorities. The nineteenth-century improvement plan was expected to harness 'nature's power' to transport silt deposits from the river into Ashbridge's Bay. The 'natural' relocation of the silt would help to fill the marshlands and relieve the city of a public health nuisance – both of which would be of considerable economic benefit. Sediment removal also plays an important role in the MVVA plan, which includes the construction of a basin in which sediment will be collected, then dried and stabilized prior to its being reused to help form the future landscape and parkland (MVVA 2007: 36), revealing another purportedly 'win-win' technical solution for both the environment and economy.

Increasing Accessibility

By accessibility we mean both opportunities for people to interact with the river and lake and, more generally, reducing the friction of interactions within neighbourhoods and the city – that is, improving transportation networks and facilities.

Both nineteenth- and twenty-first-century plans seek to increase accessibility to interact with the river. Earlier plans 'channeled nature' towards city-building ends, intending to tame it in order to produce returns for long-term infrastructure investments. The nineteenth-century plan envisioned the establishment of interactions with a straightened and encapsulated river, creating a predictable corridor for transportation (rail and shipping) and for the removal of wastes. Generally undertaken to meet utilitarian ends, the improvements were expected to attract investors who sought to secure a return on long-term and large-scale investments from the infrastructure projects. The interactions between humans and the river were to be considerably less intimate than those proposed by the MVVA plan.

In the twenty-first century, the river mouth has been 'unleashed' to provide opportunities for more up-close interactions with the river and lake and to act as an attraction for revitalizing mixed-use neighbourhoods. The MVVA plan promotes accessibility to the environment by providing opportunities to play near, swim in, boat on, or contemplate a benign socio-nature. It aims to provide extensive water-based recreation opportunities, and to bring the water's edge into the public realm so as to enrich experiences where land and water meet (MVVA 2007).While both the nineteenth- and twentieth-century plans stress the need for improved accessibility in the city, there are major differences in the transportation facilities proposed by the two plans. The nineteenth-century plan was primarily concerned with increasing the railways' access to major urban markets, better navigation on the Don, and the establishment of stronger and more reliable bridge structures across the river. The MVVA proposal, however, speaks both to linking its new neighbourhoods into the fabric of the city and to increasing the ease of movement within those neighbourhoods. It recognizes the importance of north–south connections to link the area with the city, and foresees penetrating the rail-corridor barrier with improved pedestrian and trolley underpasses. Recalling one of the plan's principal themes of sustainability, it proposes a 'responsible balance' between private automobile facilities and more environmentally friendly modes of transport (pedestrian paths, public transport, and bike lanes) to increase ease of movement within neighbourhoods (MVVA 2007: 56).

Representations of Nature and City and Their Relationships to Competitive City Processes

The two plans represent relationships between 'nature' and the city in significantly different ways. A discourse of 'improvement' featured prominently in the nineteenth-century plan (see the Introduction, this volume; Moir 1986), whereas in the MVVA plan the notion of 'sustainability' dominates.

The Don Improvement Plan, while drawing on notions of progress and modernity, also includes ambivalent representations of nature. The river was seen to be both an asset for the city and an impediment to progress. Early European colonists saw the natural harbour as attractive for both military and shipping purposes, and it was the prime reason for their settlement of the city. But by the end of the nineteenth century, both the river and the harbour were seen to be somehow less than what they potentially could be. Many of Toronto's business elite and politicians thought that human intervention was needed to improve the lower stretches of the river to bring about progress and modernization, in the form of industrialization, to the city. The improved river would attend to the interests of the railways, provide additional land for new businesses, improve the health of nearby residents, and increase tax revenues for the City. But making the river more 'natural' (in the twenty-first-century sense) was not what the improvement plan's proponents had in mind.

In the MVVA proposal, a naturalized river mouth promotes urban 'livability' and complements the complexity of contemporary lifestyles by providing spectacular images of 'sustainable habitats for wildlife, fishes, and people' (MVVA 2007: 6). The new urban estuary's two distinct worlds, the urban and the natural, are brought together as a web of ecological, economic, spatial, and social interactions. In the process, MVVA intends to 'recapture' the waterfront moment: 'We want to create a healthy ecological setting, as this is a prerequisite to sustainable habitats for wildlife, fisheries, and people, and the intractable link to ensuring market reinvestment in this place' (ibid.). Here we have an explicit recognition of and appreciation for relationships between socio-natures (i.e., a healthy socio-ecological setting) and market investments, even though these relationships are seen as diffuse and unregulated, and, in all likelihood, place more emphasis on market-based investments than on ecological integrity.

The MVVA's plan for greater complexity and diversity of socio-nature's linkages with contemporary urban life is connected with two aspects of the dominant mode of development. First, the plan envisions the production of mixed-use up-scale neighbourhoods and urban amenities that are intended to improve the city's competitive position at both the regional/metropolitan (the central city versus the suburbs) and global levels (cities competing within an international hierarchical network) (MVVA 2007). Second, the plan recognizes that, in a global economy, materials are transformed into commodities and distributed to markets through networks (spatial, technological, financial, cultural, and organizational) that are more expansive and more intricate than those that existed during the nineteenth century. Its plan to construct an urban estuary promotes post-industrial economic activities that have extensive links with globally networked production systems.

To briefly summarize this section, we have found that both the nineteenth- and twenty-first-century plans seek to produce new forms of socio-nature as a way to enhance prospects for marginal neighbourhoods and to lay the groundwork for broader urban developments. In the nineteenth century, the Don Improvement Plan envisioned a straightened river supporting development of a marginalized neighbourhood as well as efforts to industrialize the city. In the twenty-first century, the MVVA plan for an urban estuary looks to naturalize the river mouth in support of mixed-use sustainable neighbourhoods and a post-industrial economy.

Conclusions

In this the final chapter of the volume, we sought to understand better Toronto's changing waterfront by comparing nineteenth- and twenty-first-century plans for reshaping the lower stretches of the Don River. Within a relatively short historical period, city builders have decided first to straighten and encapsulate the river and then to reverse course and naturalize the river's mouth.

Both the nineteenth-century Don Improvement Plan and the twenty-first-century MVVA plan for an urban estuary and berm-park support the city's economic development. In the earlier period, the Don was altered as part of city building for an industrial era. The twenty-first-century plan aims to modernize socio-ecological relationships by reducing the risk of flooding, revitalizing a marginalized waterfront area, constructing new urban neighbourhoods in which both nature and society are seen to function for their mutual benefit, and producing an urban lifestyle that appeals to a sophisticated and cosmopolitan (and, some would say, 'creative') population. For us, MVVA's urban estuary is an exciting concept that opens up new possibilities for acknowledging a fusion between the urban and the natural. But the concept as described in the MVVA proposal does not resolve a fundamental problem – it fails to acknowledge the ideological positions and social relations that are embedded within such an urban landscape, and thus does not adequately recognize the economic and political struggles and societal tensions that will inevitably arise.

While both plans aim to transform socio-natures, they contain some important distinctions. First, the nineteenth-century plan is replete with the language of 'improvement.' Nature was regarded as both an asset and an obstruction to the city: an asset, as the foundation for large infrastructure projects; an obstruction, for its perceived inefficiency, its unpredictability, and its destructive potential. As Toronto historian Henry Scadding wrote of the nineteenth-century harbour improvements, nature could be improved by diligent human action: 'When at length the proper hour arrived, and the right men appeared, possessed of the intelligence, the vigour and the wealth equal to the task of bettering nature by art on a considerable scale, then at once the true value and capabilities of the Don were brought out into view' (1873: 559–60).

Contemporary plans for an urban estuary, by comparison, harness the language of 'sustainability' and ecological modernization. Sustainability differs from 'improvement' in its fundamental recognition that economic growth will be undermined unless society pays special attention to the ecological systems that underlie that growth – and their unlimited exploitation is understood as a threat to both economic production and human well-being. As the MVVA plan indicates, 'Our proposal embraces the use of sustainable materials and energy savings, but also goes beyond this to encompass sustainability on multiple levels: sustainable communities that provide a broad range of housing, employment, and recreation; a sustainable lifestyle that encourages pedestrian use and public transportation; a sustainable real estate value with structures that are well built and elevated above the regulatory flood levels' (MVVA 2007: 3).

Second, both plans carry important linkages between socio-natures and public health. In both periods, the plans presume an underlying fear of external nature as a serious threat to human health. In the nineteenth century, wetlands were feared because of their association with miasmas and, by extension, with a host of ailments including cholera and typhoid fever (see Jackson; Bonnell, this volume). More recently, health analysts have noted that the presence of environmental toxins in the air, water, and soil, particularly in urban areas, are potential causes of cancer, heart disease, and a number of respiratory ailments (L. Nash 2006). The MVVA plan's recognition that contaminated soils and groundwater must be cleaned up is an indication of this underlying concern.

In closing we note that the outcome of the MVVA proposal remains, of course, to be determined. Whether or not the project moves forward – and the shape it will eventually take – depends on a host of local, regional, and international contingencies that are not predictable at this time. While neighbourhood revitalization and increased value for residential properties in the new neighbourhoods are likely to result from such a proposal, the project's ability to improve the ecological viability of the highly urbanized Lower Don Lands remains uncertain. The MVVA proposal affirms, however, in clear unambiguous language that at the beginning of the twenty-first century, just as at the end of the nineteenth, the production of socio-natures are essential aspects of urbanization processes.

NOTES

1 Formed in 2001 with representatives from the federal, provincial, and municipal governments, the Toronto Waterfront Revitalization Corporation (TWRC) later changed its name to Waterfront Toronto. We have used the name 'Waterfront Toronto' throughout, to avoid confusion.
2 On 25 March 1886, the Ontario Legislature approved An Act Respecting the River Don Improvements (Statutes of Ontario Act 49 Vic., c. 66); the act was passed subject to the approval of the eligible electors of the City of Toronto.
3 British American Oil first recorded its objection to the proposed Don alignment in January 1913. By June of that year it had proposed an alternate alignment for the river and, in early July, Cousins reported that a 'compromise plan ... had been arrived at as a result of his conference with the representatives of the Company' (Toronto Harbour Commissioners 1913a).

References

Acton, T.A. 1997. *Gypsy Politics and Traveller Identity*. Hatfield, Hertfordshire: University of Hertfordshire Press.

Adam, G.M. 1891. *Toronto, Old and New: A Memorial Volume*. Toronto: Mail Printing Co.

Adam, G.M., C.P. Mulvany, and C.B. Robinson. 1885. *History of Toronto and County of York*. Toronto: C. Blackett Robinson.

Adams, M., and K. Neuman. 2006. 'It's not easy being green.' *Globe and Mail*, 20 October: 21.

Allen, N. 1892. *Report on Sanitary Conditions of the City of Toronto, including an account of the operations of the Board of Health and the vital statistics: For the year 1891*. City of Toronto Archives, fonds 200, series 365, file 6.

Altvater, E. 1993. *The Future of the Market: An Essay on the Regulation of Money and Nature after the Collapse of 'Actually Existing Socialism.'* London and New York: Verso.

American Society of Landscape Architects. 2008. 'Analysis and Planning Honor Award.' http://www.asla.org/awards/2008/08winners/013.html.

Amos, M.V. 1916. Memorandum to Lord Brand, 10 May. Library and Archives Canada, Lord Brand fonds, MG 27 II G 6, microfilm reel no. A829.

Andersen, O.B., T.R. Crow, S.M. Lietz, and F. Stearns. 1996. 'Transformation of a Landscape in the Upper Mid-west, USA: The History of the Lower St. Croix River Valley, 1830 to Present.' *Landscape and Urban Planning* 35: 247–67.

Anderson, J.R., E.E. Hardy, J.T. Roach, and R.E. Witmer. 1976. *A Land Use and Land Cover Classification System for Use with Remote Sensor Data*. Geological Survey Professional Paper 964. Washington: US Government Printing Office.

Anderson, L. 1988. 'Water-Supply.' In N.R. Ball, ed., *Building Canada: A History of Public Works*, 195–220. Toronto: University of Toronto Press.

Andranovich, G., M.J. Burbank, and C.H. Heying. 2001. 'Olympic Cities: Lessons Learned from Mega-event Politics.' *Journal of Urban Affairs* 232: 113–131.

Andrew, C., K. Graham, and S. Phillips, eds. 2003. *Urban Affairs: Back on the Policy Agenda*. Montreal: MQUP.

Arce-Nazario, J.A. 2007. 'Human Landscapes Have Complex Trajectories: Reconstructing Peruvian Amazon Landscape History from 1948–2005.' *Landscape Ecology* 22: 89–101.

Archives of Ontario. Series RG 1-2-1. Correspondence relating to surveys.

Armstrong and Cook. 1887. 'Choice Building Lots for Sale, Registered Plan No. 709, November 1.' City of Toronto Archives, fonds 79, series 343, file 6, item 32.

Armstrong, F.H. 1988. *A City in the Making: Progress, People and Perils in Victorian Toronto*. Toronto: Dundurn Press.

Armstrong, J. 1992. 'Waterfront plan unveiled, "Jurisdictional gridlock" must end, Crombie says.' *Toronto Star*, 15 May: A7.

– 1993a. 'Commission blocks probe of port books.' *Toronto Star*, 10 February: A7.

– 1993b. 'Fixed link, jets urged for island airport.' *Toronto Star*, 30 November: A6.

– 1994. 'Rowlands wins fight over Port Authority[,] mayor wants Ottawa to allow name change, public access to records of Harbor Commission.' *Toronto Star*. 23 April: A4.

Atkinson, L. 2002. 'The Impact of Cholera on the Design and Implementation of Toronto's First Municipal By-laws, 1834.' *Urban History Review/Revue d'histoire urbaine* 30(2): 3–16.

Aucoin, P. 1995. *The New Public Management: Canada in Comparative Perspective*. Montreal: Institute for Research on Public Policy.

Bakker, K. 2003. *An Uncooperative Commodity: Privatizing Water in England and Wales*. Oxford: Oxford University Press.

Baldwin, D. 1988. 'Sewerage.' In N.R. Ball, ed., *Building Canada: A History of Public Works*, 221–44. Toronto: University of Toronto Press.

Baldwin, P. 1999. *Contagion and the State in Europe, 1830–1930*. New York: Cambridge University Press.

Ball, N.R. 1988. *'Mind, Heart, and Vision': Professional Engineering in Canada 1887 to 1987*. Ottawa: National Museum of Science and Technology, National Museums of Canada, in cooperation with the Engineering Centennial Board.

Ballantyne, C.C. 1918. Letter to R. Borden, 4 April. Library and Archives Canada, Sir Robert Borden fonds, MG 26 H, vol. 239, pt. 1, microfilm reel no. C-4414.

Barber, J. 1996. 'Mr. P., the Liberals, and the waterfront.' *Globe and Mail*, 16 April: A9.

– 1997. 'Federal government ambushes Toronto.' *Globe and Mail*, 17 April: A9.

Barnett, J.M. 1971. 'Ashbridge's Bay.' *Ontario Naturalist*, December: 24–6.

Barrett, S. 1991. *Pathways: Towards an Ecosystem Approach. A Report of Phases I and 11 of an Environmental Audit of Toronto's East Bayfront and Port Industrial Area*. Ottawa: Minister of Supply and Services Canada.

– 2000. *A Decade of Regeneration: Realizing a Vision for Lake Ontario*. Toronto: Waterfront Regeneration Trust.

Basset, K., R. Griffiths, and I. Smith. 2002. 'Testing Governance: Partnerships, Planning and Conflict in Waterfront Regeneration.' *Urban Studies* 39(10): 1757–75.

Bator, P.A. 1979. 'Saving Lives on the Wholesale Plan: Public Health Reform in the City of Toronto, 1900 to 1930.' PhD dissertation, Department of History, University of Toronto.

Beck, U. 1992. *Risk Society: Towards a New Modernity*. London: Sage.

Beeby, D. 1984. 'Industrial Strategy and Manufacturing Growth in Toronto, 1880–1910.' *Ontario History* 76(3): 199–232.

Bennett, A.F. 1991. 'Roads, Roadsides and Wildlife Conservation: A Review.' In D.A. Saunders and R.J. Hobbs, eds., *Nature Conservation 2: The Role of Corridors*, 71–84. New South Wales, AUS: Surrey Beatty and Sons, Chipping Norton.

Benton, T. 1989. 'Marxism and Natural Limits.' *New Left Review* 178: 51–86.

Bilson, G. 1980. *A Darkened House: Cholera in Nineteenth-Century Canada*. Toronto: University of Toronto Press.

Bird, J.H. 1963. *The Major Seaports of the United Kingdom*. London: Hutchinson.

Blaikie, P.M., and H.C. Brookfield. 1987. *Land Degradation and Society*. London and New York: Methuen.

Bonnell, J. 2008. 'Bringing Back the Don: Sixty Years of Community Action.' In W. Reeves and C. Palassio, eds., *HTO: Toronto's Water from Lake Iroquois to Lost Rivers to Low-flow Toilets*, 266–83. Toronto: Coach House Books.

– 2010. 'Imagined Futures and Unintended Consequences: An Environmental History of Toronto's Don River Valley.' PhD dissertation, Department of Theory and Policy Studies, Ontario Institute for Studies in Education, University of Toronto.

Booz, Allen, and Hamilton. 1992. *Organizational Plan and Budgets for the Toronto*

Harbour Commission: Final Report. Toronto: Toronto Harbour Commissioners and Toronto Economic Development Corporation.

Borde, A.B., R.M. Thom, and S. Rumrill. 2003. 'Geospatial Habitat Change Analysis in Pacific Northwest Coastal Estuaries.' *Estuaries* 26: 1104–16.

Bouchette, J. 1815. *A Topographical Description of the Province of Lower Canada, with Remarks upon Upper Canada, and on the Relative Connexion of Both Provinces with the United States of America*. London: W. Faden.

– 1831. *The British Dominions in North America; or a Topographical and Statistical Description of the Provinces of Lower and Upper Canada, New Brunswick, Nova Scotia, the Islands of Newfoundland, Prince Edward, and Cape Breton*. Vol. 1. London: Longman, Rees, Orme, Brown and Green.

Bouchier, N.B., and K. Cruikshank. 2003. 'The War on the Squatters, 1920–1940: Hamilton's Boathouse Community and the Re-Creation of Recreation on Burlington Bay.' *Labour/Le Travail* 51: 9–46.

Boyd, W., W.S. Prudham, and R. Schurman. 2001. 'Industrial Dynamics and the Problem of Nature.' *Society and Natural Resources* 14(7): 555–70.

Boyle, M. 2002. 'Cleaning Up after the Celtic Tiger: Scalar "Fixes" in the Political Ecology of Tiger Economies.' *Transactions of the Institute of British Geographers* 27(2): 172–94.

Brace, C.S. 1993. *One Hundred and Twenty Years of Sewerage: The Provision of Sewers in Toronto, 1793–1913*. Ottawa: National Library of Canada.

– 1995. 'Public Works in the Canadian City: The Provision of Sewers in Toronto 1870–1913.' *Urban History Review/Revue d'histoire urbaine* 23(2): 33–44.

Bradford, N. 2003. 'Public-Private Partnership? Shifting Paradigms of Economic Governance in Ontario.' *Canadian Journal of Political Science* 365: 1005–33.

– 2005. *Place-Based Public Policy: Towards a New Urban and Community Agenda for Canada*. Ottawa: Canadian Policy Research Networks.

Bradstreet. 1914. 'Report on the Financial History of the Polson Iron Works, January 29.' Toronto Port Authority Archives, Records Department fonds, RG 3/3, box 181, folder 8.

Brand, R.H. 1916. Memorandum, June 8. Library and Archives Canada, Lord Brand fonds, MG 27 II G 6, microfilm reel no. A829.

Braun, B. 2005. 'Environmental Issues: Writing a More-than-Human Urban Geography.' *Progress in Human Geography* 29(5): 635–50.

Brenner, N. 1998. 'Between Fixity and Motion: Accumulation, Territorial Organization and the Historical Geography of Spatial Scales.' *Environment and Planning D: Society & Space* 16(4): 459–81.

– 2000. 'The Urban Question as a Scale Question: Reflections on Henri Lefebvre, Urban Theory and the Politics of Scale.' *International Journal of Urban and Regional Research* 24(2): 361–78.

Bridge, G. 2000. 'The Social Regulation of Resource Access and Environmental Impact: Nature and Contradiction in the US Copper Industry.' *Geoforum* 31(2): 237–56.

British Colonist. 1843. 15 December: 1.

Brown, P.H. 2009. *America's Waterfront Revival: Port Authorities and Urban Redevelopment.* Philadelphia: University of Pennsylvania Press.

Brownill, S. 1990. *Developing London's Docklands: Another Great Planning Disaster?* London: Paul Chapman.

– 1993. *Developing London's Docklands: Another Great Planning Disaster?* 2nd ed. London: Paul Chapman.

Bryce, Rev. P. 1931. 'Jobless in Don Valley "jungle" confident work will be found.' *Toronto Daily Star*, 20 August: 1.

Bullard, R. 1990. *Dumping in Dixie: Race, Class and Environmental Quality.* Boulder, CO: Westview Press.

Bunce, S. 2007. 'Gentrifying Sustainability: Policy, Planning, and the Development of Sustainability on Toronto's Central Waterfront.' *Dissertation Abstracts International* 69: 6.

– 2009. 'Developing Sustainability: Sustainability Policy and Gentrification on Toronto's Waterfront.' *Local Environment: International Journal of Justice and Sustainability* 14(7): 651–67.

Bunce, S., and G. Desfor. 2007. 'Introduction to Political Ecologies of Urban Waterfront Transformations.' *Cities* 24: 251–8.

Burton, E., K. Williams, and M. Jenks. 1996. 'The Compact City and Urban Sustainability: Conflicts and Complexities.' In M. Jenks, E. Burton, and K. Williams, eds., *The Compact City: A Sustainable Urban Form?* 231–47. London: E&FN Spon.

Campbell, H.C. 1971. *Early Days on the Great Lakes: The Art of William Armstrong.* Toronto: McClelland and Stewart Ltd.

Canada. 1911. *Toronto Harbour Commissioners Act*, 1-2 George V, chapter 26, Canada Marine Act, R.S.C. 1998, c. 6–7.

– 1927. *Report of the Commission to Examine and Investigate the Transactions of the Toronto Harbour Commissioners, Chair: James Herbert Denton.* http://epe.lac-bac.gc.ca/100/200/301/pco-bcp/Commissions-ef/denton1927-eng/denton1929-eng.htm

– 1983. *Agreement between the Corporation of the City of Toronto; the Toronto Harbour Commissioners; and Her Majesty the Queen in the Right of Canada Represented by the Minister of Transport.* Ottawa: Department of Transportation.

– 1996. *Proceedings of the Standing Senate Committee on Transport and Communications.* 29 October. http://www.parl.gc.ca/35/Archives/committees352/port/evidence/31_96-10-29/port31_blk101.html.

– 1997a. *Proceedings of the Standing Senate Committee on Transport and Communi-*

cations. 23 April. http://www.parl.gc.ca/35/2/parlbus/commbus/senate/ Com-e/tran-e/19ev-e.htm?Language=E&Parl=35&Ses=2&comm_id=19.

- 1997b. *Proceedings of the Standing Senate Committee on Transport and Communications.* 29 April. http://www.parl.gc.ca/35/2/parlbus/commbus/senate/ Com-e/tran-e/19ev-e.htm?Language=E&Parl=35&Ses=2&comm_id=19.

- 1998a. *Proceedings of the Standing Senate Committee on Transport and Communications.* 27 April. http://www.parl.gc.ca/36/1/parlbus/commbus/senate/ Com-e/tran-e/12eva-e.htm?Language=E&Parl=36&Ses=1&comm_id=19.

- 1998b. *Proceedings of the Standing Senate Committee on Transport and Communications.* 7 May. http://www.parl.gc.ca/36/1/parlbus/commbus/senate/ Com-e/tran-e/17ev-e.htm?Language=E&Parl=36&Ses=1&comm_id=19.

- 1998c. *Canada Marine Act.* 11 June. http://tc.gc.ca/media/documents/ acts-regulations/c-6.7-acts.pdf.

Canada. Dominion Bureau of Statistics, General Statistics Branch. 1924. *The Canada Year Book 1922–23.* Ottawa: F.A. Acland.

- 1925. *The Canada Year Book 1924.* Ottawa: F.A. Acland.

- 1931. *The Canada Year Book 1931.* Ottawa: F.A. Acland.

Canada Gazette, Part 1. 1999. Letters Patent issued to the Toronto Port Authority, 133(23). Department of Transport, 5 June 1999.

- 2004. Toronto Port Authority – Supplementary Letters Patent, 138(5). Department of Transport, 31 January 2004.

- 2008. Toronto Port Authority – Supplementary Letters Patent, 142(51). Department of Transport, 20 December 2008.

Careless, J.M.S. 1984. *Toronto to 1918: An Illustrated History.* Toronto: James Lorimer & Co. and National Museum of Man, National Museums of Canada.

Carley, J. 1998. 'The Leslie Street Spit Redressing the Imbalance: The Creation and Preservation of a Public Urban Wilderness.' In G. Fairfield, ed., *Ashbridge's Bay: An Anthology of Writings by Those Who Knew and Loved Ashbridge's Bay,* 105–16. Toronto: Toronto Ornithological Club.

Carnegie, D. 1925. *The History of Munitions Supply in Canada, 1914–1918.* London: Longmans, Green.

Castree, N. 1995. 'The Nature of Produced Nature: Materiality and Knowledge Construction in Marxism.' *Antipode* 27(1): 12–48.

- 2002. 'False Antitheses? Marxism, Nature and Actor-networks.' *Antipode* 34(1): 111–46.

Castree, N., and B. Braun, eds. 2001. *Social Nature: Theory, Practice and Politics.* Malden, MA: Blackwell Publishers.

Castree, N., J. Essletzbichler, and N. Brenner. 2004. 'Introduction: David Harvey's The Limits to Capital: Two Decades On.' *Antipode* 36(3): 401–5.

Caswell, T. 1898. Letter to W.A. Littlejohn, 20 June. City of Toronto, Legal Department, Case files, box 644 (942), file: Polson Iron Wk's Co., re Dredging Princess & Sherbourne Sts Slips.

Caulfield, J. 1994. *City Form and Everyday Life: Toronto's Gentrification and Critical Social Practice.* Toronto: University of Toronto Press.

Checkoway, B. 1994. 'Paul Davidoff and Advocacy Planning in Retrospect.' *Journal of the American Planning Association* 602: 139–43.

Choi, T.Y. 2001. 'Writing the Victorian City: Discourses of Risk, Connection, and Inevitability.' *Victorian Studies* 43(4): 561–89.

Cidell, J. 2009. 'A Political Ecology of the Built Environment: LEED Certification for Green Buildings.' *Local Environment: International Journal of Justice and Sustainability* 14(7): 621–33.

Cipolla, C.M. 1993. *Before the Industrial Revolution: European Society and Economy, 1000–1700.* London: Routledge.

City of Toronto. 1881a. Report no. 56 of the Committee on Works, *Council Minutes*, appendix, line 1082, pp. 888–90.

– 1881b. *Council Minutes*, Minute 1026, 3 October; Minute 1043, 10 October; Minute 1246, 19 December.

– 1889. Mayor's Inaugural Address, *Council Minutes*, appendix, 14–15.

– 1893. Council Proceedings. City of Toronto Archives, fonds 200, series 1078.

– 1911. *Minutes of City Council 1910*, appendix C. Toronto: City Printers.

– 1913. *Minutes of Proceedings of the Council of the Corporation of the City of Toronto for the Year 1912.* Toronto: City of Toronto.

– 1991. *Agreement of Purchase and Sale (between Toronto Economic Development Corporation and Toronto Harbour Commissioners).* Toronto: City of Toronto Executive Committee.

– 1992. *Draft Official Plan Part I Consolidation: CityPlan Final Recommendations.* Toronto: City of Toronto Planning and Development Department.

– 1994. *CityPlan: City of Toronto Official Plan.* Toronto: City of Toronto.

– 1997a. *King-Parliament Secondary Plan.* Toronto: City of Toronto.

– 1997b. *TEDCO Soil and Ground Water Management Strategy for the Port Area – Memorandum of Understanding.* City of Toronto Executive Committee Report no. 18, 14 July.

– 1999a. *Our Toronto Waterfront: The Wave of the Future!* Toronto: City of Toronto.

– 1999b. 'Bold new vision announced for city waterfront.' Media release. 3 November.

– 2000a. *Toronto's 2008 Olympic and Paralympic Games Bid: Toronto Staff Report to Council.* Toronto: Commissioner of Economic Development, Culture and Tourism. 11 February.

- 2000b. *Minutes of the Council of the City of Toronto: Tuesday August 1 to Friday August 4, 2000.* Toronto: City of Toronto.
- 2000c. *Our Toronto Waterfront: Building Momentum. Staff Response to the Report of the Toronto Waterfront Revitalization Task Force.* October.
- 2000d. 'Toronto's Waterfront Development "A Reality": Mayor Lastman announces $1.5 billion to start huge project.' Media release. 20 October.
- 2000e. *Toronto Economic Development Strategy.* Toronto: City of Toronto Economic Development.
- 2006. 'The Toronto office market.' *Toronto City Planning.* April.
- 2010. 'Chester Springs Marsh.' http://www.toronto.ca/don/chester_spring.htm.
- N.d.a. Bring Back the Don, 'Task Force Projects/Accomplishments.' Toronto: City of Toronto. http://www.toronto.ca/don/taskforce.htm.
- N.d.b. 'Restoration Projects.' Toronto: City of Toronto. http://www.toronto.ca/don/restoration.htm.
- Todmorden Mills Museum. East York Foundation Collection.
City of Toronto Archives. Series 365. Department of Public Health Reports.
- Series 393. John Boyd Sr. Photographs.
- N.d. 'Toronto History FAQs.' Re: population of Toronto. http://www.toronto.ca/archives/toronto_history_faqs.htm#population.
Clark, B., and R. York. 2005. 'Carbon Metabolism: Global Capitalism, Climate Change, and the Biospheric Rift.' *Theory and Society* 34: 391–428.
Clark, N. 2002. 'The Demon-seed: Bioinvasion as the Unsettling of Environmental Cosmopolitanism.' *Theory, Culture, & Society* 19(1–2): 101–25.
CNW. 2009. 'Waterfront Toronto's Lower Don Lands Wins International Best Futuristic Design Award.' http://www.cnw.ca/en/releases/archive/June2009/16/c7024.html.
Coatsworth, E. 1901. Letter to J. Fullerton, 14 October. City of Toronto, Legal Department, Case Files, box 843 (1402), file: Toronto Dry Dock & Shipbuilding Company.
Coburn, J. 1994. 'Whose river is it, anyway?' *L.A. Times Magazine*, 20 November: 18, 19, 20, 20, 24, 48, 50, 52, 54.
Collins, B.D., D.R. Montgomery, and A.J. Sheikh. 2003. 'Reconstructing the Historical Riverine Landscape of the Puget Lowland.' In D.R. Montgomery, ed., *Restoration of Puget Sound River*, 79–128. Seattle: Center for Water and Watershed Studies in association with University of Washington Press.
Community AIR. 2007. 'Background.' http://www.communityair.org/Background/Background.html.
Conn, D. 1987. 'The War Orders: B.C. Shipbuilding 1915–1920.' *Canadian West* 8: 83–7.

Conway, T.M. 2006. 'Can Broad Land Use Policies Maintain Connections between Protected Green Spaces in an Urbanizing Landscape?' *Landscape Journal* 25(2): 218–27.

Coombes, T. 2009. Personal communication, 15 July.

Correll, D.L. 1991. 'Human Impact on the Functioning of Landscape Boundaries.' In M.M. Holland, R.J. Naiman, and P.G. Risser, eds., *Ecotones: The Role of Landscape Boundaries in the Management and Restoration of Changing Environments*, 90–109. New York: Chapman & Hall.

Courchene, T.J. 2005. *Citystates and the State of Cities: Political-Economy and Fiscal-Federalism Dimensions*. Montreal: Institute for Research on Public Policy.

Cousins, E.L. 1914. Report to the Toronto Harbour Commissioners, 7 July. Toronto Port Authority Archives, Records Department fonds, RG 3/3, box 180, folder 8.

– 1917. Letter to F.J. Blair, 6 July. Toronto Port Authority Archives, E.L. Cousins fonds, RG 6/1.

– 1921. 'Toronto Harbour Improvements.' *World Ports*, 9 May: 59–80.

– 1948. 'The Port of Toronto: The Development of a Major Port of the Lakes of Canada.' *The Dock and Harbour Authority*, September, no pagination.

Cowen, R. 2008. *Coal. The Timber Crisis*. http://www.geology.ucdavis.edu/~cowen/~GEL115/115CH11coal.html.

Craddock, S. 2000. *City of Plagues: Disease, Poverty, and Deviance in San Francisco*. Minneapolis: University of Minnesota Press.

Craig, Zeidler, and Strong, Architects. 1970. *Harbour City: A Preliminary Working Report for the Planning of a New Community*. Toronto: Craig, Zeidler, and Strong, Architects.

Creet, M. 2000. 'Fleming, Sir Sandford.' *Dictionary of Canadian Biography* 14: 359–62. Toronto: University of Toronto Press.

Cronon, W. 1990. 'Modes of Prophecy and Production: Placing Nature in History.' *Journal of American History* 76(4): 1122–31.

– 1991. *Nature's Metropolis: Chicago and the Great West*. New York: W.W. Norton and Co.

– 1996. 'The Trouble with Wilderness; or, Getting Back to the Wrong Nature.' *Environmental History* 1(1): 7–28.

Crook, F. 1983. 'Harbourfront denies wasting taxpayers' money.' *Toronto Star*, 14 December: A6.

Crouzet, F. 2001. *A History of the European Economy, 1000–2000*. Charlottesville and London: University Press of Virginia.

Cruikshank, K., and N.B. Bouchier. 2004. 'Blighted Areas and Obnoxious Industries: Constructing Environmental Inequality on an Industrial Waterfront, Hamilton, Ontario, 1890–1960.' *Environmental History* 9(3): 464–96.

Crumley, C.L. 1994. 'Historical Ecology: A Multidimensional Ecology Orienta-
tion.' In C.L. Crumley, ed., *Historical Ecology: Cultural Knowledge and Changing Landscapes*, 1–18. Santa Fe, NM: School of American Research Press.

Daily Leader. 1873. 'Launch of the new steam dredge.' 10 July.

Dale, A., and L. Newman. 2009. 'Sustainable Development for Some: Green
Urban Development and Affordability.' *Local Environment: International Journal of Justice and Sustainability* 14(7): 669–81.

Darimont, C.T., S.M. Carlson, M.T. Kinnison, P.C. Paquet, T.E. Reimchen,
and C.C. Wilmers. 2009. 'Human Predators Outpace Other Agents of Trait
Change in the Wild.' *Proceedings of the National Academy of Sciences* 106:
952–4. http://www.pnas.org.ezproxy.library.yorku.ca/gca?allch=
citmgr&gca=pnas%3B106%2F3%2F952#abstr-1.

Davidson, M. 2006. 'New Build Gentrification and London's Riverside Renaissance.' PhD dissertation, University of London.

Davidson, M., and L. Lees. 2005. 'New-build Gentrification and London's
Riverside Renaissance.' *Environment and Planning A* 37(7): 1165–90.

Davidson, T. 1976. *The Golden Years of East York*. Toronto: Centennial College
Press.

Davis, M. 1998. *Ecology of Fear: Los Angeles and the Imagination of Disaster*. New
York: Metropolitan Books.

– 2001. *Late Victorian Holocausts: El Niño Famines and the Making of the Third
World*. London, New York: Verso.

Daw, J. 1986. 'Waterfront development plan turns into conflict of wills: With
4,000 new jobs at stake, the plan by Magna International has caused a series
of tangled disputes.' *Toronto Star* 12 March: C1.

Debeir, J.C., J.P. Deleage, and D. Hemery. 1991. *In the Servitude of Power: Energy
and Civilization through the Ages*. London, Atlantic Highlands, NJ: Zed Books.

Delaporte, F. 1986. *Disease and Civilization: The Cholera in Paris, 1832*. Cambridge: MIT Press.

Demeritt, D. 1996. 'Social Theory and the Reconstruction of Science and Geography.' *Transactions of the Institute of British Geographers* 21(3): 484–503.

– 2001. 'The Construction of Global Warming and the Politics of Science.' *Annals of the Association of American Geographers* 91(2): 307–37.

Desaigues, B. 1990. 'The Socio-economic Values of Ecotones.' In R.J. Naiman
and H. Décamps, eds., *The Ecology and Management of Aquatic-Terrestrial Ecotones*, 263–94. Paris: UNSECO.

Descola, P., and G. Pálsson, eds. 1996. *Nature and Society: Anthropological Perspectives*. New York: Routledge.

Desfor, G. 1988. 'Planning Urban Waterfront Industrial Districts: Toronto's

Ashbridge's Bay, 1889–1910.' *Urban History Review/Revue d'histoire urbaine* 17(2): 77–91.

– 1993. 'Restructuring the Toronto Harbour Commission: Land Politics on the Toronto Waterfront.' *Journal of Transport Geography* 1(3): 167–81.

Desfor, G., M. Goldrick, and R. Merrens. 1988. 'Redevelopment on the North American Waterfront: The Case of Toronto.' In B.S. Hoyle, D.A. Pinder, and M.S. Husain, eds., *Revitalising the Waterfront: International Dimensions of Dockland Redevelopment*, 92–113. London and New York: Belhaven Press.

– 1989. 'A Political Economy of the Water-frontier: Planning and Development in Toronto.' *Geoforum* 20(4): 487–501.

Desfor, G., and J. Jørgensen. 2004. 'Flexible Urban Governance: The Case of Copenhagen's Recent Waterfront Development.' *European Planning Studies* 12(4): 479–96.

Desfor, G., and R. Keil. 1999. 'Contested and Polluted Terrain.' *Local Environment* 4(3): 331–52.

– 2000. 'Every River Tells a Story: The Don River (Toronto) and the Los Angeles River (Los Angeles) as Articulating Landscapes.' *Journal of Environmental Policy and Planning* 2: 5–23.

– 2004. *Nature and the City: Making Environmental Policy in Toronto and Los Angeles*. Tucson: University of Arizona Press.

Desfor, G., R. Keil, S. Kipfer, and G. Wekerle. 2006. 'From Surf to Turf: No Limits to Growth in Toronto?' *Studies in Political Ecology* 77(Spring): 131–56.

Desfor, G., J. Laidley, Q. Stevens, and D. Schubert. 2011. *Transforming Urban Waterfronts: Fixity and Flow*. New York: Routledge.

Desfor, G., and S. Prudham. 2006. 'Deep Water and Good Land: Socio-Natural Transformation of Toronto's Industrial Waterfront.' Presentation to the Annual Meeting of the Association of American Geographers, Chicago, 10 March.

Desfor, G., and L. Vesalon. 2008. 'Urban Expansion and Industrial Nature: A Political Ecology of Toronto's Port Industrial District.' *International Journal of Urban and Regional Research* 32(3): 586–603.

De Sousa, C. 2000. 'Brownfield Redevelopment versus Greenfield Development: A Private Sector Perspective on the Cost of and Risks Associated with Brownfield Redevelopment in the Greater Toronto Area.' *Journal of Environmental Planning and Management* 43(6): 831–53.

– 2001. 'Contaminated Sites: The Canadian Situation in an International Context.' *Journal of Environmental Management* 62(2): 131–54.

– 2003. 'Turning Brownfields into Green Space in the City of Toronto.' *Landscape and Urban Planning* 62(4): 181–98.

Donald, B. 2002. 'Spinning Toronto's Golden Age: The Making of a "City That Worked."' *Environment and Planning A* 34(12): 2127–54.
– 2005. 'The Politics of Local Economic Development in Canada's City-Regions: New Dependencies, New Deals, and a New Politics of Scale.' *Space and Polity* 9(3): 261–81.
Donaldson, W., and A. Coghill. 1877. Petition, 15 August. Toronto Port Authority Archives, Board of Commissioners fonds, RG 1/4, box 1, folder 7.
Dovey, K. 2005. *Fluid City: Transforming Melbourne's Urban Waterfront.* New York: Routledge.
Drache, D., ed. 1995. *Staples, Markets, and Cultural Change: Selected Essays of Harold Innis, 1894–1952.* Montreal: McGill-Queen's University Press.
Drummond, I. 1987. *Progress without Planning: The Economic History of Ontario from Confederation to the Second World War.* Toronto: University of Toronto Press.
Dryzek, J.S. 2005. *The Politics of the Earth: Environmental Discourses.* Oxford and New York: Oxford University Press.
Duncan, S.S., and M. Goodwin. 1985. 'The Local State and Local Economic Policy: Why the Fuss?' *Policy and Politics* 13(3): 227–53.
Dupouey, J.L., E. Dambrine, J.D. Laffite, and C. Moares. 2002. 'Irreversible Impact of Past Land Use on Forest Soils and Biodiversity.' *Ecology* 83: 2978–84.
Eads, J.B. 1882. *Report on Toronto Harbour, Ontario.* Ottawa: Department of Public Works.
The Economist. 2006. 'Covering the whole waterfront: Redeveloping Toronto.' 1 April: 50.
Escobar, A. 1995. *Encountering Development: The Making and Unmaking of the Third World.* Princeton, NJ: Princeton University Press.
– 1999. 'After Nature: Steps to an Anti-essentialist Political Ecology.' *Current Anthropology* 40(1): 1–30.
Evans, R.J. 1987. *Death in Hamburg: Society and Politics in the Cholera Years, 1830–1910.* Oxford: Clarendon Press.
Evening News (Toronto). 1892a. 'Cholera to come next year.' 25 August: 1.
– 1892b. 'An undesirable emigrant.' 31 August: 1.
– 1892c. 'Coming via Canada.' 2 September: 1.
– 1892d. 'No alien need apply.' 5 September: 1.
– 1892e. 'Toronto is ready.' 15 September: 1.
– 1893a. 'Cholera not stamped out.' 1 March: 1.
– 1893b. 'Extensive powers asked.' 3 March: 1.
– 1893c. 'Guardians of public health.' 16 May: 1.
– 1893d. 'Health of citizens.' 25 September: 1.

– 1893e. 'Good works at Ashbridge's Bay.' 30 September: 1.

Fainstein, S. 1994. *The City Builders: Property, Politics, and Planning in London and New York*. Cambridge, MA: Blackwell.

Fairfield, G. 1998. 'A Short History of Ashbridge's Bay.' In G. Fairfield, ed. *Ashbridge's Bay: An Anthology of Writings by Those Who Knew and Loved Ashbridge's Bay*, 1–7. Toronto: Toronto Ornithological Club.

Fairfield, G., ed. 1998. *Ashbridge's Bay. An Anthology of Writings by Those Who Knew and Loved Ashbridge's Bay*. Toronto: Toronto Ornithological Club.

Filion, P. 2001. 'The Urban Policy-Making and Development Dimension of Fordism and Post-Fordism: A Toronto Case Study.' *Space and Polity* 5(2): 85–111.

Firth, E.G. 1962. *The Town of York, 1793–1815: A Collection of Documents of Early Toronto*. Toronto: Champlain Society, Ontario Series, vol. 5.

– 1966. *The Town of York: 1815–1832: A Further Collection of Documents of Early Toronto*. Toronto: Champlain Society, Ontario Series, vol. 8.

Fenwick, G. and F.W. Campbell. 1864. 'Cholera in Canada.' *Canada Medical Journal and Monthly Record of Medical and Surgical Science* 2: 458–89.

Flavelle, J. 1917. Letter to R. Borden, 17 March. Library and Archives Canada, Lord Brands fonds, MG 27 II G 6, microfilm reel no. A829.

– 1918. Memorandum for Mr Rowell, 23 February. Library and Archives Canada, Sir Robert Borden fonds, MG 26 H, vol. 239, pt. 1, microfilm reel no. C-4414.

Fleming, S. 1853–4. 'Toronto Harbour: Its Formation and Preservation.' *The Canadian Journal: A Repertory of Industry, Science, and Art; and a Record of the Proceedings of the Canadian Institute* 2(5), December 1853: 105–7; 2(9) April 1854: 223–30.

– 1854. 'Report on the Preservation and Improvement of Toronto Harbour.' *Supplement to the Canadian Journal: Reports on the Improvement and Preservation of Toronto Harbour*, 15–29.

Flinn, M.W. 1984. *The History of the British Coal Industry*. Vol. 2, *1700–1830: The Industrial Revolution*. Oxford: Oxford University Press.

Florio, S., and S. Brownill. 2000. 'Whatever Happened to Criticism? Interpreting the London Docklands Development Corporation's Obituary.' *City* 41: 53–64.

Flyvbjerg, B. 2002. 'Bringing Power to Planning Research: One Researcher's Praxis Story.' *Journal of Planning Education and Research* 21: 353–66.

Fong, T. 2003. 'Epidemics, Racial Anxiety and Community Formation: Chinese Americans in San Francisco.' *Urban History* 30(3).

Forman, R.T.T. 1995. *Land Mosaics: The Ecology of Landscapes and Regions*. Cambridge: Cambridge University Press.

Foster, J., and L.A. Sandberg. 2004. 'Friends or Foe? Invasive Species and Public Green Space in Toronto.' *Geographical Review* 94(2): 178–98.

Foster, J.B. 1999. 'Marx's Theory of Metabolic Rift: Classical Foundations for Environmental Sociology.' *American Journal of Sociology* 105(2): 366–405.

– 2000. *Marx's Ecology: Materialism and Nature.* New York: Monthly Review Press.

Foucault, M. 1994. *The Birth of the Clinic: An Archaeology of Medical Perception.* New York: Vintage Books.

Friedmann, J. 1995. 'Where We Stand: A Decade of World City Research.' In P.L. Knox and P.J. Taylor, eds., *World Cities in a World System*, 21–47. Cambridge: Cambridge University Press.

– 1998. 'Planning Theory Revisited.' *European Planning Studies* 63: 245–53.

– 2005. 'Globalization and the Emerging Culture of Planning.' *Progress in Planning* 64(3): 183–234.

Friedmann, J., and G. Wolff. 1982. 'World City Formation: An Agenda for Research and Action.' *International Journal of Urban and Regional Research* 6: 309–44.

Gad, G. 1994. 'Location Patterns of Manufacturing: Toronto in the Early 1880s.' *Urban History Review/Revue d'histoire urbaine* 22(2): 113–38.

– 2004. 'The Suburbanization of Manufacturing in Toronto.' In R. Lewis, ed., *Manufacturing Suburbs: Building Work and Home on the Metropolitan Fringe*, 143–77. Philadelphia, PA: Temple University Press.

Gandy, M. 1999. 'The Paris Sewers and the Rationalization of Urban Space.' *Transactions of the Institute of British Geographers* 24(1): 23–44.

– 2002. *Concrete and Clay: Reworking Nature in New York City.* Cambridge and London: MIT Press.

– 2004. 'Rethinking Urban Metabolism: Water, Space and the Modern City.' *City* 8(3).

– 2005. 'Cyborg Urbanization: Complexity and Monstrosity in the Contemporary City.' *International Journal of Urban and Regional Research* 29(1): 26–49.

Ganton, I.K. 1974. 'Development between Parliament Street and the Don River, 1793–1884.' Course paper, University of Toronto, Dept. of Geography. Fonds 92, Papers and Theses Collection, City of Toronto Archives.

Gemmil, A. 1978. 'Toronto's Outer Harbour Eastern Headland: The Changing Role of a Transportation Facility.' Toronto: University of Toronto/York University Joint Program in Transportation, Research report no. 55.

Gibbs, D. 2000. 'Ecological Modernisation, Regional Economic Development and Regional Development Agencies.' *Geoforum* 31(1): 9–19.

Giddens, A. 1984. *The Constitution of Society*. Berkeley: University of California Press.

Gilbert, P.K. 2004. *Mapping the Victorian Social Body*. Albany: State University of New York Press.

– 2008. *Cholera and Nation: Doctoring the Social Body in Victorian England*. Albany: State University of New York Press.

Globe. 1845. 'Toronto and Lake Huron Railroad.' 22 April: 2.

– 1847a. 'Annual Report of the Council of the Toronto Board of Trade for 1846.' 6 January: 2.

– 1847b. 'Toronto.' 8 May: 2.

– 1854. 'Harbour of Toronto.' 3 April: 3.

– 1855. 'Ship building in Toronto – Launch of the City of Toronto.' 27 April: 2.

– 1856. 'List of Canadian vessels.' 4 August: 3.

– 1859. 'Toronto harbour.' 30 April: 2.

– 1870. 'Toronto harbour.' 26 November: 4.

– 1874. 'Eastern smells.' Anonymous letter to the editor. 16 June: 2.

– 1876. 'Toronto harbour: Mr Kingsford's report.' 28 June: 2.

– 1880a. 'Dominion Parliament, Fourth Parliament – Second Session, House of Commons.' 5 May: 3.

– 1880b. 'Toronto harbour: Inspection by the Hon. Mr. Langevin, Minister of Public Works.' 28 July: 4.

– 1880c. 'A dry-dock. A plan for the establishment of one in Toronto.' 12 August: 6.

– 1881a. 'Don River improvement.' 19 February: 9.

– 1881b. 'The Don River.' 10 October: 7.

– 1888a. 'Property committee.' 20 April: 5

– 1888b. 'City Hall notes.' 27 April: 1.

– 1892a. 'Provincial Health Board: A special meeting called to consider the isolation hospital, Ashbridge's Bay and other matters.' 3 June: 8.

– 1892b. 'Local briefs.' 3 November: 8.

– 1894a. 'Bertram Engine Works Company' [advertisement]. 10 January: 2.

– 1894b. 'City Hall notes.' 2 March: 2.

– 1894c. 'The Bertram Engine Works Company' [advertisement]. 7 March: 2.

– 1894d. 'A high chimney.' 18 June: 8.

– 1899a. 'The harbor business.' 6 January: 7.

– 1899b. 'The Bertram Co.: A reorganization with increased capital proposed.' 19 June: 5.

– 1899c. 'Independence. Canada's watchword in shipbuilding.' 9 November: 9.

– 1900. 'Iron trade is booming.' 12 October: 10.

- 1901. 'Mr Tarte talks plainly.' 27 June: 12.
- 1902. 'To build ships here. Toronto capitalists interested in a new industry.' 17 November: 8. ·
- 1906a. 'Launch of the Cayuga. Niagara Navigation Company's new vessel.' 5 March: 7.
- 1906b. 'Iron smelters will come here.' 11 October: 12.
- 1907a. 'Moose mountain furnaces will make a Canadian Pittsburg in Toronto's marsh.' 12 October: 1.
- 1907b. 'Are laying off the men. Two large Toronto companies curtail production.' 25 October: 12.
- 1909. 'Big shipbuilding plant. Polson's Iron Works Company will construct one.' 4 June: 14.
- 1910a. 'Was coincidence a sinister thing?' 22 November: 8.
- 1910b. 'Scheme killed, says Mr. Gage.' 2 December: 1, 4.
- 1910c. 'In the civic arena.' 3 December: 8.
- 1910d. 'Development of Toronto's harbor.' 31 December: 4.
- 1911. 'Band of gypsies to be deported.' 4 February: 5.
- 1912. 'Canadian Lloyds to encourage shipping.' 17 December: 9.
- 1917. 'Dry dock here: Came 1,000 miles.' 30 July: 7.
- 1918a. 'Launching of wooden ship provides many thrills.' 1 July: 9.
- 1918b. 'Shipbuilding absorbs labor.' 26 November: 11.
- 1920a. 'Gypsies turn from horses to the auto.' 1 June: 9
- 1920b. 'Assignee gives three reasons for liquidation.' 3 September: 8.
- 1920c. 'Shipyards row grows intense; Fight in a hull.' 18 December: 18.
- 1920d. 'To keep picket at shipyards; Will win fight.' 24 December: 6.
- 1921a. 'Charge threat by local union.' 27 January: 6.
- 1921b. 'King to meet Labor along with Crerar on shipyard issues.' 21 February: 7.
- 1931a. 'Don Valley not safe for policeman soon, says range officer.' 4 August: 1.
- 1931b. 'Police will watch every freight for jobless influx.' 26 September: 1.
- 1931c. 'Ho! For the road builders.' 3 October: 4.
- 1931d. 'East York policemen houseclean "jungle."' 7 October: 1.

Goad, C.E. 1884. *Insurance Plan of the City of Toronto. Vol. 1. 1880.* Toronto: Goad.

Godfrey, C.M. 1968. *The Cholera Epidemics in Upper Canada, 1832–1866.* Toronto: Seccombe House.

Godfrey, R.T. 1866. 'Cholera: A Few Practical Remarks on Its Prevention.' (Speech read before the Montreal Medico-Chirurgical Society, 26 January

1866.) In G.E. Fenwick and F.W. Campbell, eds., *Canadian Medical Journal and Monthly Record of Medical and Surgical Science*, vol. 2. Montreal: John Lovell.

Godwin, G. 1972. *Town Swamps and Social Bridges.* New York: Humanities Press.

Goheen, P.G. 1979. 'Currents of Change in Toronto, 1850–1900.' In G.A. Stelter and A.F.J. Artibise, eds., *The Canadian City: Essays in Urban History*, 54–92. Toronto: MacMillan.

Goldman, M. 1998. *Privatizing Nature: Political Struggles for the Global Commons.* London: Pluto Press in association with Transnational Institute (TNI).

– 2001. 'Constructing an Environmental State: Eco-governmentality and Other Transnational Practices, of a "Green" World Bank.' *Social Problems* 48(4): 499–523.

Goldrick, M., and R. Merrens. 1990. 'Waterfront Changes and Institutional Stasis: The Role of the Toronto Harbour Commission, 1911–1989.' In B.S. Hoyle, ed., *Port Cities in Context: The Impact of Waterfront Regeneration*, 119–53. Southampton: Transport Geography Study Group, Institute of British Geographers.

– 1996. 'Toronto: Searching for a New Environmental Planning Paradigm.' In P. Malone, ed., *City, Capital and Water*, 219–39. New York: Routledge.

Gordon, D.L.A. 1997a. *Battery Park City: Politics and Planning on the New York Waterfront.* Amsterdam: Gordon and Breach Publishers.

– 1997b. 'Managing the Changing Political Environment in Urban Waterfront Redevelopment.' *Urban Studies* 34(1): 61–83.

Gosz, J.R. 1991. 'Fundamental Ecological Characteristics of Landscape Boundaries.' In M.M. Holland, R.J. Naiman, and P.G. Risser, eds., *Ecotones: The Role of Landscape Boundaries in the Management and Restoration of Changing Environments*, 8–30. New York: Chapman & Hall.

Gottdiener, M. 1988. *The Social Production of Urban Space.* Austin: University of Texas Press.

Gourlay, R. 1913. 'Some Aspects of Commercial Value to the City of the Proposed Harbour Improvements, January 16.' Toronto Port Authority Archives, Board of Commissioners fonds, RG 1/5, box 2, folder 15.

– 1914a. *Basic Principles for a Water-front Development as Illustrated by the Plans of the Toronto Harbour Commissioners.* Address to the National Conference on City Planning, Toronto, May. THCA Archives, RG 1/5, box 2, folder 15.

– 1914b. 'Basic Principles of Water-front Development as Illustrated by the Plans of the Toronto Harbour Commissioners.' *Proceedings of the Sixth National Conference on City Planning, Toronto, May 15–17, 1914*, 17–53. Cambridge, MA: Harvard University Press.

Green, D.R. 1991. 'The Metropolitan Economy: Continuity and Change 1800–1939.' In K. Hoggart and D. Green, eds., *London: A New Metropolitan Geography*, 8–33. London: Edward Arnold.

Greenberg, K. 1996. 'Toronto: The Urban Waterfront as a Terrain of Availability.' In P. Malone, ed., *City, Capital and Water*, 195–218. London and New York: Routledge.

Greenberg, K., and G. Sicheri. 1990. *Toronto's Moveable Shoreline*, Working paper no. 5, Canadian Waterfront Resource Centre. Toronto: Royal Commission on the Future of the Toronto Waterfront.

Griffith, J.A., E.A. Martinko, and K.P. Price. 2000. 'Landscape Structure Analysis of Kansas at Three Scales.' *Landscape and Urban Planning* 52: 45–61.

Hadley, M.L., and R. Sarty. 1991. *Tin-pots and Pirate Ships: Canadian Naval Forces and German Sea Raiders, 1880–1918*. Montreal: McGill-Queen's University Press.

Hajer, M. 1995. *The Politics of Environmental Discourse: Ecological Modernization and the Policy Process*. Oxford: Oxford University Press.

Halliday, S. 2001. 'Death and Miasma in Victorian London: An Obstinate Belief.' *British Medical Journal* 323: 1469–71.

Hamilton & Pearce. 1875. Letter to J.G. Worts, 4 August. Toronto Port Authority Archives, Board of Commissioners fonds, RG 1/4, box 1, folder 5.

Hamlin, C. 1985. 'Providence and Putrefaction: Victorian Sanitarians and the Natural Theology of Health and Disease.' *Victorian Studies* 28 (3): 381–411.

– 1990. *A Science of Impurity: Water Analysis in Nineteenth Century Britain*. Bristol: Adam Hilger.

Hannevig, C. 1918a. Letter to C.C. Ballantyne, 15 February. Library and Archives Canada, Sir Robert Borden fonds, MG 26 H, vol. 239, pt. 1, microfilm reel no. C-4414.

– 1918b. Letter to J. Flavelle, 19 February. Library and Archives Canada, Sir Joseph Flavelle fonds, MG 30 A 16, vol. 35, file: Hannevig, Christoffer.

Haraway, D. 1991. *Simians, Cyborgs and Women: The Reinvention of Nature*. London: Free Association Books.

Harbour Trust. 1873. 'Toronto Harbour.' Toronto Port Authority Archives, Board of Commissioners fonds, RG 1/4, box 5, RG 1/4, box 5.

– 1892. 'Forty-first Annual Report.' Toronto Port Authority Archives, Board of Commissioners fonds, RG 1/4, box 5.

Harding, K. 2004. 'Mayor urges Ottawa to sign deal killing bridge.' *Globe and Mail*. 13 May: A13.

Hardy, A. 1993. 'Cholera, Quarantine and the English Preventive System, 1850–1895.' *Medical History* 37: 250–69.

Harms, H. 2008. *Changes on the Waterfront: Transforming Harbor Areas*. University of California Berkeley: Institute of Urban and Regional Development.

Harney, R.F., and H. Troper. 1975. *Immigrants: A Portrait of the Urban Experience, 1890–1930*. Toronto: Van Nostrand Reinhold Ltd.

Harris, L.D., and J. Scheck. 1991. 'From Implications to Applications: The Dispersal Corridor Principal Applied to the Conservation of Biological Diversity.' In D.A. Saunders and R.J. Hobbs, eds., *Nature Conservation 2: The Role of Corridors*, 189–220. New South Wales, AUS: Surrey Beatty & Sons, Chipping Norton.

Hartmann, F. 1999. 'Nature in the City: Urban Ecological Politics in Toronto.' Unpublished PhD dissertation, Faculty of Environmental Studies, York University, Toronto.

Harvey, D. 1982. *The Limits to Capital*. Oxford: Blackwell Publishers.

– 1989a. 'From Managerialism to Entrepreneurialism: The Transformation in Urban Governance in Late Capitalism.' *Geografiska Annaler* 71(B): 3–17.

– 1989b. *The Urban Experience*. Baltimore, MD: Johns Hopkins University Press.

– 1996a. *Justice, Nature and the Geography of Difference*. Oxford and New York: Blackwell.

– 1996b. 'On Planning the Ideology of Planning.' In S. Campbell and S. Fainstein, eds., *Readings in Planning Theory*, 176–97. Malden, MA: Blackwell Publishers.

– 2003. 'The "New" Imperialism: Accumulation by Dispossession.' In L. Panitch and C. Leys, eds., *Socialist Register 2004: The New Imperial Challenge*, 63–87. London: Merlin Press.

Hayes, D. 2008. *Historical Atlas of Toronto*. Vancouver, Toronto: Douglas & McIntyre.

Hayuth, Y. 1982. 'The Port–Urban Interface: An Area in Transition.' *Area* 14(3): 219–24.

Heal, S.C. 1992. *Conceived in War, Born in Peace: Canada's Deep Sea Merchant Marine*. Vancouver: Cordillera Publishing Co.

Helfield, J.M., and M.L. Diamond. 1997. 'Use of Constructed Wetlands for Urban Stream Restoration: A Critical Analysis.' *Environmental Management* 21(3): 329–41.

H-Environment. 2008. Query on Ravinelands? http://h-net.msu.edu/cgi-bin/logbrowse.pl?trx=vx&list=h-environment&month=0803&week=c&msg=jCOc5XY%2bdPl9RpftdHqwQw&user=&pw=.

Herzogenrath, B., ed. 2001. *From Virgin Land to Disney World: Nature and Its Discontents in the USA of Yesterday and Today*. Amsterdam: Rodopi.

Heynen, N., M. Kaika, and E. Swyngedouw, eds. 2006. *In the Nature of Cities:*

Urban Political Ecology and the Politics of Urban Metabolism. London and New York: Routledge.

Heynen, N., and E. Swyngedouw. 2003. 'Urban Political Ecology, Justice and the Politics of Scale.' *Antipode* 35(5): 898–918.

Hind, H.Y. 1854. 'Report on the Preservation and Improvement of Toronto Harbour.' In *Supplement to the Canadian Journal: Reports on the Improvement and Preservation of Toronto Harbour,* 1–15.

Hodge, G. 1972. 'The Care and Feeding of an Airport, Or the Technocrat as Midwife.' In A. Powell, ed., *The City: Attacking Modern Myths,* 212–16. Toronto: McLelland & Stewart.

– 2003. *Planning Canadian Communities.* 4th ed. Toronto: Nelson.

Hodge, G. and I.M. Robinson. 2001. *Planning Canadian Regions.* Vancouver: UBC Press.

Holdren, J. 1992. 'Energy Agenda for the 1990s.' In M. Hollander, ed., *The Energy Environment Connection,* 378–91. Washington, DC: Island Press.

Hooghe, L., and G. Marks. 2003. 'Unraveling the Central State, but How? Types of Multi-Level Governance.' *American Political Science Review* 97(2): 233–43.

Horn, M. 1984. *The Great Depression of the 1930s in Canada.* Ottawa: Canadian Historical Association.

Hoyle, B.S. 1988. 'Development Dynamics at the Port–City Interface.' In B.S. Hoyle, D.A. Pinder, and M.S. Husain, eds., *Revitalising the Waterfront: Institutional Dimensions of Dockland Re-development,* 3–19. London: Belhaven Press.

– 1990. *Port Cities in Context: The Impact of Waterfront Regeneration.* Transport Geography Study Group, Institute of British Geographers. London.

Hoyle, B.S., and D.A. Pinder, eds. 1981. *Cityport Industrialisation and Regional Development: Spatial Analysis and Planning Strategies.* Oxford: Pergamon.

Hoyle, B.S., D.A. Pinder, and M.S. Husain, eds. 1988. *Revitalising the Waterfront: Institutional Dimensions of Dockland Re-development.* London: Belhaven Press.

Huber, M.T. 2009a. 'Energizing Historical Materialism: Fossil Fuels, Space and the Capitalist Mode of Production.' *Geoforum* 40(1): 105–15.

– 2009b. 'The Use of Gasoline: Value, Oil, and the "American Way of Life."' *Antipode* 41(3): 465–86.

Hudson, B. 1996. *Cities on the Shore: The Urban Littoral Frontier.* London and New York: Pinter.

Human Resources and Social Development Canada. 2005. *Audit of the Toronto Waterfront Revitalization Initiative.* Ottawa: Human Resources and Social Development Canada.

Hume, C. 2005a. 'Waterfront merits great expectations.' *Toronto Star,* 16 June.

– 2005b. 'Mayor is meddling in City's waterfront rejuvenation.' *Toronto Star*, 26 October: B3.

– 2007. 'Water Affront.' *Spacing*, Summer: 24–7.

Hurley, A. 1995. *Environmental Inequalities: Class, Race, and Industrial Pollution in Gary, Indiana, 1945–1980*. Chapel Hill: University of North Carolina Press.

Imrie, R., and H. Thomas. 1999. 'Assessing Urban Policy and the Urban Development Corporations.' In R. Imrie and H. Thomas, eds., *British Urban Policy: An Evaluation of Urban Development Corporations*, 3–39. London: Sage.

International Olympic Committee, 2000. 'Questionnaire for Cities Applying to Become Candidate Cities to Host the Games of the XXIX Olympiad in 2008.' Lausanne, Switzerland. multimedia.olympic.org/pdf/en_report_288.pdf.

Interview. 2005a. Planner for South East False Creek, City of Vancouver. September. Interview by author.

– 2005b. Former director, Waterfront Regeneration Trust. 23 November. Interview by author.

– 2005c. Vice-president of Planning and Design, Toronto Waterfront Revitalization Corporation. 25 November. Interview by author.

– 2006. John Campbell, chief executive officer, Toronto Waterfront Revitalization Corporation. 18 January Interview by author.

– 2007a. Staff, Development Division, Toronto Waterfront Revitalization Corporation. 27 February. Interview by author.

– 2007b. Former planner, Old City of Toronto. July. Interview by author.

– 2007c. Former chairperson, Toronto Harbour Commission. July. Interview by author.

– 2007d. Former city councillor, Old City of Toronto. July. Interview by author.

– 2007e. Former federal official, Government of Canada. July. Interview by author.

Ircha, M. 1993. 'Institutional Structure of Canadian Ports.' *Maritime Policy & Management* 20(1): 51–66.

– 1999. 'Port Reform: International Perspectives and the Canadian Model. *Canadian Public Administration* 42(1): 108–32.

Jackson, G. 1983. *The History and Archaeology of Ports*. Tadworth, Surrey: World's Work.

Jackson, P. 1993. *Constructions of Race, Place and Nations*. London: University College of London Press.

James, R. 2004. 'Leadership the least of waterfront worries.' *Toronto Star*, 12 November: B3.

Jarvis, A. 1994. 'The Members of the Mersey Docks and Harbour Board and Their Way of Doing Business, 1858–1905.' *International Journal of Maritime History* 6(1): 123–39.

– 1996. 'Managing Change: The Organisation of Port Authorities at the Turn of the Twentieth Century.' *The Northern Mariner/Le Marin du nord* 6(2): 31–42.

– 2007. 'Daggers Drawn: Relations between the Mersey Docks & Harbour Board and Outside Bodies from Central Government Downwards, *c.*1850–1972.' *The Mariner's Mirror* 93(2): 180–95.

Jessop, B. 1990. *State Theory: Putting the Capitalist State in Its Place.* University Park: Pennsylvania State University Press.

– 1995. 'The Regulation Approach, Governance and Post-Fordism: Alternative Perspectives on Economic and Political Change?' *Economy and Society* 24(3): 307–33.

– 2004. 'Spatial Fixes, Temporal Fixes, and Spatio-temporal Fixes.' www.lancs. ac.uk/fss/sociology/papers/jessop-spatio-temporal-fixes.pdf.

– 2006. 'Spatial Fixes, Temporal Fixes, and Spatio-temporal Fixes.' In N. Castree and D. Gregory, eds., *David Harvey: A Critical Reader*, 142–66. Oxford: Blackwell Publishing.

Johnson, G. 1866. 'How Shall We Treat Cholera?' (Speech read before the Montreal Medico-Chirurgical Society, 26 January 1866.) In G.E. Fenwick and F.W. Campbell, eds., *Canadian Medical Journal and Monthly Record of Medical and Surgical Science*, vol. 2. Montreal; John Lovell.

Johnston, A. 1911. Letter to J. Simm, 19 July. Library and Archives Canada, Department of Marine fonds, RG 42, vol. 193, file 31931.

Kaika, M. 2005. *City of Flows: Modernity, Nature, and the City.* New York and London: Routledge.

Kaika, M., and E. Swyngedouw. 2000. 'Fetishizing the Modern City: The Phantasmagoria of Urban Technological Networks.' *International Journal of Urban and Regional Research* 24(1): 120–38.

Kavanagh, K. 1989. 'The 1987 Master Plan for the Leslie Street Spit (Tommy Thompson Park): An Urban Wilderness Threatened.' *Recreation Research Review* (14) 2: 27–34.

Kearney, M.S., R.E Grace, and J.C. Stevenson. 1988. 'Marsh Loss in Nanticoke Estuary, Chesapeake Bay.' *Geographical Review* 78: 205–20.

Kehm, W.H. 1989. 'Recreation and Conservation Design: The Tommy Thompson Park Case Study.' *Recreation Research Review* 14 (2): 17–25.

Keil, R. 2003. 'Urban Political Ecology.' *Urban Geography* 24(8): 723–8.

– 2005. 'Progress Report – Urban Political Ecology.' *Urban Geography* 26(7): 640–51.

Keil, R., and J.A. Boudreau. 2006. 'Metropolitics and Metabolics: Rolling Out Environmentalism in Toronto.' In N. Heynen, M. Kaika, and E. Swyngedouw, eds., *In the Nature of Cities: Urban Political Ecology and the Politics of Urban Metabolism*, 41–62. Abingdon: Routledge.

Keil, R., and G. Desfor. 2003. 'Ecological Modernisation in Los Angeles and Toronto.' *Local Environment* 81: 27–44.

Keil, R., and J. Graham. 1998. 'Reasserting Nature: Constructing Urban Environments after Fordism.' In B. Braun and N. Castree, eds., *Remaking Reality: Nature at the Millennium*, 100–25. London and New York: Routledge.

Keil, R., and M. Whitehead. Forthcoming. 'Cities and the Politics of Sustainability.' In K. Mossberger, S.E. Clarke, and P. John, eds., *The Oxford Handbook of Urban Politics*. Oxford: Oxford University Press.

Keil, R., and D. Young. Forthcoming. 'Reconnecting the Disconnected: The Politics of Infrastructure in the In-between City.' *Cities: The International Journal of Urban Policy and Planning*.

Kellogg, P.U. 1914. *The Pittsburgh Survey: Findings in Six Volumes*. New York: New York Charities Publication Committee.

Kettl, D. 2000. *The Global Public Management Revolution*. Washington: Brookings Institution Press.

Kipfer, S., and R. Keil. 2000. 'Still Planning to Be Different? Toronto at the Turn of the Millennium.' *DISP* 10: 28–36.

– 2002. 'Toronto Inc? Planning the Competitive City in the New Toronto.' *Antipode* 34(2): 227–64.

Koch, T. 2004. 'The Map as Intent: Variations on the Theme of John Snow.' *Cartographica* 39(4): 1–14.

Kohn, M. 2004. *Brave New Neighbourhoods: The Privatization of Public Space*. New York: Routledge.

Kollin, S. 2001. *Nature's State: Imagining Alaska as the Last Frontier*. Chapel Hill and London: University of North Carolina Press.

Konvitz, J.W. 1978. *Cities and the Sea: Port City Planning in Early Modern Europe*. Baltimore, MD: Johns Hopkins University Press.

Kootenay Lake Historical Society. 2008. 'SS Moyie National Historic Site.' Kaslo, BC: Kootenay Lake Historical Society. www.klhs.bc.ca.

Krajnc, A. 2000. 'Wither Ontario's Environment? Neo-conservatism and the Decline of the Environment Ministry.' *Canadian Public Policy* 261: 111–27.

Kraut, A.M. 1994. *Silent Travelers: Germs, Genes, and the 'Immigrant Menace.'* New York: BasicBooks.

Kuletz, V.L. 1998. *The Tainted Desert: Environmental and Social Ruin in the American West*. New York and London: Routledge.

Laclau, E., and C. Mouffe. 1985. *Hegemony and Socialist Strategy: Towards a Radical Democratic Politics*. London and New York: Verso.

Laidley, J. 2007. 'The Ecosystem Approach and the Global Imperative on Toronto's Central Waterfront.' *Cities* 24(4): 259–72.

Langevin, H.L. 1881. *Memorandum, with Accompanying Plans and Documents relative to the Past and Present State of the Harbour of Toronto, Province of Ontario.* Ottawa: Department of Public Works.

Latour, B. 1988. *The Pasteurization of France.* Cambridge: Harvard University Press.

– 1993. *We Have Never Been Modern.* London: Harvester Wheatsheaf.

Lauria, M., ed. 1997. *Reconstructing Urban Regime Theory: Regulating Urban Politics in a Global Economy.* Thousand Oaks, CA: Sage Publications.

Lefebvre, H. 1991. *The Production of Space.* Oxford: Blackwell.

Lehrer, U., and J. Laidley. 2008. 'Old Mega-projects Newly Packaged? Waterfront Redevelopment in Toronto.' *International Journal of Urban and Regional Research* 32(4): 786–803.

Leiss, W. 1974. *The Domination of Nature.* Boston: Beacon Press.

Lemon, J. 1985. *Toronto since 1918: An Illustrated History.* Toronto: James Lorimer & Co.

– 1990. *The Toronto Harbour Plan of 1912: Manufacturing Goals and Economic Realities. Working Papers of the Canadian Waterfront Resource Centre: No. 4.* Ottawa: Royal Commission on the Future of the Toronto Waterfront.

– 1996. *Liberal Dreams and Nature's Limits.* Toronto: Oxford University Press.

Leo, C. 1996. 'City Politics in an Era of Globalization.' In M. Lauria, ed., *Reconstructing Urban Regime Theory: Regulating Urban Politics in a Global Economy,* 77–98. Thousand Oaks, CA: Sage Publications.

– 2006. 'Deep Federalism: Respecting Community Difference in National Policy.' *Canadian Journal of Political Science* 39(3): 481–506.

Leo, C., and M. Pyl. 2007. 'Multi-level Governance: Getting the Job Done and Respecting Community Difference – Three Winnipeg Cases.' *Canadian Political Science Review* 1(2): 1–26.

Lewington, J. 2004. 'Waterfront corporation warns of layoffs.' *Globe and Mail,* 5 March: A11.

– 2005. 'Ottawa pays $35-million to abort bridge.' *Globe and Mail,* 4 May: A1.

Lewis, A.C. 1914. Letter to A.C. McMaster, 17 August. Toronto Port Authority Archives, Records Department fonds, RG 3/3, box 180, folder 8.

Ley, D. 1996. *The New Middle Class and the Remaking of the Central City.* Oxford: Oxford University Press.

Loney, B., and R.J. Hobbs. 1991. 'Management of Vegetation Corridors: Maintenance, Rehabilitation and Establishment.' In D.A. Saunders and R.J. Hobbs, eds., *Natural Conservation 2: The Role of Corridors,* 299–311. New South Wales, AUS: Surrey Beatty & Sons, Chipping Norton.

Lorimer, J. 1972. *A Citizen's Guide to City Politics.* Toronto: James Lewis and Samuel.

Luckin, B. 2006. 'Revisiting the Idea of Degeneration in Urban Britain, 1830–1900.' *Urban History* 33(2).

Lukes, S. 1974. *Power: A Radical View*. London: Macmillan.

Lyon, J.T. 1998. '"A Picturesque Lot": The Gypsies in Peterborough.' *Beaver* 78(5): 25–30.

MacArthur, John J. 1931. Letter to the editor. *Globe*, 19 September: 4.

Macaulay, R. 1992. *Report on the Toronto Harbour Commission and Recommendations for the Future*. Toronto: Waterfront Regeneration Trust.

Macdonald, L. 1997. 'Going Global: The Politics of Canada's Foreign Economic Relations.' In W. Clement, ed., *Understanding Canada: Building on the New Canadian Political Economy*, 72–196. Montreal & Kingston: McGill-Queen's University Press.

MacDougall, H.A. 1982. '"Health Is Wealth": The Development of Public Health Activity in Toronto, 1834–1890.' PhD dissertation, Department of History, University of Toronto.

Magnusson, W. 1983. 'Toronto.' In W. Magnusson and A. Sancton, eds., *City Politics in Canada*, 94–139. Toronto: University of Toronto Press.

– 1996. *The Search for Political Space*. Toronto: University of Toronto Press.

– 2005. 'Are Municipalities Creatures of the Provinces?' *Journal of Canadian Studies* 39(3): 5–29.

Manning, W.J., J.H.W. Cavey, and F.K. Devos. 1968. *Study of Harbour Administration in Canada*. Ottawa: National Harbours Board, Department of Transport.

Mariport Group Ltd. 1999. *Evaluating the Port of Toronto: Markets and Impacts on the GTA*. Toronto: Mariport Group Ltd.

Markel, H. 1997. *Quarantine!: East European Jewish Immigrants and the New York City Epidemics of 1892*. Baltimore: Johns Hopkins University Press.

Markel, H., and A.M. Stern. 2002. 'The Foreignness of Germs: The Persistent Association of Immigrants and Disease in American Society.' *Milbank Quarterly* 80(4): 757.

Marston, S.A. 2000. 'The Social Construction of Scale.' *Progress in Human Geography* 24(2): 219–42.

Marston, S.A., and N. Smith. 2001. 'States, Scales and Households: Limits to Scale Thinking? A Response to Brenner.' *Progress in Human Geography* 25(4): 615–19.

May, R. 2006. 'Connectivity in Urban Rivers: Conflict and Convergence between Ecology and Design.' *Technology in Society* 28: 477–88.

Mayall, D. 1988. *Gypsy-travellers in Nineteenth-century Society*. Cambridge and New York: Cambridge University Press.

McCallum, T. 2004. '"Still Raining, Market Still Rotten": Homeless Men and the Early Years of the Great Depression in Vancouver.' Unpublished PhD dissertation, Department of History, Queen's University, Kingston, ON.

– 2006. 'The Great Depression's First History? The Vancouver Archives of Major J.S. Matthews and the Writing of Hobo History.' *Canadian Historical Review* 87(1): 79–107.

McDougall, A. 1907. *Shipbuilding in Canada: The Handicaps, and the Remedy Therefor Suggested.* Niagara Falls, ON: n.p.

McIlwraith, T. 1991. 'Digging Out and Filling In: Making Land on the Toronto Waterfront in the 1850s.' *Urban History Review/Revue d'histoire urbaine* 20(1): 15–33.

McKay, I. 2000. 'The Liberal Order Framework: A Prospectus for a Reconnaissance of Canadian History.' *Canadian Historical Review* 81(4): 617–45.

McKenzie, J.I. 2002. *Environmental Politics in Canada: Managing the Commons into the Twenty-first Century.* Don Mills, ON: Oxford University Press.

McLaughlin, K., S.P. Osborne, and E. Ferlie, eds. 2002. *New Public Management: Current Trends and Future Prospects.* London: Routledge.

McLaughlin, S.G. 1987. *Federal Land Management in the Toronto Region: A Report for Ministerial Consideration on the Effective Management of Federal Lands in the Region of Metropolitan Toronto.* Toronto: Stephen G. McLaughlin Consultants.

McLeod, K.S. 2000. 'Our Sense of Snow: The Myth of John Snow in Medical Geography.' *Social Science & Medicine* 50: 923–35.

McPherson, E.G. 1998. 'Structure and Sustainability of Sacramento's Urban Forest.' *Journal of Arboriculture* 24(4): 174–90.

Mellen, F.N. 1974. 'The Development of the Toronto Waterfront During the Railway Expansion Era, 1850–1912.' Unpublished PhD dissertation, Department of Geography, University of Toronto.

Melosi, M.V. 2000. *The Sanitary City: Urban Infrastructure in America from Colonial Times to the Present.* Baltimore: Johns Hopkins University Press.

– 2001. *Effluent America: Cities, Industry, Energy, and the Environment.* Pittsburgh, PA: University of Pittsburgh Press.

Mercer Delta Consulting. 2004. *Toronto Waterfront Revitalization Corporation: Review of Alternative Governance Structures and Delivery Models, Final Report.* 10 September.

Merrens, R. 1988. 'Port Authorities as Urban Land Developers: The Case of the Toronto Harbour Commissioners and Their Outer Harbour Project, 1912–1968. *Urban History Review/Revue d'histoire urbaine* 17(2): 92–105.

– 1989. *A Selected Bibliography on Toronto's Port and Waterfront.* Working paper no. 1, Canadian Waterfront Resource Centre. Toronto: Royal Commission on the Future of the Toronto Waterfront.

Metropolitan Toronto Planning Board and Metropolitan Council. 1967. *The*

Waterfront Plan for the Metropolitan Planning Area. Toronto: Metropolitan Toronto.

Meyer, H. 1999. *City and Port: Urban Planning as a Cultural Venture in London, Barcelona, New York, and Rotterdam.* Utrecht: International Books.

Michael Van Valkenburgh and Associates (MVVA). 2007. *Port Lands Estuary.* Toronto: Waterfront Toronto.

Middleton, J.E. 1923. *The Municipality of Toronto: A History.* Vol. 1. Toronto and New York: Dominion Publishing Co.

– 1934. *Toronto's 100 Years.* Toronto: Corporation of the City of Toronto.

Millard, J.R. 1988. *The Master Spirit of the Age: Canadian Engineers and the Politics of Professionalism, 1887–1922.* Toronto: University of Toronto Press.

Miller, J.B. 1912. Letter to the Toronto Harbour Commissioners, 24 April. Toronto Port Authority Archives, Records Department fonds, RG 3/3, box 181, folder 8.

– 1917. Letter to R.S. Gourlay, 22 January. Toronto Port Authority Archives, Records Department fonds, RG 3/3, box 180, folder 9.

Miller, R.I., and L.D. Harris. 1977. 'Isolation and Extirpations in Wildlife Reserves.' *Biological Conservation* 12: 311–15.

Milloy, N., Hagarty & Grasett, P. Burns, W.A. Geddes, and W. Freeland. 1882. 'To the Board of the Harbor Commissioners of the City of Toronto, the Petition of the Undersigned Wharfingers and Others Interested,' 17 April. Toronto Port Authority Archives, Board of Commissioners fonds, RG 1/4, box 2, folder 2.

Mitchell, J. 1999. *The American Experiment with Government Corporations.* Armonk, NY: M.E. Sharpe.

Mittelstaedt, M. 2009. 'Natural Selection Gives Way to Human Selection.' *Globe and Mail*, 13 January: A3.

Moilanen, A., and I. Hanski. 2001. 'On the Use of Connectivity Measures in Spatial Ecology.' *Oikos* 95(1): 147–51.

Moir, M. 1986. 'Board of Trade Agitates for Changes on Waterfront.' *Port of Toronto News* 33(2): 2–5, 12.

– 1988. 'Ashbridges's Bay … from Marsh Lands to Port.' *Port of Toronto News* 34(4): 6–9.

– 1989. 'Toronto's Waterfront at War, 1914–1918.' *Archivaria* 28: 126–40.

Moloney, P. 2008. 'Don River bridge, other plans to be delayed along lakefront.' *Toronto Star* 4 September: A6.

Moloney, P., and D. DeMara. 1999. 'Plan for waterfront called "breathtaking": Ambitious scheme will require "multi-billions" of dollars.' *Toronto Star*. 4 November: A1.

Molotch, H. 1976. 'The City as a Growth Machine.' *American Journal of Sociology* 82 (September): 309–11.

Monsebraaten, L. 1987. 'Aldermen to replace citizens on Harbour Commission: Toronto seeks more waterfront control.' *Toronto Star* 16 June: A2.

– 2001. 'City taken to court over port lands: Agency seeks return of prime property.' *Toronto Star*, 1 September: B03.

Moore, S., and S. Bunce. 2009. 'Guest Editorial: Delivering Sustainable Buildings and Communities: Eclipsing Social Concerns through Private Sector–Led Urban Regeneration and Development.' *Local Environment: International Journal of Justice and Sustainability* 14(7): 601–6.

Moss, M.L. 1976. 'The Urban Port: A Hidden Resource for the City and the Coastal Zone.' *Coastal Management* 2(3): 223–45.

Moulaert, F., A. Rodriguez, and E. Swyngedouw, eds. 2003. *The Globalized City: Economic Restructuring and Social Polarization in European Cities*. Oxford: Oxford University Press.

Mulgan, R. 2000. '"Accountability": An Ever-expanding Concept?' *Public Administration* 78(3): 555–73.

Mulvaney, C.P. 1885. *History of Toronto and County of York Ontario. Volume I & Volume II*. Toronto: C. Blackett Robinson.

Munson, W. 1990. *Soil Contamination and Port Redevelopment in Toronto. Working Paper of the Royal Commission on the Future of the Toronto Waterfront*. 2nd printing. Toronto: Royal Commission on the Future of the Toronto Waterfront.

Musolf, L. 1959. *Public Ownership and Accountability*. Cambridge, MA: Harvard University Press.

MVVA. *See* Michael Van Valkenburgh and Associates, 2007.

Naiman, R.J., and R.E. Bilby. 1998. *River Ecology and Management: Lessons from the Pacific Coastal Ecoregion*. New York: Springer.

Naiman, R.J., and H. Décamps. 1997. 'The Ecology of Interfaces: Riparian Zones.' *Annual Review of Ecology and Systematics* 28: 621–58.

Nairn, A.S. 1880. Letter to M. Baldwin, 6 April. Toronto Port Authority Archives, Board of Commissioners fonds, RG 1/4, box 1, folder 10.

Nash, L. 2006. *Inescapable Ecologies: A History of Environment, Disease, and Knowledge*. Berkeley: University of California Press.

Nash, R. 1982. *Wilderness and the American Mind*. New Haven, CT: Yale University Press.

National Research Council. 1980. *Urban Waterfront Lands*. Washington: National Academy of Sciences.

National Round Table on the Environment and the Economy. 1997. *Backgrounder: Improving Site-specific Data on the Environmental Condition of Land*. National Round Table on the Environment and the Economy. Ottawa.

- 2003. *Cleaning Up the Past, Building the Future: A National Brownfield Redevelopment Strategy for Canada*. National Round Table on the Environment and the Economy. Ottawa.

Neuman, M. 2000. 'Communicate This! Does Consensus Lead to Advocacy and Pluralism?' *Journal of Planning Education and Research* 194: 343–50.

New York Times. 1921a. 'Receivers named for Hannevig & Co.' 12 February: 20.

- 1921b. 'Hannevig in Norway for funds, he says.' 21 July: 29.

- 1927. 'Norway takes up case for millions.' 22 May: E1.

Nixon, L. 1911. 'Shipbuilding in Canada: An interview with Lewis Nixon.' *Busy Man's Magazine* 21(3): 21.

Norcliffe, G.B. 1981. 'Industrial Change in Old Port Areas: The Case of the Port of Toronto.' *Cahiers de géographie du Québec* 25(65): 237–54.

Norcliffe, G., K. Bassett, and T. Hoare. 1996. 'The Emergence of Postmodernism on the Urban Waterfront: Geographical Perspectives on Changing Relationships.' *Journal of Transport Geography* 4(2): 123–34.

Norrie, K., and D. Owram. 1996. *A History of the Canadian Economy*. Toronto: Harcourt Brace.

O'Connor, E. 2000. *Raw Material: Producing Pathology in Victorian Culture*. Durham: Duke University Press.

O'Connor, J. 1988. 'Capitalism, Nature, Socialism: A Theoretical Introduction.' *Capitalism, Nature, Socialism* 1: 11–38.

OECD [Organization for Economic Co-operation and Development]. 1995. *Governance in Transition: Public Management Reforms in OECD Countries*. Paris: OECD.

Oetter, D.R., L.R. Ashkenas, and S.V. Gregory. 2004. 'GIS Methodology for Characterizing Historical Conditions of Willamette River Flood Plain, Oregon.' *Transactions in GIS* 8: 367–83.

Ogawa, M. 2000. 'Uneasy Bedfellows: Science and Politics in the Refutation of Koch's Bacterial Theory of Cholera.' *Bulletin of the History of Medicine* 74: 671–707.

Oliver Wyman–Delta Organization & Leadership. 2007. *Value-for-Money Audit/ Organizational Review: Final Report*. Toronto: Toronto Waterfront Revitalization Corporation. 26 June.

Olivier, D., and B. Slack. 2006. 'Rethinking the Port.' *Environment and Planning A* 38(8): 1409–27.

Olds, K. 1998. 'Canada: Hallmark Events, Evictions, and Housing Rights in: Azuela.' In A. Duhau and E. Ortiz, eds., *Evictions and the Right to Housing: Experiences from Canada, Chile, the Dominican Republic, South Africa, and South Korea*, 1–46. Ottawa: IDRC.

Olson, D.J. 1988. 'Public Port Accountability: A Framework for Evaluation.' In M.J. Hershman, ed., *Urban Ports and Harbour Management*, 307–33. New York: Taylor & Francis.

O'Mara, J. 1976. *Shaping Urban Waterfronts: The Role of the Toronto Harbour Commissioners, 1911–1960.* Discussion paper no. 13. Toronto: Department of Geography, York University.

– 1984. *The Toronto Harbour Commissioners' Financial Arrangements and City Waterfront Development, 1910 to 1950.* Toronto: York University, Department of Geography, Discussion paper no. 30.

Ontario. 1990. Environmental Protection Act, R.S.O. 1990, c. E-19.

– 1992. Waterfront Regeneration Trust Agency Act, 1992. S.O. 1992, c. 2.

– 1996a. 'Changes to Ontario's Planning Process.' Media release. 22 May.

– 1996b. *Greater Toronto: Report of the GTA Task Force.* Toronto: Queen's Printer.

– 2000. '$1.5 Billion for Toronto Waterfront Re-development an Investment in the Future: Harris.' Media release. 20 October.

– 2002. Toronto Waterfront Revitalization Act, 2002. S.O. 2002, c. 28, Bill 151, 37th Legislature, 3rd session (Royal Assent 13 December).

– 2005a. Budget Measures Act, 2005. S.O. 2005, c. 31, Bill 18, 38th Legislature, 2nd session (Royal Assent 15 December).

– 2005b. *Memorandum of Understanding between Ministry of Public Infrastructure Renewal and Ontario Realty Corporation and the Toronto Waterfront Revitalization Corporation: West Don Lands Revitalization Phase One Implementation Strategy.* Toronto: Queen's Printer.

Ontario Department of Planning and Development. 1950. *Don Valley Conservation Report.* Toronto: Ontario Department of Planning and Development.

Ontario Ministry of the Environment. 1996. *Guidelines for Use at Contaminated Sites in Ontario.* Toronto: Queen's Printer for Ontario.

Ontario Ministry of Natural Resources. 2006. *Review of the Status and Management of Double-crested Cormorant in Ontario.* Peterborough: Ontario Ministry of Natural Resources.

Orr, R.B., ed. 1894. 'The Approaching Cholera Conference at Paris: The Extinction of Cholera.' *Ontario Medical Journal* 2 (8).

Osborne, D.E., and T. Gaebler. 1992. *Reinventing Government: How the Entrepreneurial Spirit Is Transforming the Public Sector.* New York: Perseus Books.

Otter, C. 2004. 'Cleansing and Clarifying: Technology and Perception in Nineteenth-century London.' *Journal of British Studies* 43: 40–64.

Paneth, N., P. Vinten-Johansen, H. Brody, and M. Rip. 1998. 'A Rivalry of Foulness: Official and Unofficial Investigations of the London Cholera Epidemic of 1854.' *American Journal of Public Health* 88(10): 1545–53.

Pankratz, H.J. 2000. 'Preface.' In T. Wickson, *Reflections of Toronto Harbour: 200 years of Port Activity and Waterfront Development*, 9. Toronto: Toronto Port Authority.

Park, R. 1952. *Human Communities: The City and Human Ecology*. Glencoe, IL: Free Press.

Park, R., E.W. Burgess, and R.D. McKenzie. 1925. *The City*. Chicago: University of Chicago Press.

Passfield, R. 1988. 'Waterways.' In N.R. Ball, ed., *Building Canada: A History of Public Works*. 113–42. Toronto: University of Toronto Press.

Patriot. 1853. 10 February.

Peet, R., and M. Watts. 1996. *Liberation Ecologies: Environment, Development, Social Movements*. New York: Routledge.

Pelango, P. 1992. 'A Smart Person's Word for "Doomed from the Start": Atara-tiri project.' *Eye Weekly*, 30 April. www.eyeweekly.com/eye/issue_04.30.92/news.

Pelling, M. 1978. *Cholera, Fever and English Medicine, 1825–1865*. New York: Oxford University Press.

Peluso, N.L. 1992. *Rich Forests, Poor People: Resource Control and Resistance in Java*. Berkeley: University of California Press.

Perlman, D.L., and J.C. Milder. 2005. *Practical Ecology for Planners, Developers, and Citizens*. Washington, DC: Island Press.

Petry, F. 1999. 'The Opinion–Policy Relationship in Canada.' *Journal of Politics* 61(2): 540–50.

Peuramaki, D. 1998. 'The Remaining Wildlife.' In G. Fairfield, ed., *Ashbridge's Bay: An Anthology of Writings by Those Who Knew and Loved Ashbridge's Bay*, 100–4. Toronto: Toronto Ornithological Club.

Pierson, P. 2000. 'Increasing Returns, Path Dependence, and the Study of Politics.' *American Political Science Review* 94(2): 251–67.

Pigg, S. 1989. 'Ontario plans to protect lakefront, but for whom?' *Toronto Star*, 23 October: A17.

Pitsula, J.M. 1980. 'The Treatment of Tramps in Late Nineteenth-century Toronto.' *Canadian Historical Association: Historical Papers* 15(1): 116–32.

Platt, H.L. 2005. *Shock Cities: The Environmental Transformation and Reform of Manchester and Chicago*. Chicago: University of Chicago Press.

Polson Iron Works. 1910. Letter from J.J. Main, Vice-president and manager, to Alderman J.O. McCarthy, with Memorandum of Facts in Connection with Sale of Water Lot from City of Toronto to the Polson Iron Works, Limited. City of Toronto, Legal Department, Case files, box 1452, file: Polson Iron Works vs. Toronto – suit H.J.C.

Port Industry Task Force. 1975. *Report*. Toronto: Metropolitan Toronto.

Porter, D. 1991. '"Enemies of the Race": Biologism, Environmentalism, and Public Health in Edwardian England.' *Victorian Studies* 34(2): 159–78.

Pringle, C. 2003. 'What is Hydrologic Connectivity and Why Is It Ecologically Important?' *Hydrological Processes* 17: 2685–9.

Prudham, W.S. 2003. 'Taming Trees: Capital, Science, and Nature in Pacific Slope Tree Improvement.' *Annals of the Association of American Geographers* 93(3): 636–56.

Pukonnen, E. 1998. 'The Canadian Experience: Bringing People, Ideas, and Resources Together.' *Proceedings of an International Symposium: Redeveloping Brownfields, A Different Conversation*. Toronto: Waterfront Regeneration Trust.

Puth, L.M., and K.A. Wilson. 2001. 'Boundaries and Corridors as a Continuum of Ecological Flow Control: Lessons from Rivers and Streams.' *Conservation Biology* 15(1): 21–30.

Raco, M. 2005. 'Sustainable Development, Rolled-out Neoliberalism and Sustainable Communities.' *Antipode* 37(2): 324–47.

– 2007. *Building Sustainable Communities: Spatial Policy and Labour Mobility in Post-war Britain*. Bristol, UK: Policy Press.

Ramlalsingh, R. 1975. *A Study of the Decline of Trade at the Port of Toronto*. Discussion paper no. 12. Department of Geography, York University.

Redclift, M., and T. Benton, eds. 1994. *Social Theory and the Environment*. New York, London: Routledge.

Redhill, M. 2006. *Consolation*. Mississauga, ON: Anchor Canada.

Reeves, W. 1992. *Visions for the Metropolitan Waterfront: Planning in Historical Perspective*. Toronto: Metropolitan Toronto Planning Department.

Reid, R., R. Lockhart, and B. Woodburn. 1989. *A Green Strategy for the Greater Toronto Waterfront: Background and Issues*. Toronto: Royal Commission on the Future of the Toronto Waterfront.

Richardson, H. 1854. 'Report on the Preservation and Improvement of Toronto Harbour.' *Supplement to the Canadian Journal: Reports on the Improvement and Preservation of Toronto Harbour*, 34–8.

Richmond, D., and D. Siegel, eds. 1994. *Agencies, Boards and Commissions in Canadian Local Government*. Toronto: Institute of Public Administration of Canada.

Risser, P.G. 1990. 'The Ecological Importance of Land-water Ecotones.' In R.J. Naiman and H. Décamps, eds., *The Ecology and Management of Aquatic-Terrestrial Ecotones*, 7–22. Paris: UNESCO.

Robbins, P. 2002. 'Obstacles to a First World Political Ecology? Looking Near without Looking Up.' *Environment and Planning A* 34(8): 1509–13.

Roberts, V.M. N.d. *Memorabilia*, vol. 10. Toronto Port Authority Archives, SC 26/2, box 7, folder 2.

Robertson, J.R. 1894. *Robertson's Landmarks of Toronto: A Collection of Historical Sketches of the Old Town of York from 1792 until 1833, and of Toronto from 1834 to 1893*. Vol. 1. Toronto: J. Ross Robertson.

Roland, C.G., ed. 1984. *Health, Disease and Medicine: Essays in Canadian History: Proceedings of the First Hannah Conference on the History of Medicine, McMaster University, June 3–5, 1982*. Toronto: Hannah Institute for the History of Medicine.

Rosenberg, C.E. 1987. *The Cholera Years: The United States in 1832, 1849, and 1866*. Chicago: University of Chicago Press.

Royal Commission on the Future of the Toronto Waterfront. 1989a. *The Future of the Toronto Island Airport: The Issues*. Toronto: Royal Commission on the Future of the Toronto Waterfront.

– 1989b. *Interim Report: Summer 1989*. Ottawa: Minister of Supply and Services Canada.

– 1989c. *Jobs, Opportunities and Economic Growth: Report of the Jobs, Opportunities and Economic Growth Work Group to the Royal Commission on the Future of the Toronto Waterfront*. Ottawa: Minister of Supply and Services Canada.

– 1989d. *Persistence and Change: Waterfront Issues and the Board of Toronto Harbour Commissioners*. Toronto: Royal Commission on the Future of the Toronto Waterfront.

– 1990. *Watershed: Interim Report, August*. Ottawa: Minister of Supply and Services Canada.

– 1992. *Regeneration: Toronto's Waterfront and the Sustainable City. Final Report*. Ottawa: Minister of Supply and Services Canada.

Royal Norwegian Consul for Canada. 1917. Letter to A. Johnston, 22 June. Library and Archives Canada, Department of Marine fonds, RG 42, vol. 262, file 38360.

Ruddick, S. 1996. 'Constructing Difference in Public Spaces: Race, Class, and Gender as Interlocking Systems.' *Urban Geography* 17: 132–51.

Rutherford, P. 1979. 'Tomorrow's Metropolis: The Urban Reform Movement in Canada, 1880–1920.' In G.A. Stelter and A.F.J. Artibise, eds., *The Canadian City: Essays in Urban History*, 368–92. Toronto: Macmillan Company of Canada Ltd.

Safieddine, H., and R. James. 2005. 'Bridge battle finally over.' *Toronto Star*, 4 May: B1.

Sancton, A. 2006. 'City Politics: Municipalities and Multi-level Governance.' In T. Bunting and P. Filion, eds., *Canadian Cities in Transition: Local through Global Perspectives*, 306–19. Toronto: Oxford University Press.

Sandercock, L., and K. Dovey. 2002. 'Pleasure, Politics, and the "Public Interest": Melbourne's Riverscape Revitalization.' *Journal of the American Planning Association* 682: 151–64.

Sandwell, R.W. 2003. 'The Limits of Liberalism: The Liberal Reconnaissance and the History of the Family in Canada.' *Canadian Historical Review* 84(3): 423–50.

Saunders, R.M. 1947. *Flashing Wings*. Toronto: McClelland and Stewart Ltd.

Savoie, D. 1994. *Thatcher, Reagan, Mulroney: In Search of a New Bureaucracy.* Toronto: University of Toronto Press.

Scadding, H. 1873. *Toronto of Old: Collections and Recollections Illustrative of the Early Settlement and Social Life of the Capital of Ontario.* Toronto: Adam, Stevenson & Co.

Schaeffer, R. 1981. *The Board of Trade and the Origins of the Toronto Harbour Commissioners, 1899–1911.* Discussion paper no. 27. Toronto: York University, Department of Geography.

Schmidt, A. 1971. *The Concept of Nature in Marx,* London: NLB.

Schoenberger, E. 2004. 'The Spatial Fix Revisited.' *Antipode* 36(3): 427–33.

Schultz, S.K., and C. McShane. 1978. 'To Engineer the Metropolis: Sewers, Sanitation, and City Planning in Late-nineteenth-century America.' *Journal of American Historians* 65(2): 389–411.

Seton, E.T. 1940. *Trail of an Artist-Naturalist: The Autobiography of Ernest Thompson Seton.* New York: Charles Scribner's Sons.

– 1998. 'Seton's Ashbridge.' In G. Fairfield, ed., *Ashbridge's Bay: An Anthology of Writings by Those Who Knew and Loved Ashbridge's Bay,* 41–8. Toronto: Toronto Ornithological Club.

Sewell, J. 1971. *Inside City Hall: The Year of the Opposition.* Toronto: A.M. Hakkert.

Sewell, W.H., Jr. 1992. 'A Theory of Structure: Duality, Agency, and Transformation.' *American Journal of Sociology* 98: 1–29.

Shaw, K., and F. Robinson. 1998. 'Learning from Experience? Reflections of Two Decades of British Urban Policy.' *Town Planning Review* 69: 49–63.

Shields, R. 1991. *Places on the Margin: Alternative Geographies of Modernity.* London and New York: Routledge.

Shipbuilding in Canada: A Memorial Presented to the Canadian Government. 1913. N.p.: n.p.

Sibley, D. 1995. *Geographies of Exclusion: Society and Difference in the West.* New York: Routledge.

Silcox, P. 1973. 'Government by Special Purpose Agencies.' Seminar Proceedings: Government by Special Purpose Agencies. Toronto, 16 February: 73–95.

Sinclair, G.A. 1931. 'Men of Don Valley Jungle a Healthy and Husky Lot.' *Toronto Daily Star*, 30 September: 1.

Sing, J.G., et al. 1912. *Report upon the Existing Water Works System and upon an Additional Water Supply.* Toronto: City of Toronto.

Skånes, H. 1997. 'Towards an Integrated Ecological-Geographical Landscape Perspective: A Review of Principle Concepts and Methods.' *Norsk Geografisk Tidsskrift* 51(3): 145–71.

Skogstad, G. 2003. 'Who Governs? Who Should Govern?: Political Authority and Legitimacy in Canada in the Twenty-first Century.' *Canadian Journal of Political Science* 36(5): 955–73.

Slack, B. 1980. 'Technology and Seaports in the 1980's.' *Tijdschrift voor Economische en Sociale Geografie* 71: 108–13.

Small, C. 2001. 'Estimation of Urban Vegetation Abundance by Spectral Mixture Analysis.' *International Journal of Remote Sensing* 22(7): 1305–34.

Smith v. Disero et al. 1991. 'Statement of Claim.' Ontario Court, General Division; Court file no. 91-CQ-4710.

Smith, J.R. 1919. *Influence of the Great War on Shipping.* New York, Toronto: Oxford University Press.

Smith, M.P., ed. 1995. *Marginal Spaces: Comparative Urban and Community Research*, vol. 5. 5 vols. New Brunswick, NJ, and London: Transaction Publishers.

Smith, N. 1984. *Uneven Development: Nature, Capital and the Production of Space.* Oxford and New York: Blackwell.

– 1996. 'The Production of Nature.' In G. Robertson, M. Mash, L. Tickner, J. Bird, B. Curtis, and T. Putnam, eds., *Future/Natural: Nature/Science/Culture*, 33–54. London: Routledge.

– 2008. *Uneven Development: Nature, Capital and the Production of Space.* Athens, GA.: University of Georgia Press.

Smith, W.H. 1846. *Smith's Canadian Gazetteer, comprising Statistical and General Information respecting all parts of the Upper Province, or Canada West.* Toronto: H. & W. Rowsell.

Somerville P. 2004. 'State Rescaling and Democratic Transformation.' *Space and Polity* 8(2): 137–56.

Spears, J. 1994. 'Dream of a jackpot: Dennis Mills has a vision of two, or even three, casinos on the waterfront in Toronto, anchoring a tourism corridor on public lands that would create 50,000 new and permanent jobs – if only politicians at all levels of government could agree.' *Toronto Star*, 10 September: E1

Speight and Van Nostrand. 1930. 'The Old Don Channel,' 7 March. Toronto Port Authority Archives, Records Department fonds, RG 3/3, box 262, folder 23.

Stallybrass, P., and A. White. 1986. *The Politics and Poetics of Transgression*. London: Methuen.

Stamp, R.M. 1991. *Bright Lights Big City. The History of Electricity in Toronto*. Toronto: Ontario Association of Archivists.

Stanford, G.H. 1974. *To Serve the Community: The Story of Toronto's Board of Trade*. Toronto: University of Toronto Press for the Toronto Board of Trade.

Statistics Canada. 2003. Shipping in Canada: 2001. http://www.statcan.gc.ca/pub/54-205-x/54-205-x2001000-eng.htm.

– 2007. *Toronto: Community Profiles*. http://www12.statcan.ca/english/Profil01/CP01/Details/Page.cfm?Lang=E&Geo1=CSD&Code1=3520005&Geo2=PR&Code2=35&Data=Count&SearchText=toronto&SearchType=Begins&SearchPR=35&B1=All&Custom=.

Stedman Jones, G. 1974. *Outcast London: A Study in the Relationship between Classes in Victorian Society*. Oxford: Oxford University Press.

Steiner, D., and M. Nauser, eds. 1993. *Human Ecology: Fragments of Anti-fragmentary Views of the World*. London and New York: Routledge.

Stinson, J., and M. Moir. 1991. *Built Heritage of the East Bayfront. Royal Commission on the Future of the Toronto Waterfront. Environmental Audit of the East Bayfront/Port Industrial Area*. Phase 2, Technical paper no. 7.

Stren, R., and M. Polese. 2000. 'Understanding the New Sociocultural Dynamics of Cities: Comparative Urban Policy in a Global Context.' In M. Polese and R. Stren, eds., *The Social Sustainability of Cities: Diversity and the Management of Change*, 3–38. Toronto: University of Toronto Press.

Sutcliffe, J.B. 2007. 'Local Government in a Multi-level Setting: Lessons from England and Ontario.' *Regional & Federal Studies* 17(2): 253–73.

Sutherland, A. 1975. *Gypsies: The Hidden Americans*. London: Tavistock Publications.

Suzuki, D. 1992. 'Toronto's "ecosystem approach" generates hope.' *Toronto Star*. 29 August: D6.

Sway, M. 1988. *Familiar Strangers: Gypsy Life in America*. Urbana and Chicago: University of Illinois Press.

Swift, J. 1991. *An Enduring Flame: The History of the Toronto Gas Workers*. Toronto: Energy Chemical Workers Union.

Swyngedouw, E. 1996. 'The City as a Hybrid: On Nature, Society and Cyborg Urbanization.' *Capitalism Nature Socialism* 7(2): 65–80.

– 1997. 'Neither Global Nor Local: "Glocalization" and the Politics of Scale.' In K. Cox, ed., *Spaces of Globalization: Reasserting the Power of the Local*, 115–36. New York: Guilford Press.

– 1999. 'Modernity and Hybridity: Nature, Regeneracionismo, and the Production of the Spanish Waterscape, 1890–1930.' *Annals of the Association of American Geographers* 89(3): 443–65.

– 2004. *Social Power and the Urbanization of Water: Flows of Power.* Oxford: Oxford University Press.

– 2007. 'Technonatural Revolutions: The Scalar Politics of Franco's Hydro-social Dream for Spain, 1939–1975.' *Transactions of the Institute of British Geographers* 32 (1): 9–28.

Swyngedouw, E., N. Heynen, and M. Kaika. 2005. *In the Nature of Cities: Urban Political Ecology and the Politics of Urban Metabolism.* New York: Routledge.

Swyngedouw, E., F. Moulaert, and A. Rodriguez. 2002. 'Neoliberal urbanization in Europe: Large-scale Urban Development Projects and the New Urban Policy.' *Antipode* 34(3): 542–77.

Sypher-Mueller International. 2001. *Toronto City Centre Airport General Aviation and Airport Feasibility Study: Small Footprint, Big Impact.* Toronto: Sypher-Mueller International, Inc.

Tarr, J. 1996. *The Search for the Ultimate Sink: Urban Pollution in Historical Perspective.* Akron, OH: University of Akron Press.

Task Force to Bring Back the Don. 1991. *Bringing Back the Don.* Toronto: The Task Force to Bring Back the Don.

Tasse, R. 2006. *Review of Toronto Port Authority Report.* Toronto: Gowling Lafleur Henderson LLP Barristers & Solicitors.

TEDCO. 1997. *A Soil and Groundwater Strategy for TEDCO Lands in the Port Area.* Prepared by Angus Environmental Ltd., INTERA Consultants Ltd., and E. Addison Lall & Associates. Toronto: TEDCO.

– 2001. *Preliminary Environmental Liability Assessment.* Prepared by Decommissioning Consulting Services Ltd. Toronto: TEDCO.

Telegram. 1910a. 'Advance Toronto.' 3 December: 14.

– 1910b. '"Oh, shut up" said McBride repartee at council meeting.' 6 December: 1.

Thomas, L., and W. Cousins. 1996. 'The Compact City: A Successful, Desirable and Achievable Urban Form?' In M. Jenks, E. Burton, and K. Williams, eds., *The Compact City: A Sustainable Urban Form?* 53–65. London: E&FN Spon.

Thomas, N. 2007. 'Global Capitalism, the Anti-globalization Movement, and the Third World.' *Capital and Class* 92: 45–78.

Tindal, C.R., and S.N. Tindal. 2004. *Local Government in Canada.* 6th ed. Scarborough, ON: Thomson Nelson.

Tischendorf, L., and L. Fahrig. 2000. 'On the Usage and Measurement of Landscape Connectivity.' *Oikos* 90: 7–19.

Todd, G. 1996. 'Restructuring the Local State: Economic Development and Local Public Enterprise in Toronto.' In J. Caulfield and L. Peake, eds., *City Lives and City Forms: Critical Research and Canadian Urbanism*, 173–95. Toronto: University of Toronto Press.

Torgerson, D. 1999. *The Promise of Green Politics: Environmentalism and the Public Sphere*. Durham and London: Duke University Press

Toronto City Council. 2004. Policy and Finance Committee Report 9, clause 1: Governance Structure for Toronto Waterfront Revitalization. City Clerk's Office. 2 December.

Toronto Daily News. 1918. 'Steel carrier launched with due ceremony.' 26 September: 7.

Toronto Daily Star. 1909. 'Civic Cabinet visited marsh.' 15 July: 3.

– 1910a. 'Toronto's harbour.' 18 June: 6.

– 1910b. 'Policy for harbour.' 10 September: 1.

– 1910c. 'Gypsy's camp in North Toronto.' 5 November: 9.

– 1912. 'Toronto's harbor and waterfront equal to any on the entire continent of America.' 14 November: 1, 6–7.

– 1919. 'Shipbuilding plant may have to close.' 5 February: 2.

– 1920a. 'North Toronto column.' 25 May: 10.

– 1920b. 'Gypsies at York Mills.' 2 June: 3.

– 1920c. 'North Toronto column.' 21 August: 22.

– 1930. 'Forty-two homeless men snoozed on heated bricks.' 2 December: 2.

– 1931a. '300 jobless sleep nightly along Don River's banks.' 19 June: 1.

– 1931b. 'He enlisted in Toronto.' 9 July: 6.

Toronto Harbour Commissioners. 1913a. Minute book, minutes nos. 401, 673, and 702. Toronto Port Authority Archives, Board of Commissioners fonds, RG 1/1/1, vol. 4.

– 1913b. *Toronto Waterfront Development, 1912–1920*. Toronto: Toronto Harbour Commissioners.

– 1914. Minute book. Toronto Port Authority Archives, Board of Commissioners fonds, RG 1/1/1, vol. 5.

– 1915a. *A District Created for Manufacturers*. Toronto: Toronto Harbour Commissioners.

– 1915b. 'There is room for 1,000 more factories in the Toronto Harbor Industrial District' [advertisement]. *Industrial Canada*, 16 June: 157.

– 1930. *Facts concerning Toronto Harbour 1930*. City of Toronto Archives collection, Fonds 2, series 1242, file 70.

– 1934. *The Port and Harbour of Toronto, 1834–1934: Centennial Year*. Toronto: Hunter-Rose.

– 1970. *Annual Report*. Toronto: Toronto Harbour Commission.

– 1985. *Toronto Harbour: The Passing Years*. Toronto: Toronto Harbour Commissioners.

– 1989. *Port of Toronto News*, 361.

– 1992. *Port of Toronto News*, 392.

Toronto Harbour Commission Investigation. 1926. 'Dominion Shipbuilding.' Toronto Port Authority Archives, Denton Inquiry fonds, RG 17/1, box 2, folder 5.

Toronto Port Authority Archives. N.d. Archival folder RG 3/3, box 54, folder 7.

Toronto and Region Conservation Authority. 2008. 'History of Tommy Thompson Park.' Toronto, ON: Toronto and Region Conservation Authority. http://www.trca.on.ca/enjoy/locations/tommy-thompson-park.dot.

Toronto Star. 2000. 'A vision for Toronto: Seize the dream, or rue the day.' 1 April.

Toronto Star Weekly. 1931. 'Two harbors for Toronto!' 14 March: 1.

Toronto Waterfront Revitalization Corporation. 2002. *The Development Plan and Business Strategy*. Toronto: TWRC.

– 2005a. *Annual Report 2004–05*. Toronto: TWRC.

– 2005b. *Sustainability Framework*. Toronto: TWRC.

– 2005c. *West Don Lands Precinct Plan*. Toronto: TWRC.

– 2006a. *Performance Specifications for Green Building Initiative for West Don Lands*. Toronto: TWRC.

– 2006b. *West Don Lands Block Plan and Design Guidelines*. Toronto: TWRC.

– 2007. *Toronto's Lower Don Lands: Innovative Design Competition – Competition Brief, v 1*. Toronto: TWRC.

Toronto Waterfront Revitalization Task Force. 2000. *Our Toronto Waterfront: Gateway to the New Canada*. Toronto: Toronto Waterfront Revitalization Task Force.

Toronto World. 1913. 'Harbor development.' 14 April: 8.

– 1918. 'New shipbuilding plant is already hive of industry.' 17 July: 4.

Treasury Board of Canada. 2010. 'The Financial Administration Act: Responding to Non-compliance – Meeting the Expectations of Canadians.' http://www.tbs-sct.gc.ca/report/rev-exa/faa-lgfp/faa-lgfp03-eng.asp.

Treasury Board Secretariat, Canada. 2007. *Annual Report to Parliament: Crown Corporations and Other Corporate Interests of Canada 2007*. Ottawa: Treasury Board of Canada Secretariat.

Trump, H.J. 1974. 'The Port of Teignmouth and the Teignmouth Harbour Commission 1836–1932.' *Maritime History* 4(1): 49–64.

Tucker, E.J. 1948. *First Century of Consumers' Gas*. Toronto: Consumers' Gas Company of Toronto.

Tully, K. 1853a. 'Toronto Harbour,' 10 February. Toronto Port Authority Archives, Board of Commissioners fonds, RG 1/4, box 3, folder 1.
– 1853b. 'Toronto Esplanade,' 26 August. Ibid.
– 1854. 'Report on the Means to Be Adopted for the Preservation and Improvement of the Harbour of Toronto.' *Supplement to the Canadian Journal: Reports on the Improvement and Preservation of Toronto Harbour*, 29–33.
– 1872. 'Toronto Harbor Works,' 20 January. Toronto Port Authority Archives, Board of Commissioners fonds, RG 1/4, box 5(A): 56.
Tunbridge, J. 1988. 'Policy Convergence on the Waterfront? A Comparative Assessment of North American Revitalisation Strategies.' In B. Hoyle, D. Pinder, and M.S. Husain, eds., *Revitalising the Waterfront: International Dimensions of Dockland Redevelopment*, 67–91. London: Belhaven Press.
Turner, M.G., R.H. Gardner, and R.V. O'Neill. 2001. *Landscape Ecology in Theory and Practice: Pattern and Process*. New York: Springer-Verlag.
Tweedale, I. 1998. 'Waterfront Redevelopment: Economic Restructuring and Social Impact.' In B.S. Hoyle, D.A. Pinder, and M.S. Husain, eds., *Revitalising the Waterfront: Institutional Dimensions of Dockland Re-development*, 185–98. London: Belhaven Press.
Uitermark, J. 2002. 'Re-scaling, "Scale Fragmentation" and the Regulation of Antagonistic Relationships.' *Progress in Human Geography* 26(6): 743–65.
Upper Canada Journal of Medical, Surgical and Physical Science (Toronto General Hospital). 1853–4. Vol. 3(2): 69–77.
Urban Design Associates. 2005. *West Don Lands Precinct Plan*. Toronto: Urban Design Associates.
Urban Strategies. 2005. *Toronto Waterfront Plan*. www.urbanstrategies.com/projects/proj_b3.html.
Valencius, C.B. 2002. *The Health of the Country: How American Settlers Understood Themselves and Their Land*. New York: Basic Books.
Valpy, M. 1990. 'Waterfront report heady stuff.' *Globe and Mail*, 14 September: A10.
Valverde, M. 1991. *The Age of Light, Soap, and Water: Moral Reform in English Canada, 1885–1925*. Toronto: McClelland & Stewart.
Vancouver Daily Sun. 1918. 'Offered $215 per ton for steamers.' 26 April: 9.
Van Dyke, E., and K. Wasson. 2005. 'Historical Ecology of a Central California Estuary: 150 Years of Habitat Change.' *Estuaries* 28: 173–89.
Velkar, A. 2006. 'Institutional Facts and Standardisation: The Case of Measurements in the London Coal Trade.' In *Working Papers on the Nature of Evidence: How Well Do Facts Travel?* no. 11. London: London School of Economics, Department of Economic History.

Vienneau, D., and P. Moloney. 1997. 'Ottawa springs surprise on harbour: Bill abolishes commission created in 1911.' *Toronto Star*, 16 April: A6.

Wade, J., 1997. 'Home or Homelessness? Marginal Housing in Vancouver, 1886–1950.' *Urban History Review/Revue d'histoire urbaine* 25(2): 19–29.

Wagner-Chazalon, A. 2007. 'Wanda returns to Lake Muskoka.' *The Muskokan.* 28 June: A12. http://209.200.253.26/special/muskokan/data/pdfs/19/A12.pdf.

Wainwright, M. 2001. 'Microbiology before Pasteur.' *Microbiology Today.* 28: 19–21.

Walker, W. 1987. 'Ontario to attack problems on Toronto's waterfront.' *Toronto Star*, 4 November: A14.

Walkom, T. 2003. 'Bridge over troubled waters.' *Toronto Star*, 14 October: A23.

Wallerstein, I. 2000. 'From Sociology to Historical Social Science: Prospects and Obstacles.' *British Journal of Sociology* 51(1): 25–35.

Wang, J.J., ed. 2007. *Ports, Cities and Global Supply Chains*. Aldershot, UK: Ashgate Publishing Ltd.

Ward, J.V., K. Tockner, and F. Schiemer. 1999. 'Biodiversity of Floodplain River Ecosystems: Ecotones and Connectivity.' *Regulation of Rivers: Resource Management* 15(1): 125–139.

Waterfront Regeneration Trust. 1993. *Lower Don Lands Site Remediation: Challenges & Opportunities: Workshop Proceedings.* 25–6 May. Toronto: Waterfront Regeneration Trust.

– 1995a. *Lake Ontario Greenway Strategy*. Toronto: Waterfront Regeneration Trust.

– 1995b. *The West Don Lands*. Toronto: Waterfront Regeneration Trust.

Waterfront Toronto. 2007a. *Annual Report 06/07*. Toronto: Waterfront Toronto.

– 2007b. *Policies on Public Access to Information*. 24 August. Toronto: Waterfront Toronto.

– 2008a. *Annual Report 07/08*. Toronto: Waterfront Toronto.

– 2008b. *Integrated Communications Strategy*. Presentation to the Board of Directors, 12 June. Toronto: Waterfront Toronto.

– 2008c. *Long Term Plan Update*. Presentation to the Board of Directors, 3 September. Toronto: Waterfront Toronto.

– N.d.a. *Don River Park*. http://www.waterfrontoronto.ca/dynamic.php?first=43fa75b221b08&second=442c3d68acd91&third=4501812159d81.

– N.d.b. Waterfront Toronto home page. http://www.waterfrontoronto.ca/index.php?home=true.

– N.d.c. Flood Protection Landform. http://www.waterfrontoronto.ca/explore_projects2/west_don_lands/flood_protection_landform.

Watts, M. 1983. *Silent Violence: Food, Famine, & Peasantry in Northern Nigeria.* Berkeley: University of California Press.

– 2003. 'Development and Governmentality.' *Singapore Journal of Tropical Geography* 24(1): 6–34.

– 2006. 'Empire of Oil: Capitalist Dispossession and the Scramble for Africa.' *Monthly Review* 58(4): 1–17.

Watts, S. 2006. 'Cholera and the Maritime Environment of Great Britain, India and the Suez Canal: 1866–1883.' *International Journal of Environmental Studies* 63(1): 19–38.

Weaver, J.C. 1979. '"Toronto's Metropolis" Revisited: A Critical Assessment of Urban Reform in Canada, 1890–1920.' In G.A. Stelter and A.F.J. Artibise, eds., *The Canadian City: Essays in Urban History*, 393–418. Toronto: Macmillan Company of Canada Ltd.

Whatmore, S. 2002. *Hybrid Geographies.* London and New York: Routledge.

While, A., A.E.G. Jonas, and D. Gibbs. 2004. 'The Environment and the Entrepreneurial City: Searching for the Urban "Sustainability Fix" in Manchester and Leeds.' *International Journal of Urban and Regional Research* 28(3): 549–69.

Whillans, T.H. 1998. 'The Fishes and Fish Habitat of Ashbridge's Bay.' In G. Fairfield, ed., *Ashbridge's Bay: An Anthology of Writings by Those Who Knew and Loved Ashbridge's Bay*, 16–19. Toronto: Toronto Ornithological Club.

White, R. 1995. *The Organic Machine: The Remaking of the Columbia River.* New York: Hill and Wang.

Whittick, A., ed. 1974. *Encyclopedia of Urban Planning.* New York: McGraw-Hill Book Co.

Wickson, T. 2002. *Reflections of Toronto Harbour: 200 Years of Port Authority and Waterfront Development.* Toronto: Toronto Port Authority.

Wiens, J.A., C.S. Crawford, and J.R. Gosz. 1985. 'Boundary Dynamics: A Conceptual Framework for Studying Landscape Ecosystems.' *Oikos* 45: 421–27.

Wiens, J.A., R.L. Schooley, and R.D. Weeks, Jr. 1997. 'Patchy Landscapes and Animal Movements: Do Beetles Percolate?' *Oikos* 78: 257–64.

Wiese, Andrew. 2006. '"The house I live in": Race, Class, and African American Suburban Dreams in the Postwar United States.' In K.M. Kruse and T.J. Sugrue, eds., *The New Suburban History*, 99–119. Chicago: University of Chicago Press.

Williams, K., E. Burton, and M. Jenks. 1996. 'Achieving the Compact City through Intensification: An Acceptable Option?' In M. Jenks, E. Burton, and K. Williams, eds., *The Compact City: A Sustainable Urban Form?* 83–96. London: E&FN Spon.

Wilmot, S. 1811. Letter 112, Correspondence Relating to Surveys, 1795–1832. 12 February. Archives of Ontario, RG 1-2-1, vol. 35, Microfilm MS 7434.

Wilson, G. 1994. *A History of Shipbuilding and Naval Architecture in Canada*. Ottawa: National Museum of Science and Technology, Transformation series, 4.

Wingrove, J. 2009. 'Ottawa names second Tory to port board.' *Globe and Mail*, 20 January: A9.

Winter, J. 1999. *Secure from Rash Assault: Sustaining the Victorian Environment*. Berkeley, Los Angeles, and London: University of California Press.

Woods Gordon. 1994. *A Review of the Proposed Economic Development Corporation*. Toronto: City of Toronto.

Worboys, M. 2000. *Spreading Germs: Diseases, Theories, and Medical Practice in Britain, 1865–1900*. Cambridge: Cambridge University Press.

Worster, D. 1990. 'Transformations of the Earth: Toward an Agroecological Perspective in History.' *Journal of American History* 76(4): 1087–1106.

– 1993. *The Wealth of Nature: Environmental History and the Ecological Imagination*. New York: Oxford University Press.

Worts, J.G. 1878. 'To the Mayor and Council of the City of Toronto,' 25 February. Toronto Port Authority Archives, RG 1/4, box 3, folder 1.

Yergin, D. 1991. *The Prize: The Epic Quest for Oil, Money, and Power*. New York: Simon & Schuster.

Yiftachel, O. 1999. 'Planning Theory at a Crossroad: The Third Oxford Conference.' *Journal of Planning Education and Research* 183: 267–9.

Young, R., and C. Leuprecht. 2004. 'Introduction: New Work, Background Themes, and Future Research about Municipal–Federal–Provincial Relations in Canada.' In R. Young and C.L. Leuprecht, eds., *Canada, The State of the Federation 2004: Municipal–Federal–Provincial Relations in Canada*, 3–22. Kingston: McGill-Queen's University Press.

Zalasiewicz, J., M. Williams, W. Steffen, and P. Crutzen. 2010. 'The New World of the Anthropocene.' *Environmental Science and Technology* 44(7): 2228–31.

Zalik, A. 2008. 'Liquefied Natural Gas and Fossil Capitalism.' *Monthly Review* 60(6): 41–53.

Zukin, S, 1991. *Landscapes of Power: From Detroit to Disney World*. Berkeley: University of California Press.

Zunino, H.M. 2006. 'Power Relations in Urban Decision-making: Neo-liberalism, "Techno-politicians" and Authoritarian Redevelopment in Santiago, Chile.' *Urban Studies* 43(10): 1825–46.

Contributors

Richard Anderson is a part-time instructor in the Department of Geography, York University, Toronto, with a research specialty in the historical geography of the environment.

Jennifer Bonnell has a PhD from the Department of Theory and Policy Studies in Education at the Ontario Institute for Studies in Education at the University of Toronto.

Susannah Bunce is Assistant Professor of Human Geography at the University of Toronto, Scarborough, Ontario.

Tenley Conway is Associate Professor of Geography at the University of Toronto–Mississauga, Ontario.

Gene Desfor is Professor Emeritus at the Faculty of Environmental Studies, York University, Toronto.

Gabriel Eidelman is a PhD candidate in political science and environmental studies at the University of Toronto.

Pierre Filion is Professor of Urban Planning at the School of Planning of the University of Waterloo, Ontario.

Gunter Gad is Professor Emeritus in the Department of Geography, University of Toronto.

Paul S.B. Jackson is a doctoral candidate in the Department of Geography at the University of Toronto.

Jennefer Laidley holds a Masters in Environmental Studies from York University, Toronto. She is currently Research and Policy Analyst with the Income Security Advocacy Centre, Toronto.

Hon Q. Lu is an associate with the MMM Group, in Planning and Environmental Services, and holds a Masters in Environmental Studies from York University, Toronto.

Michael Moir is University Archivist and Head, Archives and Special Collections, at York University, Toronto.

Scott Prudham is Associate Professor in the Department of Geography and the Centre for Environment at the University of Toronto.

Christopher Sanderson is a doctoral candidate at the University of Waterloo's School of Planning, Waterloo, Ontario.

Lucian Vesalon is Assistant Professor in the Faculty of Political Science, Philosophy and Communication Studies in the West University in Timisoara, Romania.

Index

Redway, William E. 102, 105, 118
referendum of January 1911, 45, 53,
59–64, 68, 73
Richardson, Captain Hugh 27, 28, 30,
32, 33
Rolling Mills wharf 38
Roma 18, 94, 135–41, 142, 147, 150
Royal Commission on the Future of
the Toronto Waterfront 9, 70, 223,
225, 230, 254, 263, 264
Russell, John 112, 113, 117, 121

St Lawrence River/canal/Seaway 12,
30, 46, 56, 97, 106, 112, 181, 235
sanitation 35, 76, 80, 90, 91
sewers/sewage 5, 12, 31, 32, 33, 34,
35, 36, 40, 43, 44, 47, 58, 67, 85, 87,
88, 89, 90, 91, 92, 95, 156, 176, 310
shipbuilding 5, 12, 15, 18, 97–122, 193
silt 16, 28, 31, 32, 33, 35, 38, 40, 43, 88,
89, 90, 99, 106, 164, 169, 309, 310,
318, 320
Simcoe, Elizabeth 314
Simcoe, John Graves 24, 25, 46, 128,
314
socio-ecological: approaches 9, 10;
distinct from Urban Ecology 10;
change, institutionalization of 19,
260, 262, 284; change along the
Don River 305–25; developments
3, 16, 245, 315; dynamics 19,
50, 65, 152; literature 6, 7–11;
perspectives on urban change 5,
6, 9, 10; politics 62, 72, 73, 252,
264; relationships, modernization
of 313; relationships during
industrialization 17, 305
socio-nature: and changes to the
Don River 313, 317, 319, 320, 321,
322; definition of 50, 64, 65, 74,

308; and 'metropolitan natures'
309; production of 65, 323, 325;
and public health 310, 322, 324;
representations of 317–23, 324;
and urbanization 308–10, 315, 316,
322
Spence, Francis 45, 47
squatters 124, 135, 149
staples 23, 29, 30, 53
Sunnyside 46
sustainability 13, 15, 121, 203, 212,
287, 288, 289, 291, 292, 295, 298,
299–302, 306, 318, 321, 324
sustainability fix 206, 223

Task Force to Bring Back the Don
151, 160, 171, 315, 316
Thor Iron Works 112, 113, 114
Toronto Board of Trade 30, 58, 63, 73,
107, 119, 229, 235
Toronto City Council 60, 63, 229, 233,
235, 237, 242, 311
Toronto Dry Dock and Shipbuilding
Company 101
Toronto Economic Development
Corporation (TEDCO) 257,
259, 260, 261, 262, 275, 278, 279;
environmental site evaluations
257; groundwater management
strategies 248, 252, 259; mandate
and governing structures 247, 261;
property holdings 236, 239, 247,
258, 285
Toronto Harbour Commission
(THC) 12, 14, 17, 24, 37, 45, 46,
47, 50, 54, 60–74, 98, 107, 111, 112,
114, 117, 119, 120, 121, 162, 165,
167, 169, 179, 193, 224, 247, 248,
252, 269, 276, 279, 312; and the
Royal Commission on the Future